SCIENCE, IDEOLOGY, AND
THE MEDIA

Photo courtesy of Dr. Charlotte Banks.

SCIENCE, IDEOLOGY, AND THE MEDIA

The Cyril Burt Scandal

Ronald Fletcher

Transaction Publishers
New Brunswick (U.S.A.) and London (U.K.)

Library of Congress Catalog Number: 90-40836
ISBN: 0-88738-376-9
Printed in the United States of America

Library of Congress Cataloging-in-Publication Data

Fletcher, Ronald.
    Science, ideology, and the media : the Cyril Burt scandal / Ronald Fletcher.
        p. cm.
    Includes bibliographical references and index.
    ISBN 0-88738-376-9
    1. Burt, Cyril Lodowic, Sir, 1883–1971. 2. Fraud in science-
-England—Case studies. 3. Mass media—Influence—Case studies.
4. Science news—Case studies. 5. Psychologists—England.
I. Title.
BF109.B88F44   1990
150′.92—dc20
                                                90-40836
                                                CIP

In Memory of
Miss Gretl Archer,
whose loyalty never wavered

Contents

III   MALFEASANCE AND FRAUD?
Summing Up, Additional Evidence, and Verdict

IV   QUESTIONS AND CONCLUSIONS

Acknowledgments

I would like to express my gratitude to all those who have been generous and helpful in many ways throughout some three years of investigation.

First were those who, during correspondence, visits, and conversations, provided me with invaluable documentation, information, and advice. Miss Gretl Archer, Burt's last secretary, made fully available all the manuscripts and letters she possessed, and allowed me to question her exhaustively (during a number of meetings) about matters on which, by that time, only she had personal knowledge. With equal generosity, Dr. Charlotte Banks, Burt's last colleague and assistant, provided me with copies of articles and letters, undertook a detailed study of Burt's diaries, and made herself continually available for consultation and advice. Professor Brian Cox (of Manchester University) also examined Burt's diaries, provided many significant documents and letters, and was continually ready—in meetings and by correspondence—to discuss those aspects of the Burt case of which he had special knowledge. The same was true of Professor John Cohen (also of Manchester University) before his death. Robert Reid, for twenty years editor of the *Journal and Newsletter,* which became the *AEP Journal* (of the Association of Educational Psychologists), who was in close touch with Burt throughout that period, provided copies of Burt's regular articles and much other information and advice, including his testimony about the nature of the BBC film, *The Intelligence Man.* Adrian R. Allan (Assistant Archivist at the University of Liverpool) always responded readily to questions about the Burt papers there,

providing copies of letters, documents, and some crucially significant notes. Similarly, Mr. A. R. Neate (then Record Keeper for the
Director General of the Greater London Record Office) provided
copies of some records and, in addition, many suggestions and
much useful advice about other sources of information. Mrs. Emma
Robinson (of the University of London library), besides providing
general information, was particularly helpful in the efforts to trace
assistants mentioned in Burt's footnotes; and David Eames (Deputy
Academic Registrar) was similarly helpful in providing articles and
newspaper cuttings on the Burt case that had been collected in a
file of the university's Court Department. Also helpful at the
University of London (at the Institute of Education) were Denis
Baylis (Information and Publications Officer) and Dr. Kathleen
Barker. Dr. William Hammond, too, gave me a detailed confirma-
tory account of his recollections of being tested by the two "missing
ladies," as well as many other observations on the entire controversy. Finally, the Newspaper Library of the British Library was
enormously helpful in tracing (and supplying copies of) the chief
articles in the controversy and the many items of correspondence
that followed.

Second were the editors and editorial boards of newspapers and
journals who first gave me the opportunities to revive the controversy, which—it was assumed—had so long been definitively settled. I am especially indebted to Professor R.A.B. Leaper and the
editorial board of *Social Policy and Administration* (at the University of Exeter) for giving me space to set out my defense of Burt
for the first time: a subject, and an approach, then decidedly
unpopular. Next, I am grateful to the (then) editor and staff of the
Sunday Telegraph—Peregrine Worsthorne, Desmond Albrow, and
Graham Turner—for being prepared to mount and help me with a
major article that gave the reopening of the controversy something
approaching the same wide publicity that the scandal itself had
originally enjoyed. The *Times,* at the hands of Stuart MacLure,
picked this up, and later I was grateful to Stuart MacLure for giving
me the opportunity of a subsequent article in the *Times Educational
Supplement.* Victor Serebriakoff (president of MENSA) and Simon
Clark (editor) gave the matter much space and exposure in the
MENSA magazine, and Norris McWhirter, too, invited me to
contribute a critique of the BBC film on Burt to the *Free Nation,*

and did his best to give this maximum publicity. Taken together, all these formed a kind of academic and journalistic prelude to the larger study of this book, and my gratitude is all the more strongly felt because of the widespread resistance that then existed to the voicing of any support whatever for Burt—whose reputation of fraudulence had become an apparently universally accepted and commonplace matter of fact.

Third were many who had known Burt and his work well (some having themselves been closely involved in the controversy and its aftermath), and others who, for various reasons, had been in communication with him, who proved very informative and helpful in correspondence. Professor Raymond Cattell, Dr. Geoffrey Cohen (statistician at the University of Edinburgh and son of Professor John Cohen), Professor Arthur R. Jensen, Dr. Gertrude Keir (a colleague of both Burt and Charlotte Banks), Professor John C. Loehlin (of the University of Texas), and Dr. John Fraser Roberts were all supportive in their readiness to answer questions and provide materials where possible. Among all these, however, I must express my special gratitude and indebtedness to Professor Arthur Jensen. From the appearance of my first articles on Burt, he has remained in close touch in correspondence, and has been most generous in letting me have his detailed recollections of the affair as it took place, in sending me a copy of his many-sided correspondence with participants in the affair at that time, and in giving me permission to quote from these materials or to use them as I think fit. He has been perhaps my strongest supporter in seeking to uncover the truth of these matters, and indeed was also enormously helpful in advising me on the matter of publishing this book. In all fairness, I should add that I had some helpful early correspondence with Professor Ann Clarke of the University of Hull, although regretfully I had ultimately to be radically critical of the part she played in the controversy.

Fourth were the many people who wrote to me after the appearance of the several articles—offering comments, materials of various kinds, and help in looking further into particular aspects of the case. Many of these were past students, colleagues, and friends of Burt, who had long felt that the BBC's film and the persistent efforts to smear Burt with charges of fraud were travesties. Christopher Brand and Ian Deary (of Edinburgh University), John Burrows (of the Extra-Mural Department of London University), Mrs. Joan Clarke (formerly Joan Mawer—one of Burt's ladies who was not missing!), Dr. Sybil Crane, Mrs. Josephine Freeman, Dr. James Hemming, Lady Priscilla Norman, Dr. Neil O'Connor, Mrs. Jessica Phillips, Dr. Leslie Phillips, Ray Ward (of MENSA), F. M. White (formerly of the Cambridge Institute of Education), and Dr. Moyra Williams, all helped in these ways.

My warm thanks are therefore due to all of these. Without their generously given and substantial help I would not have been able to assemble all the evidence presented in this book.

Grateful acknowledgments are also due to all those authors and publishers of the newspapers, journals, and books to whom reference is made, and from which relevant quotations have been drawn, in the ongoing argument. Full details of all of these are given where they occur in the text, and are listed also in the bibliography.

Last—and decidedly not least—I am grateful for the promptitude, clarity, and efficiency of the entire production team of Transaction Publishers, and especially, within this context, for the generous response and helpful advice of Professor Irving L. Horowitz. I do not know to what extent he agrees with all the arguments and conclusions of this book, but what is certain is that its form, presentation, and readability have benefited greatly from his editorial criticism and suggestions.

Preface

I wrote this book, as the preamble will describe, as a straightforward defense of Sir Cyril Burt. This, throughout, has been its chief objective, and remains so.

During the course of writing it, however, I came with ever-increasing certainty to the conclusion that, under the entire Burt affair—initially giving rise to it, and thereafter fueling its long-continued intensity—there lay two particular issues that were much deeper and went far beyond the matter of the alleged fraudulence of Burt himself. These I will touch on shortly.

Now that the book has been for some time completed, however, I have also come to believe, on reflection, that the scandal carries a significance far wider even than its connection with these two issues. In a way neither intended nor expected, the very particularity of this examination of the Cyril Burt scandal makes it, I think, a case study within the context of a much larger story—a story peculiarly, and perhaps increasingly, relevant to the intellectual and moral condition of our time—and it is with this that it seems best to begin.

The story I have in mind, which is far from having yet been fully told, is one about the intrusion of the mass media into science (indeed into every field of serious intellectual discourse—philosophical, religious, artistic, and so on); the *power* of the new media within the context of modern mass communications; and—perhaps above all—the *success* of this invasion, amounting to no less than a usurpation and replacement of intellectual authority in matters of truth and justice alike. It is a story about the ways in which, motivated by ideological aims and linked personal allegiances and animosities, the calculated employment of the many avenues and techniques of the media can achieve totally convincing character assassinations; can establish intellectual positions about issues of the greatest importance (and of the greatest relevance to practical public policies) in so decisive a manner that they become unassailably entrenched in public opinion—so ineradicable, so completely taken for granted, that the issues at stake are no longer thought to merit any further consideration whatsoever. It seems hardly too much to say that it is now the media, and no longer scientific study and philosophical discourse, that formulate and establish the uncritically accepted "paradigms" of the period.

Every element of testimony I will consider in cross-examination will exemplify one way, reveal one avenue, through which today— just because of the nature of the masscommunications open to us, and the uses to which these are put —intellectual issues are *misjudged*. The continual repetition of banner headlines (and the frequently simplistic substance of the stories they cover); the equally superficial and slanted productions of radio documentaries (always of necessity limited in terms of time and selective treatment); and, perhaps especially, the impressive use of apparently factual television dramatizations—all these successfully establish intellectual positions, judgments, and points of view, that are far from being grounded in truth and show little concern for the reputations of individuals or the niceties of justice. Aggressively publicized, widely broadcast, endlessly repeated before a mass audience of millions of individuals—the vast majority of whom cannot possibly have the requisite knowledge, time, opportunity, or even inclination to scrutinize the evidence further—careless errors, distortions, deliberate misrepresentations, simplistic interpretations, and direct falsehoods are able to masquerade freely and come to be accepted as the truth. It is quite clear that this publicly exposed arena of strictly contemporaneous, highly pressured, competitive disputation among parties (whether individuals or groups) who have powerful interests at stake, is not the fitting place for careful, detailed investigation, for the prolonged scrutiny and consideration of the evidence on all sides of a question, and for a deliberate suspension of judgment until informed conclusions can be drawn. Yet this is the most influential arena in which, in our time, "truths" are presented, conveyed, and established in the minds of the public.

All this would be sufficiently serious if it was merely a playground of egotistical journalists and producers ambitiously making the most of their stories—something of which we are all well aware. It becomes infinitely more serious, however, when scientists themselves are seen to collaborate with these middle-men of the media, lending apparent authority, and therefore credibility, to the positions being advocated; and more serious still when they themselves (supporting these positions) neglect to check them against the facts and the evidence on which they supposedly rest, even adding dubious testimony of their own; neglecting, in short, the most elementary tenets of the methods and procedures of science that it is their vocational commitment to uphold. But even this dire state of affairs is worsened to a condition almost beyond redemption when it becomes evident that some of the most eminent scholars in the world fall victim to the same continued repetitions in the media (of unfounded allegations, character assassinations, and the like), and go so far as to repeat them themselves, so reinforcing their influence and strength; accepting the prevailing fashion, it seems, just as uncritically as the most untutored members of the public, who simply swallow the day-to-day banner headlines as taken-for-granted truth. Does it not prove that none of us, no matter how scrupulous and careful we may consider ourselves, can be confident of being and remaining entirely free from susceptibility to the media's insidious and persuasive power?

All of this amounts to the fact not that human evil, whether in the battle for truth or in any other area, has increased (that would be hard to achieve!) but that, given the nature of modern mass communications, the calculated pursuit of ideological ends, the related pursuit of personal vendettas, and prolonged campaigns of vilification, now enjoy far more scope than was ever the case in times past. In the last analysis, this is a matter of the most serious concern for the maintenance of intellectual standards, no doubt in all fields of human activity but particularly in those of truth and justice.

This point, briefly outlined by way of introduction, is no more—literally—than a prefatory note on this matter, but as the full story of the Cyril Burt case unfolds, I believe that its relevance to this larger theme will become progressively clear. It may serve, I think, as a stark reminder of the dangers we face, and count as one small but telling contribution to the history of the human sciences during this second half of the twentieth century.

I turn now to the two issues that underlay the Burt scandal from first to last; that have kept it alive from long after Burt's own death to the present time; and that, indeed, remain the source of passionate intellectual and political controversies even today, still engendering powerful opposing commitments.

It could always be expected, of course, that the revelation, after his death, of serious fraud on the part of any scientist of worldwide reputation—who had, during his lifetime, come to be accepted as a leading authority in his field—would attract serious public attention. But why, before there had been any considered scientific investigation of the matter, was Burt's alleged misdemeanor launched in so immediate and sensational a manner in the popular press? Why was it at once simultaneously announced and *denounced* as "the most sensational charge of scientific fraud this century" and, the very next day, likened in seriousness to the fraud of the Piltdown skull in palaeontology? Why was it so avidly taken up by other newspapers and journals as to be made into a worldwide scandal overnight? We will arrive at detailed and specific answers to these questions, but there is no doubt that the immediately aggressive and sensationalist nature of the attack had its roots in two controversies that had, for a long time, given rise to powerful feelings of antagonism between those who stood on one side or the other as opponents.

The first of these was the "heredity versus environment" controversy. The Hereditarians had long insisted that the evidence of such scientific investigation as had been carried out demonstrated that (among other qualities) the mental abilities of individuals—their level of general intelligence and their possession of marked particular aptitudes—were chiefly established by heredity; though they readily agreed that environmental factors could be highly significant in either encouraging and favoring the fulfilment of these abilities, or standing as serious obstacles in the way of their development. The Hereditarians held, therefore, that there was a natural basis for the distribution of the diversity of kinds and levels of ability, and of the inequalities in such abilities, throughout the population of society—affected though this would obviously be by the differing environmental situations of families and individuals— and that this had to be accepted as a fact that education should take into account in formulating its policies and making its provisions.

Opposed to these were the Environmentalists, who insisted that all the evidence so far advanced in support of this viewpoint was unreliable—as were the methods of testing employed—and who argued that mental abilities were environmentally determined. The great range of the inequalities in general intelligence and the posses- sion of special aptitudes as measured (and supposedly demon- strated) by mental tests was no more than a reflection of the great range of diversity and inequality in the environmental conditions within which families and individuals were placed in society—with the possession and enjoyment of great privileges of wealth, status, and opportunity at the top end of the scale and the total lack of them at the other. Educational selection on this basis could there- fore be no other than a self-perpetuating social selection. Further- more, it was argued that even the mental tests on which the "demonstration" of the distribution of abilities rested were them- selves reflections of this environmental hierarchy of privileges and opportunities: so constructed (in their linguistic usage, for exam- ple), and so weighted, as inevitably to produce the results that they did, which suggested that the hierarchy had a natural ("genetic") basis rather than being something economically, socially, and polit- ically created and therefore open to change, reform, and improve- ment.

All we need to say here is that all the social surveys Burt undertook, and all the later and more specific studies that stemmed from them, led him firmly to adopt the Hereditarian position. Throughout his working life, he continually held and defended this point of view.

It is immediately evident, however, that it was well nigh impossi- ble that this Hereditarian versus Environmentalist dispute could be a purely scientific controversy. Inescapably, it held a political dimension—one in relation to which ideological persuasions were almost bound to arise—and a little more must be said.

The Hereditarian position had long been the basis of the eugenics movement, and some of the more extreme pronouncements of this movement or of some of its members—stemming from a concern for maintaining and if possible improving the quality of the "genetic stock" of society—had argued for the desirability of "selective breeding": of restricting and even preventing the breeding of some unfortunately endowed individuals. Within the context of this argument, too, the members of some races or social classes were regarded as being superior or inferior to those of others. Understandably, such a position and all those of its implications that smacked of arbitrary authoritarianism (who, for example, was to decide who was "inferior" and who "superior"; who was fit to reproduce their kind and who was not?) provoked much opposition. Taking something of a seven-league stride of argument, this opposition was greatly reinforced by the actuality of the horrors of the distinctions drawn between those considered fit and unfit to survive (including racial as well as other criteria) in the extermination policies later uncovered in Nazi Germany.

These extremes, both theoretical and actual, extended the heredity versus environment controversy into the second controversy, which was inextricably (whether justifiably or not) connected with it: the "left versus right" controversy in politics. The Hereditarian position came to be considered essentially conservative (at the worst extreme, fascist), essentially on the right in its implications for the formulation of social policies. Some of the inequalities of individuals, and the range of them manifested in society, were established by heredity, and no political changes could eliminate them. The ongoing actuality of some range of diversity and inequality of abilities was therefore recognized and accepted as a fact, together with the equally factual implication that educational policies should take them into account and provide for them. The Hereditarian position was therefore not only conservative but also essentially inegalitarian, and reactionary in insisting that there were limits to what progressive reforms could achieve; indeed, in going beyond this and claiming that great harm could come from pressing forward with political changes while biological, psychological, and social facts were ignored. Furthermore, it came to carry the stigma of the worst extremes of the eugenics movement and the Nazi atrocities. It came to be thought of as the theorectical and ideological basis of the extreme right in politics.

By contrast, the Environmentalist position, as the basis of the left in politics, was essentially egalitarian and progressive. If unequal abilities were the result of unequal environmental advantages and disadvantages, these inequalities could be progressively eliminated by political, economic, and social reforms that changed these unequal environments. The left therefore stood for radical reform, the radical transformation of society, and by this means the achievement of real, actual equality and therefore real equality of educational opportunity. The right—essentially guarded—remained always resistant to what was claimed, and what could actually be achieved, by such progressive policies; which meant that its outcome could be none other than the protection and conservation of the status quo.

Clearly, this is not the place to enter into either of these two controversies or to take sides in them; indeed, this introductory mention of them may well be regarded by professional psychologists and social scientists as being all too elementary. Even so, it is essential for our understanding of the Burt case that they should be borne in mind, and, well known though they may be considered to be, there are some aspects of them that deserve the very strongest emphasis.

The first of these is that far from being "fringe" controversies, they had lain at the very heart of scientific disputation and party political antagonisms from the beginning of our own century (being rooted, indeed, in the earlier scientific upheavals of the nineteenth century and the political upheavals that immediately followed Victorian times). Second, carrying this long history of passionate disagreements with them, they not only continued up to the time of the Burt affair but even cumulatively increased in intensity after the experienced extremes of the Second World War; and in the immediate postwar years, as reformist educational policies—in one direction, then in another—were actually initiated, encountered unexpected outcomes and problems and were from all sides militantly criticized, and as academic studies and intellectuals (as individuals) ranged themselves more emphatically (in a more engaged way—sometimes in close conjunction with politicians and political parties) on one side or other of the controversy.

The fierceness of these disagreements, and the extent to which they affected what was discussed and not discussed, what was published and what was not published, in the entire field of the life sciences and education, cannot be underestimated. Later (in the

"Burt's Detractors" section of Chapter 14) we will see that a large group of the most eminent scholars in the world within the field of behavioral genetics thought it necessary to make public advertisement of the fact that articles and books on the Hereditarian side of the question could no longer gain serious consideration by editors and publishers. This, it may be noted, was less than twenty years ago. A third point, however, is that it is clear that these controversies remain just as active, with just the same degree of virulence and intensity—though sometimes hidden rather than overt—today. Even as I write (February 1990), the reviews of the recent book by Robert Joynson on *The Burt Affair* can be plainly seen to be as strongly slanted from precisely the same opposing ideological viewpoints as were the contemporary press arguments at the time of the Burt affair itself. Similarly, a London BBC producer, approaching me in a telephone conversation about the possibility of another television treatment of the affair, said rather complainingly: "But, you know, there is a widespread and considerable resistance in and outside the corporation to giving any sympathetic presentation of the hereditarian viewpoint." When I asked him why, his answer was: "Well, it flies in the face of all that we believe about equality. Or at least that, at any rate, is how it is seen."

An additional point that I state in the simplest fashion now, but that is of vast importance, is that at the present time—just as much as has been the case throughout the long life of these disputations—the arguments relating to these two controversies, as pursued by leading scientists and politicians alike, are characterized by the most stark, unclarified, and unresolved illogicalities. It is not only that issues of political ideology have been inextricably mixed up with issues of scientific investigation and evidence, but also that issues that are matters of fact—whether of science or politics alike—have been inextricably mixed up, and more often than not completely confused, with matters of ethics or moral philosophy.

It is a most common assumption, for example, that a Hereditarian, accepting the existence of inherited inequalities of ability, cannot but be opposed to equality as a principle of social justice, and also to political reforms aimed at improving the circumstances and educational opportunities of those who are suffering severe environmental disadvantages. It is a most common assumption, similarly, that an Environmentalist cannot be other than opposed to any form of selection in education; is bound to be—in public policy and personal (parental) practice—a strict egalitarian; and is bound to believe that equality of opportunity in education means an exact uniformity of educational treatment for all. It is a most common assumption, too, that equality as a principle of social justice in education can only rest on (essentially requires) the recognition of the *factual* equality of abilities among children (other than those inequalities that have resulted from varying environmental circumstances); and therefore, again, that it also means equality of *treatment*.

Now, all of these assumptions, and many others that could be listed and that commonly occur in educational arguments, are plainly false. Yet they are the very stuff of educational theory, debate, and contentious political practice at the highest level. In Britain, for example, the entire tangled history of educational reform—from the 1944 Education Act, through the almost universal imposition of the "comprehensive principle" in secondary schools, and the subsequent efforts (through the reforms of successive ministers of education, parallelled by an enormous expansion of private education) to change and disengage from this—has rested upon the militant play, one way and another, of false assumptions of this kind. Now these issues of scientific fact, ethics, and political policy *do* permit of clarification. Yet year after turbulent year, in education itself, in political conflict, and in intellectual discourse, the continued and obdurate mix-up of science and ideology prevents such clarification from taking place.

It is enough to say for our purposes, therefore, that as well known as these two controversies may be, they have been, and have always remained, intensely active (a confused mixture of scientific and ideological claims and courses of political action), and were specifically so during the postwar years (indeed, from the early 1940s onward) when Burt's later studies were beginning to be published; studies that, increasingly during the 1950s and 1960s, were to provoke such animated criticism.

Throughout his life, and increasingly so towards the end of it, Cyril Burt was not only one of the most eminent adherents and exponents of the Hereditarian position, but also one of the most forthright defenders of it—always ready to enter into public debate and to exchange argument in articles with his opponents. To be able to demonstrate after his death that his life's work had no basis whatever, that indeed his very data and methods had been fabricated and fraudulent, could therefore be expected, from the point of view of committed Environmentalists, to be a telling blow against the Hereditarian position itself. To destroy the credibility of Burt would be, in large measure, to belittle and destroy the credibility of the position for which he stood.

In all that follows, readers will judge for themselves whether this was a motivation underlying the attack that clearly aimed at bringing Burt's reputation and work into disrepute; and indeed, whether it was sufficient to explain the virulence of it. All we need note here is that the Cyril Burt scandal arose within the context of these two areas of continuing and deeply felt disputation.

I come now to my treatment in this book itself, a treatment that has been affected by, and has deliberately tried to take into account, these contextual issues, and about which—just because of the mixture of scientific, ideological, ethical, and personal dimensions involved—I wish to be totally honest and clear.

First, on my defense of Burt. As will be seen, this began with my strong impression—resting on some matters about which I had at least some definite knowledge—that a great injustice had been done. Subsequently, during the long course of examining all the evidence advanced by Burt's detractors, as well as all that in Burt's own work, and especially in that which lay behind his many footnotes (which the detractors had ignored), I came with increasing conviction to the conclusion that this was indeed the case. I became thoroughly convinced that Burt was innocent of the charges of fraud made against him. In all that follows, then, it has to be borne clearly in mind that in acting as "counsel for the defense," I really do believe in the innocence of my client!

Bearing in mind, however, the need for objectivity and truth in this, and the all-pervasive sway of ideological bias, I have meticulously given the most detailed documentation on which every point rests—all of which is therefore open to test. Also—and this is where honesty even more necessarily comes in—I not only came to believe in Burt's innocence, but also to be increasingly incensed at the stance, purported evidence, and some of the consciously shared tactics of Burt's opponents, all of which amounted (in my view), as time went on, to a deliberate and sustained process of vilification. Increasingly, in my judgment, the questionable cloud of intellectual impropriety came to hover much more heavily and ominously over Burt's detractors than over Burt himself. In defending Burt, I found, in short, that I felt increasingly opposed to, and had to attack, those who had denounced him. This partiality in argument too, then, has to be borne in mind.

To demonstrate an objective and impartial appraisal of the evidence, I have deliberately set out my questions and arguments in the legalistic form of a trial: entering (as though in a courtroom) into a cross-examination of each of Burt's "witnesses for the prosecution," examining each item of their evidence in turn, but during the course of this, making the grounds of my opposition (as well as my feelings) clear, and ending each section with a number of forthright questions that are transparently open to, and invite, public answer. That is to say, the conclusions I have drawn are completely open to confirmation or rebuttal. And finally—with truth in this whole matter in mind—though defending Burt against the charges brought against him, it has not at all been my wish or intention to present him as a man without fault. Indeed, my knowledge falls far short of being able to enter such a sphere of personal judgment. Having, however, had experience of the intensity, extremities, and sheer evil of some academic politics, my assumption is that no man at Burt's level of seniority in university affairs is likely to be completely without fault. With this in mind, wherever the record of Burt's conduct seems to indicate something questionable, or perhaps foolish, I have deliberately been at pains to be quite clear about it.

A second matter of presentation has caused difficulty. It will be understood that, in considering all sides of each allegation, I have deliberately wanted (indeed, have felt it necessary) to present *all* the relevant evidence. Burt's articles typically contain many footnotes referring to earlier studies, the findings of which he assumes or takes for granted as the basis for his current arguments. Very frequently, his detractors, in making their charges, have failed to take these into account. It is vitally important, then, that this evidence should be presented. Much of it, however, is very detailed, and to present all of it within the text itself, as the argument proceeds, would in all probability make the text too loaded with technicalities and militate against its readability. I have therefore placed such large or complicated items of evidence in appropriate appendices. These are (1) on the mental tests Burt and his colleagues employed, (2) on Dr. Banks' statistical criticisms of Hearnshaw, and (3) on some additional qualitative information on Burt's final sample of fifty-three pairs of twins—a letter from Burt that I believe had never yet been noted and considered. I beg the reader to study these appendices in close relation to the argument, and not (because they are appendices) to ignore them. A great deal, in fact, depends upon them.

A third point has to be made, for which I can do nothing more than apologize. In presenting such a range of tables and diagrams, it could well be thought desirable that they should be brought into some degree of uniformity of design. I have given much thought to this, but have to say that I have failed, and do not think it feasible. I have wanted to give the evidence in its original form, for obvious reasons (this is how it appeared in the long cumulative course of Burt's work), and I cannot see how some diagrams can be usefully redesigned to be brought into relation with others. At the same time, Burt's own tables of correlations in his twin studies are clear and readily comparable as they stand. On this point therefore, I must simply beg the reader's indulgence, hoping that he or she will share the preference for originality over any attempt at standardization.

With these introductory points in mind—some of them broad, some very specific—I turn now to the real task in hand: conducting and considering the case for the defense.

I
CASE FOR THE DEFENSE

1

Preamble

Introduction

My purpose in this book is very simple: to try to right what I believe to have been a great wrong; to demonstrate beyond reasonable doubt—indeed, in many respects, beyond any doubt whatever—that a great injustice has been done to the name, reputation, and character of Sir Cyril Burt, to the entire body of his work, and in particular, to his views on mental ability and educational opportunity. The many criticisms following the accusations of scientific fraud made against him toward the end of 1976 quickly grew into a campaign of strangely virulent vilification that has been sustained from that day to this. The most unwarranted distortions and misrepresentations of his studies and views have been put forward, and aggressively and widely popularised. My concern, therefore, is simply to see justice done; to present a case for the defense; and it is this, as already indicated, which has led me to adopt a rather legalistic form of argument.

This chief purpose, however, entails others, each important within its own area of social and educational considerations. These, too, I must set out as preliminary matters, but before that something of a personal statement must be made. This controversy has been nothing if not personally abusive. The attack on Burt has clearly stemmed from ideological and personal feelings of the most powerful kind—some understandable, some obscure. For the sake of frankness and clarity, then, let me set out, as part of this preamble, my own approach to the matter—the way in which I became concerned about it and the reasons that led me to scrutinize the testimony of Burt's detractors.

Approach

Although during the course of this inquiry I have come increasingly to support Burt, to have an increasingly high regard for his aims, judgments, and achievements, my defense is in no way rooted in personal attachment, any early and special devotion to his work, or any political persuasion. I did not know him, nor was I in any way associated with him.

My defense stemmed only from an initial, and then a growing sense that an injustice had been done. Before the explosion of the 1976 scandal (in the *Sunday Times*), my awareness of Burt and his work was limited. I knew some of his books. I thought, and still think, *The Backward Child* one of the most excellent, humane, and practically useful investigations of the century. On the basis of this alone, I certainly regarded him as one of the great contributors to psychology, the social sciences, and education—one of those (following investigators such as Booth and Rowntree) who had most effectively exposed the extent of the ravages of poverty, squalor, and deprivation in Victorian times that had been inherited by post-Victorian society. As a junior teacher in the University of London, I also knew that Burt was held in the highest regard by people who had a long acquaintance with him as a person and an intimate knowledge of his work (Professor Mace of Birkbeck College and Professor Ginsberg of the London School of Economics, for example) and who I myself held in the highest regard. I accepted their judgment, and, within the work of the university at that time, never had any reason to doubt it.

The sudden charges of fraud (in 1976) at once, therefore, strained my credulity, and even at the outset aroused my suspicion. Some of the testimony against him gave me a feeling of disquiet, of discomfort, as though something more than a dispute about the truth was afoot. Alan and Ann Clarke, for example—already going far beyond the charges of fraud proper (which were concentrated on the study of identical twins)—accused Burt of writing articles in their names, and, after they had agreed on alteration of proofs with him, changing them in such a way as to be critical of Hans Eysenck.

But what sort of scholars were these, I wondered, who would even allow someone else to write articles in their names? Also, Burt's detractors seemed, in general, unduly intense; to be protesting too much; to be bringing to their arguments a certain inexplicable animus; but it was not a field in which I was knowledgeable, and I simply watched with growing distaste the subsequent skirmishes in the correspondence columns (chiefly of the *Times*). With every additional article in the "weeklies," however, with every new sensationalist headline, with every new radio discussion—a series of features that continued year after year—my suspicions deepened, until the 1984 BBC film, *The Intelligence Man,* proved the last straw. So flagrantly one-sided a character assassination was this, containing, even in terms of my own limited knowledge, what I knew to be such gross distortions of Burt's work, such defamatory and libelous statements, that I felt bound to inquire in thoroughgoing detail into the grounds on which these allegations had been made. On what actual evidence did they rest?

The more I have examined this, the more the entire situation has astonished me. The more, too, have I found it hard to understand the long silence and lack of objections from academic psychologists in Britain, Burt's own country, and indeed throughout the world. Have they not seen these distortions? If not, why not? And if so, why have they not spoken? The clear upshot for me, at any rate, is that I have now become quite sure that there is a matter of injustice to rectify and of truth to be established. Assembling the demonstrable evidence, presenting demonstrable arguments, my aim is no more than to reopen the case so that justice and truth—rather than a quiescent acceptance of a fashionably reiterated denunciation—can be arrived at.

There remains, however, the issue of ideology—already to a degree touched upon.

On this, little that is worthwhile can be said, since the claim to have no ideology at all is itself seen as an ideological stance by those who think in this manner. My position, in any event, is strangely mixed, but a few points can be made.

I should make it clear, first, that I do agree with Burt's emphasis on *selection* in education, and with his belief that much that has gone wrong with British education since the 1944 Act—and which remains wrong with it now—is the outcome of mistaken conceptions and practices in relation to this matter. Burt held that there should be as accurate an appraisal as possible of the level of general intelligence and the special aptitudes of each child, and that all children should then be provided with those different kinds and levels of education, and educational opportunities, which were most appropriate to their individual natures and needs. I am completely in agreement with this, but held these views on ethical grounds before embarking on the examination of the Burt affair, and had already set them out in some detail.[1]

Second, I do not regard myself as being either "right" or "left" wing in this controversy. These terms, indeed, seem to me to have become increasingly nonsensical in educational arguments. Even so, when one takes a personal stand in a dispute carrying public notoriety, suspicions are aroused. Following my early articles that sought to re-open the Burt controversy,[2] several people eminent within the field of education quizzed me as to whether a movement of the "New Right" was afoot, suspecting that I might be acting as its front man. This most emphatically was not, and is not, so, and it is worthwhile to make it quite clear (though in more detail later) that Burt himself was decidedly not right wing either. His entire emphasis was on the extension of educational opportunity to children from disadvantaged social backgrounds, and he was not, for example, on the basis of any principle, opposed to the "comprehensive" school.

Third, because of the stance of Burt's detractors, what I called a "strangely mixed" position must be stated. I actually and actively sympathize with the ideological stance lying at the root of some of the attacks on Burt, and that indeed gives rise to the virulence of their motivation. Professor Kamin, for example, detests many political policies of a racially discriminatory kind that have stemmed from some IQ testing coupled with the belief that intelligence is largely determined by heredity. He detests political proposals and policies rooted in the most extreme views of the eugenics movement: the conception and practice of "selective breeding" that found their worst embodiment in the extermination policies of the Nazis. Similarly, he detests the wholesale judgment of social classes as being superior or inferior to each other on the grounds of differences in their average measured IQ. I share these detestations. However, I am equally certain that, possibly because of the strength of his feelings, he has completely misconceived and misrepresented Burt's position on these matters, and has—whether consciously and deliberately, or unconsciously and carelessly in the "selective perception" of his sheer ideological zeal—distorted both Burt's studies and his views. In what follows, I will demonstrate that Kamin's characterization of Burt is unfounded and false, but will also have to go further than this and claim that—not only in Kamin, but also in Gillie and others who followed him—a deliberate distortion of Burt's position has been promulgated in order to discountenance this in the eyes of public and political opinion, and so advance, in its place, an Environmentalist point of view. Not argument towards truth, but calculated and slanted rhetoric, has characterized the campaign. Deliberate defamation has followed upon initial criticism.

These points, mixed though they may seem, encompass my approach to this issue, although other dimensions and nuances will doubtless emerge in what is to come. I believe that a man has been undeservedly maligned, and want to see the truth made clear and justice done.

I turn, now, to preliminary explanations of the form my defense will take.

Jury

In the first place, deliberately and directly, I address this book to you, the individual reader, as to a member of a universal jury— "universal" in that *throughout the world* it has become a deeply entrenched assumption that a fully considered judgment has been arrived at in this case, after expert scrutiny, and that the verdict is "guilty." This, most decidedly, is not so. The judgment and the verdict are for all of you to make. Deliberately, too, I do not say an "academic" jury. The denunciation of Burt has been shouted aloud in glaring headlines in all forms of the media. The assumed guilty verdict has gone far beyond academic walls. Furthermore, as we have intimated, the standards of judgment of some academics on other academics is by no means to be relied on. Going beyond such academic boundaries, too, I can suppose you to be committed to thoroughness, exactitude, and integrity in establishing testable and reliable knowledge in your own field of work (whether theoretical or practical) and that you share the same standards of truth-seeking in the pursuit of justice. It is not at all my objective to "whitewash" Burt, whatever the evidence; to deal only in exchanges of rhetoric; to counter clever and belligerent argument with belligerent argument that tries to appear more clever. Though certainly arguing as clearly and strongly as I can, my aim is to set out the relevant evidence systematically and impartially so that you may be in a position to form your own considered judgment. My request is only that you approach the entire matter with a fresh, open, and unprejudiced mind, and defer your judgment, considering your verdict only at the end of the argument, when the case for the defense has been put and all the evidence is before you. This initial request is all the more important because of the nature of the prosecution.

Prosecution

So far, no fair trial has been conducted. Only the case for the prosecution has been vociferously presented, and this has followed a strange course of development. Though it cannot be said to have been planned from the beginning, it stemmed initially from, and was subsequently orchestrated by, only a handful of contributors. The allegations have been many. Their influence has been worldwide. But the individuals who have pressed them with such sustained vigour have been surprisingly few—so much so as to raise the suspicion I have already voiced of some shared underlying grounds of malevolence; some ideological, political, or personal roots of malice. I will ask, as the evidence is revealed, whether these things do not seem to be so.

Though not planned, the few responsible for the prosecution have become more closely related as their attack has proceeded, and the nature of this attack has been quite distinctive. Beginning in academic circles proper in the criticisms of Kamin, it was brought into full public gaze by the journalism of Oliver Gillie, and since that time has been conducted through channels of the widest degree of publicity: the weekly newspapers, radio documentaries and discussions, and television drama. It has been loud, sensationalist, insistent, prolonged; Gillie in particular having been apparently drawn in to support every new occasion of defamation. All this will be fully documented. So far, however, their testimony has never been subjected to systematic cross-examination; their evidence has never been exposed to critical scrutiny; the only counterarguments having been those of letters to the press or occasional articles, and even these spasmodic protests have fallen off. For many, therefore, the case has long seemed settled.

It has become a commonplace assumption—accepted without question—that Burt faked his data, was a "fraud," a "con man," a "psychopath." It can be found taken for granted in the pages of variable but influential writers such as Medawar, Vaizey, and Germaine Greer, just as in the minds and mouths of many students who have never (perhaps because of the controversy) had any acquaintance with his work. And the whole of Burt's work, all his methods of working—going quite beyond the initial, specific charges themselves—have been thrown into disrepute. He stands portrayed as a man of warped character throughout his life, having moved "from early plagiarism to later outright fraud." The case for the prosecution has culminated in an entire character assassination. All this, however, waited for Burt's death. Had it been published during Burt's lifetime, it would have been seen to be plainly libelous. The dead, however, are not legally dangerous, as they are not available for cross-examination or even able to answer back. It is time, therefore, that a systematic investigative defense should be conducted, and this is what I now propose: looking with genuinely critical eyes at the evidence cited in the charge of fraud itself. Turning the demands for justice on those who, with such readiness, intensity, zeal, and persistence, have publicly declared their condemnations, how will their own testimony now appear before the same bar of justice?

This nature of the prosecution so far also makes necessary a clear statement of a few other specific points of a preliminary nature. Without such preliminary indications, these might not remain evident with sufficient clarity once the thick of the argument is entered into. Some signposts to paths through the thickets need to be erected.

Cross-Examination

One central and essential feature of a trial is the careful cross-examination of witnesses. In this way the opposing advocates bring forward all the arguments bearing on the case and all the evidence supporting them, so that every fact and deduction for arriving at a fair judgment is critically appraised and brought openly and fully before the court. Because of the nature of the prosecution in the Burt case so far, the first task, here, is clearly a critical cross-examination of these witnesses—from the side of the defense—and a critical exposition and examination of their evidence. This must therefore form the first and longest section of my argument, and there are certain points I want to make.

First, since the charges brought against Burt have been so defamatory, and since many of the items of evidence on which they are based will be shown to be highly questionable, sometimes disreputable, and with every appearance of being deliberate distortions, the questions to which they give rise call for clear public answers. Since the individuals concerned cannot appear in the witness box, I shall do the next best thing and end each section of cross-examination with a summary list of clear questions to which public answers are now required. Answers may then be given by these individuals in their own subsequent publications, and the case can then be completely judged in the most thorough and satisfactory way.

A second point is extremely important. It will be demonstrated that many of the claims of the prosecution and many of the items of supposed evidence on which these claims rest have been more disgraceful than anything of which Burt has been charged. Much of the evidence is careless in the extreme, highly selective, put forward in a deliberately distorted form, and then endlessly repeated in a completely irresponsible, uncritical, and vituperative manner—and all with a strangely intense animus—by scholars, journalists, and producers alike. The point of significance here is this: Quite independent of the validity or otherwise of the charges of fraud made against him, a great injustice has been inflicted on Burt by the prosecution in its wide-ranging, intense, and long-sustained process of vilification. Putting this differently: Even if the specific charges of fraud against Burt were to be proved true, the range and nature of the denigration perpetrated by the prosecution, the ways in which its evidence has been presented and the characterization of this evidence, can all be shown to have entailed great injustice. This point may well be difficult to appreciate here, at the outset, but will be fully realized and amply demonstrated as the cross-examination proceeds. My point is—to belabor this for a moment—that my first section of cross-examination will in itself, and on the grounds there revealed, demonstrate that a great injustice has been done, whatever the truth or falsity of the allegations of fraud. The evidence indicts the denigrators of Burt themselves with intellectual misconduct of the gravest kind—for which they themselves must answer. Burt's accusers stand accused.

Fraud? True or False?

To disclose the malodorous nature of the prosecution, however, is clearly not enough. The crucial question of Burt's "fraud" remains, and must be examined equally scrupulously and impartially. How does this charge stand? It will be found here, unfortunate though this is from the point of view of every side of the argument, that some aspects of the matter lie unavoidably, given the present state of the evidence, in the realm of the unprovable. Quantities of documents that would have been of crucial importance have been both lost and destroyed (not by Burt, but since his death). Conjectures about these, and about work done on them, must remain conjectures. Even so, much can be said about the nature and consistency of Burt's arguments in the long sequence of his publications, the cumulative nature of his data, the tests he used and the evidence accumulated, on which these arguments rested, which will be shown to be convincing. At the same time, side by side with this, many of the objections raised against his work by his critics will be shown to be unreliable, false, and unconvincing.

The chief critic of Burt is undoubtedly Leon Kamin, and though I will radically criticize his evidence, one can at least pay this tribute to him: He did read, analyze, and criticize Burt's work far more thoroughly than most. The other critics, by comparison, are smallfry—even Professor Hearnshaw, Burt's "official biographer." But the conclusion that has to be reached here is highly significant. What is certain is that *the charge of fraud has, most decidedly, not been proved*. The evidence for the defense against this charge is very substantial and, I will argue, convincing, even though some aspects cannot be conclusively proved. Impartial judgments of probability may be arrived at on a balance of the considerations advanced, and the verdict will then lie with you—the members of the jury.

Rehabilitation?

One other point has to be borne centrally in mind throughout this consideration of the Burt case. The charges of fraud against Burt were initially focused on one strand, or aspect, of his work only: the study of identical twins reared apart, with reference to the theory that intelligence was largely determined by heredity, and Burt's claim to have increased the number of such twins from 21 in 1955, to 42 in 1958, to 53 in 1966. Even if fraud on this one specific matter could be proved, a much wider body of work would remain entirely unaffected. Burt's earlier surveys stand in their own right, and are not in any way dependent on the studies of twins; indeed, the study of twins only gradually, but consistently, emerged from them. It is important, therefore, by way of preliminary preparation and consideration, to remind ourselves of the nature of Burt's work as a whole, and of his emphases within it for improving the lot of individuals and extending their educational opportunities within the deplorable social conditions of his time—from the end of the Victorian era up to, and during a substantial period after, the Second World War; to what amounts, in fact, to almost three-quarters of our own century.

From first to last, Burt's central interest lay in the reliable identification of individual differences, the implications and consequences of these for individuals and society alike, and the opportunities society should provide for their development. Not race, not class, not any other abstract conceptual category, but *individual persons and their destinies* were the focus of his concern. And "from first to last" was a long time: from a first 80-page article in 1909[3] (already emphasizing a "general factor" of intelligence established largely by heredity, and a number of "special aptitudes") to his last book, completed just before his death in 1971, on *The Gifted Child*. In all this work, certain features were clearly marked.

First, it was essentially *pragmatic*. Beginning as an assistant lecturer,[4] he was appointed very early in his career as an "official" psychologist,[5] his work taking shape when authorities were confronted with the need to identify the kinds and causes of backwardness, and to discover the distribution of backward children in the areas for which they were responsible, so that they could estimate the sufficiency of their educational provisions. Burt was essentially, therefore, an *applied psychologist,* employed explicitly in an investigative and advisory capacity, and this he remained through the greater part of his career. Second, as a consequence, Burt's data were always *cumulative*—derived from surveys undertaken for administrative bodies or committees; continually growing in an *additive* way: from early studies in Liverpool and Birmingham to more thorough studies for the London County Council. His data were not the systematic outcome of one study meticulously designed in advance, carried out by himself alone or an appointed research team, and as his facts were collected and brought together, so his statistics had to be continually reworked, adjusted, and rescaled,[6] to make them comparable.

Third, and also in consequence, this wide-ranging work of surveys and testing was possible only with the help of *a vast number of different assistants*—local government officials, headteachers, teachers, social workers, Care Committee workers—all of whom were ready and pleased to be involved, and some categories of whom were never officially recorded and have long since ceased to exist. Fourth, it was only within the context of this cumulative work that a *study of twins* emerged. There never was a planned study of twins, identical or otherwise. It was simply discovered in early surveys that a certain number of identical twins had been identified who had been brought up separately. Gradually, as later surveys were carried out, other cases were added and statistically incorporated into what had been established before. Knowledge of such cases may also have stemmed from personal contacts with (and reports to) both Burt and his helpers, just as some may have been added to the *statistics* when the records of earlier tests had been worked through to Burt's satisfaction. Certainly, Burt was always advertising for such information.[7] But the study of twins was never either the central core of Burt's work nor an independently planned study; it arose only within the context of the much wider investigations. Burt's data were therefore always drawn from complex sources and for practical purposes. Even so, the tests and methods employed were always clearly set out, just as the many helpers were always fully acknowledged.

Fifth, in this effort towards accurate methods for identifying individual differences, Burt's essential concern was for *the provision of appropriate opportunities*. Well aware that social advantages and disadvantages often obscured and gave a distorted picture of levels of ability, he was tireless in the pursuit of equality of opportunity—his methods of mental testing being so devised as to discover the *actual* ability and aptitudes of individual children whatever the family and social conditions from which they came. Working-class children brought up within abominable home and neighborhood conditions, by parents ignorant through no fault of their own, neither displayed nor had the opportunity of developing their true levels of ability in the elementary schools of differing neighbourhoods, and therefore rarely secured places in secondary and higher education. The tests then employed to judge fitness for secondary education were only "attainment tests," which did little more than reflect the advantages or disadvantages of background. Burt introduced tests of mental ability to probe *beyond* these disadvantages, to discover the child's true ability being masked by them, and he deliberately employed nonverbal kinds of tests having discovered (in tests of canal boat children, for example) that even the *language* required in normal tests was itself a distorting obstacle. Burt began with studies in backwardness because it was here, in particular, that knowledge was sought, that the very criteria of backwardness were difficult to clarify, the features difficult to discern, the influences of social origin and background difficult to estimate. Much backwardness had direct physical causes, and it is often forgotten that a considerable part of Burt's work was devoted to uncovering, diagnosing, and making authorities aware of the sheer physiological facts (and conditions of poor health) that underlay the educational retardation of many children.[8] Much, however, was due also to the massive social disadvantages of poverty, deplorable home conditions, ignorance, and abysmal levels of cultural and linguistic deprivation, all of which Burt emphasized, analyzed, and weighed in careful detail. All these kinds, conditions, and distributions of backwardness had to be uncovered and then appropriately treated—provided with special schools, special classes, differential treatment—just as those found to have high levels of mental ability had, whatever their social backgrounds, to be given the opportunity of secondary and higher education.

But sixth, by equality of opportunity, Burt decidedly did *not* mean *equality of treatment*. This, he thought, would be absurd. Given distinctive levels and kinds of abilities among individuals, there should be an appropriate *diversity of opportunities* to maximize their fulfilment. In view of the allegations made against him, these concerns of Burt need to be meticulously substantiated. In his 1943 article on "Ability and Income"—looking ahead to post-war reconstruction, and later so much criticized—Burt pointed out the existing *inequalities* in no uncertain manner.[9]

In London (to take one of the most striking illustrations) a survey of junior county scholarship awards during the years preceding the last war showed that in certain electoral divisions (N St Pancras, N Hackney, Lewisham, Dulwich, and Hampstead) the average number of scholarships annually awarded was about six or seven per 1,000 pupils in attendance; in others (S St Pancras, Finsbury, Bethnal Green, S Islington, W Southwark, N Lambeth) it was less than one per 1,000. A study of entrants to the universities reveals a still more startling anomaly. Taking figures for all England and Wales, it appears that, out of a total age-group, comprising something like 700,000 persons, about 660,000 belong to the elementary school or non-fee-paying class, and only 40,000 to the fee-paying class; yet of the former less than 5,000 annually enter the universities, and out of the latter more than 6,000; that is, only 0.7 per cent in the one case, and nearly 15.0 per cent in the other. This means that, if a child's parents can afford fees for his early education, his chances of going to a university are more than twenty times as great as they would be if such fees could not be afforded.

As psychologist to the L.C.C., one of my first tasks was to inquire into the causes for these persistent discrepancies.

His detailed study concluded that the inequality of incomes in society seemed "to be largely, though not entirely, an indirect effect of the wide inequality in innate intelligence"; not supporting the view that "the apparent inequality in intelligence of children and adults is in the main an indirect consequence of inequality in economic conditions"; not supporting, in short, an Environmentalist explanation of the determination and distribution of intelligence. But this was no argument for leaving things as they were. His final conclusions were plain and forceful.[10]

(1) Nevertheless, mental output and achievement, as distinguished from sheer innate capacity, are undoubtedly influenced by differences in

social and economic conditions. In particular, the financial disadvantages under which the poorer families labour annually prevent three or four thousand children of superior intelligence from securing the higher education that their intelligence deserves.

(2) The most striking instances of this are to be found at the final stage of education. With the available data a simple calculation shows that about 40 per cent of those whose innate abilities are of university standard are failing to reach the university; and presumably an equal number from the fee-paying classes receive a university education to which their innate abilities alone would scarcely entitle them.

There was no denial of the inequalities of opportunity here, no approval of them, no suggestion of resting content with them. On the contrary, Burt's concern was to *extend* opportunity for the disadvantaged, to eliminate such unwarranted inequalities.

But a seventh emphasis in Burt's work is almost always overlooked. He was not *deterministic* in his analysis. The genetic endowment of a child might set limits to what was possible (sometimes severely restricted, sometimes not so). The social context of family, neighborhood, community, and economic conditions might well enshroud a child from its earliest years with unchosen features of a deeply influential kind. But none of these *determined* what an individual person might become. Also important was the *character* of a person in facing and dealing with the facts his personal and social heritage presented. Depending upon the cultivation and government of his own nature and conduct, resting on principles, guided by ideals, aims, and values (as of self-discipline, application in work, endeavor, perseverance), sustained by continuing motives, an individual could make much or little of the nature and situation he had inherited. *Morality* was of central importance in education, as in life. All these elements were clearly stated time and time again throughout Burt's work—not only in his many books and professional articles, but also, and quite distinctively, in his regular column written for the *News Letter of the Association of Educational Psychologists* (of which he was patron) throughout the first seven years of its existence, which were also the last seven years of his life.[11]

This brief note is, of course, an extremely condensed characterization only of an enormously complex body of work that occupied a period of some 60 years, but the features emphasized are important because the image of Burt presented by his opponents has been of almost the *exactly opposite* character. Insisting on his consistent finding that mental ability was largely inherited, and not determined chiefly by environmental conditions, he was attacked as the archenemy of equality of opportunity; as one who paid little attention to social conditions and took little account of their effects; as one of the chief architects of the threefold structure of segregated schools with selection on the basis of examination and the IQ test at 11+; as the great champion of "right wing elitism." These characterizations too, as we shall see, were even smeared with charges of racism stemming from the most extreme pronouncements of eugenics. All these issues will be examined, but is it not beyond doubt, even at the outset, that the subjects to which Burt devoted himself remain of the greatest importance in society and education today? Yet all have been thrown into disrepute. If the charges of fraud are shown to be false, if the allegations of his detractors are shown to be sheer calumnies resting on no foundation, then the case for the rehabilitation of both Burt and his work will be incontestable.

Relevance?

This is especially true because of the relevance of Burt's ideas to the condition of crisis in which British education now finds itself. It is hardly too much to say that the present widespread disaffection evident within British education at all levels has stemmed from an ignoring of the plain matters of fact to which Burt pointed, a complete misunderstanding of the concepts of equality and equality of opportunity that underlay and ran through all the arguments that left-wing critics had with him, and a reliance on the politically simplistic reorganization of schools that followed. One minister of education after another now steps into the misguided footprints of the one who preceded, and proceeds by instituting new "reforms" to compound the manifold mistakes. It is arguable that only a return to the basic truths of Burt's position can provide a satisfactory remedy for our condition. All this, however, remains to be argued more fully when the case for the defense is completed.

With all these provisos, our initial cross-examination can now begin.

Notes

1. Fletcher, Ronald. *Education in Society: The Promethean Fire*. London: Penguin Books, 1984.
2. Especially "The Doubtful Case of Cyril Burt," *Social Policy and Administration,* spring 1987; and "The Progressive Vendetta Against the IQ Man," *Sunday Telegraph,* August 2, 1987.
3. "Experimental Tests of General Intelligence," *British Journal of Psychology* 3, 94–177.
4. 1908, University of Liverpool.
5. 1913, by the London County Council.
6. Much mathematical criticism has been levelled at Burt's adjustments of his tests and statistics. When he spoke of "adjustments", he seems, usually, to have meant one of three things: (1) retesting and adjusting tests when they seemed greatly out of keeping with the teacher's experience of a child and estimation of his or her ability (his concern was always for fairness to the individual child), (2) adjusting test scores to try to take into account obvious environmental advantages and disadvantages, and (3) rescaling findings in terms of a normal distribution to render them comparable. Dorfman (*Science,* September 1978) may well have failed to take this into account in believing that Burt's figures were "too normally distributed," and Stigler (October 1978) has in turn criticized Dorfman for this.
7. In the *News Letter of the Association of Educational Psychologists,* no. 3, Easter 1965, for example, Burt wrote: "During the past 50 years my colleagues and I have kept a careful watch for cases of this kind— 'identical' twins reared apart from infancy. At first we could discover only a handful. But as soon as our results were published, more cases kept coming in, and we have now located as many as 53 pairs. We should still be grateful for additional names and addresses."
8. At least six out of the sixteen chapters in *The Backward Child,* together with some appendices, are concerned with these alone.
9. *British Journal of Educational Psychology* 13:83; 1943.
10. Ibid. p. 98. In the same place, Burt also "readily endorsed" the pronouncement of Marshall, the economist: "No extravagance is more prejudicial to the growth of national wealth than the wasteful negligence which allows genius that happens to be born of lowly parentage to expend itself in lowly work; and there is no change that would conduce so much to a rapid increase in that wealth as an improvement in our schools and scholarships such as would enable the clever son of a poor man to rise gradually till he has the best education the age can give."
11. Issue no. 1, September 1964. Burt died in 1971.

II
WITNESSES FOR THE PROSECUTION

CROSS-EXAMINATION

Introduction

We now turn to the testimony of those who made the allegations against Burt. From the beginning, the accusers seemed to be waging a war, conducting a vendetta, rather than pursuing an argument, but it was the BBC's television dramatization, broadcast early in 1984, that provided the final and convincing evidence that this was so; that something was seriously and massively wrong. The entire attack seems now—seven years or so after the initial charges were made—to have become not only an organized campaign but also one that was most emphatically slanted. *The Intelligence Man* must rank as one of the most vicious and patently one-sided character assassinations ever seen on the television screen; a character assassination of the worst kind, of a dead man who could not answer back; one of the worst blemishes on the record of the BBC. It was *so* one-sided, took for granted in so unqualified a way the truth of the charges of fraud, presented so unrelieved and blackened a picture of Burt's character, as to be totally and disquietingly out of keeping with the BBC's professed concern for balance, fairness, and impartiality. It cried out for justice; for some indication, at the very least, that there was another side to the story. Had it been made about a living person, it would have been plainly seen to be defamatory and libelous. As such, without the most careful qualification, it would not have been shown. It was about the dead, however, so that this consideration did not apply. Therefore it was shown. This was surely—on the part of all those who wrote and produced it, and approved its transmission—a disgrace.

Lord Denning, one of the most eminent British judges, has voiced his distaste at the libel of the dead, but has also pointed out the apparent impossibility of dealing with it within the law. The dead are not available for cross-examination. This is a matter, therefore, where justice must seek ways outside the law. Those who traduce the name and reputation of a man, who throw his whole character and the entire body of his work into disrepute, should nonetheless, in some way, be publicly required to justify their testimony and defend the soundness and veracity of the evidence on which it rests. I propose, therefore, to begin by examining this film. It is a kind of compendium of items of evidence from many of the contributors we shall have to consider later. Working backwards from it (that is, to the evidence that had been presented before it appeared), we will then be able to look at the further testimony of each contributor in turn.

2

The BBC: *The Intelligence Man*

The Billing

Having long suspected the substance and manner of the charges made against Burt by Gillie, Kamin, and the Clarkes from 1976 onwards, and having, subsequently, been even more deeply skeptical about the apparent impartiality of Leslie Hearnshaw's "official biography" that appeared in 1979, I was at once disturbed by the billing of the film. Without raising any question whatever, it took completely for granted the view that these charges of fraud were true; that the matter was settled; that proof had been decisively established. The subtitle boldly described the film as "A Story of Scientific Fraud." The introductory blurb in the Radio Times (January 7–13, 1984) plainly stated that "after his (Burt's) death in 1971 much of his work was shown to be fraudulent." Burt was "a character . . . who betrayed himself." Why, asked Stephen Davis, the author, did Burt "pervert his career in such a bizarre way?" "Was Burt born a villain?"

Such assertions and assumptions—exposed to so much many-sided argument, if only in letters to the press and book reviews, from 1976 onwards—had most certainly *not* been settled. Why were they so stated, then, in such a settled and conclusive way to a wide viewing audience whose members, clearly, could not possibly be aware of the details of the controversy or possess the knowledge on which to assess it? Why, too, in this billing of so serious a matter as a factual drama-documentary exploration of a man's entire character, was this introduction by the author accompanied by almost as long a piece by Oliver Gillie, the journalist chiefly responsible for initiating the charges of fraud? This too stated, as settled matters of fact, that five years after Burt's death "his reputation was in ruins; that he had "not only created an immense body of fradulent scientific findings but invented a whole team of non-existent characters to bolster his credibility"; that "as recently as 1969 he was still inventing data"; that "his work was used in America to support the theory that black Americans were innately inferior to whites"; and that, when Kamin had "put Burt's work through the scientific mincing machine . . . there was little left." Given the known degree of disagreement, every one of these statements seemed inexcusable in its exaggeration and total lack of qualification. Every single one had been challenged, critically considered, and (for some) satisfactorily rebutted, yet here they were all presented to a general audience as settled matters of fact. This kind of introduction led to similar repetitive billings elsewhere in the press.

> *Horizon: The Intelligence Man.* A drama-documentary by Stephen Davis about the scientific fraud perpetrated by Sir Cyril Burt. . . . A story that begins in 1970 and works back, studying the development of Burt's character from when he was at the height of his powers and influence in the University College of the 1930s, when he was secretive and preoccupied with his theory of inherited intelligence. (Program description, *Radio Times,* Monday, 9 January 1984)

Reviewers were led to exactly the same matter-of-fact judgments. The film, wrote Dennis Hackett in the *Times* (January 10, 1984), was

> an ingenious documentary . . . on Sir Cyril Burt, whose psychological prejudices about inherited intelligence, and the relationship between it and income, dominated British educational thought for so long and pleased those who were disposed to believe it anyway. Five years after his death in 1971, his research was shown to be fictitious, a gigantic fraud.

In such ways are judgments about a man's character, work, and ideas now disseminated and entrenched. The film itself, however, was even worse than these preliminary forebodings.

Misrepresentations

Throughout, "clips" from interviews with authoritative psychologists (intermingled with dramatized scenes exemplifying the supposed deviousness, dishonesty, overbearing dogmatism, and egocentricity of Burt's nature) were linked together and presented in such a way as solidly to confirm Burt's guilt and the one-sided picture of his character. But one thing puzzled me. I knew that, among those taking part, two had been close friends, supporters, and (to some extent) co-workers of Burt. These were Professor Arthur Jensen of Berkeley, California, and Professor Raymond Cattell, now retired in Hawaii. Although both would no doubt have criticisms of Burt (Jensen, especially, had already published some criticisms), I could not believe that they would testify against him in so total a way as the short "clips" from their interviews suggested. Knowing the ways of film editing, I wrote to both of them telling them frankly of my doubts and expressing my bewilderment. Professor Cattell replied as follows:

The answer to your question about how far we were appraised of what the presentation would turn out to be is that we were distinctly misled. I had expected a documentary and I gave an hour of my time to a BBC team which came out here to Hawaii to get my reactions, as one who knew Burt well in the past. In my presentation I dwelt not only on the twins reared apart but also on other scientific and political aspects of the question. For example, I pointed out that the consensus of scientific work in the area fell exactly at Burt's figures and that the removal of Burt's data would not affect the scientific issue at all. I also pointed out that I thought the British educational system had retreated from a very fine renovation that it had been given by Burt's eleven plus system, which was as near a just meritocracy as one could get. Finally I dwelt at some length on the psychological causes of resistance to heredity as a principle in the general population, a resistance which has come to extreme forms in the left wing politically. . . . It is quite clear that these people—Gillie, Kamin, and others—thought that by a thorough character-assassination of Burt they could disprove the importance of heredity in intelligence. This they have conspicuously failed to do. . . .

The team that came to Hawaii consisted of three intellectuals and assorted mechanics, and I sometimes think that since they took an hour's recording from me and apparently gave only one minute of it in the final appearance that they came primarily to get in a visit to Hawaii! We had a friendly and amicable interaction, but I sensed that I was dealing with the products of the 1960 revolt of students. One of them did tell me that he proposed to present it not as a documentary but as a drama in which I gathered that Burt was likely to play the part of the popular image of "the mad professor." Now I have not seen the product myself, but my brother in Devonshire and others who have written to me fully concur with your opinion of a very biased presentation. I have written twice, once a year ago and once a month ago,[1] to ask if they will send me a cassette of the presentation or at least of the account they took from me which I think might have some use as a lecture on the subject. I get evasions in terms of the technical difficulties in putting an English version upon an American machine.

In a later letter, referring to "that absurd BBC film", he wrote:

Both Jensen and I became aware they had a pre-arranged concept that took no notice of all that we gave them.

Professor Jensen, not going as far as Professor Cattell, in not being sure to what extent he was "actually misinformed," wrote nonetheless:

The BBC people who came to Berkeley to interview me did describe the general format of the program, i.e., as a dramatization of episodes in Burt's career, interspersed with excerpts from interviews with people who had some connection with Burt, or who had figured in the controversy over the authenticity of Burt's twin data. They also told me that that they were taking a nonjudgmental stance regarding Burt's ideas and contributions, and the script writer (I forgot his name) emphasized that he was fascinated by the *complexity*[2] of Burt's personality. I was led to believe they were attempting to present a rounded, balanced picture of Burt's great career in psychology. I was of course dismayed when I saw the final product, and dismayed by such a monolithically *simple*[2] portrayal of Burt; rarely have I seen such an overly simplified one-dimensional character on any TV drama. Burt came across . . . as uniformly cold and sinister. The real Burt was a wonderfully engaging person, rather than the stiff, cold and calculating prig we saw on the BBC show. This kind of thing, however, is typical of the popular media. I have long since learned that the popular media (in all its forms) regard the uninspired fictions of its own creation as more interesting than the actual truth.

What conclusion can be drawn from this testimony other than that at least two of the authorities taking part had been in various ways and to varying degrees misled as to the nature of the program to which they were contributing, and that the clips from their interviews had been selected in order to seem to confirm the one-sided picture of Burt? But the testimony of Cattell and Jensen was by no means all.

Indefensible Judgments

The film was scattered with extreme and damning judgments from other authorities. Two examples will suffice—one from Professor Eysenck, one from Professor Kamin—and in both cases we will examine their testimony in more detail later.

For a long time Professor Hans Eysenck, while admitting mistakes on the part of Burt, had staunchly defended him against the charges of fraud. Finally, he was won over by the apparent balance and impartiality of Hearnshaw's "official biography." His conversion, however, seems to have been not only complete but extreme. This was his judgment of Burt in the film.

> He really is to me a mystery wrapped up in an enigma. Outwardly he was always polite, gentlemanly, kindly, helpful and so on, but the evidence indicates very conclusively that he was very vengeful, hostile, aggressive, and extremely devious. . . . Psychopaths unfortunately are usually able to conceal their motivation and their wrong-doing extremely well. They are the typical con-men, and in a sense, of course, Burt was a con-man.

As a matter of received fact, the evidence being "very conclusive," Burt was here labelled both a "psychopath" and a "con-man." Are these statements defamatory and libelous, or are they not? Did the writer or the producer question this? The film raised no question and offered no criteria as to what evidence justified the diagnosis of psychopath. Could, and would, such things have been publicly said about Burt had he been alive—or indeed, about any living person?

The testimony of Professor Leon Kamin (of Princeton) was, if anything, even more reprehensible because it is demonstrably false. The following was his account of Burt's 1943 paper on "Ability and Income."[3]

> The argument that Burt made there was really quite simple and quite astonishing I think—if you listen to it carefully. He says "Look—there

are vast inequities of income in our society, and some people think that unjust, but it is not unjust at all because there are vast inequities in innate ability in society as well; so since we know that ability is innate, then it follows that the distribution of income where some people get a great deal and many people get very little corresponds closely to the distribution of innate ability.''

He then presents the correlations—these, to say the least, sketchily documented (there are no sources given, there are no details given, he simply says our statistics have shown that the correlation in IQ between cousins is .22, whatever number he used), these radically undocumented numerical . . . in retrospect I will call them numerical *fictions* . . . are presented to bolster the argument that ''indeed here I have data that show that results on IQ tests are genetically determined. So since ability as measured by IQ tests is genetically determined, then the differences in income in our kind of society are perfectly good, beautiful, and true.''

No one, having tried their best to make sense of this statement, could possibly recognize from it the article to which it refers. Who could suppose from this caricature that in this article the sources of the statistics to which reference is made are given in precise detail from the very first page onwards; that questions of the ''output'' of individuals, as well as the distribution of intelligence, are very deliberately and specifically gone into in relation to large inequalities (*not* inequities) of income; and that the entire motive in writing it had stemmed from a concern about the inequalities of opportunity in education in society (the figures on the very first page demonstrating these inequalities in many London districts, and between fee-payers and non-fee-payers)? The conclusion at which the article arrived was the one that we have already noted:

The financial disadvantages under which the poorer families labour annually prevent three or four thousand children of superior intelligence from securing the higher education that their intelligence deserves.

The most striking instances of this are to be found at the final stage of education. With the available data a simple calculation shows that about 40% of those whose innate abilities are of university standard are failing to reach the university; and presumably an equal number from the fee-paying classes receive a university education to which their innate abilities alone would scarcely entitle them.

Kamin's account of this article was deplorably superficial and misleading. But there was an even more abominable example. "I was tremendously interested," Kamin said,

> in some of his earlier notebooks—obviously lecture notes from his undergraduate days at Oxford in 1902 and 1903. Talking about the problem of the very poor and the perpetuation of poverty, for example, Burt has written out in his hand "Of the Problem of the Very Poor: they must be segregated; prevented from producing their own kind." This is the kind of atmosphere obviously to which he was exposed.

Elsewhere,[4] Kamin has repeated the same quotation, commenting:

> With beliefs of that sort it was not surprising that Burt could interpret the fact that slum children did poorly on Binet's test as a sign of their genetic inferiority.

In one place, Burt's notes are described as his "lecture notes" indicating "the atmosphere to which he was exposed," in another as his own beliefs. But what in fact were they? They were notes that Burt had taken of an essay by A. C. Pigou, the welfare economist, on "Some Aspects of the Problem of Charity" (forming a section of a book published in 1901[5]). Had either Kamin or Stephen Davis taken the trouble to read this section, they would have discovered that its entire sympathy was with the very poor who, in the wreckage of society, had suffered so much of deprivation and degradation that their own plight, for their own generation, within their own time, seemed incapable of solution. Its entire emphasis was upon the humanitarian task of finding the most effective way of overcoming these problems of poverty. They would have seen, furthermore, that the book of which this essay was a part began very forthrightly with the sentence "The Victorian era has definitely closed," and that its many sections (on "Realities at Home," "The Housing Problem," "The Children of the Town," "The Distribution of Industry," "Temperance Reform," "The Church and the People," "Past and Future," and so forth) were all discussions of ways in which the appalling conditions of society that remained could be improved. The very idea that Burt or Pigou, were reactionary in these many respects, advocating extreme eugenicist policies of "selective breeding," is either an outrageous distortion or rests on the most careless of errors. The significant point here, however, is the fact that Kamin's gross misrepresentations were neither questioned nor checked by the author, the producer of the film, or (let it be noted) by Professor Hearnshaw, who it seems was their chief consultant. "Professor Kamin," Stephen Davis has written in defensive correspondence, "has written very cogently on the subject." Were these examples of such cogency? Did Stephen Davis agree with them—and approve them?

Such judgments—presented as plain matters of fact, and in a slighting superior, derogatory manner—were an outrageous traducing of Burt's character and the nature and objectives of his work. Seeking in his surveys to establish the truth about the harshness of social and economic conditions, concerned about the considerable inequalities of opportunity they entailed and desiring to redress them, Burt was made to appear exactly the reverse. And no question was raised.

A Disallowing and Rejection of All Qualifications

All such issues could have been properly dealt with as elements in the ongoing Burt controversy had both sides been given, had appropriate qualifications been introduced; but there were none. What is more seriously damaging, however, is that some were proposed—and rejected. Again, a few examples will suffice.

None of Burt's supporters appeared in the film, a fact in itself significant. But why, when they expressed the wish that qualifications should be made, were their wishes ignored and their views excluded? Dr. Charlotte Banks, in addition to correspondence, spent some two hours with Martin Freeth, the producer, explaining her wish that—minimally—some sentence should be inserted at the start of the program to let the public know that there was another side to the Burt story. But her request was refused and her views discounted. Why? Chiefly, it seems, because Leslie Hearnshaw, Burt's "official biographer," who had somehow gained the impregnable reputation of being "impartial and magnanimous," had written to Freeth saying that Charlotte Banks was very loyal to Burt but biased in his favor and not to be relied on. Such magnanimity! The supporters of Burt were biased and unreliable. His traducers were not. Such impartiality! Following a limited correspondence after the showing of the film, Martin Freeth wrote in the Radio Times that "Burt's impartial and magnanimous biographer, Leslie Hearnshaw, described *The Intelligence Man* as an interesting and enjoyable film which was "reasonably fair to Burt'." There was an oracle, it seems, who had spoken.

Why, too, when Robert Reid—who had worked very closely with Burt during the last seven years of Burt's life as editor of the Journal of the Association of Educational Psycholigists—also suggested to Martin Freeth that some qualification was called for, did Freeth ignore his objection, claiming that such qualification would spoil a good story? Reid met Freeth on at least three occasions, letting him see articles and letters from Burt; and, having looked at them, Freeth told him that he "wouldn't like the play . . . you're not going to like it," the gist of his point being that they were basing it upon Hearnshaw's opinion. Reid's comment: "I was surprised and hurt that my account of Burt's character was completely ignored and he was given a character I would never have recognised." But there is a perhaps even more telling piece of evidence of this kind.

Ann Clarke (now Professor at Hull University) was one of Burt's sternest and most severe critics from the beginning of the controversy—to my mind unjustly so—but she refused to take part in this film. Why? Because the assurance of a fair treatment of the subject, which she had requested, was refused. In correspondence (in the *Sunday Telegraph*), Stephen Davis said of one of my own early articles: "It is both mischievous and inaccurate" to try to "insert into his tale" the suggestion that Dr. Ann Clarke "refused to take part unless given certain assurances of fairness which were not forthcoming." But Ann Clarke's own words in personal correspondence were precisely this: "I was invited to take part, but in the absence of certain assurances about fairness, declined to do so."[6] Furthermore, she subsequently expressed appreciation of the fact that, while criticising her on many grounds, I said that this was much to her credit.

To what conclusion does such testimony lead other than that the portrait of Burt presented in this film was not only one-sided but also deliberately so?

Stephen Davis said, in the same correspondence, that his drama-documentary rested on research that "took many months, involved thousands of miles of travelling, interviews with a great many of Burt's former associates and colleagues, and the sifting of every relevant paper, archive, and journal." He certainly travelled thousands of miles—to visit Raymond Cattell in Hawaii and Arthur Jensen in California. What are his answers to their stories of misrepresentation and grave dissatisfaction over the ways in which their contributions were used? He "sifted every relevant paper, archive, and journal." What, then, are his answers to the misleading caricatures and distortions of the archive material and the paper presented by Kamin? What are his and Martin Freeth's explanations, too, of the fact that qualifications from supporters of Burt were not allowed, and that assurances of fairness even to a critic of Burt could not be given? Martin Freeth quotes the "impartial and magnanimous" Leslie Hearnshaw (a kind of god looking on from the wings) as his final authority. But among the papers so thoroughly sifted out, had neither he nor Stephen Davis noticed that Hearnshaw's own impartiality was by no means universally accepted? Lee Cronbach of Stanford, for example, in a widely known review,[7] had said "Hearnshaw, once convinced, wrote a prosecution brief." Indeed he did; one raising questions we will itemize and that he too must answer. One wonders whether, for example, as consultant, he had himself questioned and approved Kamin's interpretations in the program he thought "reasonably fair to Burt"? But a final important area of criticism lies in the many dramatized scenes.

Dramatized Incidents and Scenes: Evidence?

Interspersed with the interview-type pronouncements were over 35 dramatized scenes all of which (with perhaps one or two exceptions) were such as to exemplify and buttress the charges made against Burt. They portrayed him as having an egotistical, dogmatic, hectoring manner in the lecture-theatre, and with a crass intolerance of questioning by students, insensitively humiliating one such student before others. They claimed, showing pictures of long queues waiting in vain in the corridor outside his study, that he had little interest in his students—all of which runs totally counter to the actual testimony of his students and colleagues, which overwhelmingly emphasises his great kindliness, helpfulness, and concern for their own work and personal problems. They showed him "guessing" the IQs of adults; claiming the ability to assess the IQs of the parents of children he was testing without at all subjecting them to tests; rigging an investigation to arrive at the "evidence" desired; secretively hiding from his secretary the fact that he had invented an assistant who did not really exist. They dwelt, throughout, on the supposed flaws in his work and character, on the deceit and subterfuge he allegedly practised.

Since this program was not fictional, however, but a supposedly factual presentation of Burt's character in relation to the "story of scientific fraud," the simple question is: On what concrete evidence did these dramatic reconstructions and sequences of dialogue rest? This question could be asked of every one of the dramatized incidents, but for the sake of brevity just a few are ennumerated.

1. Burt and his secretary, emerging from their door to go for a walk, bump into a butcher's boy on his bicycle. After his departure, Burt estimates his IQ as being 90, but says that "we must not look down on butchers," even though "intelligence is correlated with occupational status." Questioned by his secretary as to how he can possibly estimate a person's IQ on just meeting them, Burt simply says "Practice!"

2. Some colleagues are drinking coffee in a common room. One colleague from another department, who turns out to be a Jew, is being irately castigated for "scoffing at eugenics, scoffing at Galton, scoffing at psychology" and for being ignorant of the fact that "the breeding stock is of prime importance" and the danger that "the lower classes will outbreed the superior stock." Burt is called into the conversation to "tell him about *data* (having "tested thousands of slum children"). It is said that "in Germany they've got some good ideas", and the Jew, claiming that he is a "positivist" and that "even your concept of intelligence is metaphysical," leaves. The conversation continues: "He's touchy about Germany because he's a Jew." "I'm well aware he's a Jew. He also seems to be a communist. . . . Perhaps you ought to tell him about twin studies. . . ." "There's no doubt about the genetic basis of intelligence. All you need are the figures . . . the *data,* I mean."

3. Burt's father, a doctor, takes "Loddy" (Burt as a boy) on a visit

to Francis Galton. "Loddy" (Lodovic) is already a scholarly prig. "Are you good at your school work, Loddy?" "Oh yes, sir, very good!" The conversation dwells on the continuity of high ability from fathers to sons among judges, and, at a much lower level, the existence of a "large number of defectives and ne'er-do-wells. . . . The sheer size of slum families makes me concerned. . . . Society must take steps in the matter." Later, there is a fantasy-type repetition of this scene. "You can sit on my throne," says Galton to Loddy. "I have an IQ of 200, father," says Loddy, and then voices float vaguely about the scene in a dreamlike way. "Was he a slum boy?" "He was never a slum boy." "I was nearly a slum boy, father."

4. Jack Flugel, a colleague, is called in hush-hush fashion into Burt's room. Against Flugel's wish (he clearly thinks the whole matter improper), Burt presses him to act as a second "independent investigator" in a study of occupation, social class, and intelligence, because "you and I are likely to agree. . . . We need two independent testers who have a high level of agreement . . . and two looks better than one!"

5. Miss Archer hands Burt a letter addressed to Margaret Howard, c/o Professor Cyril Burt, 4, Aldous Grove, Aberystwyth, asking "Where would you like me to send it?" Guiltily, Burt takes it. "Leave it with me." As Miss Archer leaves the room, he surreptitiously slips the letter under his blotter.

On what concrete evidence can these reconstructions and conversations possibly rest? On what evidence, according to the author and producer, *do* they rest?

The question is all the more pressing because at least one such scene has been said by the person who described it to have been falsified. Miss Archer (Burt's last secretary) initially told a Columbia Broadcasting interviewer of a dinner scene when Burt and his wife argued about a gynecological operation that (she claimed) employed a new technique. Burt disagreed and, referring to a medical book, was proved right. Lady Burt then made a kind of mock-despairing gesture with her hand towards the floor and pulled a "lips-turned-down-at-the-corners" face, indicating "Oh dear, downed again!" But no anger was involved and there was no violent altercation. In the film, the scene ended in a violent row, Lady Burt leaving the table in outrage without finishing her meal, Burt being depicted as an insensitive, overbearing, uncaring bigot. Why was Miss Archer's account taken over and distorted in what can only have been a deliberate way?

Doubt—grounded in evidence—having been thrown on the validity of one of these scenes, answers are required on the rest. There are over 30 such scenes—but answers should be easy to provide on the few examples specified.

Did You See?

It also seems worthwhile to point out that, as though to add insult to injury, a *Did You See?* panel discussed the film closely after its showing. No question whatever was raised about the truth or otherwise of the allegations. The "story of scientific fraud" was again taken completely for granted as having been conclusively settled—even by Professor Tessa Blackstone who presumably must at least have known that there were other sides to the argument. Some time afterward, when I had begun to inquire into the whole of the Burt case, Professor John Cohen wrote:

> I thought that Ludovic Kennedy's opening remarks in his *Did You See?* programme, after the drama, were absolutely monstrous libels, especially as he knew nothing at all about Burt. I phoned his secretary in advance to warn him to tread carefully and to brief him, but he took no notice at all. I was really shocked, and his panel, equally ignorant, were just as bad.

Also, having explicitly refused Charlotte Banks' request for the insertion of a qualifying sentence at the start of the film, Martin Freeth promised: "I shall inform the producers of *Did You See?* of your views on the evidence for fraud." Whether or no this promise was kept cannot be known, but there was certainly no evidence of it in the discussion. Only Robert Robinson (for which he deserves much credit) seemed disquieted at the very end of the discussion and made a brief comment to the effect that Burt had been portrayed wholly as a "baddy." But the discussion was rounded off quickly with some statement that Burt, in any event, was not likely to be remembered for having made any contribution of great or lasting worth to psychology—and that was the end of the matter. The panel had corroborated the film.

I repeat: In such a way does the media now judge a man and his life's work. In such a way is popular opinion formed.

Conclusion

I come back, finally, and in general terms, to Stephen Davis and Martin Freeth as writer and producer of this film. It is arguable that Stephen Davis as a dramatist (not, as far as I am aware, a qualified psychologist) genuinely believed that the picture he was creating and projecting—in imaginative drama as well as by authoritative statements in documentary fashion—was the received, established, consensus; that the matter was in fact settled. If, however, he had actually "sifted every relevant paper, archive, and journal" and considered these responsibly, it is difficult to believe this, as letters, documents, and articles existed in plenty showing beyond doubt that alternative views were held. Furthermore, we have seen that some contributors and consultants clearly wished to make qualifications, wished to have assurances of fairness, all of which were denied. It is arguable, similarly, that Martin Freeth's single-mindedness was simply that of a zealous television producer who—realizing the weakening effect of qualifications—wanted to achieve and sustain the strength of a good story. The evidence as it stands, however (from Cattell, Jensen, Banks, Reid, and Ann Clarke, at least), points overwhelmingly to the conclusion that misleading misrepresentations took place and that the indication of alternative views, the making of qualifications, the assurance of fair treatment of the subject, were denied: in short, that the one-sidedness of the presentation was deliberate.

I return to what seems the most crucial consideration.

This program was a factual program about the reputation of a man, his character, his life, his work. It was (as it seems to me) defamatory and libelous on many counts, both in the testimony of some of those interviewed and in the plain implications of the dramatized scenes. It stood as a damning character assassination of a man—called a "psychopath," a "con man"—actually guilty of a fraud actually committed. Had this man been alive, would the BBC have transmitted this film without the fullest consideration of the possible grounds of libel? I cannot believe it. The man, however, was dead. Libel did not count.

I leave the matter here, for you—as members of the jury—to consider, but let us now set out a clear list of questions to which public answers are required.

Questions Requiring Public Answers

Of Stephen Davis (author), Martin Freeth (producer), and the editor of the Radio Times, it must be asked:

1. Why was the billing of the film, as "a story of scientific fraud," such as to claim without any question or qualification, that fraud had in fact been committed—that Cyril Burt was, without any doubt, guilty? And why was Oliver Gillie, in addition to Stephen Davis, called upon, in the Radio Times introduction, to reiterate his charges—again without qualification?
2. Why were Professors Cattell and Jensen, in various ways and to varying degrees, misled about the nature of the film?
3. Why were Leon Kamin's plain misrepresentations allowed and passed for transmission without check, correction, or qualification?
4. Why was Dr. Banks' request for the introduction of even the most minimal qualification in the program (simply to indicate that there was another side to the story) refused? Why was the description of Burt's character by one of his supporters who knew him well—Robert Reid—ignored? Why were assurances of "fair treatment" of the subject so fully refused to Ann Clark that, even though a forceful critic of Burt, she refused to take part?
5. On what firm evidence did the five dramatized scenes specified rest? Could the items of evidence, in each case, be supplied?
6. Did the producer inform the *Did You See* team of Dr. Banks' view and wish, as he had promised?

Of Professor Eysenck, it must be asked:

1. After he had so long defended Burt against his detractors; on the grounds of what evidence did he become convinced that Burt was "very vengeful, hostile, aggressive, and extremely devious?"
2. On the grounds of what evidence, and on what criteria of

diagnosis, did he also conclude that Burt was a "psychopath" and a "con man"?

Of Professor Kamin, it must be asked:

1. How does he explain his complete misrepresentation of Burt's 1943 paper on "Ability and Income"?
2. How too does he explain his complete, and repeated, misrepresentation and misinterpretation of Burt's early diary notes in such a way as to smear him with the most extreme views of the eugenics movement, when these notes were clearly listed under the title of a book or essay by Pigou? Why did he never think fit to check the source of this title, and the nature of the book from which it came?

(It may be noted that these questions refer to only two of Kamin's accusations in the film. There are others, but these will be introduced later.)

Of Ludovic Kennedy and the "Did You See?" team, it must be asked:

1. Why—as the evidence at present seems to suggest—was Professor Cohen's telephone message that there was another side to the Burt story completely ignored?
2. Was the promised message (about Dr. Banks' views) from Martin Freeth received? If so, why was this also ignored?

Of Professor Leslie Hearnshaw, as Burt's "official biographer," and especially in view of his judgment after the showing of the film and some criticisms of it, that it was "reasonably fair to Burt," it must be asked:

1. Why—as he was presumably aware of Burt's 1943 paper and its conclusions, and of Burt's early diary notes—did he not point out to the producer Kamin's gross misrepresentations of both?
2. Why did he influence the producer against taking Dr. Banks' views into account, especially when her request for a qualifying sentence was so minimal?
3. Knowing well (from his perusal and consideration of all the documents) that there *was* another side to the Burt story,

strongly maintained by many of his colleagues and supporters, why did he too not request that this should, at the very least, be indicated?

4. Also, did he not question the nature and degree of reliability of the evidence on which the dramatized scenes were based? If not, why not?

These are quite straightforward questions that stem clearly from the nature and contents of this film, and to which answers would be required in face-to-face cross-examination in an open court. We should now, then, be able to expect equally clear public answers.

Notes

1. This was written on September 4, 1984.
2. These italics are Jensen's own, and these excerpts from their letters are published with the permission of both Professor Cattell and Professor Jensen.
3. *British Journal of Educational Psychology* 13.
4. *Intelligence: The Battle for the Mind*. London and Sydney: Pan Books, 1981, p. 95.
5. The Heart of the Empire. London: Fisher Unwin.
6. Her additional comment was "The Burt programme was hopeless, and I have not heard a single approval of it."
7. *Science*, 206; 1979.

3

Professor Leon Kamin

Among the "authorities" interviewed in *The Intelligence Man,* there is no doubt that the only critic to be taken seriously is Professor Leon Kamin (we have seen that Professors Cattell and Jensen were not critics in the same way). Indeed, it is almost true to say, in the controversy in general, that Kamin is the *only* critic to be taken seriously, the others doing little more than follow repetitively behind him (though noisily in the case of Gillie). Because of this, a few preliminary points—of a mixed nature—must be made.

As we have seen, one can sympathize to a considerable extent with the roots of Kamin's ideological stance, his hot indignation, and his attack on policies of a discriminatory kind resting on simplistic caricatures of race and class. One can also admire the rigor with which he has criticized the many studies (original and secondary) claiming to have established that intelligence is largely determined by heredity. *The Science and Politics of IQ,* attacking these positions, does so while undertaking a thoroughly documented critical analysis of them, including a critique of their conceptual and statistical *methods* and of their mathematical *models.* This is detailed work that compels respect and calls for serious recognition and consideratioan. Certainly, it cannot and should not be easily cast aside or rhetorically dismissed. But here at the onset must come the elements of mixed response, for this ideological frankness and intellectual stringency is accompanied by several highly questionable characteristics.

First, the ideological zeal frequently issues in a strident, denunciatory, derisive tone of voice and posture bordering sometimes on the fanatical. Of all the participants in *The Intelligence Man,* Kamin was the most deliberately defamatory in his pronouncements and his manner of making them. His absurd and misleading caricature of Burt's 1943 paper, for example, was presented in a derisory manner, each misrepresentation heaped cumulatively upon the last, and culminating in what can only be called a final spit at "numerical *fictions*." No accumulation of denunciations was so sufficient for him that he could resist the compulsive addition of just one more. "I take an even more skeptical view . . . I think it's reasonable to suppose that he never laid eyes on a pair of separated twins in his entire lifetime."

Second, a close examination of his documentation in his books and articles, detailed though it is, shows that it is nonetheless highly selective—so much so as to be seriously misleading, and always such as to denigrate Burt's position and support and advance his own. The scholarship, in short, is more apparent than real. All too often it is slanted rhetoric appearing in scholarly clothes. And here arises a great difficulty of judgment. Sometimes it seems feasible and understandable to suppose that Kamin's ideological zeal—and the sheer intensity and haste of proving and carrying forward his case—leads to a hasty selective perception, a hasty misreading of facts, and hasty mistakes (as, for example, in his eugenics interpretation of Burt's early notes). Sometimes, however (and we will cite clear examples), for a critic who is so sharpsighted to be at the same time so blind to other plainly existing aspects of what he sees, forces one to the judgment that his *selectivity* is a matter of deliberate special pleading, indeed sometimes of falsification. Kamin is a man out to kill an enemy he detests (I do not mean only Burt, but all those maintaining the Hereditarian position) and the way in which he wields his scholarly weapons has, therefore, to be watched with care. And this skepticism of judgment is reinforced by yet other considerations.

On the one hand, he gives a fair imitation of a gramophone record. His publications, lectures, and broadcast statements are many—but the same caricature-like utterances are repeated in much the same form in all. A rhetorical (psychologically well-known) process of "stamping in" is afoot. The ideological and intellectual needle seems to have got stuck in one of its few grooves.

The gramophone syndrome also revealed itself in the fact that—quite apart from publications—Kamin, it seems, did something of a "whistle-stop tour" of American universities, spreading his gospel in almost evangelical manner. He can fairly be regarded, in America at least, as the John Wesley of the Environmentalists, and it is both interesting and important to notice that—our own present judgments aside—his reputation in the United States among those who are still serious students of intelligence is that of a man who "has carefully selected facts in the service of an ideology . . . in the service of a social cause."[1] It may be this rhetorical skill appearing in scholarly clothes and issuing in simplistic and endlessly repeated ideological extremes—with commitment, zeal, and energy—that has succeeded in calling into line behind him those sharing the same persuasions. But the upshot is that Professor Kamin, to be admired in some respects, has also to be approached with the utmost care; indeed, held at arm's length and kept under the closest scrutiny.

One last point. In his detailed survey, Kamin has voiced many and many-sided *criticisms* of the methods employed by those who have sought to measure intelligence. It is not to our purpose to consider these criticisms here. Our own sole concern in this cross-examination is with Kamin's *testimony* relating to the charges of fraud against Burt. It is, of course, well nigh impossible to separate an examination of the testimony as such from a consideration of how the charges of fraud actually stand, and in questioning and criticizing Kamin's arguments and evidence, I will deliberately introduce substantive illustrative material (items of evidence) that will be of direct use and importance when, later, these charges come to be fully considered. Even so, there is a very clear difference of emphasis here. Later we will look specifically at the question of fraud itself, and will then have to bear in mind what is here revealed about the nature of Kamin's testimony. Here we are concerned with the character, truth, and validity of the testimony itself, and the nature of the evidence on which Kamin himself has rested his case.

General Charges

First, Kamin condemns Burt's work in the most sweeping and general way. It was characterised, he says, by the most "elementary flaws," In his section in *Intelligence: The Battle for the Mind* on "The Cyril Burt affair,"[2] he says:

> With hindsight, it seems almost incredible that Burt's data could ever have been taken seriously. *To begin with, Burt never provided even the most elementary information about how, where or when his purported data had been collected.* When a scientist reports results, it is essential that he provides a clear and reasonably detailed account of the procedures he employed in obtaining the results. *This was never done by Burt.* Incredibly, *in most of his papers there is not even any information about which IQ test was supposedly used to obtain the reported correlation.*

Anyone having any acquaintance going beyond the most superficial with the enormous range of Burt's work will find it not only *almost* but *totally* incredible that such a statement could be made by a serious scholar, or taken seriously by anyone else. From early papers in 1909 onward, Burt had examined the newly proposed methods of mental testing in the clearest way, had adjusted them for use in England, had actively used them—and printed them as used—in specific surveys (for example, in that for the Wood Report), had clearly delineated the scale and nature of specific investigations (for example, that in Birmingham in 1921, and of vocational guidance in 1926) and set out in considerable detail the methods employed, tests used, range of subjects to which the tests had been applied, and other data that had also been drawn upon (for example, the tests of recruits to the United States Army during the First World War and of exservice candidates for the English civil service). Furthermore, *all this work was of a cumulative nature* and remarkably consistent in the way in which the data, tests, and methods of each were presupposed and carried over (with specific references) into the nest.

By way of immediate illustration, let us consider Burt's *Investigation upon Backward Children in Birmingham,* published in 1921. I select this deliberately because we will later have to consider charges against it by Ann and Alan Clarke, and it is also relevant to some of Gillie's criticisms. Burt's part in this investigation took place during a visit of four weeks in June 1920, but the children to be tested had already been independently studied by Dr. B. R. Lloyd (who had to some extent prepared the ground for Burt), who also continued his own studies during July and September, finally submitting his report together with that of Burt. Here, our sole concern is to note that on the very first page of this report (after one paragraph briefly stating the investigation's "general conclusion") Burt set out, very precisely, the plan and the methods he had adopted. His exact statement was this (italics added):

Methods of Investigation. I append a brief account of the data upon which this conclusion is based, and of the methods of calculation employed.

Two double investigations, either one comprising both an extensive and an intensive survey, were carried out, first, through the mediation of the head teachers, and secondly by myself. There were thus *four surveys* in all, each following a somewhat different plan.

(1) A preliminary return was first asked for by the chief Education Officer from all head teachers. The head teachers reported from all departments 4,509 backward cases. Of these, however, nearly fifteen hundred were only eight years of age or less. This leaves but 3,045 in senior departments, or barely 3.9 per cent. It is a matter of common experience that (for various reasons, most of which are sufficiently obvious) such returns tend, as a rule, to underestimate very considerably the amount of backwardness obtaining in the individual schools, and further to depend upon a conception of backwardness which fluctuates very widely from teacher to teacher. In the present instance, however, the preliminary return has not been without some interest; by its aid I have been able to compare my own conclusions with teachers' first impressions, and to check my own calculations for the differing incidence of backwardness in schools of various types and various districts.

(2) Preparatory to my own visits a second return was obtained for me from the head teachers in sixteen selected schools. Upon a specially printed schedule the teacher was desired to enter the names (i) of all children whose age was above the normal or average age of their class by one or more years; and (ii) of all children (not included in the foregoing) whose attainments were below the normal or average attainments of their class by the equivalent of one or more years' progress; and further, against the name of each child so enumerated to append details as to his actual age, his approximate attainments (in terms of standards), his attendance at school, and the nature and apparent causes of his retardation.

(3) Six of these departments I myself then visited; and, by means *chiefly* of psychological and educational tests, made an *intensive study* of every child whose name appeared upon the schedules.

(4) In addition I made a rougher survey of seven other departments. Here the object was not to examine every backward child, but to check the general level of the teachers' standards, and the wider applicability of my own methods and conclusions.

Procedure in the Intensive Psychological Survey. To test the standardisation of my tests (based in the first instance upon a previous investigation in London) I also tested *small samples of normal children in the ordinary schools* and of defective children in a special mentally defective school and the residential colony of Monyhull.

During the four weeks covered by my visit to Birmingham I personally tested 562 children. This was at an average rate of rather over ten minutes to every child. The time actually spent, however, varied enormously, according to the nature of the individual case and according to the amount of discussion involved with the teachers and occasionally with the parents.

The general procedure was that each child should be examined first by an assistant by means of standardised educational tests (chiefly tests of reading and mental arithmetic), and then by myself by means of psychological tests (chiefly the Binet-Simon tests of intelligence revised for English children). Other tests and other methods of psychological observation and analysis were employed as occasion arose.

This is hardly a lack of "even the most elementary information about how, where or when his purported data had been collected." Furthermore, this investigation clearly involved the collaborative work of many others, among whom were the chief education officer, head teachers, and other teachers throughout the whole area, and Burt, as always, was precise and generous in his acknowledgments:

My work was greatly facilitated by the help given throughout the investigation by Miss Horrocks (from the clerical staff of the Education Office), and from time to time by Miss Ritchie, Miss Griffiths, and Mr. Andrews (members of the Education Department of the University). I should like here to express my gratitude both to them personally, and to Professor Valentine for thus arranging for special assistance. To the information given by teachers, both in the written schedules and in discussions upon individual cases, and to the records of the medical inspection carried out in advance so carefully by Dr. Lloyd, I found myself deeply indebted when forming my conclusions as to the causes and nature of the backwardness displayed.

Were all these people deluded about Burt's data, his methods of sampling, collecting, and studying the children he said he was studying, the several tests he said he was employing, and which they themselves helped to administer? Is there the slightest evidence of lack of openness or care in the setting out, carrying out, and reporting of the investigation? It can be said, without any question, that the same meticulous statement of detail characterized every one of Burt's surveys.

Kamin's global denunciation of Burt's work has therefore not the slightest foundation. It is not only plain nonsense, it is also false and misleading nonsense, which will be clearly demonstrated in the additional specific examples to follow. But even on this large-scale level of denigration, the gramophone record syndrome was in evidence. In *The Science and Politics of IQ,* we also find this broad statement:

> The papers of Professor Burt, it must be reported, are often remarkably lacking in precise descriptions of the procedures and methods that he employed in his IQ testing.

Such a statement could only be made either by someone so careless as not to have followed from survey to survey, from paper to paper, the descriptions of the procedures and methods Burt gave, or by someone who wished deliberately to promulgate a false picture of Burt's work. But this must be precisely evidenced in other specific instances.

The 1943 Paper "Ability and Income"

We have already noted the misleading caricature of this paper given by Kamin in the BBC's film, but a far more distorted account (nonetheless repeated) is given in his written publications. In Intelligence: The Battle for the Mind, Kamin says (italics added):

> The first large collection of IQ correlations among relatives was reported by Burt in 1943. *The paper contains virtually no information about methods or procedure.* The alleged correlations are merely presented, without supporting details. *The only reference to procedure* is the following: "Some of the inquiries have been published in LCC [London County Council] reports or elsewhere; but the majority remain buried in typed memoranda or degree theses." When scientists refer to primary sources and to documentation, they do not usually cite "else-

where" as the place where something has been published. They do not tend, when talking about genuine work, to emphasise that the work is "buried" and inaccessible. The reader should not be surprised to learn that none of the London County Council reports, typed memoranda or degree theses vaguely referred to by Burt in the cited sentence has ever come to light.

In *The Science and Politics of IQ,* the gramophone record reports:

> The first major summary of his kinship studies, a 1943 paper, presents a large number of I.Q. correlations, but virtually nothing is said of when or to whom tests were administered, or of what tests were employed. The reader is told, 'Some of the inquiries have been published in LCC reports or elsewhere; but the majority remain buried in typed memoranda or degree theses.'

. Let us take these claims point by point. First, the statement that this paper "*contains virtually no information about methods or procedure. The alleged correlations are merely presented, without supporting detail."* What is to be said about this charge?

The truth of the matter is that this paper was primarily concerned with *the inequalities of educational opportunity in Britain.* The central questions it addressed were "What proportion of the non-fee-paying population are really capable of profiting by higher education?" and "What proportion of these actually fail to obtain it?" (Later, it also discussed the question of the output of individuals in relation to the distribution of income.)

Its very first statement (already quoted in the Preamble), was such as to point clearly to the inequalities that existed, and the task with which Burt was faced, and it is worthwhile to reiterate the fact that Burt's primary concern, from first to last, was to extend opportunities to those who, meriting them, were denied them because of social, economic, and cultural disadvantage. Here, however, let us simply note the immediate footnote that Burt gave to make clear the source of these figures:

> The data are tabulated in full in the L.C.C.'s annual report on *London Statistics,* Vol. XXIV (1913–14), p. 424. Later figures will be found in *The Backward Child* (1937), Table IV.

Then, immediately following this, commenting on the data on which his article was based, Burt claimed that "there can be little question that the intelligence of children, and still more of adults, differs according to the occupational class to which they belong. Average IQs are shown in Table I." This table is reproduced here as Table 3.1.

He at once followed this table with another footnote indicating its sources:

These figures were obtained during surveys carried out for the London County Council and the National Institute of Industrial Psychology. The classification follows that which I adopted in our joint *Study of Vocational Guidance* (H. M. Stationery Office, 1926, p. 16).

If these references are checked, the following facts can be discovered. In the 1926 vocational guidance study (table 3.2), the same classification is in fact given.

Detailed information is given on all the elements of the table—the occupational detail of each "vocational category," how the IQ levels of children and adults alike were arrived at, and the percentage of each in each category. But before giving the evidence of these, let us deal with the second of Kamin's charges above—that "the only reference to procedure" is that "some of the inquiries

TABLE 3.1.
Intelligence of Parents and Children Classified According to Occupations

Occupational Category	Average I.Q.	
	Children	Adults
Class I Higher professional: administrative	120.3	153.2
Class II Lower professional : technical, executive	114.6	132.4
Class III Highly skilled: clerical	109.7	117.1
Class IV Skilled	104.5	108.6
Class V Semi-skilled	98.2	97.5
Class VI Unskilled	92.0	86.8
Class VII Casual	89.1	81.6
Class VIII Institutional	67.2	57.3

TABLE 3.2.
Distribution of Intelligence Among Children and Adults

(1) Level of intelligence (in mental ratio).	(2) Educational category or school.	(3) Number of children (in percentages).	(4) Vocational category.	(5) No. of Male adults (in percentages).
1. Over 150	Scholarships (University honours)	0·2	Highest professional and administrative work.	0·1
2. 130–150	Scholarships (secondary)	2	Lower professional and technical work	3
3. 115–130	Central or higher elementary	10	Clerical and highly skilled work	12
4. 100–115	Ordinary elementary	38	Skilled work. Minor commercial positions	26
5. 85–100	Ordinary elementary	38	Semi - skilled work. Poorest commercial positions	33
6. 70–85	Dull and backward classes	10	Unskilled labour and coarse manual work	19
7. 50–70	Special schools for the mentally defective	1·5	Casual labour ..	7
8. Under 50	Occupation centres for the ineducable	0·2	Institutional cases (imbeciles and idiots)	0·2

have been published in LCC reports or elsewhere; but the majority remain buried in typed memoranda or degree theses.''

In the context of Kamin's criticism, this charge seems to refer to the ''correlations among relatives'' and ''the presentation of correlations without supporting details.'' In fact, however, this itself is totally misleading. We are demonstrating in full measure, in all the evidence that we cite, that this comment of Burt's was very far from being ''the only reference to procedure,'' but it has to be emphasized here that—compounding and reinforcing his gross misrepresentation—Kamin has drawn it from a totally different section of the article. At one point, Burt notes the many and varied grounds on which it has come to be believed that "differences in intelligence are innate" (a "vast mass of converging evidence, general inferences, and observations" going beyond the standard tests commonly employed), and says:

> Perhaps, therefore, it will be helpful to summarize quite briefly what appear to be the most convincing lines of argument, and (since some writers have doubted whether it is fair to apply American conclusions to English children) to illustrate those arguments, so far as space allows, from material collected in British schools during inquiries carried out by myself, my colleagues, or my research students.

He then provides a summary account of seven chief arguments, and it is with reference to *these summaries* that his footnote is made:

> Some of the inquiries have been published in L.C.C. reports, or elsewhere: but the majority remain buried in typed memoranda or degree theses. I should like to repeat my acknowledgments to the many workers who assisted me.

For accuracy's sake, and since so much has been said about "missing ladies and assistants" supposedly invented by Burt to support his case, it is worthwhile to note that I did in fact look into one such specific reference in this article. On the study of the number of entrants to secondary and higher education to be expected from the various social classes, Burt made this acknowledgement:

> In addition to acknowledging my indebtedness to teachers and others who assisted in the earlier surveys, I am particularly grateful to Miss Joan Mawer for compiling much of the data on which the following conclusions are based, and for thus bringing my earlier computations up-to-date. A fuller account of sources and calculations, with detailed tables, will be found in her degree essay on *The Relative Influence of Mental Ability and Economic Class on Entrance to the Universities* (filed at the Psychological Laboratory, University College).

Fortunately, with the help of the University of London library,[3] I was able to trace Miss Joan Mawer. She is now Mrs. Joan Clarke. In reply to my letter, she wrote "Certainly I wrote an essay in 1942 whilst working for my B.A. degree under Professor Burt. I do not recollect its exact title but the title you quote is an accurate description of what it was about."[4]

This, then, was unquestionably a highly selective and quite misleading quotation on Kamin's part, whether deliberately so or not. But let us now go back to the data underlying the 1926 tables. Burt and his co-author, Winifred Spielman (vouched for, let us note, as a researcher and contributor to the Industrial Fatigue Board for which the study in vocational guidance was undertaken) made their data, procedures, and kinds of tests employed, perfectly clear. They also, with perfect honesty, made clear their limitations.

As to the *children* in the study, the main inquiry rested on a selection of 100 (of whom more in a moment), and the range of measured intelligence of these children was the outcome of detailed tests. In addition, however, the figures given in the first column of table 3.2 were "a classification of London school children":

> Based on the figures given in the L.C.C. Report on the *Distribution and Relations of Educational Abilities* (Report No. 1868, P. S. King & Son, 1917), pp. 18 *et seq.*, cf. also *Mental and Scholastic Tests*, pp. 147 *et seq.*

Kamin thought it quite "reasonable to suppose that IQ scores of children were easily available to him," but, he continued skeptically, "where and how did Burt obtain IQ scores *for adults?*"

The 1926 study makes the answer to this question perfectly clear. On the one hand, Burt and Spielman drew on studies already undertaken:

> Among adults the range of intelligence varies quite as widely as among children. This has been demonstrated by recent examinations carried out with group-tests—for example, in this country by the Civil Service tests for ex-Service candidates, and in America by the psychological tests applied during the war to recruits for the Army. When persons so tested are classified according to their several occupations, it is found that there is a broad correspondence between intelligence on the one hand and vocational requirements on the other. The correspondence is

shown by the classification of vocations indicated in the fourth column of Table III [Table 3.2].

The percentage of men following trades or professions belonging to each group or class, shown in column 5, were "computed primarily from the figures given in the Census returns for London," but here the limitations were very frankly pointed out.

> The figures finally arrived at are to be taken as nothing more than the roughest approximation. Unfortunately the divisions and sub-divisions adopted in the Census render it at times extremely difficult to reclassify the numbers on any psychological basis; sometimes a single figure in the Census lists has had to be split among two or more vocational categories; and the only guide has been the opinion of some expert, familiar with the conditions of the trade concerned, who could state what was the usual distribution of employees so described.
>
> Approximate as they are, we feel that these figures are still worth recording. A rough numerical guide is better than no guide at all, or the use of a mere unformulated impression; and the publication of a tentative table may at least stimulate other investigators to a more exact analysis of the particular problems raised.

At the same time, the "occupations and professions" included in each vocational category were very clearly specified; it is most important to note this in detail because of the grounds for the correlations between intelligence and economic status that Kamin also criticized, and also so that this can be compared later with the categories of occupational status and social class used by the sociologists of education. The occupational list is given in Table 3.3.

In addition to drawing on existing studies for this classification of IQs and occupational gradings of adults, however, Burt and his colleagues did try to estimate the IQs of the *parents* of the children studied, and here we must turn—for exactitude—to three other charges made by Kamin that are quite distinct.

First, he comments with complete skepticism on the efforts to estimate the IQs of the parents of the children studied. In *Intelligence: The Battle for the Mind,* Kamin wrote:

> There is, in fact, a telltale footnote in one of the earlier papers. With respect to a reported correlation between parent and child, Burt wrote

TABLE 3.3.

Classification of Vocations According to degree of Intelligence Required

Class I.—Higher professional and administrative work (mental ratio, over 150) :

Lawyer, physician, teacher (university and secondary), author, editor, scientist, artist, civil service clerk (Class I), managing director, company secretary, broker, chartered accountant, architect, analytical chemist, professional engineer.

Class II.—Lower professional, technical, and executive work (mental ratio, 130–150) :

Teacher (elementary), civil service (second division), accountant, secretary, executive clerk, dentist, veterinary surgeon, reporter, social worker, factory superintendent, surveyor, merchant, auctioneer, buyer, commercial traveller, technical engineer, designer.

Class III.—Clerical and highly skilled work (mental ratio, 115–130) :

Shorthand-typist, book-keeper, bank or office clerk, wholesale salesman, musician, specialist teacher (gymnasium, music, domestic science), small merchant, insurance agent, electrician, telegraphist, druggist, hospital nurse, compositor, engraver, lithographer, draughtsman, photographer, tool-maker, pattern maker, moulder, machine inspector, showroom assistant, foreman.

Class IV.—Skilled work (mental ratio, 100–115) :

Tailor, dressmaker, milliner, upholsterer, engine, tram and bus driver, policeman, telephone operator, printer, mechanic, turner, fitter, miller, finisher, hand-rivetter, cabinet maker, carpenter, plumber, blacksmith, mason, farmer, shop assistant, cashier, hair-dresser, routine typist.

Class V.—Semi-skilled repetition work (mental ratio, 85–100) :

Fairly mechanical repetition work requiring low degrees of skill, poorer commercial positions: barber, welder, tin and coppersmith, driller, polisher, miner, furnace man, carter, bricklayer, painter, carpenter, baker, cook, shoemaker, textile worker, laundry worker, packer (delicate goods), postman, coachman, waiter or waitress, page boy, domestic servant (better class).

Class VI.—Unskilled repetition work (mental ratio, 70–85) :

Unskilled labour, coarse manual work: automatic machine worker, labourer, loader, navvy, fisherman, farm hand, groom, slater, chimney sweep, packer, labeller, bottler, porter, messenger, deliverer, lift boy and lift girl, domestic servant (poorer class), factory workers generally.

Class VII.—Casual labour (mental ratio, 50–70) :

Simplest routine work, and occasional employment on purely mechanical tasks under supervision.

Class VIII.—Institutional (mental ratio, under 50) :

Unemployable (imbeciles and idiots).

in that footnote in 1955: "For the assessments of the parents we relied chiefly on personal interviews; but in doubtful or borderline cases an open or a camouflaged test was employed." That is, in assigning intelligence scores to adults, Burt did not even *claim* to have administered an objective, standardised IQ test. There was no description by Burt of which "open" IQ test might sometimes have been employed. The idea of Professor Burt administering an occasional "camouflaged" IQ test to grandparents and uncles while interviewing them might have merit as comic opera—but as science it is absurd. This work, however, was cited as "the most satisfactory attempt" to estimate the heritability of IQ. That surely tells us something about the scientific calibre of work in this area, or about the critical standards of authorities in this area, or about both.

The estimates of the IQs of parents, because they did not rest on "objective, standardized tests," came, later, to be totally dismissed as "guesses".

Second, Kamin was equally radical in dismissing all credibility about the actual nature and consistency of any tests employed. In *The Science and Politics of IQ,* he went into great critical detail about the complexity of claims made in Burt's several papers about the tests employed in the study of *children,* going so far as to make claims such as these: "There is no way of knowing what tests were in fact administered to the twins." "There is no way of knowing what test(s) he (Burt) used, how well they were standardized, or how test scores might have been combined. We do not know what was correlated with what in order to produce the co-efficient of .77." This referred to the initial (1943) study, and in critically reviewing the *kinds* of tests specified by Burt—for example, the "group test of intelligence . . . evidently used over a 45 year period"—Kamin claimed "We cannot, however, locate the test."

And third, coming back to our opening criticism, Kamin claimed that no grounds were presented by Burt for the *correlations* he claimed (between intelligence and economic status, between kinship relations, and so forth). "The alleged correlations are merely presented without supporting detail." "The first major summary of his kinship studies (the 1943 paper) presents a large number of IQ correlations, but virtually nothing is said of when or to whom tests were administered, or of what tests were employed."

Again, let us consider each of these charges point by point.

First, though it is true that the parents of the children studied were not subjected to standardized tests, it is totally false to claim that the estimates arrived at were no more than "guesses," or that the methods and procedures of arriving at them were not clearly specified. They were, in fact, very clearly set out, and furthermore their limitations were equally clearly and very frankly admitted. Again, Kamin's quotation from Burt's own 1955 paper is misleadingly limited and selective. Burt's statement was, in fact, of very modest proportions, and frank in its confession of limited range, reliability, and significance. He simply stated what he had found it possible to do. Commenting on his collection of "assessments for a 1000 pairs of sibs, as representing, as far as possible, a random selection of the London school population," he adds (my italics):

> At the same time I have endeavoured, *though with poorer success,* to secure assessments *for at least one parent.* Since these proved obtainable for only 954 cases, the analysis has to be limited to this smaller number.

Then follows his qualifying footnote:

> For the assessments of the parents we relied chiefly on personal interviews; but in doubtful and borderline cases an open or a camouflaged test was employed.

Kamin's selective quotation is, at best, an extreme and misleading, at worst a scurrilous, denunciation of what was an honest claim of what had been possible. But it was even more disreputable in an additional way. Burt's references to the 1926 vocational guidance survey did in fact contain a detailed account of these interviews, and interestingly enough it was not Burt himself who first outlined and applied these methods, but one of his co-workers, Lettice Ramsey. Furthermore, in her account, Miss Ramsey also gave a detailed description of her additional analysis of the *home conditions* of the children studied, which, supplementing the list of occupations and scale of vocational categories, made clearer the levels of economic status with which the children's IQs were correlated. In her chapter on home conditions, she described the data she collected on special visits to the homes of the 100 children tested. The details obtained for the "general description of the homes" were as follows:

1. *Home conditions.* Names, ages and occupations of all members of the family. Number, size, and condition of rooms occupied. Rent and total family income. Special conditions such as death or desertion of parents or the presence of foster-parents.

2. *Family history.* Health, intelligence and character of the various members of family.

3. *Personal history,* including a record of the health past and present of the child himself, schools attended, and changes of dwelling place.

4. *Out-of-school behaviour,* including parent's report upon child with particular reference to his intelligence, temperament, interests, special abilities, hobbies and amusements.

5. *Intended occupation.*

Again, the limitations of what proved possible were very precisely made clear:

> It proved impossible to gain full particulars for every one of the hundred cases selected for special study. No satisfactory data were available for the prosperity of the home in the case of four children, nor for the intelligence of the mother in the case of twenty-one.

Even so, the parents in general proved very responsive, cooperative, and generous in providing information.

> In nearly every case it was possible to obtain fairly full information on all the above points; and in no case did the parents seem to resent the inquiry. Many were pleased at having so much interest taken in their children; and thought the scheme for vocational guidance "an excellent idea."

On the basis of this information, the homes were classified in terms of their degree of "general prosperity" into (1) superior, (2) good, (3) moderate, and (4) poor,[5] and these, with knowledge of the occupations of the parents, were closely related to the vocational categories of Table 3.3, adding further dimensions to the economic description of these levels.

We come now to the assessment of the intelligence of parents, the correlation of the intelligence of both parents and children with the material and economic conditions of the home, and a comparison between the intelligence of parents and children. Again, the methods and procedures were set out in the most precise way, with their limitations clearly stated.

The estimated intelligence of parents proved in fact to have been that of mothers. It was based upon personal interview, but carefully, and graded again in relation to the scales of table 3.3. Miss Ramsey described the procedures in this way:

> An attempt was made to grade the intelligence of the mother—the parent most often interviewed. Only a rough estimate could be made during an interview lasting from 20 to 40 minutes; and of course this estimate was entirely a personal one based upon the judgment of one investigator only. Notes were made immediately on leaving the house, and the mother described as (1) Very Intelligent (A+); (2) Intelligent (A) (3)Moderately Intelligent (B); or (4) Unintelligent (C).

> This classification may be taken as roughly corresponding to the classification given above in Table IV [table 3.3]. A corresponds to Class IV (average mental ratio, 107); B to Class V (average mental ratio, 92); and C to Class VI (average mental ratio, 79). The few cases falling into Classes I, II, and III, are grouped together as A+ (average mental ratio, 124).

This, let it be noted, was *an attempt;* the personal interview was a sustained and careful one; and notes and classifications were deliberately made "immediately on leaving the home." We shall come back to the interviews in a moment, but it is important to see at this point that it was made perfectly clear that the intelligence of the 100 children was measured by the Binet tests.

The three comparisons described are given in Tables 3.4 through 3.6. The correlation and analysis in table 3.4 should be clearly noted here, as they must be compared in a moment with Burt's own statement in the 1943 paper.

If the homes are arranged in order of prosperity and the mothers in order of intelligence, the correlation between the two proves to be .31 (probable error, ± .07).

The correlation between the intelligence of the children and the prosperity of the home is .43 (probable error, ± .06).

The correlation for table 3.6 was .51, and the additional comment was that these findings were "consistent with those obtained by previous investigators, which tend to indicate that a child's intelligence is correlated somewhat more closely with the intelligence of his parents than with the material prosperity of his home."

TABLE 3.4
Intelligence of Parent Compared with Prosperity of Home

Class of Home	Number of Mothers	Number of Mothers in each Class showing the Grade of Intelligence specified			
		A+.	A.,	B.	C.
Superior	13	3	4	3	3
Good	27	3	16	8	0
Moderate	25	1	8	12	4
Poor	14	0	2	9	3

If the homes are arranged in order of prosperity and the mothers in order of intelligence, the correlation between the two proves to be .31* (probable error, ± .07).

TABLE 3.5
Intelligence of Child Compared with Prosperity of Home

Class of Home	Number of Children	Average Mental Ratio (Binet Tests)
Superior	14	109.5
Good	34	98.8
Moderate	32	91.5
Poor	16	89.3

The correlation between the intelligence of the children and the prosperity of the home is .43 (probable error, ± .06).

TABLE 3.6
Intelligence of Mothers Compared with Intelligence of their Children

Intelligence of Mothers	Number of Children*	Average Mental Ratio
A+	7	110.6
A	30	104.0
B	32	93.9
C	10	85.1

¹In no case was there more than one child tested from each home.

Again it must be noted that the most careful provisos were continually emphasized in this study. The kind of comment made on the correlation between the intelligence of children and their home conditions, for example—"The group is too small, and the classification too rough, to permit of much importance being attached to this figure"—was much repeated, but again, even so, its close agreement with other known findings, such as those of the Medical Research Council ("Isserlis and Wood—1923: The Correlation between Home Conditions and the Intelligence of School Children—M.R.C. Spec. Rep. Ser., No. 74, pp. 17–18"), were also diligently noted.

The presence and precise nature of these statements of methods, procedures, tests employed, and qualified findings, already provide us with suffucient grounds for a plain judgment on Kamin's charges, but a little more still has to be said about the *personal interviews* on which he heaps such total scorn and condemnation. For a satisfactory estimation of these interviews it is also necessary to note fully the nature of the tests that were being employed—even of the group test, which Kamin said could not be located—for these tests and the assessments of the intelligence of adults on the basis of the interviews are directly relevant to the correlations that Burt stated.

These oral tests and nonverbal tests (including performance tests and a nonlanguage group test) were fully described by Winifred Spielman and Frances Gaw in the *Study in Vocational Guidance* (1926), and, at much the same time, a number of "mental and educational tests" were being standardized by Burt himself for what later became the Wood Report (1929). Although it is important that these should be considered at this stage, they are too detailed to be sensibly incorporated in the text here. They are therefore given in full detail in Appendix 1.

With these tests in mind, let us consider further the estimation of the intelligence of adults on the basis of the *personal interview* coupled with (where there was doubt) "camouflaged tests." Kamin outrightly condemned and dismissed these methods and measurements as "guesses." Bearing in mind, however, that those undertaking these interviews were well acquainted with the nonverbal as well as the Binet-Simon and performance tests as outlined (in Appendix 1); that they were very experienced in administering such tests; that they graded the levels of intelligence into four bands as outlined by Miss Ramsey (each corresponding to a range of the Binet-Simon scale); that, if in any doubt about their assessment on the basis of their interview, they also asked questions embodying a "camouflaged test"; that they gave interviews for each individual of between 20 and 40 minutes; and that their notes were deliberately made immediately after the interview—could the results of such interviews, in any sense whatever, be held to be mere guesses? Would not such estimates be likely to have a considerable degree of reliability? In any event, was it not *the best that proved possible?* And was it not quite frankly stated *that this was so*—that these estimations had, in fact, these degrees of both reliability and limitation? I leave the reader to consider this—and to consider, too, whether there was any suggestion of fraudulence here.

After all these details, however, we can be quite decisive about a third point. Kamin claimed, as we have seen, that Burt "merely presented" the "alleged correlations" in the 1943 paper "without supporting detail." Let us now look at these correlations.

The first was the correlation between "children's intelligence and economic status," which, said Burt, was "found to be approximately .32." Kamin's comment on this was as follows:

> The 1943 paper, among many other findings, reported a correlation of 0.32 'between children's intelligence and economic status.' There was no clear indication of how intelligence had been measured, but the data had been 'obtained during surveys carried out for the London County Council and the National Institute of Industrial Psychology.'

The following statement, however, drawn from the 1943 paper in the very place where the correlation is reported makes it plain how superficial and false this comment is. This, together with its following comment (the italics are mine), makes quite clear the continuity from the vocational guidance report and its methods; particularly from those of Miss Ramsey. "in the L.C.C. elementary schools," Burt said, "the children from '*superior homes*' were about 10 IQ above average, and those from '*poorer homes*' about 10 IQ below." But in his footnote, he also referred to the close agreement (to the figure of .32) reported in other studies, and (on the figures for "superior" and "poorer" homes) to his own *Mental and Scholastic*

Tests (1921), in which he had commented on the significance of family size (2.9 children in "superior" and 5.2 in "poorer" homes). The grades for this correlation had therefore been made perfectly clear; and the same is true for the correlation reported for the measured intelligence of relatives.

Kamin here referred to Burt's 1943 paper as his "*first large collection* of IQ correlations among relatives," but it may therefore be something of a surprise to note that only one page in the fifteen-page article at all concerns itself with such correlations. They are in fact very few and very limited in number, the simple reason being that this article was not centrally about identical twins and other close relationships at all, but about the distribution of income in society and the inequalities of educational opportunity. The mention of identical twins arose only within the context of this much wider survey of facts and arguments. Here, however, we are only concerned with this question: How far were the correlations that were presented, presented without supporting detail, and with no information about methods and procedure?

While discussing the several grounds (or arguments) for holding the view that the level of general intelligence in individuals was largely determined by heredity rather than by the environment, Burt considered two cases: (1) that where, from early infancy, the environment of the children studied had been the same for all; and (2) that where the heredity of the children was identical (that is, in identical twins). On the first, he reported the results of his study—over a period of 15 years—of children brought up from early infancy in residential homes and orphanages, finding a wide range of differing levels of intelligence among them. The same environment had evidently not produced the same level of intelligence. Connected with this, he also reported some correlations provided in Miss Conway's[6] study of 157 children boarded out in foster homes:

(i) I.Q.'s of brothers and sisters in the same homes, .54; (ii) of brothers and sisters in different homes, .42; (iii) of foster-children with foster-parents' own children, .27; (iv) economic status of foster-parents and of foster children's own parents, .24.

His own chief correlations, however, stemmed from his study of the small number of identical twins among all the twins discovered in a London survey (using the Binet tests) of 3,510 children reported earlier in his book *Mental and Scholastic Tests* (together with a smaller number of children studied later):

> The correlations between the I.Q.'s are as follows: non-identical twins (156 cases), .54 (little, if at all, higher than for ordinary brothers and sisters); twins of like sex and 'identical' in type so far as could be judged (62 cases), .80 (almost as high as the correlation between successive testings of the *same* individuals: in the few cases (15 in number) where the 'identical' twins had been reared separately the correlation was .77). And, in general, the remoter the family relationship, the smaller the correlation: e.g., between first cousins (167 cases), .30; second cousins (86 cases), .24.

These were the correlations between relatives reported in the 1943 paper. Were they presented without supporting detail? By no means. The number of children studied and the kinds of tests used were clearly stated, and furthermore, Burt added this comment (the italics are mine):

> All the above correlations have been calculated by Fisher's formula for intra-class correlation. American investigators have used either the ordinary product-moment formula or the Otis difference formula (which assumes that the means for the two series are identical). A novel method of analysis was attempted by Miss V. Molteno, who up to the outbreak of the war, was working up data obtained for twins in London. She has applied the alternative technique of 'correlating persons' to numerous assessments for a variety of mental characteristics (collected by herself and Dr. R. B. Cattell). *The research unfortunately remains incomplete,* but indicates, so far as it goes, that the qualitative resemblances between twins are even more striking then the quantitative. (For references cf. Cattell and Molteno, *J. Genetic Psych.,* I.VII, 1940, pp. 31–47; Herman and Hogben, *Proc. Roy. Soc. Edin.,* I.III, 1933, pp. 105–129). American investigations on twins are fully summarised by Sandiford (pp. 98–121).[7]

Kamin has been critical of Fisher, as of all the investigators and methods entering into Hereditarian studies, but the point at issue is simply this: that Burt did in fact state very clearly his methods, procedures, kinds of tests, and way of arriving at his correlations. These might be disagreed with; in the light of later and more sophisticated methods they might even be criticized as being insufficient; but there is no doubt whatever about the fact that they were presented.

Kamin's representation of Burt's studies was and remains, therefore, grossly insufficient, inaccurate, and false. Apparently very sophisticated and fastidious in its documentation, close scrutiny proves it instead to be highly selective in its quotation, and misleadingly and superficially simplistic in that it never troubles to look up and consider carefully and sympathetically the detailed actuality, the substance, of the earlier surveys, and the nature of the earlier work to which Burt's brief footnotes refer. Burt is in fact enormously consistent and cumulative in all his work—from his earliest critical consideration of the new methods of "mental testing"; through his *Mental and Scholastic Tests*; through the application of the tests of various kinds in the Birmingham investigation, the vocational guidance study, and the Wood report; and from the study of *The Backward Child* onwards. The 1943 paper, still dealing with the wider issues of the inequalities of opportunity suffered by the economically, socially, and culturally disadvantaged, stemmed from, and referred back, to all of this early work; and it was only here (only as one very limited element within this very large context; in relation only to *one* Hereditarian argument among six or seven others) that the study of *identical twins* emerged as a particular focus of significance and concern. And it was only much later—in the papers of 1955, 1958, and 1966—that this became a prominent and central issue in the sharpening conflict between Hereditarians and Environmentalists.

In assessing the nature of Kamin's testimony, we must look specifically at some aspects of his criticism of Burt's twin studies—which Kamin erected as the touchstone, the major part, of Burt's work—but, before that, we must look at one other important aspect of Kamin's criticism of Burt's methods of *testing* that leads him to be scurrilously dismissive. This is Burt's insistence on the necessity in testing of "making adjustments," "making allowances," and "re-testing," if (closely following Binet scores) the test results are found to conflict sharply with "teachers' estimates." Kamin's criticism was such as to pour scorn upon these considerations since they rendered the test results insufficiently objective, inexact, and unreliable, sometimes counting teachers' estimates the more reliable criteria, overriding the tests themselves. Here too the arguments of Burt and his co-workers have to be carefully and sympathetically considered, not simply brushed aside.

In his outright denunciation of the methods of estimating the IQs of adults on the basis of personal interview, we have seen that Kamin was too brash. Burt and his colleagues were totally honest *in doing the best they could* within difficult circumstances (often with only one parent available); in working out *the most reliable method possible*. The methods adopted, and also *their known limitations*, were clearly stated. The same point has to be made about the adjustments and allowances in arriving at the final assessment of an individual's IQ on the basis of the tests. Burt made it perfectly clear that he was a *pragmatic*, not a purely *theoretical* psychologist, due to the very nature of his job—its requirements, commitments, and responsibilities (supremely to individual children, but also to the authorities employing him). In the 1943 paper, referring to the comparative study of children in residential schools and orphanages, in which "*an endeavour was made* to compare the intelligence of the children with that of their parents," Burt was quite clear and direct on this:

> These inquiries differed somewhat from similar researches reported by American investigators. Unlike the theoretical investigator, the school psychologist attached to an education authority is rarely content to assess the I.Q. of a doubtful or special case on the basis of a single test alone; even if he uses the Binet scale as his chief stand-by, he regularly supplements it by others (performance tests, for example, or tests of reasoning); and, before he reaches his final verdict, he will make numerous allowances for disturbances due to shyness, emotional instability, ill health, reading disability, fatigue, lack of interest, and the like. The I.Q.'s of the residential pupils were first assessed in this way; and subsequently the desired information procured about the parents from independent investigators.

Furthermore, he *defends* these allowances (italics added):

> If these allowances are not made, then improved (or depressed) environmental conditions appear to raise (or depress) the I.Q., as assessed *by the Binet scale* with younger or duller children or by group-tests with older children, by about five or six points. In exceptional cases (about once in a thousand cases) the distortion may amount to as much as fifteen points. The experienced psychologist, of course, always endeav-

ours to detect and allow for such distortions, before declaring that the child is mentally defective or reporting on his case to the school authority. The need in such corrections was admirably shown by the results obtained by Mr. Hugh Gordon, H.M.I., with canal boat children. He found an average I.Q. with the Binet tests of 69. When, at my suggestion, Dr. Frances Gaw applied performance tests to the same group, she found an average I.Q. of 82 (cf. *The Backward Child*, p. 59, and refs.). I may add that, in my experience, most of the alleged 'cures' of certified mental defectives are usually obtained with children certified by doctors untrained in the pitfalls of psychological testing, who have diagnosed mental deficiency by simply taking at its face value an I.Q. based on the printed version of the Terman-Binet scale (which was not standardised for English children) without any further adjustments.

Several extremely important points are to be noted in this statement. First, my italics emphasize that it is in the assessment *by the Binet scale* (involving linguistic skills) that Burt found the environmental influences especially noticeable, and this, we will see, he also found to be so in "teachers' estimates." Second, this clearly pointed to the great importance of *nonverbal* tests, which were therefore also emphasized in the 1926 and 1929 surveys. But a third consideration is one of quite crucial importance. Burt was employed as an *official psychologist*. His reports on the defective nature, deficiency, backwardness, or retardation of a child was of vital importance for the actual destiny of that child; just as his *criteria* of defectiveness, backwardness, and so on, were of vital importance for the actual *policies* of the responsible administrative authorities. His diagnoses had vital practical consequences. Of this he was always conscious, and therefore "adjustments" and "allowances" were a matter calling for great responsibility. However, though teachers' estimates (based on long acquaintance with a child, and perhaps some knowledge of his or her family and neighborhood circumstances) had to be taken seriously—so that if they differed markedly from the test results, they called for a careful reappraisal—they also had to be considered with critical caution, even guarded against, and the findings of both Burt and his colleagues threw up clear indications of this. In the vocational guidance study, both Winifred Spielman and Burt, when correlating the several tests with each other, found that

The Binet tests correlate more highly with the teachers' estimates than do the performance tests, and less highly with the non-language group test. . . . Both the Binet tests and the teachers' estimates seem to have a marked linguistic bias; while the non-language group test has no such bias, and further resembles the performance tests in that form relationships enter into several parts.

The judgment of the teacher, although certainly to be taken into account as one indicator and a check for caution, had also, they said, other drawbacks:

It not only depends on the personal impressions of a fallible individual, but is very apt to be biased by a knowledge of the child's school attainments, which themselves in turn depend upon linguistic rather than non-linguistic abilities.

Throughout Burt's work—in his accounts of all his surveys, the tests used in them, and the final presentation of his results—he speaks of such "adjustments," and seems usually to have meant one of three things:

1. Retesting and adjusting tests when they seemed greatly out of keeping with the teacher's experience of a child and estimation of his or her ability (his concern being always for fairness to the individual child.)
2. Adjusting test scores to try to take into account obvious environmental advantages and disadvantages.
3. Rescaling findings in terms of a normal distribution to render them comparable.

Later we will come to one mathematical criticism of this last practice (see the Dorfman/Stigler argument, p. 156–161), and we may well have to comment again from time to time on these methods of adjustment, but it is enough here to see that Burt was perfectly clear about what he was doing and why he did it, and furthermore, that it was the inescapable outcome of the nature of the job he was doing. Essentially committed to *practical* diagnoses for practical advice, but pursuing *fundamental theoretical* questions at the same time, he had to do *what it was possible to do;* and this he did with detailed frankness and clarity.

We come back to the flawed basis of much of the theoretical criticism of Burt and his work. Burt's study of identical twins was never a single investigation, nicely planned and carried out at one time, with a single comprehensive set of test scores and compilations. Indeed, it was never the central part of Burt's work at all, only becoming so in the mid-1950s and 1960s when the political and ideological arguments about educational policies, their relevance to "class inequalities," and their effects on educational standards, were becoming ever more intense. Only then did the Hereditarian versus Environmentalist conflict sharpen; only then did the focus upon the study of identical twins become central in the debate; and, five years after Burt's death, it was his contribution in this conflictful area that became the focus of attack and the charges of fraud. Kamin characterized Burt's 1943 paper as "the first large collection of IQ correlations among relatives," as though this was its dominant focus, but—like his deplorable caricature in the BBC television film—this gave a completely misleading picture; was a slanted exaggeration, a far too narrow falsification. Although we must leave a full investigation of the alleged fraud until much later, we must consider at least one example of the charges Kamin leveled at Burt's twin studies proper.

The "Invariant Correlations"

The crux of Kamin's criticism—the one taken to be damning, which has been repeated ad nauseam ever since it was made—was that the correlations Burt reported in successive papers were "too good to be true"; were, at the very best, miraculous, and at worst impossible. Subsequently, they have been said to be "fraudulent." Burt had reported an increase in the number of twins studied (of identical twins reared apart) from 15 in 1943 to 21 in 1955, to "over 30" in 1958, to 53 in 1966; yet, despite these increases in numbers, some of the correlations remained precisely the same "to three decimal places." Kamin pointed out several such invariant correlations, but here—considering as we are the soundness of his testimony—we will confine ourselves to the correlations resulting from the *"group test"* of the intelligence of *identical twins reared together, and those reared apart.* Precisely the same criticism is stated by Kamin in *Intelligence: The Battle for the Mind* (pp. 100–101), *The Science and Politics of IQ* (p. 59), and *The IQ Controversy* (pp. 245–246). The table he repeats, given here as table 3.7, includes

TABLE 3.7
Correlations for MZ Twins, Group Test of Intelligence[8]

Source	Twins reared apart	Twins reared together
Burt, 1955	0.771 (N = 21)	0.944 (N = 83)
Burt, 1958	0.771 (N = 'over 30')	0.944 (N = ?)
Conway, 1958	0.778 (N = 42)	0.936 (N = ?)
Burt, 1966	0.771 (N = 53)	0.944 (N = 95)

four apparently different studies: three by Burt, one by Conway. Kamin's exact accompanying criticism[9] was this:

> The IQ correlations that Burt claimed to have observed in his separated twins are quite literally incredible. The first reference to separated twins by Burt was in his 1943 paper. He claimed to have studied fifteen pairs of separated identical twins. Their IQ correlation, on some unspecified test, was said to be 0.77. By 1955, Burt had managed to increase his sample of separated twins to twenty-one pairs. The level of precision in Burt's calculations had increased, and he now adopted the unusual practice of reporting his correlations to the third decimal place. The correlation was now said to be 0.771, based on a group test of intelligence. The precision of Burt's procedural descriptions had not, alas, increased. There was no indication of which group test of intelligence might have been employed. (A group test is one which can be sat by any number of candidates at the same time, since it does not need to be individually administered.)

> By 1958, Burt claimed that his sample of separated twins had been increased to "over thirty". The correlation on the group test was *still* reported as 0.771—identical, to the third decimal, to that reported earlier for a smaller sample. By late 1958, Burt's research associate, Conway, was able to report that the sample of separated twins had been increased to forty-two pairs. This sudden swelling of the sample size did affect the reported correlation, but not much. The correlation was now said to be 0.778. When Burt last reported on his separated twins, in 1966, the sample size was said to have increased to fifty-three pairs. The correlation, almost supernaturally, had returned to the originally reported 0.771.

> This remarkable consistencey can be observed not only in Burt's work on separated twins, but also in his work on identical twins who have

been reared together, in their own families. The 1955 Burt paper claimed to have studied 83 such pairs, and to have observed an IQ correlation (on an unnamed group test) of 0.944. That correlation, it might be noted, is remarkably high. There is considerable measurement error involved in IQ testing, and it is doubtful whether if the same group IQ test were to be given on two separate occasions to the same set of people, a correlation that high would be observed between scores on the two occasions. The Burt 1958 paper, in any event, again reported a correlation of 0.944 for identical twins reared together.[10]

The Conway 1958 paper, in remarkable synchrony with her report on separated twins, observed a trivial change in the correlation for twins reared together. It was now said to be 0.936, with the number of pairs not specified. When Burt made his final report in 1966, the correlation for twins reared together had also returned to its original value of 0.944. The sample size was said to have increased to 95 pairs.

We have seen that the nature of the group test administered was not seriously in doubt, but the following facts are the most important.

First, it will be seen that the Conway paper of 1958 with the new number of 42 did *not* repeat invariant correlations. Only *three* apparent studies reported the invariant correlations of .771 and .944, and it is this repetition in all the three Burt papers that has been endlessly repeated as the chief ground indicating fraud. But here it is a second fact which is crucially important.

This is the simple but startling fact that *there never was a 1958 study by Burt of "over 30" twins reared apart*. This was either a hasty misreading and misrepresentation by Kamin—in his headlong ideological gallop—or a deliberate misrepresentation. The 1958 paper by Burt proves, on examination, to be the publication of Burt's Bingham lecture, which was delivered in *May 1957*. In it, Burt did say that in the study of identical twins "We have now collected over 30 such cases," but the table of correlations he reproduced was very plainly and decidedly *not* the outcome of working over this new number. No new, additional study was done and reported at that time. The table (in May 1957, reproduced here as table 3.8) was quite simply a *lecture illustration,* a straightforward *quotation* of the figures arrived at in his study of 1955.

Table 3.9 reproduces the full table as presented in the 1955 paper.

It will be seen that the 1957 table is quite simply a *total* reproduc-

TABLE 3.8.
Correlations Between Mental and Scholastic Assessments

	Identical twins reared together	Identical twins reared apart	Nonidentical twins reared together	Siblings reared together	Siblings reared apart	Unrelated children reared together
Mental						
"Intelligence"						
Group Test	.944*	.771	.542	.515	.441	.281
Individual Test	.921	.843	.526	.491	.463	.252
Final Assessment	.925	.876	.551	.538	.517	.269
Scholastic						
General Attainments	.898	.681	.831	.814	.526	.535
Reading and Spelling	.944	.647	.915	.853	.490	.548
Arithmetic	.862	.723	.748	.769	.563	.476

[a]In correspondence with Jensen, Burt pointed out that this was a misprint in the 1955 paper (the figure should have been .904), and the error was inadvertently repeated in the publication of the Bingham lecture, as this simply reproduced the same table.

tion of the mental (intelligence) and scholastic correlations of the 1955 table; no more than Burt's lecture illustration of the findings of this study. But one immediate fact is startlingly clear. Kamin's charge—quite plainly claiming that these figures represented the findings of a new (1958) study of the increased number of "over 30" twins—is that the correlations of .944 and .771 (for twins reared together and twins reared apart) are exactly the same, to the third decimal place. The simple truth, however, is that *all these correlations in this table are exactly the same to the third decimal place. Every figure is "invariant";* is an exact repetition of those in the 1955 study; and for the completely evident reason that they represent precisely *the quoted 1955 study itself.*

If this plain fact was not enough in itself to render questionable an investigating scientist who was supposedly diligently searching for and proclaiming the truth (which Kamin was so demonstratively claiming himself to be), the 1958 paper by Conway was such as to confirm these doubts. The paper of *November 1958*—published *a year and a half* after the delivery of the Bingham lecture (of *May 1957*)—was in fact a new and extended study of the larger number of identical twins then collected: 42 of them reared apart. It will be seen in the table reporting this study (table 3.10) that *all* the correlations for these twins *differed* from those of 1955. The total table is simply an *updating of the 1955 table,* replacing the old

TABLE 3.9.
Correlations Between Tests of Mental, Scholastic, and Physical Measurements

Measurement	A.—Burt and Conway						B—Newman, Freeman & Holzinger.		
	Identical Twins reared together	Identical Twins reared apart	Non-identical Twins reared together	Siblings reared together	Siblings reared apart	Unrelated children reared together	Identical Twins reared together	Identical Twins reared apart	Non-identical Twins reared together
Mental (Intelligence)									
Intelligence:									
Group Test	·944	·771	·542	·515	·441	·281	·922	·727	·621
Individual Test ..	·921	·843	·526	·491	·463	·252	·910	·670	·610
Final Assessment ..	·925	·876	·551	·538	·517	·269	---	...	...
Scholastic									
General Attainments	·898	·681	·831	·814	·526	·535	·955	·507	·883
Reading and Spelling	·944	·647	·915	·853	·490	·548	—	---	---
Arithmetic	·862	·723	·748	·769	·563	·476	--	---	---
Physical									
Height	·957	·951	·472	·503	·536	--069	·981	·969	·930
Weight ....·.....	·932	·897	·586	·568	·427	·243	·973	·886	·900
Head Length	·963	·959	·495	·481	·536	·116	·910	·917	·691
Head Breadth	·978	·962	·541	·507	·472	·082	·908	·880	·654
Eye Colour	1·000	1·000	·516	·553	·504	·104	—	—	--

correlations of the identical twins with the new, but leaving the rest of the table precisely the same; and this updating of the earlier table is stated quite clearly. (In short, only the new identical twins had been newly studied.) The important additional statement, however, is that *"the last review of our own cases" was that of 1955.*

The question that clearly arises is this. If Kamin was so sharp-sighted as to notice that, in the 1958 Burt (1957 Bingham lecture) paper, the correlations of .944 and .771 were exactly the same to the third decimal place as those in the 1955 paper, how was it that he failed to see, and failed to report, that *every correlation in these two tables were exactly the same to the third decimal place?* Did his sharpness of sight fail him in this connection? There seem to be only two possible explanations: (1) that his rush to prove his own case was so headlong, so careless, that his perception was rendered

TABLE 3.10.
Correlations Between Measurements for Mental, Scholastics and Physical Characteristics

Measurement	A—Burt and Conway						B—Newman, Freeman and Holzinger		
	Identical twins reared together	Identical twins reared apart	Non-identical twins reared together	Siblings reared together	Siblings reared apart	Unrelated children reared together	Identical twins reared together	Identical twins reared apart	Non-identical twins reared together
Mental (Intelligence)									
Intelligence :									
Group test	0·936	0·778	0·542	0·515	0·441	0·281	0·922	0·727	0·621
Individual test	0·919	0·846	0·526	0·491	0·463	0·252	0·910	0·670	0·640
Final Assessment	0·928	0·881	0·551	0·538	0·517	0·269	—	—	—
Scholastic									
General Attainments	0·894	0·629	0·831	0·814	0·526	0·535	0·955	0·507	0·883
Reading and Spelling	0·943	0·645	0·915	0·853	0·490	0·548	—	—	—
Arithmetic	0·870	0·726	0·748	0·769	0·563	0·476	—	—	—
Physical									
Height	0·956	0·942	0·472	0·503	0·536	−0·069	0·981	0·969	0·930
Weight	0·929	0·884	0·586	0·568	0·427	0·243	0·973	0·886	0·900
Head length	0·961	0·958	0·495	0·481	0·536	0·116	0·910	0·917	0·691
Head breadth	0·977	0·960	0·541	0·507	0·472	0·082	0·908	0·830	0·654
Eye colour	1·000	1·000	0·516	0·553	0·504	0·104	—	—	—

"selective" to an abnormally narrow degree (tunnel vision, one might say, with a vengeance!), and that seeing the figures he wanted to see, he did not stop to examine the rest; or (2) that he *did* see the entire table perfectly well, but deliberately selected and reported the replications that supported his charges against Burt, deliberately staying silent about the rest. Similarly, did he not see (through importunate haste) the relevant qualification in the Conway 1958 paper? Or, again, did he see it, but stay silent?

What is certain is that his account of these repeated correlations was a plain falsification of the facts—a falsification that has gone unseen, been widely publicized, and remained widely accepted up to this day. One is surely entitled to ask now, given these clear facts, what price the veracity and integrity of this scientific criticism?

But two other facts in this same connection deserve note and emphasis. First, the *time sequence* involved.

The reporting of both the Burt 1958 paper and the Conway 1958 paper in 1958 gives the obvious impression that the claims of both (referring to the numbers of twins and correlations reported in them) were made in the same year; were almost simultaneous. The sudden eruption of the number of twins from "over 30" to 42 (increasing to 53 in 1966) seems therefore quite incredible. The actual sequence, however, was very different and gives a far more feasible picture. In 1943, the number of twins—gathered from the wider and earlier surveys over some 15 years—was 15. At that stage, however, the study of identical twins was only then emerging as being of quite central significance in the heredity versus environment argument, and further cases began to be deliberately and actively sought. By the time of the 1955 study, 21 had been discovered and were the basis of the correlations reported then. In his Bingham lecture of May 1957, Burt mentioned that the number discovered had increased to "over 30," an increase of something over 9 in two to three years. Eighteen months later, the number had been increased to 42; and by 1966, eight years later, to 53. This increase was therefore by no means of the nature of a sudden explosion; but it is in relation to this gradual increase that the second fact is also important.

It is perfectly clear (and was then made perfectly clear throughout the whole of the following period) that from 1943 onwards, a deliberate search for cases of identical twins was begun and constantly pursued. In his 1955 paper, for example, Burt referred back to the 1943 paper and the correlations then drawn "originally from surveys in the London schools" and added that Miss Conway, who had then provided supplementary data, had now managed "thanks to numerous correspondents" to increase the number of cases (to 83 identical twins reared together and 21 reared apart). But, at that point, the further revealing footnote was added (the italics are mine):

Of the monozygotic twins, only nineteen were found in London; and, owing to the distances involved, we have been obliged to depend for measurements of the rest either on research-students or on local teachers and doctors (to whom we must extend our sincerest thanks). As a result, the correlations for this group may have been somewhat reduced. There is a natural prejudice against separating twins, especially if their sex is the same; and *we should like to repeat our appeal for further cases*. Although the handful of monozygotic twins reared apart is decidedly small *(and it is the outcome of a quest that has lasted for over forty years)*, the differences between the correlations for this group and the rest are for the most part statistically significant.

What is clear here is that Burt and his co-workers were now continually *appealing* (advertising) for news of identical twins. This was further evidenced in the Conway 1958 paper, coupled with the additional significant fact that the *nature* of the additional cases had become different as a direct result of the deliberate search.

Our earlier cases were encountered during the routine inspections of children brought up in residential institutions under the L.C.C.: not infrequently it turned out that the child in the institution was a twin, and that the other twin had been left with the mother or with relatives. Among our later cases most were discovered through personal contacts; and, as a result, many of them came of educated parents, usually school teachers or members of a University staff: when the pair was separated, one twin generally remained with the mother and shared her cultural environment, while the other was boarded out, usually with persons of much lower intellectual status.

In the *News Letter of the Association of Educational Psychologists* (no. 3) in 1965, when (say his critics) Burt had long ceased his researches and "collecting of data," Burt wrote:

During the past 50 years my colleagues and I have kept a careful watch for cases of this kind—'identical' twins reared apart from infancy. At first we could discover only a handful. But as soon as our results were published, more cases kept coming in, and we have now located as many as 53 pairs. We should still be grateful for additional names and addresses.

In the 1966 paper, this increased number, of 53 reared apart (and 95 reared together), was in fact the number on which the study was based.

The growth in the number of twins was therefore demonstrably gradual, not sudden. It was clearly the outcome of a deliberate quest that had grown gradually out of the chance discoveries in the earlier surveys; and the course of this is quite plainly marked in the sequence of papers from 1943, 1955, and 1958 (including the 1957 Burt lecture), to 1966.

Later, we will have to return to this matter of the "invariant correlations" when considering the specific charges of fraud, and at that point the 1966 paper will also have to be considered. We have seen enough here, however, to indicate the character and degree of reliability of Kamin's testimony; in this connection one final comment must be added.

Errors of Carelessness, in Haste? Or Deliberate Misrepresentations?

A fundamental question arises from all the points we have considered. It strikes at the very heart of Kamin's own integrity and cannot be escaped or avoided. It must be stated frankly and directly—but fairly. It is simply this.

Were all the misrepresentations of Burt's positions (here plainly demonstrated) genuine mistakes on Kamin's part? Were they errors of selective perception, of unwitting misinterpretation, stemming from ideological zeal and too importunate a degree of haste in attacking Burt as forthrightly as possible as an enemy in the Hereditarian/Environmentalist debate? Or were they deliberate falsifications, smears, or distortions?

I leave this question to you, the reader—as a member of the jury—to judge.

The grossly inaccurate caricatures of Burt, his views, and his work, presented in such a denunciatory manner, indeed with such condescension and venom as in the BBC film, coupled with this unbelievable failure to see some plainly visible facts while selecting others within the self-same report, do surely suggest the most disgraceful kind of character assassination—and to this possibility we will have to return after examining the testimony of those who followed readily in Kamin's footsteps. For now, however, it is enough to see that Kamin himself was not content to present what he took to be a damning *criticism* of Burt's work, claiming that its data and findings went beyond the bounds of credibility and were therefore of no use for scientific purposes; that "the absence of procedural description in Burt's reports vitiates their scientific utility" and "the frequent arithmetical inconsistencies and mutually contradictory descriptions cast doubt upon the entire body of his later work"; that "the marvellous consistency of his data support- ing the hereditarian position often taxes credibility; and on analysis, the data are found to contain implausible effects consistent with an effort to prove the hereditarian case"; that "Burt's correlations and data were useless for hypothesis testing—that is to say worth- less." He also went beyond this to make quite clear the implied charge of deliberate *fraud*. In *Intelligence: The Battle for the Mind,* he wrote:

> With some measure of restraint, I wrote, after reviewing Burt's work: "The numbers left behind by Professor Burt are simply not worthy of our current scientific attention." The clear implication—that Burt had invented the data in order to support his ideas about social and educa- tional policy—was left for the reader to make.

And he then, brushing aside one or two criticisms of his own account of Burt,[11] fully accepted and approved the outright charges of fraud made much more forcefully (in the manner of sensationalist journalism) by Oliver Gillie, and the subsequent judgments of Hearnshaw's "official biography." Not satisfied even with this— the gramophone record syndrome making its appearance again—he concluded with the extreme and sweeping statement (which we have seen that he reiterated in the 1984 BBC film) that "from the available evidence . . . it is reasonable to suggest that perhaps Burt never tested a separated twin, or calculated a genuine correlation between relatives, in his entire life."[12]

Questions Requiring Public Answers

Arising from the criticisms, discussion, and evidence presented, public answers are now required to the following questions at least:

1. Why did Kamin characterize Burt's work as (1) "containing virtually no information about methods or procedure," (2) "never providing even the most elementary information about how, where or when his purported data had been collected," and (3) giving "not even any information about which IQ test was supposedly used to obtain the reported correlations," when, as we have seen, Burt always gave detailed accounts of his methods, procedures, place, period of time, and kinds of tests used in the specific surveys in which his data had been collected?
2. Why did Kamin specify "the only reference to procedure" in the 1943 paper as being "some of the inquiries have been published in LCC reports or elsewhere; but the majority remain buried in typed memoranda or degree theses," when this comment was made only with reference to the grounds for seven arguments about the hereditary basis of intelligence, *not* about the collection of data or the bases of correlations at all; and when, going beyond these arguments, many other very detailed references were made?
3. Why did he not follow up these other references? Or if he did follow them up, why did he not fully report all the details that they contained?
4. Why did he deride dismissively the detailed and thoroughly considered ways in which Burt and his co-workers estimated the levels of intelligence of adults; and the ways in which test scores of different kinds were brought together in a "final assessment"—the ways in which teachers' estimates were taken into account, "allowances" and "adjustments" made, and on the basis of which retesting sometimes took place? And why did he not think fit to explain the considered reasons Burt gave for these procedures—even if he himself disagreed with them?
5. Why did he claim that Burt presented correlations (between the intelligence of children and economic status, between relatives, and so forth) without specifying the tests used as the basis for them, when in fact these were more often than not clearly pointed out?
6. Why did he completely misrepresent the nature of the "invariant

correlations'' in the sequence of the 1943, 1955, and 1958 Burt papers and the 1958 Conway paper, and then erect the supposed repetition of these correlations "to the third decimal place" as a crucial charge against Burt; the major ground for refusing to take his data and figures seriously, and charging him with "inventing data" to support his ideas?

7. The questions we asked earlier must also be briefly repeated here, since the grounds for asking them so clearly reveal the nature of Kamin's attack. Why, in *The Intelligence Man,* did he so grossly misrepresent the nature of Burt's 1943 paper, and the nature and significance of Burt's early notes on the essay by Pigou, claiming these as demonstrations of Burt's commitment to the views of the eugenics movement, when they were clearly nothing of the kind?

Answers to these questions will be awaited, but the very fact that an examination of Kamin's account of Burt's work makes it necessary to ask them—resting, as they clearly do, on demonstrable evidence—makes plain the character, quality, and degree of reliability of Kamin's testimony for the prosecution. Coupled with evidence proving the similar character of the testimony of others, I will later ask whether it is not far more disgraceful and more lacking in scientific veracity than anything of which Burt himself could even remotely be considered guilty.

Notes

1. *American Journal of Psychology* 95:346–49; 1982.
2. P. 99. My italics.
3. It was Mrs. Emma J. Robinson who was successful in tracing Miss Mawer's address, and who put me in touch with her.
4. This was written in November 1984—just over 40 years after her essay and Burt's article were written—but this is a verified example of the very meticulous way in which Burt always acknowledged his helpers or those on whose work he had drawn. Mrs. Clarke also wrote "I am glad that you are looking into the allegations of fraud. I could, I must admit, see him finding it amusing to bamboozle the over-confident, but a calculated major scientific fraud is another matter."
5. Quite specific elements were taken as criteria, such as the number of persons per room, condition of cleanliness and comfort, class of house, occupation of parents, family income, and family size. The classes of homes also (it was noted) closely corresponded to Charles

Booth's classes (FEC and D) in *Life and Labour of the People in London*, (London and New York: Macmillan, 1902). Booth's own division into classes had been: A. The lowest class of occasional laborers, loafers, and semi-criminals; B. casual earnings—"very poor"; C. intermittent earnings; D. small regular earnings (C and D together = the "poor"); E. regular standard earnings = above the line of poverty; F. higher class labor. G. lower middle class; H. upper middle class. (p. 33)

6. This early reference to Miss Conway is to be noted.
7. The Sandiford book referred to is *Foundations of Educational Psychology*, 1938.
8. The respective correlations given in the 1943 paper were .77 and .86.
9. *Intelligence: The Battle for the Mind*, pp. 100–101.
10. It will be seen quite definitely here that Kamin claims that the Burt 1958 paper reports a *new study* with precisely the same correlation as that reported in the 1955 study.
11. That of Loehlin, Lindzey, and Spuhler (1975, Social Science Research Council), and that offered in a review by D. Fulker (also 1975).
12. The tone of Kamin's criticism of Burt may be further judged from the following example taken from *The Intelligence Man*. Claiming that Burt "really believed that the numbers he was inventing corresponded to the truth," Kamin continued: "He had to convince other lesser intellects that this was true. Lesser intellects who hadn't received this knowledge from on high, as he appears to have, would have to be convinced by actual data and I don't think that Burt thought of himself as a manipulator and misleader of the public. I think Burt had the intellectual audacity to think that he knew the truth, prior to any actual investigation of the facts, and therefore as a kind of '*noblesse oblige*' he was letting the rest of us get a handle on the truth by presenting us with numbers that would help us to accept it. And he did us the courtesy of inventing the numbers for us."

4

Dr. Oliver Gillie and the Press

Leon Kamin, as we have seen, gave a fair *imitation* of a gramophone record, but the themes repeated on his tracks were at least his own. Oliver Gillie, by way of contrast, gives the impression of actually *being* a gramophone record—endlessly playing through the loudspeakers of the press, volume turned up high, but with this difference: the grooves engraved on his wax are loaded with the themes of others; roared out for publicity's sake in a more outrageous presentation. Had Burt been alive, Gillie would undoubtedly have been open to legal proceedings, vulnerable in the courts, for the most glaringly obvious charges of libel; the most gross, cumulative, and persistent kinds of defamation. Words and phrases such as "fraudster," "plagiarist of long standing," "outright fraud," "dishonest," and "the crowning success of Burt's career as a fraudster," roll with boldness and the confidence of some sort of self-assured authority from his pen. But Burt had been five years dead before so bold an attack upon him was made. "Courage after the enemy's decease" might be the motto painted in shining colors on this gladiator's shield.

But it may be that this warrior, too, clad in thin, rattling journalistic armor, will be proved to have been tilting at windmills. Sometimes he speaks proudly of his distinction as "the journalist who wrote the first story in which the word 'fraud' was used in connection with the work of Sir Cyril Burt."[1] Sometimes he claims to have been the forthright public mouthpiece for "leading scientists" who "are convinced that Burt published false data and invented crucial facts to support his controversial theory that intelligence is largely

81

inherited."[2] The "leading scientists" to whom he referred were Leon Kamin and Ann and Alan Clarke at the University of Hull (whom he interviewed together with their colleague Michael Mc-Askie). All of these certainly claimed to have discovered difficulties in their study of Burt's figures; Kamin, as we have seen, had evidently (he later announced) *implied* fraudulence, but had not been so unrestrained as to charge Burt with this. It was Gillie's claim to distinction to have brought all their criticisms together under the plain and outspoken charge of fraud.

Let us now examine point by point Gillie's testimony, in his first "revelatory" article of October 1976, and in the many other subsequent statements made between then and 1984.

THE MOST SENSATIONAL CHARGE OF FRAUD
THIS CENTURY

That was how Gillie's opening sentence began, and it continued: "is being levelled against the late Sir Cyril Burt, father of British educational psychology." We have first to note, simply, that even this was not true. Kamin had published his criticisms, the Clarkes were evidently making their doubts known, some London University scholars were experiencing difficulty in tracing two or three of Burt's assistants, but no charge of fraud—whether the most sensational this century or otherwise—was being made. It was Gillie himself who collated these criticisms and made this charge.

As far as it is possible to ascertain, words such as "fraud" were only being used by others in their interviews with Gillie, and it is within the context of this interviewing that their intemperate language at that time is to be noted. All of those involved, it is of interest to note, were psychologists at the University of Hull,[3] and for simplicity's sake I will refer to "The Hull department" in all that follows, though I believe two departments were involved, the psychology department and the school of education. Kamin, Gillie, and these psychologists of the Hull department—all journalistically orchestrated by Gillie—were Burt's accusers. The Clarkes, said Gillie, concluded that "scientifically Burt's results are *a fraud*" (italics mine). Burt could not have made certain observations, said Michael McKaskie, "without deliberately *fiddling the figures* to produce the results he desired." Defamatory statements of this kind were now to be found in plenty. Gillie, it seems, had unlocked and opened a door through which others were now ready to walk.

Race and Eugenics

One serious fault of Burt and his ideas, Gillie claimed, was that they had "inspired the public controversy over race and intelligence . . . led in Britain by Professor Hans Eysenck and in America by Professor Arthur Jensen, a former post-doctoral student of Eysenck." Like Kamin, Gillie's opposition to Burt and criticism of him was rooted in his evident conviction that Burt was saturated in the early literature and views of the eugenics movement, and that his claim that differences in intelligence were largely inherited entailed the view that *races* and *social classes* could clearly be said to be superior or inferior to each other, and that this resulted in and served to justify discriminatory political policies. This opening charge against Burt was subsequently made time and time again by Gillie in slightly different ways. Before looking at these, however, let us see what Eysenck himself had to say about the charge that it was Burt and his ideas that had inspired his own and Jensen's research. "Gillie," he wrote,

> is not above making statements which are, in fact, untrue. Thus he says that 'Arthur Jensen used Burt's data and argued that American blacks are innately inferior to whites'. The use of 'and' subtly suggests that in some odd way Burt had used his data to suggest black inferiority; he had not. Neither had Jensen; it is simply untrue to make such a statement, as Gillie must know perfectly well. What Jensen did point out was that the possibility of finding genetic differences in IQ between races should not be dismissed axiomatically, and that many of the arguments used to establish environmental causes of the observed differences had been disproved experimentally. This is a far cry from arguing 'that American blacks are innately inferior to whites'. In any case, it is difficult to see how Jensen comes into this whole story; is this another instance of McCarthyism?[4]

The *racist* and *eugenics* smear was subsequently made, however, in much more radical ways. In a radio discussion,[5] saying that eugenics took different forms in different countries, Gillie's comment was that whereas in Germany it had taken the form of "Hitler's excesses," in England it had taken "the much more subtle form" of selection for secondary education. Burt's arguments for *selection* in English education were mentioned in the same breath as the extermination policies of the Nazis, and so smeared with the same eugenics brush that was supposed to be necessarily one of race and class discrimination. And yet "racialism" never in any way whatever entered into Burt's work. This extreme comparison between Nazi extermination and selective education in England is not to be taken, either, as a brash comment from Gillie uttered in a moment of heated argument. It was, and has remained, his considered view. In the *Radio Times* in 1982,[6] his comments were the following:[6]

> Burt's scientific ideas were influenced by Francis Galton, a cousin of Charles Darwin who began the science of race improvement, or eugenics as he called it, at the turn of the century. Eugenics became unfashionable among scientists with the rise of Hitler.

> Nevertheless the ideas of eugenics remained buried in science and an attempt was made to resurrect them in modified form, together with Burt's research, following the passing of laws against race discrimination in American schools.

Again, in a 1987 exchange of letters in the (London) *Sunday Telegraph*,[7] he said that in an article supporting Burt's position I had minimized.

> the intellectual influence of the eugenics movement on education in Britain. This movement was not primarily concerned with selective breeding of a super-race. In Britain, the movement was preoccupied with the faster rate of reproduction of the working classes and was worried that they would swamp the intellectual and moneyed élite. It is not absurd to link ideas about educational selection with eugenics or social Darwinism. Burt was steeped in this thinking.

> In Germany, university professors endorsed the eugenics movement, and many continued to support it when it provided the Nazis with a pseudo-scientific rationale for their programme' of genocide and their attempts to breed a super-race. There is a lesson from the German experience: science may be misused to give false authority to social planning.

The slur was, and is, continually repeated. Burt, says Gillie, was "steeped" in the thinking of eugenics, which was "preoccupied with the faster rate of reproduction of the working classes" and "worried that they would swamp" the élites above them. Why, then, it has to be asked, was Burt so centrally and continually concerned to make clear the facts of economic and social inequality and extend the educational opportunities of the children of the lower classes who suffered from them? We have seen, however, the fallacious basis of the eugenics smear in Kamin's account, and it was Kamin's criticism, and fallacy, that Gillie was here repeating. He had already repeated it in a letter to the *Listener*,[8] deepening the charge of racism in the same way, and again linking selection in English education with the Nazi atrocities, this time forthrightly extending his criticism of Burt to include Eysenck and Jensen. Eysenck's own reply again deserves note. Gillie, he commented, says that

"the genetic philosophy which lies behind Eysenck's position is derived directly through Burt and others from the eugenic movement. In Germany, where eugenics was known as race hygiene, the movement had appalling consequences. In this country it was simply used to rationalise class divisions in our society and to justify an educational system which was widely criticised as unjust." It is difficult to know where to begin in putting the record straight.

(1) I am not concerned with any philosophy, but with scientific facts; the philosophy which Gillie attributes to me is wholly in his imagination. (2) My position was derived primarily from the teaching in genetics I received from J. B. S. Haldane, who was both an outstanding biologist and geneticist and a high-ranking member of the Communist Party. (3) The eugenics movement, as I have known it, has been concerned with research into genetic-problems and, on the practical side, with disseminating knowledge about, and advice concerning, genetically transmitted diseases; it had nothing to do with rationalising class divisions and justifying an educational system of any kind. This certainly was the position when I was on the council of the movement, and I have no reason to imagine that it has changed since then. (4) Hitler's absurd racial theories and his diabolical persecution of the Jews and other racial groups had nothing to do with eugenics or genetics; in fact, he banned (like Stalin) IQ testing, which provides an important plank for genetic research. (He condemned it as 'Jewish', while Stalin condemned it as 'bourgeois'.) Gillie complains that I have said that his writings produce 'a whiff of McCarthyism'; if dragging Hitler into this discussion does not justify this accusation, I do not know what might.

The Mentally Subnormal: The Wood Report

As though this was not enough, in his opening 1976 article Gillie accused Burt (with his eugenicist ideas) of having exerted an unfortunate influence on the findings of an important government report. Burt's belief, he wrote,

> that the commonest cause of educational retardation was 'inborn inferiority of general intelligence'—incorporated in the Wood Report of 1929—played a part in confirming the policy of segregating the mentally sub-normal so that they would not reproduce.

To say that Burt believed that "the commonest cause of educational retardation" was "inborn inferiority of general intelligence" is itself a statement of the most simplistic kind. As we will see, Burt very carefully took into account many environmental circumstances and influences that he thought responsible for "backwardness" and "retardation." Furthermore, and long before doing this, he had clearly set out in his Birmingham study his method of measuring a child's level of mental ability by *intelligence testing* (the Binet-Simon scale) and degree of "backwardness" by his or her level of educational *attainments*.[9] The Wood report was, however, the report of the "Mental Deficiency Committee" set up in 1924 and reporting in 1929. Its area of investigation was specifically "the problems presented by the *mentally defective child*" (emphasis mine) (not *educational retardation* in general). It sought to establish the number and distribution of "mental defectives"; extended its study to include "the adult defective"; and had to cover the entire range (to use its own carefully defined designations) of idiocy, imbecility, and the feeble-minded. The chief investigating officer was Dr. E. O. Lewis; the chief additional authority referred to, Dr. Tredgold. Burt was a member of the committee, but his contribution, as we have already seen, was that of drawing up the tests to be used. The setting up and the scope of the inquiry, and its findings and recommendations, were not his but those of the other investigating officers and the committee as a whole. But what, in any event, were their recommendations?

Essentially, they were entirely humane, regretting the insufficiency of society's recognition of the mentally defective, their

problems, and the treatment of them, and recommending considerable extensions and improvements to the provisions then existing.
For our purposes, only a few points need to be noted. First, for any
category of the mentally defective whatever (even the most help-
less), the committee was extremely opposed to any consideration
of *sterilization* or any idea of legislation for it. Having discussed
the extent to which "the sterilization of mentally defective adults
in the present generation would reduce the volume of mental
deficiency in the next," their conclusion was

> that even if this measure were rigidly applied to all the mentally
> defective the reduction would not be great. A more cogent ground for
> advocating sterilisation is that its application would ease the economic
> burden by enabling defectives who would otherwise have to be perma-
> nently segregated in institutions to return to the community with no
> risk of their becoming parents, and that a number of them could live
> happily and harmoniously outside institutions. If it could be proved that
> sterilisation could safely and profitably be applied even to certain
> groups or categories of defectives, the question of its adoption would
> no doubt deserve careful attention.

Then, having considered sterilization policies in "about twenty
American States, Alberta, Sweden, and Switzerland," they repeated their great caution.

> The Committee regard with much apprehension the tendency observed
> in some quarters to allow the discussion of this question and the hope
> of legislation on the subject to retard the provision of the institutional
> accommodation which is so lamentably insufficient in all parts of the
> country. The cases to which sterilisation could profitably be applied are
> not among those for whom this additional accommodation is required,
> for it must be borne in mind that large numbers of defectives are not
> socially adjustable and should not be left in the community in any
> circumstances, while many of those who might ultimately be returned
> to the community would first require a long period of training and
> stabilisation to fit them for life outside an institution. Moreover the view
> of many who have had wide experience of mental defectives in this
> country is that the freedom accompanying sterilisation, though it might
> increase the happiness of some defectives, would be positively harmful
> to many others.

This is hardly the kind of pronouncement to be expected from a
committee so dominated by the more extreme views of the eugenics

movement as to be advocating a policy of "selective breeding." There was here, surely, a clear and deeply felt concern for the happiness and well-being of defectives themselves—as persons—to be given the best possible conditions for their own fulfillment, and an equally clear concern to provide the most suitable institutional conditions for those where institutional care was necessary. And here again their recommendation was exactly the opposite of that implied by Gillie. Clearly distinguishing all those mentally defective children who needed care, control, and residential provisions under the Mental Deficiency Acts, from those who were "educable" and "known as dull or backward children," they designated all the latter as "the *Retarded* Group" and argued that these "should be given a type of education adapted to their degree of retardation."

But then, far from proposing a policy of *segregation,* their recommendations were such as to make provision for "the retarded" *within the educational provisions for "normal" children:* that "all these children should be retained within the Public Elementary School system and that Local Education Authorities modify the organisation of the schools in their areas so as to provide suitable education for the whole group." They further recommended "the abolition of the requirement that the Local Education Authority should certify a particular type of child as mentally defective as a necessary preliminary to providing him with the type of education he requires." These "types of education" included special schools, day schools and centers, and special classes within public elementary schools, depending on the nature of the retardation and the child's age. The detailed nature of these recommendations may be seen in the "schema" appended to the report (figure 4.1).

These recommendations of the Wood Committee—far from implying the segregation of educationally backward and mentally subnormal children—may also be seen to be entirely in agreement with Burt's own earlier recommendation following his 1921 Birmingham study. There, he had said plainly that "the most urgent need for the backward child is *the establishment of special classes in the ordinary school, where each individual child can be studied, treated, and taught.*"[10]

Gillie's comments, building themselves upon those of Kamin, and accusing Burt of "inspiring" racialist research and attitudes

FIGURE 4.1.

Diagram showing the normal stages in the education or training of a child according to age and grade.

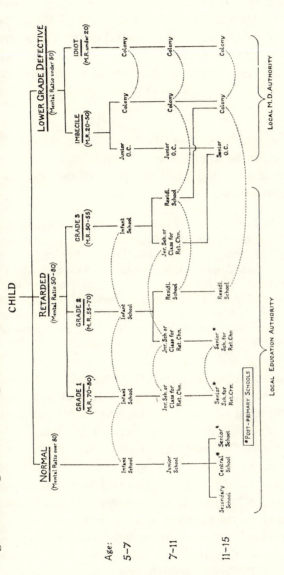

Notes: (1) The term "retarded" includes, as well as these children who are merely dull or backward, a considerable number of children who are at present certifiable as mentally defective under the Education Act. Some of these will, at some time during or at the end of their school life, require to be notified to the Local M.D. Authority for care and control.

(2) The dotted lines indicate groups of children of the same age but of different grades who, subject to proper classification, may be accommodated in the same school or institution.

(3) The brackets at the foot indicate the Authority financially responsible for the child.

(4) The upper and lower mental ratios in each grade indicate the approximate limits only.

and "playing a part" in influencing the Wood Committee's report in the direction of selective breeding—the "segregation of the subnormal so that they would not reproduce"—were therefore completely without foundation. They were smears of the worst kind, misrepresenting the character, findings, and recommendations of the members of the Wood Committee themselves, besides presenting Burt in a distasteful light that was totally undeserved.

Guessing the IQs of Adults

Like Kamin, Gillie also claimed that Burt "often guessed at the intelligence of parents he interviewed but later treated these data as hard scientific data," and here the gramophone record was playing back Kamin's groove.

> In a paper published in 1943, Burt gives an astounding figure of 153.2 for the average IQ of parents in the "higher professional" or "administrative" classes. This figure is impossibly high, exceeding by some 20 points the average IQ of Cambridge scientists tested recently. How Burt obtained such a figure is mysterious, because no standardised tests existed at that time for the proper measurement of adult IQs in the higher ranges.
>
> It now seems clear that Burt arrived at this figure by guesswork—a method he refers to as "assessment" in other papers.

We have seen that the figures given in the 1943 paper were derived from the data on recruits to the American Army during the First World War and the civil service tests for exservice candidates in Britain, and that these and the classification of "classes" and occupational grades had all been presented long ago in the 1926 vocational guidance study to which Burt, in this paper, clearly referred. All this was also fully known and had been commented on by leading educationalists such as Sir Percy Nunn,[11] and had already been stated in Burt's own *Mental and Scholastic Tests* (1921) and "Mental Differences Between Individuals" (1923).[12] Had Gillie taken the trouble to look up these references instead of accepting Kamin in the most slavish and uncritical manner, he would have been aware of this. His statement about "guess-work" is therefore, on the most generous interpretation possible, plainly astonishing. In addition, the extremely simplistic statement that

"no standardised tests existed at that time for the proper measurement of adult IQs in the higher ranges" reveals his ignorance of
these earlier studies, just as the charges of "guess-work" and
"assessment" reveal his ignorance of the care Burt and his colleagues had taken in their estimation of the level of intelligence of
adults and parents. All this was plainly set out in the earlier
literature, but Gillie, like Kamin, seems spuriously to have ignored
it.

The Missing Ladies—and Parapsychology

We will have to return to the question of Burt's "missing"
research assistants when coming to consider the present standing
of the charge of fraud itself, but here we must simply note the
definiteness of Gillie's charges on this matter and the kind of
language he used. It is not easy to ascertain the extensiveness of
Gillie's search for Miss Conway and Miss Howard (the two assistants whose existence has been most doubted) *before* his *Sunday
Times* article was written. *One week before* he had evidently
advertised in the *Sunday Times* itself, and then claimed in that first
article of 1976 that "advertisements in the personal columns of The
Times had . . . failed to locate anyone who knew of Howard or
Conway and their connection with Burt." Having searched files in
the Senate House of London University and made inquiries of
professors at University College and the Institute of Education, he
claimed that no trace at all could be found of either Howard or
Conway. "No-one," he also wrote, "with these names is listed in
the files of the British Psychological Society." What seems certain,
however, is that Gillie chiefly investigated the question of the
existence of these ladies after this first article was written and
published. In 1979, in an article on "Burt's Missing Ladies" in
Science,[13] he reported "the enquiries made by the Sunday Times
and other *over the past two years*." This, it is true, was a very
detailed report (giving the appearance of the most detailed investigation Gillie himself undertook in the whole affair), but let us note
the nature of the claims he made in, and after, this report.

First, they revealed extraordinary carelessness and inaccuracy.
In 1982,[14] introducing a radio program on the "Burt Scandal" and
referring to Burt's 1943 paper, he said that "the joint author of this

article was a mysterious J. Conway." This raises doubts as to whether Gillie himself ever saw or read this paper at all (and that his comments were therefore entirely repetitions of Kamin), for this is simply not true. There was no co-author of this paper. It was written by Burt alone, and carries his name alone. Miss Conway was referred to only in a brief footnote acknowledging the information she provided on 157 children boarded out at foster homes— something occupying *five lines* in a closely printed *sixteen-page* article. Furthermore, even in the footnote, no initial whatever was mentioned. It was a bare "Miss Conway." The initial 'J' only emerged much later in the controversy, and we will see that even the name 'Jane' seems nothing more than a supposition. Why such inaccuracy from Gillie?

Second, Miss Howard apparently proving just as insubstantial a figure, Gillie says that it was some officials of the British Psychological Society who "volunteered the opinion" that Conway and Howard were merely "pen-names" used by Burt. The degree of reliability of these officials in tracing the names of members of their society (whether "missing ladies" or otherwise) may be amusingly seen, however, in the following correspondence. In the *Bulletin of the Society* (vol. 29) published in October 1976, the following obituary of Frederick Laws appeared.

Obituary

FREDERICK LAWS (1911–19765)

Frederick Laws, who died earlier this year, was the first Editor of this *Bulletin*. From 1949, when the *Bulletin* was launched, until 1952, when he resigned the Editorship on account of pressure of other work, Fred Laws played an outstanding part in setting the *Bulletin* on its feet and in establishing it as the representative voice of the British Psychological Society.

Educated at King's College, Cambridge, Laws went into journalism and was successively art critic, radio critic and literary editor of the *News Chronicle* until the paper folded in 1955. Thereafter he worked mainly in freelance journalism and became a well-known broadcaster and script writer for radio and television. In his latter years, he became a part-time lecturer at various art schools in London.

Law's connection with psychology was in many ways close, though he never claimed to have formal qualifications in the subject. For a time, he was a graduate student at the Institute of Experimental Psychology at Oxford, where he worked under Dr. William Stephenson, at that time Assistant Director of the Institute. The fact that his first wife, Virginia (née Molteno) was an educational psychologists undoubtedly quickened his interest in the subject and gave him a shrewd appreciation of the difficulties at that time encountered by many professional psychologists in the course of their work. Later, he regularly reviewed books for the *Daily Telegraph,* including a good number in psychology.

As Editor of the *Bulletin,* Fred Laws brought not only considerable knowledge and understanding of psychology, but also wide experience in the realities of practical journalism. He envisaged the *Bulletin* not merely as a house journal for the Society but also as a vehicle for short original articles and book reviews of general interest to psychologists. He tried hard to maintain a proper balance between the academic and professional aspects of the subject as, indeed, between the various professional interests represented in the Society. In all these respects he succeeded well and his example has been closely followed by his successors.

Fred Laws served for a time on the Council of the Society and brought wide experience and shrewd judgment to its affairs. He did much to help the evolution of the Society from a primarily academic to a more manifestly professional body. He had many friends in all walks of psychology no less than in journalism, broadcasting and the Arts. By all he will be sadly missed.

O. L. ZANGWILL

Miss Virginia Molteno (who had become one of the controversial ladies—though not missing) had married Frederick Laws. Anxious to write to her in connection with the controversy, Gretl Archer (Burt's last secretary) wrote to the Society, in November, in the following way:

26, November, 1976

The Executive Secretary,
British Psychological Society,
18–19, Albemarle Street,
London W1X 4DN

Dear Sir,

I just heard that Frederick Laws, the first editor of the BPS Bulletin, recently died. I wonder whether you could kindly let me have, or find out for me, Mrs. Laws' present address to enable me to write to her. I enclose an addressed and stamped envelope.

> With many thanks,
> Yours sincerely,
>
> Gretl Archer

About a month later, she received the following reply from the Records Manager:

The British Psychological Society,
St. Andrews House,
48 Princess Road,
Leicester LE1 yDQ

> December, 1976

Dear Miss Archer,

I am sorry to say that we have no recent knowledge of the death of Frederick Laws, in fact I can find no record of him on any of our files. I am sorry that I cannot help you in any way to trace Mrs. Laws.

> Your sincerely,
>
> D. J. Griffiths,
> Records Manager

Some of these officials, however, referred Gillie to Professor J. Tizard of the University of London Institute of Education, a quest that led to others, none of whom proved able to trace them—their names not appearing as members of staff of any description in the University of London. The fact that they may not have been formal employees at all but (in Miss Conway's case) a "Care Committee worker," or (in Miss Howard's case) a mathematician, both of whom were voluntary helpers in his researches (as many others were known to be), did not seem to cause Gillie any pause for reflection, and the "lack of documentary evidence" led him to the supposition that they may never have existed "but were the fantasy of an ageing professor who became increasingly lonely and deaf." This colorful suggestion was then taken to what may well be thought extraordinary lengths. In the *Journal of the Association of Educational Psychologists* in 1984,[15] he claimed that

> from childhood, Burt may have created a fantasy world complete with imaginary intellectual companions with whom he debated and played

logical games. According to the observations of Theodore Barber of Cushing Hospital, Framingham, Massachusetts, people who have imaginary companions in childhood often continue with a rich fantasy life throughout adulthood but keep this a closely guarded secret. They also commonly have psychic experiences.

Miss Conway, Miss O'Connor and probably Miss Howard, were Burt's imaginary companions. Even if at one time they were real people, they continued to live in his imagination long after they disappeared from his life. He also had an imaginary relationship with Miss Molteno.[16] Further evidence that Burt had the type of imagination referred to by Dr. Barber, comes from Burt's interest in psychical research.

Burt, said Gillie, knew S. G. Soal, the well-known psychic researcher, who worked for several years at University College, and had described how:

> Dr. Soal invented a non-existent friend named John Ferguson, and before each sitting visualised an imaginary event in which John took part. Time and again 'John' turned up at the seance as a discarnate communicator and reminded him of these various events. In this passage Burt seems to be arguing that it is possible to create a person in the imagination who will then have a separate existence as some sort of spirit which can subsequently enter the mind of others. . . . Perhaps Misses Conway, O'Connor and Howard were discarnate communicators". Indeed Burt might have recruited a ghostly team of research workers who sent him data by means of ESP or PSI. However, when Burt does mention his research they seem anything but ethereal. According to Burt, Miss Conway (always the provider of data) helped him to study ESP in identical twins.

Burt was also interested, Gillie continued, in the "quasi-telepathic sympathy" which, he believed, seemed to occur with special frequency between identical twins, but here, Burt claimed:

> "In our own studies of monozygotic twins, Miss Conway and I encountered several stories to the same effect, but were not particularly successful when we came to test the pairs with the procedure adopted by Soal." There is no hint in this that Miss Conway could be communicating from the spirit world, but then as Barber says, the existence of fantasy companions in adulthood is generally kept a closely guarded secret.

This, we must note—itself a piece of "rich fantasy" on the character of Burt's interest in parapsychology—was what Gillie seriously put forward as *scientific* criticism! This cannot be allowed to pass without comment.

It is certainly true that, like Arthur Koestler, a friend of his, Burt was seriously and scientifically interested in parapsychology, but his discussion of this took place on the level of interest and contributions of men like William MacDougall, C. D. Broad, F. W. H. Myers, Henry Sidgwick, G. N. M. Tyrell, and in relation to the *Proceedings of the Society for Psychical Research*. All of these (including Burt) were stringently critical of all the claims made and evidence presented by "mediums" and others. The following is just one of Burt's criticisms of "the content of messages transmitted by these modern forms of necromancy." At best, he says, one has to conclude that they are "decidedly unilluminating."

> First of all they are exceedingly trivial in themselves. For the most part they are a medley of sentimental gush and sermonizing platitudes. As one writer observes, 'if these ghosts have souls, they certainly have no brains.' The account they give of 'Life in the Beyond' is often ludicrous. In the descriptions which Sir Oliver Lodge believed he had received from his son Raymond (killed in the first world war) we gather that the departed spirits drink whiskies and sodas and smoke cigars (*Raymond*, 1916). When similar communications are received from a great moral and intellectual hero of the past, the only inference that could be drawn from them would be that the surviving personality has left all the best parts of his intelligence and character behind. If (we are tempted to say) that is the kind of immortality achieved by 'this grey shadow, once a man', then surely he must be ready to echo the lament of old Tithonus:
>
> > 'I ask'd thee: "Give me immortality",
> > Then didst thou grant my asking with a smile.
> > But thy strong hours indignant work'd their will,
> > And beat me down and marr'd and wasted me.
> > And tho' they would not end me, left me maim'd,
> > Immortal age beside immortal youth,
> > And all I was in ashes.'[17]

This is hardly the judgment of a man deluded by popular mediumistic reports; and some of those who had known Burt well came readily to his defense against such fanciful condemnation. In the *Times* of October 27, 1976, Dr. Anita Gregory, who had edited a volume of Burt's writings on parapsychology, said:

> He was a very erudite and learned man, and the writings I edited were entirely of a theoretical and philosophical nature. He never did any

empirical research in the subject, or wrote on the basis of personal experiences.

Mrs. Rosalind Heywood, too, who was vice-president of the Society for Psychical Research, was just as definite:

> The idea is much too childish for the extreme normality of his approach. My impression was that his interest was very profound and that he believed telepathy was a very subtle extension of the five senses, so that if we were all blind we would regard a sighted person much as people with telepathic gifts are regarded today.

She also, despite the attacks on him, remained a great admirer of Burt:

> I was completely devoted to him as a man of the most remarkable integrity. It is possible, since he was so head and shoulders above everybody else, and working in such isolation that he might make mistakes or assumptions. But I would deliberately shoot myself rather than attribute any nefarious motive to him.

Third, however, Gillie went on to claim that Burt had written articles with both Conway and Howard as co-authors, and some articles using their names alone. This is true, but Gillie (although touching on this in his first 1976 article) nowhere gives full weight to the reasons Burt himself gave for this—particularly to his last secretary, Miss Gretl Archer. There were several such reasons. First, and most important, Conway and Howard had helped him very substantially over many years in carrying out tests, collecting and collating evidence, and—in Howard's case particularly—collaborating with him in the mathematical and statistical aspects of his studies. Though they were no longer with him, he wished to acknowledge their contributions, as he had always done with those who had collaborated with him. Second, he was no longer in touch with them because (he believed) they had emigrated. Third, it was a very widely held opinion of him (of which he was well and sensitively aware) that he himself "published too much." Always meticulously acknowledging his helpers, no matter how small their contribution might have been, he had in fact written articles with co-authors before; these, of course, having been quite undisputed.

Clearly these reasons cannot be *proved* or *disproved,* but they are such as to be taken into account, at the very least, before arriving at a definitive judgment; and Gillie's pronouncements are thrown into doubt as being too dogmatic by some of his own related claims.

Before leaving this point, however, bearing in mind my concern not to evade any reasonably founded criticism of Burt, it does seem totally fair—whatever may be thought about these various reasons he supposedly gave for it (which all lie in the realm of hearsay and conjecture, the truth and soundness of which it is therefore impossible to judge)—to say that, at the very least, Burt was foolish in publishing some articles under Miss Conway's name alone. Joint authorship is common, but to attribute to someone else, and to publish under their name (no matter how great one's degree of indebtedness) an article one has written oneself, is not. Foolish, therefore, this most certainly was, and was undoubtedly and understandably something on the basis of which his critics could call into question the articles' actual subject-matter. We will consider the dispute over the content of the articles later, but here it can readily be conceded that, on the face of it, this publication under another's name (without explanation) was a foolishness and a fault on the part of Burt.

Returning, however, to Gillie's claims, one of these is particularly important because it demonstrates either the sheer inaccuracy (the careless reporting) or the deliberate distortion of what he put forward as *evidence.* But let us note before this (it is an essential ground of Gillie's argument that follows) that by 1979 Gillie had in fact uncovered *some* concrete evidence of Miss Howard's existence, and even some connected evidence of the existence of Miss Conway.

Although Gillie only says (in several places) that Professor John Cohen claimed to have "once met a woman called Miss Howard in the Psychology Department at University College, London,"[18] John Cohen in fact remembered her very well. In an article in *Encounter*[19] following Gillie's attack on Burt, Cohen wrote:

> I had, indeed, often met her, and I recall her roundish face, her pleasing smile, her brown eyes and bobbed auburn hair, her slightly tinted spectacles, and her competence in mathematics.

Donald MacRae, at the London School of Economics, also had quite definite and unmistakable recollections of her, still actually possessing the corrected proofs she brought to him. In a letter to the *New Statesman*[20] toward the end of 1978 (following yet another article by Gillie attacking Burt, of November 24, 1978, entitled "Sir Cyril Burt and the Great IQ Fraud"), he wrote:

> I hold no brief for Burt, but I do know that he did not invent Miss Howard. When *The British Journal of Sociology* was first founded, I was appointed Review Editor and was also in charge of the production of the *Journal*. On the advice of the late Morris Ginsberg, I approached Burt for what was intended to be a review article on *The Trend of Scottish Intelligence* (1949). Burt very quickly produced a long article which appeared in *The British Journal of Sociology,* Vol. 1, No. 2, June 1950, as *The Trend of National Intelligence.* I have in my hands the corrected proofs of that article. They were brought down from University College London to the London School of Economics by a lady who introduced herself to me as Miss Howard 'who worked for Professor Burt.' I have a fairly clear recollection of her appearance, but on looks, over so long a time, memory can lie. What I can say with confidence is that Miss Howard came to me here once with these proofs and once again on some question connected with offprints.
>
> When the controversy about Burt first blew up, I thought of writing to this effect in some public place, but as, in fact, at least one psychologist also vouched for Miss Howard's existence, I did not bother. Now, however, I feel that I must put at least this point on record.

There is nothing in the slightest degree undecided about that testimony, and it may be noted that it was written two years after the initial scandal—MacRae clearly having assumed that the full testimony of John Cohen would have been accepted as being adequate and conclusive. But there was other evidence of the same kind. Dr. William Hammond very clearly remembered being tested by Miss Howard *and* a "Miss C." It also turned out, after all, that a Miss M. A. Howard *was* among the list of members of the British Psychological Society in 1924, her address being 39, Brunswick Square, London WC1 (just across the road, more or less, from both University College and the Institute of Education). How much evidence, one wonders, is enough?

All this Gillie knew well enough by 1979—after his two years of further inquiry—and though playing down, if not actually seeming to discount, all these references, the important thing to note is that he had come to believe that the existence of the missing ladies *"now seems possible at least for Howard"*; hardly a great concession given the evidence we have mentioned. But, even after having conceded this, he then went on to claim, about these ladies, that they were "not the people Burt said they were and did not do at least some of the things that he said they did."[21] This it was, he said, that had led him on to identify the "mechanism of fraud" Burt employed, and this is the argument it is most important to note.

Gillie said that among the assistants he was able to trace (as I was readily able to trace "Miss Mawer"), one was *Miss Molteno.* And, he continued (my italics), Elizabeth Virginia Molteno

> is particularly interesting because Burt acknowledges her help, together with that of Howard and Conway, *in finding twins*. I have been in touch with Miss Molteno, now Mrs. Moody, who tells me that she never knew Howard or Conway; but even more curious, she never assisted Burt with his research work *as Burt said she did,* although she did study in his department and did publish work on twins with R. B. Cattell. This suggests the mechanism of the alleged fraud: Burt used the name of a real person and attributed work to her that she did not do.

This, it will be seen, again repeats the assumption by this time that Conway and Howard may well have been "real persons" but the paper to which he referred concerning Burt's acknowledgment was once again the 1943 paper. But in the particular acknowledgment Burt made, two things are outstandingly clear. First, in it there is no mention of Howard or Conway at all. Second, and more important, nowhere does Burt make the claim that Miss Molteno helped him *in finding twins*. His precise acknowledgment is this:

> A novel method of analysis was attempted by Miss V. Molteno, who, up to the outbreak of war, was working up data obtained for twins in London. She has applied the alternative technique of 'correlating persons' to numerous assessments for a variety of mental characteristics (collected by herself and Dr. R. B. Cattell). The research unfortunately remains incomplete but indicates, so far as it goes, that the qualitative resemblances between twins are even more striking than the quantitative. (For reference, cf. Cattell and Molteno, J. Genetic Psychology, 57, 1940, pp. 31–47.)

What Gillie asserts about Burt's claim is patently false. Burt nowhere acknowledges Molteno's help (together with that of Conway and Howard) in finding twins. But the falsity put forward here by Gillie is compounded by the fact that the reference he himself gives for the "work on twins Miss Molteno published with R. B. Cattell" is *precisely* that which Burt himself mentioned, as above. Furthermore, Burt's account of all this has been fully confirmed by Raymond Cattell himself. Gretl Archer told me that Burt and Cattell had a mutual working agreement, and that when Burt was interested in some particular problem or needed evidence on it, he would be in touch with Cattell, who would—as and when possible—introduce it into his own investigations. I wrote to Cattell about this, and about this specific instance of the part played by Miss Molteno, and he replied "Re. the 'missing women', yes, Virginia Molteno and I worked at Burt's suggestion on the paper 'Inheritance of Perseveration . . .' in which I was personally interested as an inheritable trait," going on to say what happened to Miss Molteno subsequently (her marriage, and so forth).

This entire claim is therefore a falsification, a distortion. How then are we to judge Gillie's next step: of claiming, on this completely false basis, that this suggests "the mechanism of fraud," of "using the name of a real person and attributing work to her which she did not do"? It was patently untrue about Miss Molteno, the one instance that Gillie cited as his crucial example. How, then, can it be hypothetically extended to Miss Conway and Miss Howard? What degree of credence or reliability can such an argument have? How can one regard it as being anything other than intellectually scandalous?

We will have to come back to the case of the missing ladies, but here it is enough to have plainly shown that Gillie's testimony— even on this one apparently demonstrable matter—was questionable throughout in the extreme, and in some respects quite clearly and deliberately false.

The Invariant Correlations and Working Backwards

Gillie's charge here was "gramophone record criticism" at its best (or worst, depending upon how one chooses to describe it). His precise accusation was:

that Burt miraculously produced identical answers accurate to three decimal places from different sets of data—this is a statistical impossibility and he could have done it only by working backwards to make the observations fit his answers.

He added to the charge of "working backwards," the "supplying of data to fit predictions of his (Burt's) favourite genetic themes." But what then are the repeated, identical three-decimal-place correlations he reports? Why . . . they are precisely Kamin's mistakes! Gillie wrote in the 1976 article:

The number of twins he used changed from 21 in a paper published in 1955 to "over 30" in 1958, to 53 in 1966. Amazingly, the figures for the statistical correlations of IQs remained the same to three decimal places—0.771. Furthermore, the figures for the correlation of IQs of twins raised together (0.944) remained the same—despite three changes in the number of twins.

We have seen that *there was no new study of "over 30" twins in 1958,* and that the figures repeated in Burt's paper published in that year was simply a repetition of *all* the correlations of his 1955 study, quoted by way of illustration in his 1957 Bingham lecture. Gillie here simply repeated Kamin's errors. He did not check his facts, something which is not only bad science but surely bad journalism.

Furthermore, anyone who looked at the full range of some 60 to 70 correlations reported in each of Burt's tables would see, at a glance, the utterly *preposterous* nature of the idea that Burt "worked backwards" and "invented" spurious data to produce them. If the repetition of two three-decimal-place correlations is a statistical impossibility, then working backwards to produce sixty-odd three-decimal-place correlations is even more so. And indeed, it seems clear that the very idea of working backwards ultimately stems from one source only. During the last few years of his life (from about 1963 onwards) Burt was frequently asked by several scholars for various details of his twin studies. Two of these have been chiefly mentioned as a basis of criticism. In December 1968, Professor Jencks asked Burt for a "listing of the pairs (of twins) with IQ scores and class positions of each." In his diary, Burt recorded that he spent a week, from January second onwards, "calculating data on twins for Jencks," and on January eleventh "finished checking tables for Jencks." His reply went off to Jencks on January twenty-fifth. This, says Hearnshaw, constitutes fraud.[22]

> Had the IQ scores and social class gradings been available they could have been copied out in half an hour at the most. So quite clearly the table of IQ scores and social class gradings was an elaborately contrived piece of work, and we are forced to the conclusion that he simply did not possess detailed data, at any rate for the whole sample of his separated MZ twins.

This is a strangely conclusive verdict from someone with no first-hand knowledge of the actual condition of Burt's data—whether they were, indeed, test scores of Burt's usual kind, whether they had already included "class gradings," and so on—and concerning figures prepared and collated over a period of little more than a month from the receipt of Jencks' request, a period that included the Christmas and New Year period.

Hearnshaw dismisses all Burt's excuses for delays as "lies," when it is surely one of the commonest things in correspondence to give easy-to-hand (or plausible) excuses for not having done something at once. Has Hearnshaw himself, one wonders, never given such excuses? Most of us (I would hazard a guess) have told such "lies" by the yard! And Burt was then a man of 86 years of age, with very meagre secretarial help.[23] In November 1969, Dr. W. Shockley also asked him for the data of his latest twin studies. Again Burt replied—a month later—that the lack of secretarial help accounted for his delay, but sent the table already sent to Jencks.[24] This twofold Jencks-Shockley incident was the ground for arguing that Burt worked backwards, inventing data to support his correlations. We will come back to this when considering the present standing of the charges of fraud, and more of significance on the Shockley correspondence may be seen in Appendix 3. Here, however, it is enough to note that at the hands of Gillie, this alleged method of "working backwards" had become a wholesale accusation referring to all Burt's tabulated correlations, "to make the observations fit his answers," a task which would be infinitely more impossible than the alleged recurrence of the *two* correlations themselves.

Here too, then, Gillie is shown to merely repeat Kamin's error and the judgment of others, simply extending them in an unwarranted way to further his argument and deepen and augment his portrait of Burt as a man guilty of scientific misconduct.

"Early Plagiarism to Outright Fraud"

A final example of Gillie's standards of rigor and impartiality in scientific criticism is to be seen in his charge of plagiarism. In 1980 an article appeared in *The History of Science* by Gillian Sutherland and Stephen Sharp.[25] This discussed the appointment of Burt as the first official psychologist of the London County Council (LCC), comparing his claims for this appointment disadvantageously with those of W. H. Winch, who at that time was already a member of the LCC inspectorate. Winch, said these authors, was "plainly the front runner," and Burt's success only came "after the Committee had voted three times according to some preferential system of mind-boggling complexity." The article went on to belittle Burt's work in relation to that of others, but in particular claimed that Winch's publications "closely parallelled and even anticipated" those of Burt. Winch "began to publish nine years earlier than Burt" (he was 48 at the time of Burt's appointment; Burt was 29); and, they pointed out, a 1914 paper by Burt on the Binet tests "coincided with a series by Winch on the same topic." In all this, they contrasted the "casualness" of Burt's work with the "impeccable reporting" of Winch. In short, Burt was deplored, Winch was extolled. The impression given was that there was conflict between the two men, a marked contrast in the quality of work between them, and Burt was presented as the more deliberately calculating of the two in actively promoting both the publicity of his own work and his own prominence and self-advancement.

The strange thing about this article is that two of its appendices, which list the bibliographies of both Winch and Burt, seem conclusively to disprove its authors' claims. The early publications of Winch, from 1900 onwards, have practically nothing to do with intelligence testing. His earliest paper relating to this—"Social Class and Mental Proficiency in Elementary School Children"[26]— was published in 1911, and his first articles on "Binet's Mental Tests" were published from 1913 to 1915.[27] These were also a series of very short pieces. Burt's first two articles on the Binet tests (two parts forming a substantial and detailed article) were also published in 1914,[28] but these had been preceded by very detailed articles on "Experimental tests of general intelligence" from 1909 onward. There is no doubt whatever that Burt preceded Winch in this, and there is no shred of evidence to suggest that Burt borrowed from Winch or at all relied upon him.

All such argument, however, suggests that bad blood existed between the two men, but in Burt's own publications it can be seen that he made much reference to the work of Winch and testified to its value. In *Mental and Scholastic Tests,* for example, there are no fewer than thirteen references to Winch, three of these quite substantial. Indeed, Burt acknowledged his indebtedness to Winch (among others) for having read and criticized his earlier typescript, and in some instances he mentions his preference for suggestions made by Winch (in the use of tests) over those of others (often, indeed, pointing out their "excellence") and makes it quite clear that he and Winch were in correspondence with each other over materials to be used in the Binet-Simon tests. Winch's "age-assignment" for the several tests referred to are also fully reported among those of others; and indeed, Winch's articles on the Binet tests are in fact recommended, Burt's judgment of them being: "A free but excellent revision of the tests as far as Age VIII, based upon experiments with London school children." The same appraisal is given in *The Backward Child* in his reference to "a detailed and interesting account of such tests applied to London school children: W. H. Winch, 'Children's Perceptions: An Experimental Study of Observation and Report in School Children (1914)."

The truth is that there appears to have been no kind of cleavage between Burt and Winch at all, and no overlapping of their work such as to raise any suspicion, but it suited these authors (having requested details about Burt from Miss Archer, who was subsequently disgusted with the use to which they had been put) to add to the smearing of Burt's reputation, an exercise that by this time had become so fashionable; the bandwagon now being well set on its rails. And Gillie was ready to take a seven-league stride of judgment from the basis they supplied. His judgment was this:

I think it most likely that Burt was a plagiarist of long standing, and that a habit of plagiarism developed by stages into fraud. Burt was appointed as the first London County Council (LCC) psychologist over the head of W. H. Winch—a modest and retiring man who was an impeccable scientist. It appears from research published by Dr. Gillian Sutherland and Stephen Sharp of Cambridge University (England) that early in his career, Burt's work shadowed that of Winch. Burt came behind Winch in publishing original research but came ahead of Winch in promoting himself and in obtaining a reputation. In 1917, for example, a paper by Burt on reasoning tests covered much the same ground as a paper by Winch published in 1911. Yet Burt, who was always an effective self-publicist obtained five times as many citations for his work in The British Journal of Psychology.[29]

Winch was for Gillie "modest, retiring, and an impeccable scientist"; Burt a "plagiarist" and "effective self-publicist." Again, Gillie could not possibly have taken the trouble to read both the Winch and the Burt publications in sequence. But Gillie was not content with just this pronouncement. It had to be taken further. "By 1950," he wrote, "Burt had moved from plagiarism to outright fraud."

Of such a nature was Gillie's testimony on this other quite specific manner.

General Denunciations

This enumeration of such criticisms could be continued well nigh endlessly, but here we will bring together, briefly, a few final instances, while noting the wide-ranging denunciation and generally exaggerated and intemperate nature of the language Gillie used.

In his first 1976 article, he claimed that Burt had strongly influenced the 1944 Education Act. The division of secondary education into three kinds of schools—grammar, technical, and secondary modern—"echoed," said Gillie, "Burt's theory that intelligence was innate and unlikely to change during teenage years." Burt certainly did think that assessment, selection, and the provision of different kinds of educational opportunities appropriate to different levels of general intelligence and special aptitudes were essential in any satisfactory system of education, but even this statement of Gillie's was far too simplistic. Burt had contributed to the Spens Committee, but the division of "secondary education for all" into the three kinds of school was chiefly the proposal of the Norwood Committee, and in this report *intelligence* was not mentioned at all—either as a criterion for selection to, or a criterion of the nature of education within, each of the three types of school. Children of the highest intelligence might well be suited for, and attracted to, any one of them. Neither was Burt himself, or his ideas, at all mentioned.

Furthermore, Burt was never, on the grounds of any principle, opposed to the conception and institution (where it might be well-suited to a community and its conditions) of the comprehensive school. The truth is that he thought it a mistake to divide schools on the basis of different kinds of subject (or simple vocational) orientations; just as he believed that no *one* particular kind of *school organization* could possibly satisfactorily meet the needs of all the differing geographical and administrative areas of the country. All the arguments about the equality of opportunity had, he thought, been grossly politicised; just as selection had been grossly conceived in terms of social class. His own position was that the *opportunities* in education should be enriched by a *greater diversity,* and this was stated quite clearly in what was one of his last articles.

> In England the issues that arise have of late been canvassed chiefly in reference to their bearing on school organization; and it seems widely assumed that those who subscribe to the hereditarian view are wholly at variance with the establishment of comprehensive schools. That is by no means an inevitable inference. . . . There is no one universal scheme equally suited to every type of educational area. Recent enquiries have demonstrated that so-called comprehensive schools differ far more from one another than is commonly imagined, and the various types of organization are constantly being revised. We should therefore suspend our judgment as to the relative efficiency of different kinds of school.
>
> The paramount need is not equality of educational opportunity, but diversity. Each child should in an ideal system, be provided with the peculiar types of opportunity that can best minister to his needs. Inevitably that must entail some kind of segregation or selective streaming. A year or two ago a questionnaire circulated to a number of practising teachers indicated that the majority of the older (and therefore presumably the more experienced) favoured relatively homogeneous classes as being far easier to teach. "The dull pupil," said one, "when working in a class with pupils of average intelligence quickly

becomes disheartened by the daily evidence of his own inferiority; the exceptionally able soon get bored and restive.'' But unless the teacher is prepared to sift and sort he cannot secure the intellectual homogeneity that he wants.[30]

The whole matter of selection and equality of opportunity had been vastly oversimplified; as had the issue between heredity and environment. One of Gillie's chief charges was that in his emphasis on the hereditary basis of intelligence, Burt had greatly ''underrated the importance of social factors.'' In fact, however, Burt had always emphasized the importance of environmental influences, both in presenting difficulties in the *recognition* of the mental ability and educational potentiality of children, and in blocking and obstructing, or encouraging and facilitating, its development and fulfillment. But there was more than this. Within the context of both hereditary and environmental influences, he also emphasized the central importance of aims, ideals, values, and personal *character*. This, again, was made quite clear in the same article[30]:

> Intelligence is by no means the only factor determining the child's educational progress. There are the special abilities and disabilities that emerge and mature during the years of growth; there are his qualities of temperament and character—the ambitions that he cherishes and the aims that he forms. These, like general intelligence, are also largely influenced by the child's inborn constitution; but they are far more liable to be swayed by the conditions and events of his daily life, at home, at school, and wherever he meets his boon companions. Hitherto, our notions about the kind of school, curriculum, and teaching methods best fitted to this or that type of child have been for the most part decided by purely theoretical deductions. What is most urgently needed therefore are systematic experiments, deliberately planned and conducted, in order to secure first-hand empirical evidence as to the merits and limitations of the various alternatives now proposed.

Gillie certainly knew of this paper; he accused Burt of having ''invented data'' in it; but one wonders, did he ever actually read it? And if he did, why did he choose to ignore Burt's quite clearly stated position?

The one-sidedness of his judgment is plain to see, too, in his extolling of Professor Dorfman's denunciation (it was far more than a scientific criticism) of the statistical methods Burt employed in his 1961 paper on "Intelligence and Social Mobility." "Burt's 1961 fraud," wrote Gillie, "was elegantly exposed" by Dorfman—and consider here the nature of the language he then used:

> The 1961 fraud provides false data to support a substantial theory which is supposed to account for the success and upward mobility of those who have inherited a high IQ. This is possibly the crowning success of Burt's career as a fraudster. What had developed as a habit of plagiarism turned into an elaborate technique of fraud, using numerical methods to work backwards from theory to 'data.'[31]

The gramophone record was rotating yet again, but this laudation of Dorfman's criticism fails to mention that Dorfman's own "Exposure" of Burt's statistics was itself found to be very gravely flawed by Professor Stigler.[32] Not both sides of the criticism, only the one side—the side that denigrated Burt—was presented.

It is surely telling as well that this intemperance of Gillie's language marked all his of writing on Burt. Both in small, insidious, and in large and conspicuous ways, it was and is always present. In the opening 1976 article, for example, it was not said that Burt consistently maintained the conclusions resulting from his studies that "differences in intelligence were largely inherited" but that he was "dedicated" to the idea. He was, says Gillie, quoting from his journalistic interviews with the Clarkes and McAskie of Hull, "obsessed" with it; and his "gross inconsistencies" could only be explained by "the probability of dishonesty." But we have seen enough of this in the way in which the words "fraudster" and "confidence trickster" liberally sprinkle his writings, and it only remains to note how extensively the intemperate nature of Gillie's attack was furthered by the accompanying journalistic practices of the press, supported by the immediate and unbelievably overreaching comments of one of the members of staff of the Institute of Education who had been one of Burt's former colleagues: Professor J. Tizard.

The headline of Gillie's first *Sunday Times* article—"Pioneer of IQ Faked His Research Findings"—could hardly be said to suffer from doubt or the temper of scientific criticism. Neither did that which followed in the next day's *Times,* which must have been written with foreknowledge of Gillie's article before it actually appeared. It read "Theories of IQ Pioneer 'Completely Discredited,' " this, the piece reported, being the judgment of Professor Tizard. Again, it was said that Burt's work had "led to burning debates in America and Britain over whether black people are genetically bound to be of inferior intelligence to white"; that Burt had "manufactured evidence", "guessed the IQs of parents", and so forth. The gramophone record was played again, and loudly. But Professor Tizard's pronouncement—magically commenting on an article that had appeared on Sunday in sufficient time for this further article to be written and printed on Monday—was as extravagant as the paper's headline:

> Professor Tizard said the discrediting of Burt's work cast doubt on his whole line of inquiry. It would have the same effect on that branch of science as the finding that the Piltdown Skull was a forgery had had on paleontology. "But Burt not only discovered the bones, he gave the vital dimensions and estimated the intelligence quotient. It has been immensely damaging to science."

And again, the denunciation of Burt's work immediately went far beyond the last few papers on identical twins, which was the focus of Kamin's original criticism.

> Professor Tizard also challenged the findings of two of Sir Cyril's most important works, *The Young Delinquent,* published in 1924, and *The Backward Child,* published in 1937.

> "All the research work in these books is very difficult to pin down. You can get no indication of when the field-work was carried out."

Those who take the trouble to read these books will see how fantastic this claim is. But the newspaper headlines went on, year after year: "How Heredity Research Was Faked," "Burt's Warped Personality Led Inevitably to Fraud," "More Flaws Found in Intelligence Theory Data," "Call for Burt Fraud Inquiry," "The Decline and Fall of Burt," "Sir Cyril Burt and the Great IQ Fraud." It is the editors and subeditors of newspapers—not usually the authors of articles—who are responsible for titles and headlines. Gillie's strident shout of "Fraud" gave them a field day, a good story that never ceased until its inglorious culmination in *The Intelligence Man*. And Gillie's pronouncement, like that of Tizard, had become total. Going far beyond the later twin studies, he concluded that "Burt's whole corpus of work must now be suspect."

A matter of personal choice and testimony also remains. I will make little of it, though it is of considerable significance. After all these denunciations of Burt—condemning his defense of selection in secondary education, his supposed opposition to the idea of equality of opportunity, his class consciousness and elitism, and in particular his Hereditarian theory as the basis for these inegalitarian positions—one would have supposed Gillie to have been an egalitarian par excellence, opposed to all forms of privilege and privileged opportunity in education. But surprisingly, not so! The *Camden New Journal* (January 19, 1984) reported that Gillie sent his own children to private schools. Commenting on his belief "that intelligence is shaped by environment," the article continued:

> Oddly enough, it is because he believes this, that, although he supports comprehensive schools, he is sending his children to private schools. This makes sense once you accept that the environment of some comprehensive schools can be so bad that kids who go there don't stand a chance!

In an exchange of letters in the *Sunday Telegraph*, I pressed Gillie for his explanation of this, finding it incongruous with all he had maintained. Having attacked my "sexist assumption" that the choice was entirely his, he replied:

> My wet, soft-focus, centre-of-the-road politics are a disappointment to those people who deduced that I must be some sort of raving red because of my part in the Burt controversy. I am proud to be an egalitarian if that means every child should be given the best chance possible of getting a good education. The 11-plus encouraged obvious inequality, I believe, because it selected into two broad streams when human ability exists as a continuous spectrum of various talents. However, I don't think that egalitarian arguments should preclude individuals from spending money on their childrens' education.

> We considered that private schools would give our children the best environment for learning in London. So I am an environmentalist just as are others who seek to give their children a better environment by paying for it.

This is Gillie's conception of equality and equality of opportunity. Quite apart from his own personal choice, and more profoundly, does not his action, and even more, his defense of it, prove that an Environmentalist theory of the determination of intelligence can itself entail inequality, selection, élitism, just as much as a Hereditarian theory is supposed to do—but now served by the long-established and often arbitrary power of the purse, which was what Burt specifically opposed?

Such was the nature of Gillie's testimony. Confining these only to those matters on which evidence has been presented, and which are quite straightforward and specific, anwers are now required from him on at least the following questions.

Questions Requiring Public Answers

1. Why did Gillie, like Kamin, smear Burt with the charge of racism, of being uncritically steeped in the most extreme views of the eugenics movement, and of having inspired the research on the intelligence of blacks and whites in America and Britain, when this was not true, when there is no evidence whatever of racialism or race discrimination in Burt's own work, and when this had no bearing whatever on his later twin studies?
2. Why, similarly, did he misrepresent the report of the Wood Committee of 1929, Burt's contribution to its work, and, in general, Burt's views about the placing of backward or retarded children for their most appropriate kinds of education—so smearing Burt with the worst interpretation of the views of the eugenics movement, recommending the "segregation of the mentally subnormal so that they would not reproduce"?—when this too had no bearing on the controversial twin studies?
3. Why, on these questions of eugenics, did Gillie go so far as to compare selection for secondary school education in England with the Nazi atrocities in Germany? Why did Gillie also link this with social class, suggesting that Burt was opposed to giving opportunities to the "lower classes" out of the fear of their relative rapidity of breeding?
4. Why did he completely falsify what Burt had claimed about the contribution of Miss Molteno, and then base upon this falsification his account of Burt's "mechanism of fraud"?
5. Why did he repeat, and therefore reinforce by his published repetition, Kamin's error in claiming that there had been a 1958 study of "over 30" twins, and that therefore there were three repetitions of the "invariant correlations" (.770/.944) when this

was clearly not so? If this was just a mistake on his part, why had he not read the relevant papers and checked his facts before repeating what was clearly a damaging and false assertion?

6. Why has he consistently and repeatedly extolled Dorfman's critique of Burt's statistics, while making no mention whatever of Stigler's damaging criticism of Dorfman?

7. Why did he not check the charge of "plagiarism" before immediately accepting the judgment of others, let alone extending it to claim that Burt had moved "from early plagiarism to later outright fraud"? Did he read and check the early writings of Winch and Burt before, in wholesale fashion, accepting this judgment? If not, why not?

8. Why did he persistently claim that Burt "underrated social factors" when in fact Burt had especially itemized, analyzed, and emphasized these—in precisely the same way as was subsequently done by the sociologists of education (whose work we will compare later)?

9. So deeply committed to egalitarianism; so vehemently opposed to Burt's ideas on the desirability of selection; so radically opposed to the segregation of children in different kinds of schools, and to elitism; does he not concede that his decision to send his own children to private schools, together with his defense of this decision, gives rise to a fundamental question at the heart of the whole controversy? Does it not make abundantly clear the fact that inequality, inequality of opportunity, the practice of privilege, and élitism are just as possible on Environmentalist as they are on Hereditarian grounds?

As these questions cannot be either asked or answered in the open forum of a court, Gillie's public, published replies will be awaited with interest.

Notes

1. *Science* 204:1035; 1979.
2. *Sunday Times,* October 24, 1976.
3. With the exception of Tizard of the University of London.
4. *Listener,* letter on "The Burt Scandal." May 13, 1982.
5. January 1, 1979.
6. April 24–30.
7. August 9.
8. May 6, 1982.

9. Details of this, together with a table showing chronological age, mental age, and standards, are to be found in *Report of an Investigation upon Backward Children in Birmingham,* City of Birmingham Stationery Dept., 1921, p. 17.
10. P. 28. My italics.
11. *Education: Its Data and First Principles.* London: Arnold, 1920 (2d ed. 1930), pp. 122–26.
12. "The Mental Differences Between Individuals." British Association Annual Report, Presidential Address, Psychological Section.
13. Vol. 204, p. 1035.
14. *Radio Times,* April 24–30, p. 12.
15. Vol. 6, no. 3, pp. 1–4.
16. For this "imaginary relationship" see p. 00.
17. From "The Pros and Cons of a Religious Metaphysic" (unpublished), p. 67.
18. *Radio Times,* June 7–13, 1984, p. 11.
19. "After the Cyril Burt case: The Detractors," p. 86. Later, in correspondence, when I was checking all this (and other matters) with John Cohen, he reiterated "Yes. I *do* remember Miss Howard."
20. Vol. 96, p. 820, 1978.
21. *Science* 204:1037; 1979.
22. *Hearnshaw, L. S. Cyril Burt, Psychologist.* London: Hodder & Stonghan, 1979, p. 247.
23. It is a point of interest and perhaps significance that throughout his whole career Burt was never provided with a secretary. The only secretarial help he had was that for which he paid himself. This, clearly, is why so many (the preponderance) of his letters were handwritten—with an absence, presumably, of file copies.
24. This table was later published by Jensen: *Behavioral Genetics,* 4:15; 1974.
25. "The First Official Psychologist in the World." *History of Science* 18; 1980.
26. *Journal of Experimental Pedagogy* 1:9; 1911.
27. *Child Study,* volumes 6 through 8.
28. *Eugenics Review* 6:36; 1914.
29. *Journal of the Association of Educational Psychologists* 6(3):3.
30. "Intelligence and Heredity: Some Common Misconceptions." *Irish Journal of Education,* Winter 1969.
31. *Journal of the Association of Educational Psychologists* 6(3):3; 1984.
32. See pp. 156–161).

5

The Clarkes and Hull

The testimony of Ann and Alan Clarke (both now Professors of Psychology at the University of Hull), linked, quite early, with that of Dr. Michael McAskie (also of Hull), is perhaps the strangest testimony of all in the entire case. So too is its bitterness, tenacity, and—progressively as the controversy continued—the determination of its effort to extend the charges against Burt further and further, and blacken his character completely. Kamin—whether justifiably or not—was clearly motivated by a deep aversion to anything that he saw contributing to policies of racial or class discrimination. Gillie clearly shared the same abomination of eugenics and the Hereditarian position as he saw it. The Clarkes, however, did not agree with Kamin, and wanted to make this disagreement clear. Presumably, therefore, they did not share much that lay at the root of Gillie's position. What, then, could it have been that fired their own deeply felt hostility to Burt? This remains a mystery; but on the basis of it the "Hull department" could justifiably be designated the one conspicuous anti-Burt department among all the universities of Britain. Let us consider the substance and character of the Clarkes' testimony by taking each of their allegations in turn.

Collaboration in the Public Charge of Fraud

The Clarkes began examining two of Burt's papers in 1971 and 1972 (soon after Burt's death), and published their judgment in a few pages of criticism in 1974[1] that the papers contained "puzzling features" and "surprisingly high correlations," left some "question begging," and contained results that "appear suspiciously perfect." This, however, they said later, was "very much less ambitious" than Jensen's paper of the same year, which reviewed all Burt's data and statistics, was much milder than Kamin's attacks, and did not then lead them "to their shame" to "suspect fraud." These deeper suspicions came with Ann Clarke's collaboration with McAskie in 1976.[2] We have seen, however, that the forthright charge of fraud was made by and in conjunction with Gillie in his 1976 *Sunday Times* article. In that article, the Clarkes and McAskie were involved by way of interview and consultation with Gillie. There, it was said by Gillie that "having checked the consistency with which Burt's figures fitted his theories"[3] the Clarkes had concluded that "scientifically Burt's results are a fraud." McAskie added: "It is impossible to see how Burt could have obtained these observations without deliberately fiddling the figures to produce the results he desired." And he and the Clarkes then said: "Since no one who knew Burt could possibly accuse him of incompetence,[4] there remains only the probability of dishonesty."

What becomes perfectly clear, however, from the Clarkes' own later writing, is that they actively collaborated with Gillie in the production of his original article. They were active partners in this making public of the outright charges of fraud. In 1980, in the *Bulletin of the British Psychological Society,* the Clarkes wrote: "Our motive for cooperating with Gillie was neither personal, political, nor ideological. Indeed, he allowed us to include a statement in the *Sunday Times* article which effectively indicated the substantial difference between Kamin and ourselves."

One of the questions we will ask is what precisely was this statement, and where is it to be found? My own close scrutiny of the article has failed to disclose or identify it. The clear point at issue, however, is that the Clarkes—from this very beginning— were actively in cooperation with Gillie. This cooperation continued (in the case of Ann Clarke particularly) over many years, and soon very specific charges emerged. It is in one of them, in particular, that the strangeness of the Clarkes' testimony lies.

The Famous Articles

This one, among their several charges against Burt, was persistenly reiterated throughout the controversy, and it too first made its appearance in a shorter article by Gillie. After an exchange of letters in the *Times,* some of which had defended Burt, Gillie published a piece in the *Sunday Times* (November 7, 1976) entitled "IQ Researchers 'Did Exist' "—the main point of which was to persist in throwing doubt on their existence. In this, he wrote:

> Professor Alan Clarke, his wife Dr. Ann Clarke, and Dr. Michael McAskie of Hull University, say: "An attempt is being made to white-wash Burt. We (the Clarkes) had personal experience of Burt's intellectual eccentricities. Articles were published in our names by Burt which we did not write ourselves.

That the Hull trio was beginning to be clearly identified as an anti-Burt group is to be seen in Professor John Cohen's immediate reply:

> Dr. Gillie then cites two or three people at Hull who say: "An attempt is being made to whitewash Burt." The boot, I am afraid, is on the other foot: an attempt is being made to denigrate him. Perhaps on the North East coast it is the practice to consider a man guilty until he is proved innocent.

> Five years after Burt's death, the Hull group suddenly decide to make an unverified allegation about the publication of certain unspecified papers. Why did they not take action or protest while Burt was still alive?[5]

The trio was quick to respond with many criticisms, among which the famous articles were mentioned again.

> In addition, there is also the surprising experience of two of us in having articles written by Burt on our behalf changed after we had seen them, and then published in our names to give a misleading account of our work. Such irregularities cannot be dismissed as carelessness.

> In the circumstances we have regretfully concluded that Sir Cyril Burt was either a fraudulent scientist or a fraud as a scientist.

This conclusion was by no means indecisive, but let us stop for a moment and see clearly what was being said. The Clarkes were saying (1) that Burt had written articles on their behalf, (2) that they had seen and approved them (3) that Burt had subsequently changed them without their further consultation in such a way as to be misleading, and (4) that Burt had then published them under the Clarkes' names.

But is this sequence in itself not extraordinarily strange? If the Clarkes were shown articles Burt had written on their behalf, why did they not object at once and end the matter there and then? What self-respecting scholar would entertain the idea of someone else writing an article on his or her behalf? The Clarkes, however, were shown these articles, agreed with Burt on any changes they wanted to make (see the evidence for this later), and raised no objection. They must clearly, therefore, have known about, and approved of, their subsequent publication. The gist of their charge against Burt was that (according to them—for there is no evidence of this other than their own word) he had subsequently altered them in a misleading way. But, as Cohen's question implied, which exactly *were* these unspecified articles, and why had the Clarkes not taken action or protested while Burt was alive—indeed, at the very time when the articles had first been written?

The story of the two articles was stressed in further repetitions. Another example was Alan Clarke's statement in a radio program of January 1979. Claiming that Burt "misused his role as editor," he said

> Perhaps the most florid example that we ourselves know was one relating to ourselves. He published two articles allegedly written by each of us, and these publications were not, indeed, written by us at all, and they gave a quite slanted account of the research work we'd been doing.

It was at the end of this same program that (in both substance and tone of voice) Ann Clarke's was by far the most forceful condemnation. Burt, she said, "was a man who used his position to deceive two generations. . . . He was a Con Man, and he took the Con-way to fame and fortune."

A fraud as a scientist, a fraudulent scientist, . . . and now a con man! But even that was not the end of it. Commenting on Hearn-shaw's *Balance Sheet on Burt* in 1980, the Clarkes wrote:

> We were registered PhD students of Burt although working in Hans Eysenck's department at the Institute of Psychiatry at a time when the former was putting numerous obstacles in the way of the latter. Our

relations with Burt were on the whole amicable, although we were both surprised and angry when he wrote and published articles under our names which appeared to be slanted against Eysenck in a way with which we disagreed.

The newly emerging dimension in this repetition was that the articles were not only slanted and misleading in their account of the Clarkes' own work, but were also *slanted against Eysenck,* and at a time when Burt *was putting numerous obstacles in the way of Eysenck.* How, one wonders, were the Clarkes, as Ph.D. students, so intimately aware of the interpersonal and interdepartmental affairs then taking place between Burt and Eysenck, University College and the Maudsley? And again, which exactly *were* these articles? Where were they to be found? What was their nature?

More information was disclosed in Hearnshaw's biography. There[6] Hearnshaw quoted a letter written to him by Alan Clarke in September 1976 (the italics are mine):

> After the Ph.D. vivas [writes Clarke] Burt said that we were both to glance at some brief summaries he had made of our theses and approve them, because "I like to publish some of the more promising results". These summaries proved to be a little inaccurate. We corrected them, and almost forgot about the incident. In the autumn, to our astonishment, we found two articles under our authorship in the *British Journal of Educational Psychology* implicitly attacking Eysenck. We did not recognise them as the same summaries (of which of course we had no copies) we had corrected at University College. Our theses had indeed been critical of the 'dimensions of personality' approach, but the whole emphasis of 'our' articles were slanted. We went personally to apologise to Eysenck, who, hearing our disclaimer, was exceedingly generous, saying that this sort of ploy was typical of the old man. *When I asked him for advice he suggested that I should let the matter drop. Nevertheless I wrote an angry letter to Burt, and was told that he thought we were out of the country and hadn't therefore sent galley proofs.* By this stage we had become quite clear that Burt was dishonest, and predictably he later quoted 'our' two articles as independent support for his attack upon Eysenck.

The whereabouts of Burt's attack upon Eysenck is not mentioned, and much that is said in this letter lies clearly within the realm of uncorroborated personal testimony and hearsay. The essential revelation, however, is that the two articles were summaries Burt had evidently made of the Clarkes' theses, and were to be found in the *British Journal of Educational Psychology*. I therefore looked them up. To my utter astonishment I found, quite simply, that the two articles had never existed! The two publications were no more than brief abstracts of the Clarkes' theses.

It should be noted that one requirement for the Ph.D. examination in the University of London is that the bound thesis should contain (before presentation) a short abstract of approximately 300 words, setting out its nature. Valentine, the editor of the journal who had preceded Burt, had thought it worthwhile to draw attention to interesting and successful Ph.D. theses by publishing the abstracts of them. Clarke, in his letter, quoted Burt as having said "I like to publish some of the more promising results," but in doing this for the Clarkes, he was doing no more than carrying out Valentine's policy. And what was it in Burt's apparently amended version of their abstracts that the Clarkes found so offensive? I decided to compare them with the abstracts in the theses themselves. The following is Alan Clarke's own abstract.

THE MEASUREMENT OF EMOTIONAL INSTABILITY BY MEANS OF OBJECTIVE TESTS: AN EXPERIMENTAL INQUIRY.

Thesis Abstract.

Two main groups of subjects were tested, 68 neurotic soldiers (subdivided into anxiety-states and hysterics), and over 100 controls. The experiments were designed to show differences both of theoretical and practical interest between these groups.

Results showed that the subsidiary tests investigating colour-form attitudes, mirror-drawing and motor tension ("point-pressure") had no great discriminatory value. The main investigation, however, involving an extended version of Luria's association-motor technique, yielded some most suggestive findings. One of these tests involved response to an emotionally-loaded word list; the other used electric shock stimuli with free association.

The results for the first test showed that neurotics were highly differentiated from controls on both motor and verbal scores. The fact that rather high negative correlations were found between these scores and a verbal intelligence test indicates that disturbance is not only associated with affective arousals. This important relationship has not previously been noted. Further, it was shown that the same words tended to produce disturbance in both groups, but significantly different in degree.

Selective remembering was investigated by asking subjects to recall the stimulus words after the test. Results did not corroborate the psycho-analytical hypothesis of "repression" in that no negative correlation was found between words remembered and the corresponding disturbance. Moreover, neurotics and controls tended to remember the same words.

The electric-shock test differentiated between the groups only on the verbal level, with relatively greater motor disturbance than previously.

In addition, a test of static ataxia discriminated between the groups. The addition of suggestion to the situation, however, minimised the difference, thus failing to confirm previous work.

Although many theoretically interesting relationships have been demonstrated, the tests, as they are at present constituted, are limited in practical screening efficiency on such populations.

Alan D. B. Clarke.
April, 1950.

The following is the version printed by Burt.

Summaries of Researches Reported in Degree Theses

The Measurement of Emotional Instability by Means of Objective Tests.

By A. D. B. CLARKE.

(Abstract of a Thesis for the Ph.D. Degree, University College, London.)

PROBLEM.—The purpose of the following research was to assess the validity of certain objective tests which have been put forward as methods of assessing what may briefly be designated 'emotional instability.' For working purposes Warren's second definition was accepted. Those who have maintained the existence of a factor of 'general emotionality,' analogous to that of 'general intelligence,' have argued that, in addition to the so-called 'temperamentally defective,' we should recognize the existence of a milder, non-certifiable group consisting of the 'temperamentally unstable' (just as, in addition to the 'intellectually defective,' we recognize the existence of a non-certifiable group who are 'intellectually dull').[1] On this hypothesis the emotionally unstable may be regarded as potentially neurotic. Hence, it is of special importance to the Services to have some practicable method for screening out such cases.

TESTS.—The tests employed were all individual tests, and were selected in consultation with Dr. Eysenck as being in his view the most promising for the purpose. The following were eventually adopted.

(1) *Mirror Drawing.*
(2) *Motor Tension:* (a point pressure test).

(3) *Body Sway:* (*a*) spontaneous ('static ataxia'); (*b*) induced by suggestion.

(4) *Association Motor Tests:* (*a*) Motor and verbal disturbance with Luria technique; (*b*) motor and verbal disturbance with electric shock.

(5) *Preference for Colour or Form:* (*a*) Lindberg's ring test; (*b*) a sorting test.

SUBJECTS.—168 persons were tested, all drawn from the Services. 68 had been diagnosed as neurotic by Army psychiatrists, and the remainder were normal adults used as controls. It was later found that the control group had a slightly higher average intelligence.

RESULTS.—In the tests for emotional instability the difference between the average score obtained by the neurotic and the normal, respectively, was statistically significant in three cases only, namely, for motor disturbance in the Luria test (but not for verbal), for verbal disturbance in the shock test (but not for motor), for spontaneous movement in the body-sway test (but not for suggested movement). The remaining tests showed no significant difference whatever.

Even for these three tests the correlations with the criterion were decidedly low, namely, 0.48 for the Luria test, 0.27 and 0.24 for the other two. Were these tests used for preliminary screening, one case out of every four would be misclassified. On eliminating intelligence by partial correlation, it appeared that the number of misclassifications would be even greater.

CONCLUSION.—None of the tests proposed has a sufficiently high validity coefficient to claim any practical value for purposes of screening or diagnosis. Moreover, being individual tests, and requiring somewhat elaborate apparatus, they would, in their present form, consume as much time, and need as much expert control, as would be required for an ordinary psychiatric interview. However, these defects might no doubt be overcome by further research; and the detailed findings of the present investigation suggest the more promising lines for improvement.

---

[1]See *Report of Joint Committee on Mental Deficiency* (H. M. Stationery Office, 1929), Pt. I, pp. 8–9, Pt. II, pp. 49f. The concept of the 'emotionally unstable' appears to have been first introduced in this sense by BURT (*Child Study*, X, 1917, pp. 61–78). Cf. EYSENCK, H. J.: *Dimensions of Personality (1947), p. 55, footnote 1; and Warren, H. C.: Dictionary of Psychology (1934).*

I ask the reader to consider which of these two versions, printed in the British Journal, would do Alan Clarke most credit. The substance and conclusion are the same, but set out more precisely and in a more systematic form in the printed version, the chief difference lying only in the initial statement of the problem. I ask the reader to consider, too, any way in which Burt's printed version can be said to be either a misleading account of Alan Clarke's own work or "slanted against Eysenck"—and (particularly) so egregiously so as to call for a personal apology on Clarke's part to Eysenck? Where was the fault? The only evidence of Burt's own intrusiveness and/or "vanity" lies in the footnote, but this seems unexceptionable in view of Alan Clarke's own generous acknowledgment of Burt's help in his preface to the thesis:

> The writer wishes to record with gratitude his debt to his Supervising Teacher, Professor Sir Cyril Burt, who has at all times been ready, both in correspondence and in personal discussion, to offer advice when difficulties arose; such advice has proved invaluable.

Ann Clarke (then Ann Gravely) had studied exactly the same subjects as Alan Clarke, the "168 adult men from the services," her own investigation being into the value of "perceptual tests" as measures of "temperament," whereas Alan Clarke's had focused on various "objective tests" as measures of "emotional instability." The following is the abstract printed by Burt in her name.

Summaries of Researches Reported in Degree Theses

An Investigation of Perceptual Tests as Measures of Temperament.

By ANN M. GRAVELY.

*(Abstract of a Thesis for the Ph.D. Degree,
University College, London.)*

PROBLEM.—The object of the inquiry was to examine the claim that "tests of temperament have reached a stage where they can take their place with the usual tests of cognitive function and special abilities,"[1] and, in particular, that non-verbal (or perceptual) tests may successfully be employed to discriminate between the neurotic and the non-neurotic members of the population and between those suffering from different types of neurotic disorder, such as hysteria and anxiety states. The idea of diagnosing such disorders by means of psychological tests has come much into favour among a small group of psychiatrists and psychologists working in mental hospitals both in this country and in America. On the other hand, the majority of the medical profession, and probably the majority of British psychologists appear to be sceptical of the possibility of diagnosing mental illnesses by such means.

TESTS.—The majority of the tests employed were suggested by those described by Dr. Eysenck and his fellow-workers at the Maudsley Hospital in their investigations of 'temperamental types.'

(1) *Flicker.*—A measure of the threshold for visual flicker obtained with an electronic 'stroboflash.'

(2) *Dark Adaptation.*—A measure of the threshold of adaptation obtained after 10 minutes in a dark room.

(3) *Autokinetic Illusion.*—A measure of (*a*) the time taken for apparent movements to be noted; (*b*) the amount of apparent movement perceived, and (*c*) the influence of suggestion on the direction of apparent movement.

(4) *Fluctuation of Ambiguous Figures.*—A measure of the rate of fluctuation in the perception of the Necker cube.

(5) *Estimation of Distances.*—A measure of the accuracy of the visual estimation of line-lengths.

(6) *Motor Perseveration.*—Measured by the success with which the subject can write reversed 'S's after writing ordinary S's and *vice versa*.

(7) *Motor Stability.*—A measure of (*a*) the amount of spontaneous movement while standing with eyes closed (so called 'static ataxia') and (*b*) the amount of bodily sway induced by suggestion (Eysenck's test).

As a check on the perceptual tests, the following were also included.

(8) *Verbal Association Test.*—This was introduced by way of comparing the results of the non-verbal or perceptual tests with those of a standard verbal test: it was used in the 'closed choice' form (Maller).

(9) *Vocabulary Test of Verbal Intelligence.*

(10) *Questionnaire on Neurotic Symptoms.* (The version adopted was that prepared for use in investigations at the Maudsley Hospital by Dr. Eysenck.)

SUBJECTS.—168 adult men from the Services, aged for the most part between 19 and 31, consisting of (1) 100 normal persons, used as controls, and (2) 68 diagnosed by Army psychiatrists as neurotic and divided into two main 'types,' viz. (*a*) 134 suffering from hysterical conditions and (*b*) 34 suffering from anxiety states.

RESULTS.—(1) *Statistical Discrimination: (a) Between Neurotic and Normal.* The averages for the two main groups were significantly different in the case of the following tests: (i) dark adaptation; (ii) quickness of autokinetic reaction; (iii) motor perseveration (production score); (iv) static ataxia; (v) word association test; and, of course (vi) the questionnaire on symptoms. No significant differences were found with (i) flicker; (ii) amount of autokinetic reaction; (iii) fluctuations of ambiguous figures; (vi) estimation of distances; (v) body-sway as induced by suggestion.

(*b*) *Between Hysterical Conditions and Anxiety States.*—No significant differences were found with any of the tests. There is, therefore, in the present experiments no confirmation of the belief that perceptual and other tests of the type here described can be used to discriminate temperamental types, although the contrast between hysteria and anxiety exhibits such differences in an extreme form.

(2) *Correlations. (a) With External Criterion.* The dichotomy be-

tween normal and neurotic subjects was made the basis of a set of biserial correlations for the five tests noted above as yielding a statistically significant discrimination. The questionnaire on symptoms gave a correlation with the criterion of 0.58 (raised to 0.62 when verbal intelligence was partialled out); the other tests gave correlations ranging (after correction) from 0.36 to .024. Of these the verbal test (word association) gave decidedly the highest correlation (0.34); but was appreciably reduced when intelligence was partialled out. Multiple correlations were calculated by reducing the correlation table to a triangular matrix of semi-partial correlations.[2] It was found that the addition of the two next best tests to the questionnaire on symptoms only raised the correlation by 0.08.

(b) With Internal Criterion. A factor analysis was carried out by Burt's method of simple summation. A small general factor was found, accounting for 21 per cent of the total variance. With this non-perseveration (production score) gave the highest saturation and the questionnaire the next highest. The correlation of the general factor with the criterion amounted to 0.64; this seems due chiefly to the presence of the questionnaire.

CONCLUSION.—Although with several of the tests there are small positive correlations between the results of the test and the subject's neurotic condition, these correlations (with the possible exception of the questionnaire on symptoms) are far too low for the methods to be of any practical value. There is little evidence for the suggestion that non-verbal or perceptual tests might yield better indications of temperamental differences than verbal, at any rate in their present condition.

---

[1]EYSENCK, H. J.: *Dimensions of Personality,* 1947, p. 259. A fuller description of most of the tests here used will be found in that volume. The writer wishes to express her indebtedness to Dr. Eysenck for further explanations and assistance.

[2]Cf. Lab. Notes on *Multiple Correlations computed by Hierarchical Subtraction* and FRAZER, R. A., DUNCAN, W. J., and COLLAR, A. R.: *Elementary Matrices* (1938), pp. 971.

The strange fact in Ann Clarke's (Gravely's) case is that her own thesis contains *no abstract at all.* On the face of it the Ph.D. examination regulations do not seem to have been complied with. The essential point, however, is that this printed abstract is the *only* abstract that exists, and again, I ask the reader to consider in what way it can be said to be "slanted against Eysenck." It is also to be noted that the acknowledgment of Eysenck's assistance is exactly in the style of Ann Clarke's similar acknowledgment of Burt's assistance in the preface of her thesis, which reads:

The writer wishes to thank her supervising teacher, Professor Sir Cyril Burt, for the generous way in which he has put his time at her disposal, and for the very valuable advice he has given during the course of the work.

It is important to note as well that the Clarkes' Ph.D. registration *had* to be in Burt's name, although their work was chiefly with Eysenck, simply because at that time Eysenck was not yet a "recognized teacher" of the University of London. It was not, in short, a matter of either choice or insistence on the part of either Burt or Eysenck.[7]

The tale of the "famous articles," therefore, which sounded like a big bang of criticism, turned out to be a whimper of two brief abstracts. Why, one wonders, was such a sheer misrepresentation made in the first place? And why was it then repeated so insistently, sustained for so long?

Clearly, much that is almost bound to remain undisclosed or undiscovered lies in the supposed conflict between Burt and Eysenck, which must also have entailed Aubrey Lewis and the whole relationship between the Maudsley Hospital department and University College. There is the possibility, of course, that if such conflict existed, Eysenck and Lewis—as well as Burt—might have had something to do with it! And there is a lack of clarity about the timing of events that makes the several statements of the Clarkes—in their thesis prefaces, about their "protest" against the "articles," about their knowledge of the supposed Burt/Eysenck antagonism, and so forth—questionable at the very least.

Hearnshaw had pointed out to Alan Clarke that in the Twenty-Sixth Maudsley Lecture, Burt's reference to both his own and Ann's Ph.D. work at the Maudsley had been "quite fair." Clarke accepted and agreed with this, but at the same time (in a November 3, 1977 letter) still claimed that Burt had used "our articles" in an attack on Eysenck—using, however, the pseudonym of WLG. In the same letter, he mentioned "the appendix in my thesis criticizing criterion analysis which Burt forced me to write." Again, is it not strange that a graduate scholar should accept the situation of being *forced to write* anything? And is it not stranger still that, having done so with quite obvious resentment, he should write so fulsome an expression of gratitude to Burt in his preface?

Similarly, the position claimed by the Clarkes is that their thanks to Burt in June 1950 were entirely genuine, and that their doubts and protests arose in the October of the year when the famous "articles" were published. Yet Alan Clarke had already been *forced* to write an offending appendix against his own will and judgment, and both the Clarkes had had "earlier warnings from Sir Aubrey Lewis and Eysenck" that they "should not assume" that they "would get their Ph.Ds."[8] Also, referring to a letter from Burt to his sister of February 4, 1949, in which a "German Jew" was mentioned in relation to a Maudsley readership, Ann Clarke wrote: "The German Jew was Eysenck (who happens not to be Jewish), who Burt did everything in his power to suppress, including using us as pawns in his battle." But if all this was so in 1949, during the period of the Clarkes' research, and "earlier warnings" had come from Lewis and Eysenck, how could their thanks to Burt have been so "genuine" and untainted with other feelings in June 1950? And how could they have been drawn in such an intimate manner into what they claim to have been such a malicious cleavage between the personalities of Burt and Eysenck and the two departments? All this speaks of a strange quality of relationships. None of this, presumably, can possibly be unraveled, but needs to be noted since it has clearly left indelible marks in the consciousness of the Clarkes and, in some way or other, their motivation in attacking Burt is clearly rooted in it. Hearnshaw himself certainly believed this. "The incident that took place with Professor A. D. B. Clarke and his wife in their student days," he wrote, "is of particular importance, as it *sowed the seeds for their later role as instigators of doubts as to Burt's integrity.*"

The essential point, however, in whatever way it was rooted in this early situation of graduate experience, is that the Clarkes' persistently repeated reference to Burt's having "written two articles in their names" was a vast misrepresentation, and such as to add a deepening dimension to the picture that was being painted of Burt as a man lacking integrity and practising deceit. At the same time, it had nothing whatever to do with the supposedly fraudulent study of identical twins. It had gone far beyond this.

Beyond Hearnshaw: The "Confidence Trickster"

The Clarkes were in correspondence with Professor Hearnshaw during (at least) the later part of the writing of his official biography, supplying him with apparent "evidence" of Burt's misdemeanors, and its publication gave their attacks a new lease of life. Indeed, two things are noticeable. First, there seems to have been a strange selectivity in the reviewing of this book. It was chiefly the *adversaries* of Burt who were called upon to do so. Second, the members of what might now have been called "the Hull brigade" were dominantly represented. The 1976 start of the controversy had been reported in *Newsweek,* in December 1976, by "Charles Panati with Malcolm MacPherson in Hull, England," and it turns out that even then it was the Clarkes who had been talking to "Newsweek's Malcolm MacPherson," telling him that they had been "suspicious about Burt's integrity" even when they had "worked with Burt in the 1940s and '50s." Now, the Clarkes themselves reviewed the new biography in *Nature*[9] and in the *British Journal of Psychology*.[10] McAskie also reviewed it in the *Guardian*.[11] They all praised Hearnshaw's scrupulous scholarship, and applauded his conclusion that Burt *had* been guilty of fraud as something that had finally set the seal on the whole matter. The charges, they claimed, had now been convincingly proved.

But the slanted nature of their judgment could be seen, again, in the even more intemperate language they now used. The supposed authority of the official biography seemed to embolden them to indulge in new excesses. "The Cardinal Sin" was the title of the *Nature* review. Burt was accused of "deception, fraud, and irregular conduct over many years." He was "an unscrupulous man who deserves a high place in science's rogues' gallery." And the review was packed with the usual catalog of charges. In the *British Journal of Psychology* review, the twin studies were referred to as "perhaps the most *florid* of Burt's deceptions," and on "the missing ladies" it was said that Professor Cohen had "*thought* that he remembered Howard in the late 1930s" (my italics). McAskie, too, in his *Guardian* piece, saluted Hearnshaw's "competence and impartiality" in providing "clear evidence for frauds committed by Burt in his later years," but now raised the question: "What of his earlier work?" And here, he found Hearnshaw's arguments that Burt's early work was "unblemished in this respect" unconvincing. The Hull contingent now wanted to press their charges beyond those of Hearnshaw, and this was most conspicuous in an article by the Clarkes in the *Bulletin of the British Psychological Society*[12] in

which they very deliberately took issue with Hearnshaw's judgment. The nature of the further charges they then made deserves
very careful note.

Hearnshaw had claimed that Burt's "misdemeanors" were
rooted in the coming together of a number of serious personal
problems, and had started when he was in his late 50s. This,
however, was far from being enough for the Clarkes. Their argument ran on as follows:

> An alternative possibility to this discontinuity model is that from early
> adulthood, using his charisma and unusual linguistic gifts, Burt was a
> successful confidence trickster. Hearnshaw's contrary evidence seems
> to us unconvincing in view of what he himself has written. Dr Marion
> Burt did not doubt her brother's honesty, and confidently believed that
> Professor Hearnshaw's investigations would clear him of all the
> charges. Dr Charlotte Banks testified to his integrity, so did Professor
> Cohen; their association was prolonged. It seems probable that others
> earlier in Burt's career were as similarly deceived, before 1940, as the
> rest of us were afterwards; the hallmark of a *successful* confidence
> trickster is precisely that people are persuaded of his honesty. We make
> no secret of our distaste for Burt, now that the truth about him is
> known. For a man to rise to his position both as an applied psychologist
> and also as an accredited scientist with such a record of cutting corners
> and active deception of honest and trusting colleagues is for us horrify-
> ing.

Let us note clearly two very strange aspects of this charge. First,
it simply *assumes*—and then *rests on the assumption*—that Marion
Burt, Charlotte Banks, and John Cohen were *deceived*. Not the
slightest evidence is given for this; not a single piece of evidence is
even suggested or considered. Without the slightest semblance of
critical consideration, it is merely *assumed*. Then, however, it is
firmly asserted as a probability "that others earlier in Burt's career
were as *similarly deceived*." All this, too, is simply put forward as
"an alternative possibility to the discontinuity model." Yet it is the
basis of the charge that Burt was a "successful confidence trickster." Is this an example of the Clarkes' own scientific reasoning,
of the standard of scientific criticism they themselves think it fitting
to employ in scientific argument?

We may also recall the forceful pronouncement of Ann Clarke
that ended the radio program of 1979: that Burt was "a Con Man,
and he took the Con-way to fame and fortune."

Second, what is the suggested proof of the truth of the accusation, the ground that supposedly makes it persuasive and convincing? Astonishingly, it is that in his character and all his conduct over so many years, Burt gave no sign of it! "The hall-mark of a *successful*[13] confidence trickster is precisely that people are persuaded of his honesty."

In short, arising from no grounds whatever, put forward only as a conjectural "alternative model," the accusation that Burt was a "confidence trickster" of long standing—now extending the charges of "fraud" to all of his earlier work—was grounded only (as the basis of its supposed truth) on the fact that not the slightest evidence for it was at all apparent in Burt's nature or behavior. The proof of it lay . . . in its absence! On that ground, clearly, all of us who are well-behaved are, under the surface of our highly successful pretenses, confidence tricksters! On what criteria one determines the existence of an honest man is a question rather left in the air!

Is this not the strangest of arguments? Particularly so in coming from two such ardent scientists accusing another scientist of scientific chicanery? We must also note that in this the Clarkes at last "make no secret of their distaste for Burt" and, as though becoming increasingly relentless in the pursuit of their quarry, as though remaining dissatisfied until they have finally hunted him to the death, the Clarkes (in the same article) added yet another charge: that of shoddy work.

"A Poor Applied Psychologist"

Believing that Hearnshaw had provided "extensive evidence of shoddy work" (and rather going back on their earlier claim that no one who knew Burt could possibly have any doubt as to his competence), the Clarkes said that this confirmed their feeling "that Burt, unlike some of his contemporaries, was a poor applied psychologist." The contemporaries with whom Burt was compared were not specified, but given the range and detail of all Burt's investigations, from the earliest decades of the century onwards, such a pronouncement goes beyond the bounds of credulity. The Clarkes, however, seem to have had no difficulty in believing themselves in so lofty a position of superiority and authority as to be able to deliver such a judgment. And which was the particular investigation of Burt's on which they chiefly rested this accusation? It was the Birmingham study of 1921.

We have a copy of a little-known 'Report of an Investigation upon Backward Children in Birmingham' undertaken in 1921. In it, Burt alleges that he assessed, mainly with the Binet–Simon test, 562 children at a little over 10 minutes each, in just four weeks. Having ourselves a good deal of experience of testing such children, we find this a disturbing additional example of the sort of applied psychology in which Burt was indulging.

This, literally, is *all* that is said about this study. We deliberately noted earlier, however, the systematic and detailed way in which (in collaboration with other highly competent professional colleagues) Burt had set out his methods of investigation in undertaking this survey.[14] It is absolutely clear that the Clarkes' brief statement is the most gross oversimplification, and grossly misleading. Burt's *average* time of ten minutes over each of his own tests was only one component in a much more thorough investigation, all the other elements of which the Clarkes failed even to mention. Furthermore, in his *Mental and Scholastic Tests* and *The Backward Child,* and long before the Clarkes' reading of the Birmingham study, Burt had clearly described his methods of testing (including group testing, the reliability of median sampling, and so forth) and here it had been said—within the context of careful provisos, and without any earlier adverse comment from the Clarkes or anyone else—that tests reliably estimating a child's level of ability could be conducted within an average of *six* minutes. Why, then, was this comment on the methods employed in a study undertaken fifty-five to sixty years earlier (and openly declared by Burt) thrown out in so unqualified a way as to be bound—within the context of heated controversy—to be misleading? Could it have been for any other reason than that of wanting to denigrate Burt further? Were the Clarkes looking for every bit of ammunition they could find?

Whatever the reason, the truth is clear. The Clarkes did not stop at charges of fraud; they also accused Burt of shoddy professional standards, of bad workmanship, and in such ways as to throw into disrepute not only his later twin studies but also, as with Gillie, "the whole corpus of his work."

The questions to which answers are required from the Clarkes are very clear.

Questions Requiring Public Answers

1. Which is the statement Gillie "allowed" in his first 1976 article that "effectively indicated the substantial difference between Kamin" and the Clarkes themselves? Where in that article is it to be found?
2. Why did the Clarkes from the very beginning claim that Burt had "written two articles in their name" when these were, in fact, no more than the amended abstracts of their Ph.D. theses, which it was the editorial policy of the journal (established before the time of Burt's editorship) to publish?
3. What were the inaccuracies in the abstracts Burt published? In what ways were they misleading about the nature of the Clarkes' own research?
4. In what ways were the abstracts "slanted against Eysenck"?
5. What were the numerous obstacles Burt had put in the way of Eysenck? In what ways had he used the Clarkes as "pawns in his battle"?
6. How, why, and when, did Aubrey Lewis and Eysenck warn the Clarkes that they should not assume that they would get their Ph.Ds? On what grounds?
7. Since many elements of their own testimony (published by themselves, or in letters, or reported in interviews with others) make it plain that they were suspicious of Burt from the late 1940s onwards, that they were aware of being used as pawns in the battle between Burt and Eysenck, that Alan Clarke had been forced by Burt to write an appendix he had not wanted to write in his thesis, and so forth, why did they preface their theses with such fulsome acknowledgments to Burt for generously putting his time at their disposal, and being always ready to give them valuable advice?
8. Why, for the same reasons, did they not bring at least some of these charges of misdemeanors, fraud, and poor standards of workmanship against Burt before his death?

Notes

1. See (1) letter to the *Bulletin of the British Psychological Society* 83; March 1977; (2) "Comments on Professor Hearnshaw's 'Balance

Sheet on Burt,' " the *Bulletin* 33:17–19; 1980; and (3) *Mental Deficiency: The Changing Outlook,* 3 ed. London: Methuen, 1974.
2. McAskie, M., and Clarke, A. M. "Parent–Offspring Resemblances in Intelligence: Theories and Evidence." *British Journal of Psychology* 67:243–73; 1976.
3. It may be noted that Eysenck and Jensen alike, having studied the mistakes and misprints in Burt's papers, found on the contrary that these did *not* consistently *support* his theories but sometimes worked *against* them.
4. See, however, the Clarkes' criticism of Burt as a "poor applied psychologist" (p. 130–131).
5. Letter to the *Sunday Times,* 14 November 1976.
6. Hearnshaw, L. S. *Cyril Burt: Psychologist.* London: Hodder & Stoughton, 1979, p. 148.
7. Indeed, this may have been an example of Burt's generosity, because unless I am much mistaken, Eysenck should not (officially) have been examining graduate theses at this time. While an assistant lecturer in the University of London, for example, but before I had become a "recognized teacher," I taught a course in "The Theories and Methods of Sociology." I was not, however, a member of the Board of Studies in the subject, and should (officially) neither have set the final examination paper nor acted as examiner. I did both, however—with everyone's knowledge—by having my setting of the paper submitted to the board by Professor Acton (Professor of Philosophy) who was of course himself a "recognized teacher" and a member of the board. In short, in some situations, some latitude was responsibly extended from senior scholars to those as yet "unrecognized," and this latitude was most probably extended from Burt to Eysenck, though everything would still of necessity have to be recorded in Burt's own name.
8. Personal correspondence from Ann Clarke, July 1984 and June 19, 1987.
9. Vol. 282, November, 8, 1979, p. 150.
10. Vol. 33, 1980,m p. 172.
11. July 20, 1974.
12. Vol. 33, 1980, pp. 17–19.
13. The Clarkes' own italics.
14. See pp. 44–47.

6

Professor Leslie S. Hearnshaw:
The Official Biography

With Professor Hearnshaw, we come to a category of criticism completely different from those we have dealt with so far, but one that is curiously two-edged. His sword—wielded so judiciously, as though to insist on and protect a stance of impartiality—cuts in both directions, both for Burt and against him. Like Kamin in one respect, in the meticulous thoroughness of his investigation, he is different in all others. Kamin's determined documentation is one-sided, selective, belligerent, and rebarbative throughout, stemming aggressively from his ideological roots, presenting everything entirely in accordance with his ideological aims. By contrast, Hearnshaw seems genuinely devoted to impartiality and concerned to arrive at the truth.

His testimony, judgment, and conclusions are, however, open to serious question, to grave doubts, and I shall have to argue that some of his arguments do seem to have been substantially influenced in what seem to be dubious ways by the more radical critics of Burt. His writing of the biography seems to have been deeply affected, the course of its argument seems to have been decidedly swayed, by the "scandal." At the same time, one has to recognize that the nature and tone of his critical investigation of this (as part of his biographical account of Burt) are of a different order from, and stand on a different level to, those of the other critics. Indeed, I have to some extent changed my mind and feeling about him during the writing of this book. Initially, I saw him simply as one member of the anti-Burt group, of the same ilk as the others. Now

I regard him as being in many ways quite distinct from them. He is certainly different from Gillie, the Clarkes, and the Hull Brigade. Taken together, Kamin, Gillie, and the Clarkes—whether from ideological or personal motives or both combined, who can know all that is involved?—are like vociferous hounds barking at Burt's heels, trying to drag down their quarry, baying for his blood. Hearnshaw, with certain scruples as to standards of evidence and judgment that nag him like a conscience, is a serious scientific critic. That is the difference.

A Critic of Burt's Detractors

Indeed, it is important to note that he is in quite strong agreement with many of the criticisms I have made so far of those in whose company he ultimately decided that he had to walk. His article "Balance Sheet on Burt"[1] written a year after the completion of his Burt biography, stated some very decided and telling judgments, though even here they were double-edged. He believed, for example, that Burt's radical detractors were fulfilling the useful function of "exposing Burt's delinquencies." Nonetheless, he had to "disagree strongly, with Kamin, the Clarkes and Gillie *in the virulence and extent of their denigration of Burt.*"[2] The only "vocal group" that adversely criticized his biography, he wrote with evident surprise, was

> that of the anti-Burters, who accuse me of not going far enough in my condemnation of Burt, of trying to salvage as much of his work as possible, and of obscuring his malign antisocial motives. *They wish, it seems, to strip every particle of respectability from Burt's remains.* I shall have something to say about them in due course, since *I believe that they are both wrong and prejudiced.* They must forgive me if at times I speak somewhat bluntly.

This in itself is blunt speaking, But Hearnshaw went much further on quite specific points. On the question as to when "Burt's delinquencies" could be said to begin, he claimed

> Here I differ from Burt's principal detractors. According to the Clarkes (1980) Burt's frauds 'started earlier rather than late in life', and the

deficiencies in his research reports, amounting to gross professional incompetence, are to be found even in his earliest papers.

Then, having claimed that Burt's early work suffered only from "inadequate reporting and incautious conclusions," he went on:

Inadequate reporting is possibly culpable, but it does not in itself constitute fraud. It must, too, be remembered in considering Burt's early work, that he was, for most of the time, an applied psychologist employed by a local authority. His reports were not only, and often not primarily, directed to academic readers. . . . In evaluating Burt's early work we must in all fairness keep in mind the context in which it was produced.

In saying this, Hearnshaw also pointed out that "similar weaknesses" were to be found in Spearman's early work and in that of Piaget—to such an extent in Piaget's case that it had proved quite impossible to replicate his experiments. The Clarkes' charges, he insisted, rested on no foundation of evidence whatever:

Burt's detractors will have to make out a much better case if they are to establish their claim that Burt's work was flawed from the beginning, and they will have to establish it on the basis of Burt's published work. There is almost no other documentation for the period 1913 to 1940, as Burt's own papers were completely destroyed in the air raids on University College. Apart from juvenile material, which was stored in his parents' home, and a few letters from the 1920s and 1930s retained by those with whom he corresponded, there is no biographical material extant for the first half of Burt's life. So when the Clarkes (1980) question whether Burt ever systematically collected twin material, they are going to have a hard task to substantiate their suspicions. . . . The Clarkes base their case on the fact that, to quote their own words: 'In a letter to University College during the war he catalogues an array of different material he left stored in the basement. The most important and unique, on twins, is never mentioned,' Burt's own words in the letter in question were; (the materials) 'include many files of case histories of defective, neurotic and delinquent children, rather large collections of children's drawings, compositions, etc.' . . . To call this a catalogue is indeed stretching language beyond its limits. A catalogue, according to the Oxford Dictionary, is 'a complete enumeration'. All Burt is doing is clearly instancing some of the bulkiest items of material, not providing a catalogue. To base their case on the absence of twin data from a so-called catalogue of three items (case histories, drawings, compositions) followed by the words *et cetera,* which obviously imply incompleteness, is surely a flimsy argument for the Clarkes to be advancing. Would any jury convict on evidence as full of loopholes as that?

As in other cases, we have noted the Clarkes were indulging only in biased and unfounded speculation (indulgent but slanted and rhetorical conjecture). Hearnshaw made the same point about their unwarranted speculation that, being a psychopathic "con man," Burt had succeeded in deceiving all his earlier colleagues, many of them of very long standing:

> For the early phase of Burt's life we have to rely a good deal on the reports and recollections of contemporaries. And these are wholly favourable. I have been in touch with most of Burt's colleagues of those days, some of them now deceased, such as Professor T. H. Pear, Dr. R. R. Rusk, and Mrs. Winifred Raphael; others still happily alive, such as Professor R. B. Cattell, Dr. William Stephenson, Professor P. E. Vernon and Dr. R. H. Thouless. I have been in touch with many of his former students from the 1930s. All of them speak, without exception, in glowing terms of Burt as a psychologist, as a teacher and as a man. All of them reject decisively the idea that, at this stage of his career, Burt could have been guilty of deception and was simply a confidence trickster. As I said in my book, to dismiss these unanimous tributes is just arrogant, and it is certainly not impartial scholarship. . . . If Burt was always a psychopath, as Dr. Ann Clarke, for example, asserts, psychologists as sophisticated as Professor J. C. Flugel, who had known him intimately from undergraduate days, were not likely to have been blind to the fact. I do not believe that this unanimous testimony can be set aside. So I stand by my statement, that if Burt had died at the age of 60, in 1943, his reputation would have been unblemished, and that he would have been regarded, as an honourable pioneer in British psychology, our first applied psychologist.

For Hearnshaw, Burt's "delinquencies" came only late in his life, were practised only in his later work, and we will consider his views on this later. But, continuing here with his specific rejection of the claims of Burt's detractors, it is important to see that he was just as firm in rejecting Gillie's and Kamin's smears of racism and class discrimination, and his testimony is particularly valuable, containing some dimensions beyond those we have already noted. Mentioning Harold Laski and his wife, among others, who had been serious students (and teachers) of eugenics, he wrote:

It is unfair to regard an interest in eugenics and membership of the Eugenics Society as a badge of racism and reaction. Yet this is what Gillie (1978) appears to suggest. Burt was certainly sympathetic to eugenics, and contributed to the journal of the Eugenics Society on several occasions from 1912 onwards. But what are we to conclude from that? . . . The truth is that eugenics was highly fashionable in the intellectual world of the early years of the century, and an interest in eugenics carried no special implications. It certainly does not mean that Burt was racist and reactionary,

Equally biased are Kamin's strictures. 'If you look at his [Burt's] early work', says Kamin,[3] you will find him describing delinquent boys in London as having "the face of a chimpanzee", or "cow-like intelligence". Far from liking these children, as his admirers suggest, he seems to me to hold them in contempt. This statement of Kamin's is not merely biased, it is obtuse. It is biased because Kamin could equally well have selected entirely opposite descriptions; e.g., 'a diminutive child with a happy and cherubic face—an angel' (*Young Delinquent*, p. 137); 'a handsome lad with fair hair' (*Young Delinquent*, p. 183); 'A happy, captivating child with golden curls, a sunny smile, and an arch affectation of babyish simplicity' (*Young Delinquent*, p. 590). One can pick out almost as many flattering as disparaging descriptions. But Kamin didn't, because Kamin went out of his way to paint Burt in the blackest colours. This is bias, and, I think, malicious bias. It is also obtuse, because it is totally blind to the vivid powers of character portrayal which for two generations have made Burt's *Young Delinquent* a live and readable book.

Again, it is important to see that here we have a moderate detractor of Burt seriously and severely criticizing an extreme detractor of Burt for "going out of his way to paint Burt in the blackest colours," and being guilty not only of bias but also of *malicious* bias. Hearnshaw found the same bias at work in Kamin's condemnation of Burt as a right-wing reactionary, in his assertion that Burt

manifested a class bias which was strongly and continuously present from the beginning. This is a peculiar accusation against a man who came from a pretty humble background, and who spent a good part of his working life helping the underdog in the most deprived areas of London. It also happens to be completely at variance with the truth. Burt was a very non-political animal. He played no part, and wished to play no part, in politics. He was often critical of 'the establishment', and privately often made fun of those in high places. On most social questions his attitudes were, at any rate until towards the close of his life, progressive. It is impossible to read Burt's correspondence—and I must point out that this is something my critics have not yet done—without being struck by the breadth of his sympathies and his frequent helpfulness to those in difficulties or distress. The Kamin view is blinkered, and completely contrary to the evidence.

On this same count, Hearnshaw was equally strong in his rejection of Gillie:

Socially, it is claimed, Burt's influence was wholly malign. According to Gillie (1979) he victimized a whole generation of children. This is an astonishing claim, which depends on a good many assumptions. It assumes that selective education is necessarily victimization (was I victimizing students when I selected some, but not others, for postgraduate work?); it assumes that Burt was personally responsible for the system of 11 + selection; and it fails to weigh any good that Burt did in his many years as an educational psychologist with the alleged harm that he did through his support for selection. I tried to show in my book that, though Burt was influential during the 1920s and 1930s in the discussions which finally resulted in the 1944 Education Act, he was in no sense responsible for the system that finally emerged. True he backed the principle of selective education; he believed that because of the wide range of human ability diversity of educational provision was essential. But he neither initiated, nor fully supported, the system that flourished in the 1950s and 1960s. Quite apart from this question however it is absurd to overlook Burt's many years of educational work—the hundreds of cases he assisted clinically, his work for the backward and maladjusted, and the help he gave on their upward path to dozens of the gifted, who otherwise might have had a far harder struggle to rise. To put the matter mildly I regard Gillie's accusation that Burt victimized a whole generation of children as unfounded. This is not to say that Burt was always right in his views; but I believe we must be fair to him and keep some sense of proportion, and this Gillie has not done.

After all these points, one wonders what is left of the combined attack of Kamin, Gillie and the Clarkes. Even this critic of Burt whose "objectivity, balance, impartiality and fairness" they themselves profess to hold in high esteem, has only severe criticism to mete out to them, leaving them in disarray, and proving that their most far-reaching charges lack all foundation and are characterized by unwarranted "virulence" and even "malice." Yet it is their view that has prevailed and gained dominance, partly by the sheer cumulative force of much-repeated *media-publicity,* and partly by the apparent fact that Hearnshaw has been thought to be, in most things, on their side; has come to be seen as someone walking with them, accompanying them on the same campaign; indeed, as the most reliable scholar of all who has finally signed, sealed, and conclusively delivered their own judgment in the case. Why is this?

It is because of the fact we have already noted: that Hearnshaw's criticisms have been "two-edged." Castigating extreme condemnations, they have nonetheless rested on the considered conviction that, when all is said and done, when all the evidence is scrupulously examined, Burt was in fact guilty of "delinquencies"; that the charges of fraud were in some crucial respects true.

What, then, was Hearnshaw's own testimony against Burt? For the moment, we will simply note his view that Burt's "delinquencies" came only late in his career, brought about by a coming together of a number of serious misfortunes: the loss of much of his earlier data and many of his papers by wartime destruction, the retirement from his chair at University College under troublesome circumstances, the relinquishing of the editorship of the journal that for many years he had managed almost alone, the break-up of his marriage, the onset of serious ill health, and a mounting volume and intensity of hostile criticism from those who opposed his views on intelligence and education. We will consider the validity of this claim later. First, however, in Hearnshaw's view of this situation what were the elements of fraud of which he did believe Burt guilty? There were four.

The Charges

First, he concluded that Burt had fabricated the data on twins (and other relationships) in the papers from 1943 onwards. These later papers, he claimed, put forward "bogus findings." Second, and similarly, he believed that Burt in his 1969 article for the *Irish Journal of Education* (to which we will come later) had invented tables to demonstrate a decline in educational standards. There was no doubt, he said, "that these figures were in part a fabrication." Third, he charged Burt with having deliberately distorted the early history of factor analysis in such a way as to belittle Spearman and claim originality for himself. And fourth, he maintained that Dorf-man had made "suspect" some of Burt's statistics (on parent–child correlations in intelligence). The last three of these are of a relatively minor nature, and the interpretations on which they rest have been seriously challenged—without, so far, having received any answering response. But let us now examine Hearnshaw's own testimony on these "frauds"; on the first charge is particular; and this can best begin by noting the actual order of some of the events in the writing of his biography.

The Biography

Having gained a reputation as a historian of psychology, Hearnshaw was asked after Burt's death to deliver the address at his memorial service in October 1971. This having impressed Dr. Marion Burt (Burt's sister) very favorably, led her to invite Hearnshaw to write Burt's "official biography." During the course of writing this, however, "the scandal" broke with Gillie's *Sunday Times* article of 1976. This, as Hearnshaw himself said, "put a very different complexion on my task"; undeniably and understandably, it did. From that point on, he deliberately delayed the completion and publication of the book, gained permission to extend its length, and entered into detailed discussions and correspondence with those (the Clarkes, for example) who might help in clarifying the background and detail of the various charges. He appears, in fact, to have been much influenced by the scandal, and from that point on the two-edged nature of his sword of criticism can be seen to have become increasingly evident.

"Burt's exposure," he wrote, "encouraged witnesses to talk frankly about matters of which they had previously been reluctant to speak." Some of this testimony satisfied him that, from the late 1940s onward, Burt could be "high handed, devious, and corrupt." As one person who remained in touch with Burt until the time of his death said to me, "perhaps all this meant, though, was that he had been a better committee man than them!" Bearing in mind the nature of university politics, such an interpretation is far from being unlikely. It is highly unlikely that Burt—the unscrupulous manipulator—was surrounded by noble innocents. The scandal following Burt's death undoubtedly provided a bandwagon on which many could jump with alacrity; and indeed, on which many others might now feel themselves constrained to ride, or at least beside which they might feel constrained to stand in circumspect silence as the show rolled by. Academics, it seems, do not relish standing in the way of a juggernaut. Their judgments become qualified to an unaccustomed extent by caution; their tongues cease to speak. This alternative possibility seems not to have occurred to Hearnshaw, however, even though he was himself subsequently astonished at the strange and telling silence of Burt's colleagues and supporters. This seems to have been one of those occasions when silence seems to have spoken louder than words.

> From the pro-Burt faction, which had been fairly vocal following Gillie's exposé, there has been not a murmur of dissent. I expected them to be at my throat; but even Professor Eysenck appears calmly to have accepted my conclusions, and Professor Jensen has manfully recanted his former views on Burt. Quite as surprising has been the complete absence of response from University College, London. Not a single member of the staff or of the establishment of that institution has uttered even a whisper of condemnation or approbation. My book has been received with a stunned silence, though one would have imagined that it did concern them, and that it was a contribution, though not perhaps a very flattering one, to their history.

The silence of onlooking psychologists (after the press exchanges immediately following the scandal) has indeed been a strange feature of the campaign against Burt throughout its course, no matter how evident and blatant the distortions from the detractors have become. But before touching again on a possible reason for this, we can note an even stranger fact in Hearnshaw's own testimony; and it is here, in this, that questions begin to raise their head about the depth of his own veracity and the extent of his supposed impartiality.

Misrepresenting Dr. Marion Burt

When he decided to delay and extend his biography, Hearnshaw informed Marion Burt and gave his reasons. In the introduction to his book, he described her response in this way:

> At the beginning of April 1978 I felt that I could no longer honourably refrain from telling Dr Marion Burt the gist of my conclusions regarding

her brother's later work. (She had up till then only seen drafts of my first and third chapters.) I had been reluctant to do this earlier, while my investigations were still in progress, as she was over 85 years of age, and had an enormous admiration for her brother. When Dr Gillie's article appeared in the *Sunday Times* Dr Marion Burt regarded it 'as a storm in a tea-cup', and remained 'convinced of Cyril's integrity' (Letter, 18 November 1976). It was painful for me to have to inform her that the evidence had finally forced me to accept the accusations. Her response, I thought, was rather remarkable. She simply said that if I was to substantiate the charges I should need much more space than the 100,000 words originally agreed with the publishers. When I informed her that I had been granted permission to extend the length of the book she replied, 'I am *delighted* to know that you have been granted more space for the biography' (Letter, 15 April 1978). This was my last letter from Dr Marion Burt. I had arranged to visit Malvern and talk with her the following month, but she died suddenly at the age of 87 on 14 May 1978.

This description of Marion Burt's "remarkable response" and her "delight" at the extended length "to substantiate the charges" was such as to convince at least one reviewer that she "seemed to have acknowledged that her brother might have been dishonest."[4] Even Cronbach, the most fair-minded of all the reviewers, said "to her credit, Marion Burt encouraged Hearnshaw in a searching enquiry"—which was true, but by no means implied her acceptance of the possibility that her brother had been a fraud. What, however, was the strict truth of this matter?

At the time of which Hearnshaw wrote, Marion Burt was in close touch with Gretl Archer (Burt's last secretary) and Dr. Charlotte Banks (Burt's last assistant). On April 11, 1978, she wrote in some distress to Charlotte Banks, enclosing a copy of her reply to Hearnshaw (who, having told Dr. Banks he was going to see Marion to tell her of his decision, then decided not to see her, but instead to inform her by letter). In her letter to Charlotte Banks, she wrote about Hearnshaw's judgment:

I tried to avoid getting temperamental about it. I am very willing to grant Cyril making mistakes, but that he was fool enough to bring out wilfully and consciously fraudulent productions I cannot believe, since he would have known that subsequent exposure was inevitable.

And the following is the copy of her letter to Hearnshaw:

Dear Prof Hearnshaw,

Thank you for your letter. Of course I knew that you collaborated with C over some time, but I still don't think your contact was close enough for you to know him personally.

I do not think he was ever stupid enough to bring out wilfully fraudulent work which he must have known would sooner or later be proved against him.

You appear to regard him as schizophrenic, & if so I take it you will be using up quite a proportion of the 250 pages allowed for the book to develop & substantiate the theory. So when it comes to what you may consider the ethical part of his career, I hope you may, none the less, find ample space to expand & amplify its value, (even though it might mean cutting some of his interesting early life story). Otherwise I foresee reviewers will seize upon the former as something they can sensationalize, while minimising any commentary on his notable achievements which they can less well understand. What a pity the book must be kept so small, for the trouble, time and patience you have spent in sifting all these matters deserves more space.[5]

On May 14th, Marion Burt had died.

On June 11th, Hearnshaw wrote to Gretl Archer. Voicing his "admiration and respect" for Marion, he again said "When I told her about my conclusions she took it extremely calmly, and simply said that she was delighted that Mr. Foster had agreed to my book exceeding the originally arranged length." The following is Miss Archer's reply, which makes it clear that Marion had also written to her on April 12th. The extent of Marion Burt's distress may be gathered from the fact that she had written to both Miss Archer and Charlotte Banks almost simultaneously.

Dear Professor Hearnshaw,

Thank you for your letter of 11th June, which was awaiting me on my return from Malvern, where I attended the interment of Dr. Burt's ashes into the family grave and helping to clear out her room at Woodgate.

I am astonished that you think Dr. Burt took your 'conclusions' "extremely calmly". She wrote me a most distressed letter on the 12th of April saying: "To say that I feel indignant at my last letter from Prof. H. is putting it mildly. He says ". . . (and goes on quoting what you wrote to her, with her own comments) ending with "But my contention is that *Cyril would not have been such a fool* as to bring out and publish wilfully fraudulent work which he'd certainly have known would be subsequently detected and proved against him!!! And this I shall tell him (meaning you). She also mentions that she is sending your letter to Charlotte to ask for her help in refuting your 'conclusions'.

It was not only my own impression that Dr. Burt was very much upset and worried about "your seeming to take the opponents side and turning against Cyril", as she put it during her last telephone conversation with me; but now, during my stay in Malvern, I was also told by some of her friends there that Dr. Burt was very worried and depressed lately, succumbed to a flu, which further weakened her heart, so that they were not too much surprised when she collapsed on her way upstairs and died shortly after. So you can imagine that your impression that Dr. Burt took it 'extremely calmly' surprised me.

Even to Marion Burt, and even then, Hearnshaw had clearly seemed to be "taking the opponents' side and turning against Cyril." Even then, she was clearly suspecting that, having become convinced, Hearnshaw was on the point of writing a "prosecution brief." This letter, we must note, was written a month before Hearnshaw handed over his manuscript to his publisher.[6] I ask the reader—again, as a member of the jury—to consider: Was his published account of this not a falsification? Did it not distinctly misrepresent Marion Burt's reaction to his conclusion, and in so doing obscure her obvious criticisms of it, indeed her plain and undoubted expressions of dismay and disbelief about it? Did it not give the quite wrong impression that she had not been greatly disturbed by Hearnshaw's acceptance of the "revelations" of fraud? And what, one wonders, could have been Hearnshaw's reasons for persisting in this clear misrepresentation, when it had been plainly pointed out to him, and he had had plenty of time in which to amend and correct it?

These letters and questions do at least seriously question the accuracy, if not the veracity, of Hearnshaw's presentation of evidence, and this doubt is deepened when other elements of testimony are examined and other relevant letters are brought to light.

Burt's Supporters: Ignored and Excluded

Hearnshaw had noted, as we have seen, that "the pro-Burt faction . . . had been fairly vocal following Gillie's exposé," subsequently, rather quietly but decidedly, castigating them for having voiced no criticism of his own biography. Might it have been, however, that the grounds of their silence were not deserving of so cynical an interpretation as the one I voiced a moment ago, but that on the contrary they were genuinely bemused, disturbed, and perplexed at the *appearance* Hearnshaw's treatment gave of impartiality and "balanced" scholarship—the marshalling of evidence that did *seem* to demonstrate and confirm Burt's guilt, and was at the same time so systematic and detailed as not easily or quickly to be criticized or faulted? Was the confirming blow so conclusive in its effect simply because of the appearance it gave of integrity and genuine scholarship? And where was the considered representation of Burt's supporters (and their arguments) in Hearnshaw's own biography? Some of them at least having been vocal immediately after the outbreak of the scandal, where in the biography was the mention, the elaboration, the critical appraisal of their views? In fact it was strangely nonexistent! The claims of Burt's opponents were there in plenty; Gillie, the Clarkes, Kamin, and so forth, were much mentioned, as was Burt's considered judgment of them. But there was barely any sign at all of Burt's supporters: John Cohen is mentioned only twice in the entire biography, Jonckheere only once, Lawlor not at all, and Summerfield not at all (except in relation to the Summerfield Committee and its report). Is not this in itself evidence of serious—though not conspicuously displayed—imbalance and bias? There were, however, more substantial and serious omissions. Hearnshaw was in close correspondence with the Clarkes during the later stages of writing the biography, apparently letting them see copies of Burt's letters to others; but, writing to Professor Brian Cox on January 27, 1984, John Cohen said:

> I do not think Hearnshaw's book is conclusive. Far from it. He completely ignored a huge stack of letters and memoranda from Burt, extending over nearly four decades, which I showed him when he came to consult me about the subject of his biography. I probably knew Burt better, more intimately, and for a longer period, than anyone else now living. Hearnshaw only saw him at a few meetings, and not almost daily, as his research student, as I did, for some seven years. . . . Hearnshaw took his information far too much from Burt's enemies. Of many of his really competent friends (Fraser Roberts, Jonckheere,

Pilliner, Birch, Summerfield, Lawlor, etc) we hear very little or nothing at all.

Of course Burt was *not* a fraud. A man more staunchly faithful to authenticity I cannot imagine.

Similarly, Brian Cox had himself let Hearnshaw know about an impropriety of the *Sunday Times* in dealing with accusations made against Burt in their pages on the very matter (the 1969 article written for the *Irish Journal of Education*) on which Hearnshaw had claimed that Burt had fabricated evidence. In a letter to me of July 23, 1984, Brian Cox wrote:

> Did you know that in 1969 the *Sunday Times* published lies about Sir Cyril Burt? They claimed that he had invented his statistics about school performance and that the *Irish Journal of Education* had never heard of his supposed article. All this was untrue, and eventually I arranged for the *Sunday Times* to publish a letter admitting their error. By this time much damage had been done to his reputation. I supplied this information to Professor Hearnshaw, but there is no reference to the matter in his book. This is strange.

The *Sunday Times* had reported, after Burt had claimed that his statistics on educational standards were to appear in the *Irish Journal,* that "the editor of the journal says he has neither published nor received any article from Professor Burt which would substantiate his remarkable claim." Their reporter, however, had certainly not contacted the editor of the *Irish Journal,* and its editor (Dr. Kellaghan) wrote to the paper to say so. The *Sunday Times,* however, did not publish his letter. Professor Cox pressed the paper again, and was told by the personal assistant to the editor (Richard Vickers):

> I apologise for the long delay in acknowledging and replying to your letter. My difficulty has been that the member of our staff who was responsible for handling the matter in relation to Professor Burt has since left us for another post and although I have asked him for details of the episode I have still not heard from him.
>
> However, I have renewed my request to him and as soon as I hear from him I will get in touch with you again.

Professor Cox, however, was clearly concerned about what seemed the deliberate reflection of all this on Burt's character and reputation, and felt that some speedy restitution should be made:

Your reviewers claimed that they had rung the editor of the *Irish Journal of Education* in which Professor Burt's full statistics were to appear and that the editor knew nothing about Professor Burt's article.

Your report was completely untrue. A letter from the editor of the *Irish Journal,* saying this, was not published.

At first I thought this was a trivial mistake and did not matter, but this false story has now been repeated in newspapers and in the *Times Educational Supplement.* There is a suggestion abroad that Professor Burt is an old man who does not know what he is doing. I hope you will agree with me that the *Sunday Times* should publish an apology to Professor Burt. It is most unfortunate that a man of his great reputation and public service should have his reputation tarnished by this unfounded rumour. Professor Burt's article is to apear in the *Irish Journal of Education* within the next few weeks.

I should be glad if you would let me know what action you intend to take, and trust you will feel, as I do, that this is most urgent.

Finally, the response of the *Sunday Times* editorial office was this:

Thank you for your latest letter which I propose to publish this week. In the meantime I have been able to clarify the situation. Our information about non-publication of Professor Burt's article came from two very reliable sources in the educational world and our correspondent did not think it necessary to check with him directly. He agrees now he should have done so. . . . We accepted the word of our informants.

So much for the standards of professional journalism, and the editorial standards, then operating in the *Sunday Times*. One also wonders about the "two very reliable sources in the educational world"—hardly reliable in this particular case!—but sources, of course, following the rules of good journalism, cannot be disclosed.

The essential and significant point, however, about this incident and this correspondence (of which these quotations are only a very brief selection); about what seems to have been a clearly intended denigration of Burt (and his "remarkable claim"); was that Hearnshaw completely ignored it, still, in his biography, claiming "fraud" in this connection. "Hearnshaw," writes Cox, "was shown my letters about the Sunday Times . . . but he published none of this. It is extraordinary!" But, he adds, "I am learning that Hearnshaw made little effort to check his sources. . . . I have read him with care, and he seems to me to jump very easily to conclusions.''

The Diaries: "Decisive Evidence"

Perhaps the most serious of Hearnshaw's charges, however, was his agreement with the Kamin-Gillie-Clarkes claim that Burt had invented or "fabricated" the data for the later papers on twins. On this, he was not only very decided but equally definite about the basis of evidence on which he rested the claim. This was the record contained in Burt's diaries; and the specific and apparently minor details of Hearnshaw's criticism, as well as its large and essential nature, must be scrutinized with care. Burt's claim, said Hearnshaw, to have increased the number of identical twins reared apart from 21 in 1955 to 53 in 1964 (when, it is claimed, his 1966 article was sent for publication) could not be substantiated.

> On this issue *the evidence from diaries is decisive*. Though there are some gaps in the diary record, the diaries are so nearly complete, for fifteen of the last eighteen years of Burt's life, and record so many trivia (haircuts, tea in the garden, walks on the hill, the temporary disappearance of the cat, etc.) as well as listing engagements of his own and visitors to the flat (even the weekly Saturday visits of Charlotte Banks), that we can be reasonably confident that no important activity or contact has been omitted. On the basis of this evidence we can be sure that Burt himself did not collect any data on twins, or any other topic, during these years, and that he was never visited either by Miss Howard, or by Miss Conway, or by any other assistant actively working for him. . . .[7]

Indeed, Hearnshaw was even more definite on this. "It was," he wrote, "the pretence of on-going research which the evidence from the diaries reveals as a complete fabrication.'' This is very strong language—"decisive evidence" for "complete fabrication"—but what in fact is the nature of the diary record? Charlotte Banks, in particular, has fully scrutinized the diaries, and to quite a considerable extent, her report on them has been confirmed by Brian Cox. The following is a relatively brief picture drawn by Brian Cox in a letter to me of September 4, 1984, incorporating some of Dr. Banks' findings. "Anyone who consults the diaries," he wrote, "will be astonished at Hearnshaw's remarks. They give a false impression, and for me this casts doubt on all his assertions." The facts about the diaries, he went on, are these:

a) For many days and weeks there are no entries. Dr. Banks calculated that in 1953 there were 317 days without an entry and in 1954 the number was 284. She worked out that in the years 1955–60 the days without entries for each year were 261, 95, 101, 177, 298 and 81. This looked right as I skimmed through these diaries.

b) I didn't have time to complete Dr. Banks's count for the 1960's. In the late 1960's Burt used his diary more often, but gaps remain. For example, in 1961 there are no entries from April 20–30, Oct. 27–Nov. 12, Nov. 14–25, Dec. 4–6, 16–21. There are other blank days in 1961. In 1963 there are seven blank days in January, and no entries on Feb. 4, 5, 6, 7, 8, 11, 18, 19, 20, or on March 15, 18, 20, 22, 25, 26, 27, 28, 29, 30, 31 or on April 1st. And so on.

c) These are not engagement diaries. Entries are brief and scrappy. They are usually about the weather, his walks, his ailments or the people closest to him—Gretl, Charlotte, Marion. He seems to have filled the diary in after the day was over. Many significant meetings and events are not recorded (Dr. Banks mentions the death and funeral of Miss Bruce which does not appear). He kept no record of telephone calls, and it seems likely that many visitors were not mentioned in the diary. He occasionally writes something like "11 letters posted" but there is usually no indication of the name of the recipients.

d) To give the flavour of the diaries here are the *total* entries for January, 1965:
Jan. 1. Out ½/hour. 2. Charlotte to tea. 3. A sunny January but wind was too cold to go out. 4–6. No entry. 7. Out ½ hour. 8. No entry. 9. Charlotte poorly. 10. Writing draft of paper on ESP for Mrs. Heywood's new book. 11–13. No entry. 14. Q. Paper for Advertising Association. 15. Very windy. Snowy. Collated papers for Teachers Diploma. 16. Charlotte to Archdeacon at Truro. 17–18. No entry. 19. Out 30 minutes. Charlotte to tea. 20. Snowing. 21. Out over hill and nearly round. Feet wet from snow. Hot foot bath. 22. Rang up Booth to be excused Examiners' meeting. 23. Charlotte to tea. 24. Churchill dies. George and Cohen on TV. Very mild. 30′ out p.m. 20′ walk to seat. At Harley Street and K. Coll road. 25. Colder. Out 20′ church and road. 15′ walk. 26–31. No entry.

This general characterization of the diaries is enough in itself to completely discountenance, if not conclusively belie, the decided nature of the claim Hearnshaw made on the basis of them. But Cox also noted many specific points that also demonstrate the "false impression" that Hearnshaw's account gave.

For example, the reference in the January record above to cancelling an examiners meeting "is one of the very few references to such meetings. He did *not* usually record such events in his diary." Similarly, on the apparently trivial matters Hearnshaw emphasises as being indicative of the *detail* of the diaries, "I found only one reference to a haircut (July 21, 1956). Presumably on other occasions there was no diary entry. Hearnshaw's reference seems deliberately misleading." There was also evidence of Burt's continued contacts and his continuing search for materials. For example, "July 6, 1966, saying 'Marked Teachers Certif.—Chelsea and Borough Road.' He must have been meeting or in touch with many people who never appear in the diaries." Or "In November, 1969, Burt wrote to Gertrude Keir of the Department of Psychology, University College, asking for examples of English composition from students. He did keep looking for such material."[8] There were also facts that made it clear that Burt's diaries were very far indeed from being a complete record. For example, "In a letter to me of Nov. 11, 1969, Burt mentions his Conference paper. In the diary there are almost no references to this kind of event." Or again, "My co-editor, A. E. Dyson, visited Burt in 1969. I could find no reference to this in the diaries. Cohen arranged an appointment by letter on July 21st, 1969. There is nothing about this in the diary." And finally, "Because Burt wrote letters in longhand, most are missing. The correspondence is not complete."[9]

It is clear, then, beyond any shadow of a doubt, that Burt's diaries were not the complete record Hearnshaw claimed them to be. His most "decisive" evidence therefore—for the most important charge of fraud against Burt—falls to the ground completely. It was no evidence at all.

Spearman and the History of Factor Analysis

Hearnshaw's charge here was that though Burt had publicly acknowledged Spearman's priority and preeminence "in the field of Factor Analysis up to the point of Spearman's death in 1945; had considerably (though not entirely) agreed with him and recognised his 'leadership'; from 1947 onwards—in a stream of articles on the mathematics and conclusions of factor analysis . . . [he] largely re-wrote the early history of the subject," his main concern being to "de-throne Spearman as the founder of factor analysis, and assert his own claims to priority as *the first user of factorial methods in psychology*" (my italics).

In his argument, he compared a Spearman article of 1904 with Burt's articles of 1909, and in general claimed that Burt was demonstrably derivative, and that his claims to the originality of both Karl Pearson and himself were false. The mathematical argu-ments involved are extremely complicated, but it is enough for our purposes to see that on this subject—in the considered opinion of those competent to judge these mathematical matters—Hearnshaw himself seems to have lacked a basic understanding of the issues involved, in addition to not having examined sufficiently scrupu-lously the papers on which he rested his claims. Three substantial criticisms have been made of Hearnshaw's judgment.

In his review of the biography,[10] Professor Cronbach took issue with this "major charge."

Hearnshaw accuses Burt of falsifying the history of factor analysis to aggrandize himself and detract from his mentor Spearman. This should be placed in context. Spearman's theory of a unified ability *g* was superseded by multiple-factor theories that Burt pioneered. Thurstone's important book *Multiple Factor Analysis,* published in the United States in 1947, underplayed Burt's influence and ignored his priority"[11]; this stimulated Burt to tell the story his way. The defense can read many of Burt's supposed falsifications as consistent with the printed record of 1909 and after, making Hearnshaw's reading seem tendentious and defusing the charge.

A much more detailed criticism of Hearnshaw, however, was published by Charlotte Banks in 1983,[12] attacking Hearnshaw's very decided charge that Burt's claim that "his own early work was derived from Pearson's 1901 articles and not from Spearman at all, and that therefore he was the *first factorist in psychology* . . . were *completely false*" (my italics). It is enough to say that, bearing in mind, as she pointed out, that "Burt did not claim to have origi-nated the idea nor to have been the instigator of the necessary formulae. He only claimed to be the first to do it in psychology," she completely demolished Hearnshaw's account and demonstrated that in the claims that he had made, Burt was entirely justified. Her own sources and arguments were also very detailed, but for our purposes one example will suffice, the historical mistake Hearnshaw made because of his confusion over Spearman's tetrad equation and the proportionality criterion. Hearnshaw had argued that the results of the intercorrelation of tests in Burt's 1909 papers were "analysed using the tetrad equation which was derived from Spearman's work." Charlotte Banks showed that Burt "did not use the tetrad equation for his analysis" and that certain things would not have been possible had he done so. Furthermore, she showed that Burt and Spearman were in communication about these theoretical correlations; that Burt accepted and acknowledged a formula suggested by Spearman, and quoted the proportionality equation in his 1909 paper, making it quite clear that the equation was Spearman's. Hearnshaw's historical account, and therefore his charges against Burt's claims, were again shown to be inaccurate through a lack of basic understanding.

This one example was then followed by a letter in the *AEP Journal* from Dr. R. B. Joynson[13] that voiced concern about a wider range of historical inaccuracies.

Sir,

In your special issue on Sir Cyril Burt, Dr Banks claimed that there are many inaccuracies in Professor Hearnshaw's account of Burt's historical views. This particularly interested me, because it occurred to me some time ago that, before one accepted Hearnshaw's allegations concerning Burt's falsifications, one ought to check at least a sample of the sources.

The first point I examined was Hearnshaw's assertion (in 'Cyril Burt', 1979, p. 171) that Burt had deliberately misrepresented Spearman when he, Burt claimed in 1947 that Spearman had proposed the identification of general intelligence and general sensory discrimination. I quickly discovered that Spearman's famous 1904 paper contains a number of statements which seem abundantly to justify Burt's view. In his 'summary of principal conclusions', for instance, Spearman writes that ". . . there is also shown to exist a correspondence between what may provisionally be called 'General Discrimination' and 'General Intelligence' which works out with great approximation to one or absoluteness" (Amer. J. Psychol., 1904, 15, p. 284; Spearman's italics). In addition, Burt was already ascribing this view to Spearman in 1909 (Brit. J. Psychol., 1909 3, p. 159), and what he said in 1947 was merely a repetition of this. Thus, so far from Burt's view being part of a 'new story' which Burt maliciously invented in the 40s to discredit Spearman, as Hearnshaw supposes, it was simply an accurate re-statement of what the two men had been saying some forty years before.

It should be added that the view which Burt ascribes to Spearman is in accordance with Spearman's well-known doctrine of the 'general factor'. On the other hand, to deny this view—that is, to hold that there is a capacity for general sensory discrimination, distinct both from general intelligence and from a capacity for discrimination in specific senses— is in accordance with Burt's well-known belief in 'group factors'. to accuse Burt in this context of misrepresenting Spearman is like accusing a man of misrepresenting Freud by saying that Freud supported the doctrine of infantile sexuality.

I have examined many further aspects of Hearnshaw's account of Burt's historical claims; and I can confirm, quite independently, the accuracy of the examples of Hearnshaw's unreliability which Banks provides. I wonder whether any of your readers have noticed other instances?

Your faithfully,

R. B. Joynson.

Hearnshaw's response to Charlotte Banks' very long, precise, and fully documented criticism, however, was in fact a nonresponse, a shrugging off of her arguments rather than a considered reply. Joynson wrote again (May 21, 1984), coming back specifically to the matter of the tetrad equation and the proportionality criterion.

Professor Hearnshaw (his Journal, 1984, p. 6), referring to Dr Banks' contribution to the recent Burt Symposium, declares that he can find nothing in her paper which forces him "to amend in the slightest detail" what he wrote on factorial history in Chapter IX of his biography of Burt. However, as I mentioned in a previous letter (ibid, 1984, p. 39), I think the points raised by Banks are sound; and Hearnshaw does not examine them, he only brushes them aside.

Dr Banks has, indeed, provided Hearnshaw with much to answer. Perhaps he might begin by re-considering his assertion that in 1909 Burt analyzed his results using Spearman's tetrad equation. This is a particularly important 'detail' in view of Hearnshaw's further assertion that "Burt's 1909 work was entirely derived from Spearman" (see Banks, This Journal, 1983, p. 23). The tetrad equation was not formulated until several years later. Hearnshaw is confusing it with the proportionality criterion, a closely related statistic. Burt obtained this latter from Spearman, but again there are no good grounds for supposing that Burt used it in his paper. It is odd that Hearnshaw should profess to correct Burt's account of factorial history when he himself plainly does not understand such basic points.

To the best of my knowledge, Hearnshaw has never yet replied to these criticisms. Yet another of his charges, then, falls to the ground.

Dorfman and Stigler on Burt's Statistics

Another stark example of Hearnshaw's selectivity and one-sidedness in the presentation of evidence (an example equally well-marked in the testimony of Gillie)[14] is that of Dorfman's supposed demolition of Burt's statistics. In the September 1978 issue of Science,[15] the lead article was entitled "The Cyril Burt Question: New Findings"; its subtitle being (without any qualification) "The eminent Briton is shown, beyond reasonable doubt, to have fabricated data on IQ and social class." In it, D. D. Dorfman, Professor of Psychology at the University of Iowa, analysed and criticized Burt's statistics in his 1961 article "Intelligence and Social Mobility."[16] Dorfman quoted the charges of fraud from Kamin, Gillie, the Clarkes, and McAskie; the repudiation of these charges by Jensen and Eysenck; and the judicious open-ended conclusion of a reviewer, Nicholas Wade, that it would still be of interest to decide whether the "flaws" in Burt's work were the results of "systematic fraud, mere carelessness, or something in between" and that "the facts so far available did not allow any of these explanations to be ruled out." Dorfman then set out to supply further evidence on the basis of which the question could be resolved "beyond a reasonable doubt."

Again (as with Charlotte Banks' mathematical arguments on the Burt/Spearman matter) the statistical critique of Dorfman was more complicated than need be entered into here, our chief concern being with the nature of Hearnshaw's testimony about it. It is enough to note that his chief criticism focused upon (1) the assumption (and assertion) that the "row totals" and "column totals" of some of Burt's tables were "simply totals per mille" and (2) Burt's method of rescaling assessments of intelligence to fit a normal distribution curve. Dorfman wrote that

> The fit of Burt's data to the theoretical normal distribution appears extraordinarily good; . . . the almost perfect fit of Burt's adult and child distributions to the normal curve suggests that his 'actual' distributions are not actual distributions. . . . Beyond a reasonable doubt, the frequency distributions (of Burt's tables) were carefully constructed so as to give column marginals in agreement with the normal curve.

Throughout, Dorfman's language was very decidedly judgmental. Burt's figures and statistical practices were said to be "bizarre," his correspondences "too good to be true," his claims for the distribution resulting from reclassification "fraudulent." Burt, he claimed, "fabricated data." It was the kind of derogatory language used by Kamin and Gillie, and the essential point to note here is that Hearnshaw accepted it. Dorfman's analysis of 1978, Hearnshaw wrote in 1980,[17] made Burt's "extremely doubtful material on parent–child correlations in intelligence . . . look even more suspect." Dorfman was not mentioned in the biography, most probably because the book was then already in the press, but the fact of this 1980 mention will be seen to be significant.

What must be noted now, however, is that Dorfman's attack on Burt was almost immediately rebutted in no uncertain manner. In October 1978, Stephen Stigler, Professor of Statistics at the University of Chicago, replied to his criticism in *Science*. The charges of fraud in Dorfman's article, he wrote, were "unfortunate" because "Dorfman is in error on two major points, and his other points are sufficiently open to reasonable doubt to call his conclusions into serious question."

On Dorfman's assumption and assertion about the row totals, Stigler wrote:

> First, I wish to call attention to a significant misrepresentation of Burt in Dorfman's section entitled "Burt's row totals." Dorfman writes "The row totals of Burt's tables I to IV and the column totals of his tables III and IV would appear on the basis of Burt's descriptions and discussions to be "simply totals per mille." He then goes on to show that the row totals (the proportions in each class) agree perfectly with 1926 data of Spielman and Burt, saying "the coincidence is bizarre indeed." Dorfman's contention that Burt described his row totals as

"simply totals per mille" is simply wrong, and his conclusion that the agreement is "bizarre" is uncalled for. What Burt in fact wrote was,

"In constructing the tables the frequencies inserted in the various rows and columns were proportional frequencies and in no way represent the number actually examined: from class I the number actually examined was nearer a hundred and twenty than three. To obtain the figures to be inserted (numbers per mille) we weighted the actual numbers so that the proportions in each class should be equal to the estimated proportions for the total population."

Presumably he got the "estimated proportions" from Spielman and Burt, or some other publication of these data. In other words, Burt is *saying* he has weighted the counts to get precisely the agreement that Dorfman presents as evidence of fabrication. It is hardly "bizarre" when an author is found to have done what he said he was doing.

On the rescaling of assessments to fit a normal distribution curve, Stigler's comments were:

One of Dorfman's major contentions relates to Burt's column totals, his grouped intelligence assessments for all classes together. Dorfman demonstrates convincingly that Burt's column totals fit a normal distribution exactly, if rounding is allowed for. What does Burt say about that? . . . Burt wrote:

"Finally, for purposes of the present analysis we have rescaled our assessments of intelligence so that the mean of the whole group is 100 and the standard deviation 15. This is done because the results of so many intelligence tests nowadays are expressed in terms of conventional I.Q.'s conforming to these requirements."

The question is, what did Burt mean by "rescaled"? For if he meant that he followed the by no means unknown practice of "curving" the scores to fit a normal curve (with mean 100 and standard deviation 15), either by transforming his pooled (over classes) I.Q. scores individually, or by reweighting his columns (as he did his rows) to fit "estimated proportions," then Dorfman's case collapses. It is clear that for his purposes, Burt would need the father scores and son scores to be comparable. It seems plausible that if the raw data (which were gathered over a half-century under widely varying conditions) were in fact "crude" (and thus possibly skew or otherwise markedly non-normal) and the assessments of adult intelligence "less thorough and reliable"[18] (and hence possibly more variable) then Burt would rescale the marginal totals to agree with one another, so that he could make direct comparisons of within row variability. Contrary to Dorfman's implication, Burt did believe I.Q. scores were approximately (though not exactly) normal,[19] and in a "pilot study" he might well choose to rescale using a normal distribution. In fact, Dorfman's Table 7 could be interpreted as showing just how he might have proceeded in scaling Tables III and IV. It may be significant that Burt used the word "rescaled" instead of "standardized", which would be more suggestive of a linear rescaling. . . .

It must be admitted that Burt's description of his procedure is extremely vague . . . and one can easily see how many readers could be misled into believing the counts were frequencies, but Dorfman does Burt and the readers of *Science* a great disservice by not even mentioning a reasonable alternative explanation that does not involve either fabrication or fraud.

Stigler also demonstrated other faults: (1) that Dorfman had used "the wrong formula" in his calculation of regressive coefficients, (2) that he showed "serious faults of logic" in his conclusions, and (3) that he was wrong in claiming that Burt was practicing an "abuse of statistical terminology" in still referring to his distribution tables as "data." He concluded:

I do not wish to be interpreted as endorsing either Burt's statistical procedure or his unclear explanation of what he did (and his refusal to present the raw data), but given the standards of Burt's time, and his repeated disclaimers (it was "merely a pilot inquiry," "data are too crude and limited") the charges of fabrication or fraud seem (at least in this instance) to be totally without foundation.

Stigler's was also by no means the only criticism of this kind. In December 1978, Arthur Cohen of New York also wrote to the editor of *Science* in perhaps an even more condemnatory tone:

Dear sir,

I read Science mostly for pleasure. That is, until I read your September 29, 1978 issue and the article by D. D. Dorfman entitled "The Cyril Burt Question: New Findings" (pages 1177–1186). I am amazed that your Editorial Board allowed this attack on Burt to be published (and being the lead article makes the error in judgment even worse). . . .

In addition . . . the article's subtitle states: "The Eminent Briton Is Shown, Beyond Reasonable Doubt, to Have Fabricated Data on IQ and Social Class." Only one thing in this article is beyond reasonable doubt . . . it was not publishable as written. As I shall show, there is much doubt in Dorfman's allegations.

Cohen went on to criticize the same points as Stigler and on the same grounds. His comments on the question of rescaling were as follows:

> Burt's paper of 1961 was 22 pages long. Only 10% of the paper was devoted to discussions of table construction and row and column totals. His main focus was on social mobility and its relationship to intelligence as well as other causal factors. Dorfman seems to completely miss the mark in criticizing Burt's rescaling of his tables to new borderlines. Dorfman goes through much detective work, but . . . misses the point completely.

And he described Dorfman's conclusions that the results of Burt's rescaling were bizarre, fraudulent, and so forth, as "pure nonsense." Cohen's repudiation of Dorfman was quite independent of Stigler, and in stating his conclusions, like Stigler he made it quite clear that he himself did not necessarily share Burt's substantive views, and would by no means want to be altogether uncritical of him. Quite obviously, though defending Burt, these critics were in no sense whatever one-sided and uncritical supporters; their criticisms of Dorfman were prompted only by a sheer concern for correctness and veracity.

> The above criticism of Dorfman's analysis and conclusions should not be taken as indicating my agreement with Burt's hypothesis or conclusions. I would well understand criticism of Burt's paper as vaguely written with questionable methodology. But, Dorfman cannot say beyond a reasonable doubt that the "distributions were systematic constructions", and that "they were observed frequencies per mille", and other such statements.

> On the contrary, Burt probably carefully sampled 1000 pairs of observations from a larger collection of data based on occupational class proportions in the population and found skewed occupational distributions. He scaled his total distributions to N (100,15) according to standard practice. He transformed borderlines legitimately to match percentiles in occupational and intelligence distributions.

> Professor Dorfman's attack on Burt's work is immoderate and unfounded, and Burt deserves a retraction by Professor Dorfman and *Science*.

To the best of my knowledge no such retraction was ever forthcoming from either source; but what, now, of Hearnshaw's judgment? Hearnshaw probably did not know of Cohen's letter at all,[20] and probably knew of Stigler's criticism too late to take it into account in his biography. We have seen, however, that he mentioned Dorfman with approval in 1980, but with no mention whatever of Stigler's counterarguments. Yet he quite clearly knew about these toward the end of 1978. In a letter to Miss Archer of November 20, 1978, he wrote:

> I have seen Dorfman's article and Stigler's reply. The reply I found unconvincing. It failed to answer a great many of Dorfman's points. I'm afraid, moreover, that evidence from other sources, not available to Dorfman or Stigler, fully confirms Dorfman's conclusions.

And that was all! He did not say what was mistaken about Stigler's criticism. He did not say which of Dorfman's points remained unanswered. He did not indicate what the "evidence from other sources" was. And though he subsequently upheld Dorfman's judgment, no mention whatever was made of Stigler. Where, it has to be asked, was the objectivity, balance, and impartiality, the rigorous consideration of all sides of the question to arrive at the truth, in this? As with Charlotte Banks' objections to the judgment on Spearman, so in the matter of Stigler's objections to the judgment of Dorfman (which became the judgment he accepted) they were (to the best of my knowledge) never dealt with but simply ignored or brushed aside.

The Journal and Burt's Editorial Practices

The strangeness of Hearnshaw's reasoning may also be seen in one or two other examples, one of which is his attitude toward the part Burt played as contributor to and editor of the *British Journal of Statistical Psychology*. One of the charges against Burt was that he himself wrote articles for the journal but published them under the names of others, sometimes using their names alone, sometimes as co-authors. Miss Conway and Miss Howard were examples. Quite apart from these two cases, however—which were to become the most notorious (the two ladies having been said never to have existed)—it was said that Burt wrote many letters in the journal using pseudonyms, in this way offering a wide range of views and criticisms, and perhaps enjoying this anonymity as a way of putting forward a multiplicity of positions.

Many seem to have recognized Burt's practice in this, to have been aware of it, sometimes referring to the journal as "Burt's own journal," but none thought of "fraud" in this connection or at least gave expression to such a judgment. Hearnshaw's view, however, was very severe. Though conceding that Burt's long editorship was in the tradition of "the old days, when editors had unlimited tenure . . . and virtually absolute discretion in running their journals" (F. C. Bartlett edited the *British Journal of Psychology* for 24 years, to 1948; and C. W. Valentine edited the *British Journal of Educational Psychology* for 25 years, to 1956; both of them assisted by Burt), Hearnshaw castigated Burt for his "autocractic control." Burt's assumption that it was "in some sense his personal journal," he said, "was indefensible." The story of the British Psychological Society's alteration of this state of affairs, however, has its decidedly amusing sides.

In 1953, the society established a publications committee and a new six-year rule for editorship, but, wrote Hearnshaw, in addition to financial problems that meant that the journal had difficulty in surviving, at that time it was not easy "to suggest a well-qualified successor for Burt; and, indeed, this proved so difficult that Burt remained *de facto* editor for five years after he had been replaced." "There is no doubt," Hearnshaw concluded, "that he fooled the Society."

Anyone who has had experience of (I almost said suffered at the hands of) academic "publication committees" will be deeply disposed to say "Good for Burt!" But they might also be inclined to ask if there were not other sides to the story. Indeed, there were. First, being himself extraordinarily many-sided and prolific, Burt was always sensitive to the evidently widespread criticism that "he published too much." Second, he was always (throughout the whole of his written work, from first to last) meticulous in acknowledging the help he received from others, and co-authorship was one way of doing this (as with Conway and Howard, but others besides). But also—a third and very telling point—the journal was, as Charlotte Banks gently put it,[21] "never over-full." Putting this in another way: material of worth was not always plentifully submitted! As responsible editor, Burt may well have decided to fill in its pages and do something to bring a little life to them. Furthermore, it was largely owing to Burt's own indefatigable efforts and the secretarial and financial help he provided out of his own pocket that the journal survived at all. There is no doubt whatever about Burt's generosity in this. It must (again) be borne in mind that Burt *never,* in the whole of his academic life, in any of his appointments, was provided with a paid secretary. His secretaries—Miss Bruce and later Miss Archer—had to be paid out of his own resources. But it was this private secretarial help that bore the brunt of the journal's work. Charlotte Banks wrote of Miss Bruce: "She read proofs upside down and found more errors than authors and editors of the *British Journal of Mathematical and Statistical Psychology* put together, not to mention the printer's reader." But this was by no means all. In 1965, Charles Valentine said:

> I should like to pay tribute to Burt's generosity in helping others engaged in psychological research. . . . It was brought home to me over many years when I submitted to him articles sent to me for the *British Journal of Educational Psychology*. He was not content with brief approval or disapproval; he corrected figures, made recalculations, offered various suggestions and constructive criticisms, often including detailed references for further study. In this way he has put many a young psychologist on his first path to advancement. . . . incidentally, may I mention (in the founding of a new journal dealing with mathematical aspects of psychology) he paid for much of the necessary secretarial help—the re-typing of manuscripts, and the heavy correspondence— out of his own pocket.
>
> Many others have experienced the same generosity. Nor has he forgotten his earlier fields of work. . . . This . . . is a tribute to a great psychologist and a great man.[22]

Could anyone who had known Burt and his work so intimately, and for so long, have been so remarkably wrong as the testimony of Hearnshaw and the other detractors suggested? Burt also remained, by invitation, the Patron of the Association of Educational Psychologists, and was, unfailingly, a regular contributor to its *News Letter* (which developed into the *AEP Journal*) during the last seven years of his life, being accorded many warm tributes on his death.

The journal (its very survival and subsequent development) was largely Burt's own creation. Can it be at all surprising that he felt aggrieved at the attitude of the British Psychological Society and the machinations of its newly established "publications committee" (even if he may have been at fault in not being ready to recognise the need for change)? Especially when he had to "continue as the *de facto* editor for five years after he had been replaced"! Is this not a strange, even comic, situation? But I spoke of the strangeness of some of Hearnshaw's reasoning; what did I mean by this?

In his biography, when writing about Burt's editorial practices, Hearnshaw claimed that over half of the "more than 40 'persons' who contributed reviews, notes and letters to the journal . . . were unidentified," but that "judging from the style and content of their contributions were pseudonyms for Burt." This, clearly, can be no more than conjecture, but Hearnshaw continued (p. 245): "no doubt this exercise, *which other editors are known to have indulged in,* tickled Burt's well-developed sense of humor, as well as very often providing him with excuses to expound his own views under his own name by way of reply" (italics added).

Apart from very well-known examples such as that of Schumann, in music, I myself know of only a few "other editors" who have indulged in this practice. One such, however, richly deserves a note in passing. Writing about Tom Paine—a great, energetic Englishman—Augustine Birrell had this to say:

Paine made his appearance in Philadelphia, where he at once obtained employment as editor of an intended periodical called the *Pennsylvanian Magazine or American Museum,* the first number of which appeared in January, 1775. Never was anything luckier. Paine was, without knowing it, a born journalist. His capacity for writing on the spur of the moment was endless, and his delight in doing so boundless. He had no difficulty for 'copy', though in those days contributors were few. He needed no contributors. He was "Atlanticus"; he was "Vox Populi"; he was "Aesop". The unsigned articles were also mostly his. . . . He spent the rest of his days with a pen in his hand, scribbling his advice and obtruding his counsel on men and nations. Both were usually of excellent quality.[23]

A parallel between Tom Paine and Cyril Burt—if something of an exaggeration—does not seem altogether wide of the mark, at least in this respect! (It is pleasant, anyway, to recall Paine!) Hearnshaw, however, clearly implied that he himself did know of other instances of such editorial practice, and clearly saw good-humoured and plausible reasons for it. But knowing and believing this, is it not strange that he should have judged Burt so harshly for it as to make it seem yet another piece of evidence supporting the charges of fraud? In this matter of "having fooled the British Psychological Society," might not Miss Mawer's (Mrs. Clarke's) judgment be quite apposite? "I could, I must admit, see him finding it amusing to bamboozle the over-confident, but a calculated major scientific fraud is another matter."

Strange Conjectures

A final example of this strange reasoning can be very briefly given. Supporting his claim (based on the diaries) that Burt's "pretence of on-going research" was "a complete fabrication," Hearnshaw cited one piece of "evidence."

> "So in 1960," (he wrote), "we are told in the statistical journal that 'for a more conclusive answer . . . we must I imagine await the results of Miss Conway and others who are applying tests of various abilities to twins who have been brought up separately from birth'."

But then he gave the source of this comment in a footnote which is surely astonishing. The source, he said, was E. D. Williams, "The General Aesthetic Factor," *British Journal of Statistical Psychology* 13 (1960), p. 89, and he added (my italics):

> Miss Eliz. D. Williams *was a real person,* who took an M.A. under Burt in 1937. She must have derived this 'information' about Miss Conway from Burt, who as editor was responsible for passing it. It is also possible that Burt 'planted' the statement. He was in the habit of making additions and alterations to contributions from others.

Now this, quite plainly, can be nothing more than purely slanted conjecture, reinforcing the picture of Burt's "fraudulence" and "malfeasance" by no more than an indication of possibilities. This lady clearly *could* be, and *had been,* traced. Even so (placed in quotation marks to indicate its dubious nature) her "information" could not be assumed (by Hearnshaw) to be her own. Burt *possibly* had "planted" (again in quotation marks) the statement. And again we are treated to a repetition of the charges (chiefly from the Clarkes) that Burt "was in the habit" of altering and adding to the manuscripts of contributors. But this latter is merely *hearsay*, from the unsubstantiated claims of the Clarkes about the abstracts that they themselves had represented as articles. There is, of course, the other clear possibility, which Hearnshaw never even considered, that Mrs. Williams herself actually meant what she said, and had herself actually written what was published. For Hearnshaw, however, the possibility of surface truth was not enough. There had, it seems, to be a hidden, darker side of deceit, falsehood, impropriety. And so conjectural possibilities were adduced as evidence, their effect being the same: to add to the blackened picture of Burt.

Inordinate Language

In many ways, then, a careful examination of Hearnshaw's testimony shows that beyond any doubt whatever it is in many ways seriously questionable, inaccurate, flawed, insufficiently cautious, and much too ready to be influenced by Burt's detractors—often giving the appearance of being deliberately deployed to touch in additional colors to the portrait of a guilty Burt that these more extreme critics had more garishly outlined. He does not seem to be one of them, yet has chosen to place himself in their company, to walk by their side. As Marion Burt originally suspected, he seems to be "turning against Cyril and taking the opponents' side," and as Cronbach had also detected, under the apparent balance and impartiality of Hearnshaw's account there lurked a "prosecution brief"—all the more persuasive because of the apparent moderation and reluctance of its adverse judgment. Charlotte Banks offers the same testimony. When, distressed and concerned about the falsifications she saw in the attacks on Burt, she tried to defend him, Hearnshaw wrote to her (February 21, 1979) saying "It would be prudent to wait before nailing your flag so firmly to the mast—unless you are determined to go down with a sinking ship!"

Hearnshaw himself, it seems, was too prudent to nail his flag firmly anywhere, but would walk the deck of the ship that floated.

His estimation, however, of which ship would float and which would sink, might well prove to have been much mistaken.

This anti-Burt disposition and persuasion—indeed, conviction—underlying the surface appearance of academic balance and impartiality also showed itself in the last characteristic that deserves mention: the use, within the context of apparently calm, good-tempered, and well-considered argument, of inordinate language.[24] We are told, from the time of the Kamin-Gillie-Clarkes attack onward, of "Burt's exposure," "delinquencies," and "demonstrable lies," of the "autocratic control" of his editorship and the "abuse" of this position. We are told that Burt's claims about his own early work were "completely false," and that his claims of ongoing research in relation to his later work were "a pretence" resting on a "complete fabrication" of data and evidence. On the testimony of three London professors, Hearnshaw was satisfied that Burt was "high-handed, devious, and corrupt." This is hardly impartial language. Hard knuckles lay inside the white glove. A fist was clenched tight within the polite handshake.

And this kind of language was plentifully scattered about in the making of other judgments that Hearnshaw felt himself in a sufficiently exalted position to make. For example, that Burt was too much of an applied psychologist to be a good scientist ("Neither by temperament nor by training was he a scientist."[25]) and that Burt's later "delinquencies" were to be explained not only in terms of his broken marriage, retirement from his chair, loss of his editorship, declining health, and so forth; and not only by his egocentricity, vanity, loneliness and insularity, introversion, paranoia, and the like: but also by such factors in his make-up as his mixed genetic ancestry (of part-Saxon, part-Celtic stock), an "innate instability in his psychosomatic make-up," and the lasting effects of disturbing experiences in his early childhood. Coupling these with mention of the fact that "a number of personality tests note a preponderance of obsessional-compulsive types" among sufferers from Ménière's disease, Hearnshaw found that "all this evidence fits the known facts of the Burt case extremely well."

Later we will look in more detail at Hearnshaw's imaginative account of Burt's personality and character, but, even now, on the basis of a little reflection on these supposedly factual ingredients, I leave the reader to consider whether this judgment of one man by

another—in an "official biography"—is an example of the reliable
science and careful scrutiny of evidence possessed and practiced
by Hearnshaw but lacking in Burt; or whether, again, Cronbach
was not much closer to the mark in declaiming "This Burt is a
figure worthy of Moliérè!"

What is proved beyond doubt, given all the evidence we have
examined, is that "the official biography" seems in many ways that
are of clear and grave significance, and therefore profoundly disturbing, very far from being the impartial document it has been
held up to be. Hearnshaw, like the early and more overtly aggressive accusers, has many questions to answer. We will confine
ourselves here, however, to those few for which it has been possible
to produce the evidence and demonstrate the grounds.

Questions Requiring Public Answers

1. Why did Hearnshaw so completely and conspicuously misrepresent Dr. Marion Burt's response to the news about the charges
   of fraud against her brother, and in relation to this, her attitude
   towards the proposed extension of the biography? Why, too, did
   he proceed to publish this misrepresentation when he had been
   made plainly aware of it—certainly by Miss Archer—with plenty
   of time left for an alteration to his manuscript before it had to go
   to his publisher?
2. Why did he so conspicuously ignore the testimony of Burt's
   supporters in his biography? Why, in particular, did he ignore
   the materials offered and presented by John Cohen and Brian
   Cox, especially when some of this had a direct bearing on one
   or other of the charges of fraud?
3. Why did he insist that the near-complete record of Burt's diaries,
   and the nature of their record, constituted "decisive" evidence
   proving Burt's "pretence of ongoing research" a "complete
   fabrication," when this account of the diaries was so radically
   incorrect as to have been termed false? Why, too, did he
   misrepresent the nature of the record the diaries contained?
4. Why did he misrepresent the record of the relationship between
   Spearman and Burt in the history of factor analysis in such a
   way as to denigrate Burt? And why, in particular, if this was a
   genuine and understandable mistake, has he never replied to the
   criticisms of this account very clearly articulated by Charlotte

Banks and Dr. Joynson? Indeed, what now are his answers to these criticisms?

5. Why, upholding Dorfman's criticism of Burt's statistics, has Hearnshaw never taken into account Stigler's criticism of Dorfman—even if only to show why he considered Dorfman's account the more correct of the two, and especially when he knew of this as early as 1978, and must have known that Gillie in particular had been repeatedly mentioning Dorfman, but not Stigler, ever since the publication of Dorfman's article?

6. Why did he so severely criticize Burt's (alleged) writing under pseudonyms in the British Journal of Statistical Psychology while readily conceding that this was a practice of other editors (of other journals)? Why, too, did he not take into account, in criticizing Burt's tenacity in not wishing to relinquish his editorship of the journal, the long and many-sided efforts Burt had devoted to it, including much financial support, to secure its continued existence and development?

7. What is his explanation of the conjectural account he gave of Mrs. Williams' mention of Conway in her journal article?

We will come back to some of Hearnshaw's testimony when considering the present standing of the fraud charges, and especially his conjectural account of the development of Burt's personality, but the above are questions clearly requiring answers regardless of what may be said later.[26]

Notes

1. *Bulletin of the British Psychological Socity* 33:1–8; 1980.
2. The italics in these quotations are mine.
3. In an interview in the *Guardian,* November 5, 1979.
4. Hawkes, Nigel. *Science* 205; August 17, 1979.
5. October 1, 1979, following Nigel Hawkes' review, Charlotte Banks sent a letter to *Science,* but *Science* did not publish it.
6. Mentioned in his letter of June 14th. In the same letter, Hearnshaw said that he had written to Marion on May 18th and had had no reply, and was "planning to visit her in Malvern next month." In the biography, he wrote "I had arranged to visit Malvern and talk with her the following month, but she died suddenly at the age of 87 on 14, May, 1978."
7. *Cyril Burt, Psychologist;* (London: Hodder & Stoughton, 1979), 240; italics added.

8. This, it may be noted, was the date of the *Irish Journal* article comparing standards of educational attainment for which Burt was said to have fabricated data.

9. Again, it is worthwhile to recall that Burt was never provided with a paid secretary.

10. "Hearnshaw on Burt." *Science* 206: 1392–94; 1979.

11. This "underplaying" of Burt by Thurstone may be borne in mind when considering Eysenck's comment on Thurstone's judgment of Burt.

12. "Professor Cyril Burt: Selected Reminiscences." *AEP Journal* 6:21–42; 1983. Also see Appendix 2.

13. Joynson has since published his book *The Burt Affair* (Routledge, 1989), in which these criticisms are elaborated.

14. See p. 113.

15. Vol. 21, pp. 1177–86.

16. *British Journal of Statistical Psychology* 14 (3); 1961.

17. "Balance Sheet on Burt."

18. *British Journal of Statistical Psychology* 14:3; 1961.

19. *British Journal of Statistical Psychology* 13:83; 1943; and *Mental and Scholastic Tests*. London: P. S. King, 1922, p. 162.

20. I am not sure that it was published.

21. *AEP Journal* (1):32; 1983.

22. *Cyril Burt—A Biographical Sketch and Appreciation*. London: University of London Press, 1965. Also published in *Studies in Psychology: Presented to Cyril Burt*. London: University of London Press.

23. *Self-Selected Essays*. London and Edinburgh: 1916, Thomas Nelson & Sons, p. 113.

24. This also showed itself more recently in Hearnshaw's response to Robert Joynson's book, *The Burt Affair*. The "balanced scientist" disappeared in a flash from the scene! Taking his place, smarting under unaccustomed criticism, appeared something very different: a tetchy and aggrieved anti-Burt antagonistic at bay. In this exchange ("The Psychologist," *Bulletin of the British Psychological Society* 2, 1990: 61–68) it was Joynson, with his quiet and sober mode of argument—meticulously documented—who emerged as the balanced scholar; Hearnshaw, by contrast, as the angry disputant distastefully attempting to discountenance Joynson's defense in its every detail—as a total and dismal failure.

25. "Balance Sheet on Burt," p. 2. On this judgment, the exacting nature, great detail, and wide range of Burt's work deserves comparison with *any* psychologists or social scientists who were working then or who have followed him in this field, and we will see something of this when considering the sociologists of education.

26. We may also remind ourselves of the answers required of Hearnshaw in connection with questions raised by the BBC film; see p. 38–39.

7

Professors Jensen and Eysenck

A final and very brief note is now necessary on the positions of two men in particular who are indeed "leading scientists" and who have been of quite central importance in the controversy: Professor Arthur Jensen and Professor Hans Eysenck. Both had long acknowledged the influence of Burt upon their own work. Both had been in many ways and over a long period supporters of Burt, and were indeed loyal supporters during the greater part of the period of "scandal." But the judgments of both were converted—though in different degrees—by the detailed evidence marshaled in the official biography and the apparent impartiality of Hearnshaw's treatment. Our consideration of Jensen can be very brief indeed, because his position is by no means yet decided in a hard-and-fast manner. That of Eysenck, however, calls for more serious question and comment, the conversion in his case having involved so extreme a swing of the pendulum as to be difficult to understand and indeed to call for some explanation.

In the beginning, Professor Jensen was very emphatic indeed in defending Burt against *all* the charges of fraudulence in statistics advanced by Kamin and Gillie, his judgments resting in a rigorously demonstrated way on his own first-hand study of Burt's figures—probably the most thorough examination of all Burt's tables yet carried out. His distaste, too, for Kamin's and Gillie's "post-mortem" attitudes could hardly have been more forcibly expressed. In a long letter to the *Times* on December 9, 1976, he wrote:

Sir, If the late Sir Cyril Burt, who died in his 89th year in 1971, were still living, he should easily win a libel suit against the London *Sunday*

171

Times and perhaps the small band of psychologists who have irresponsibly charged Burt with "faking" scientific data and publishing "fraudulent" results on the inheritance of mental abilities.

The central fact is that absolutely no evidential support for these trumped-up charges of fakery and dishonesty on the part of Burt has been presented by his accusers. The charges, as they presently stand, must be judged as the sheer surmise and conjecture, and perhaps wishful thinking, of a few intensely ideological psychologists whose antipathy for Burt's hereditarian position in the so-called "IQ controversy" was already well known to researchers in this field long prior to *The Sunday Times* broadside. Professor Leon Kamin, who apparently spearheaded the attack, has been trying for several years now, in his many speeches and a book (*The Science and Politics of IQ*), to wholly discredit the large body of research on the genetics of human mental abilities. The desperate scorched-earth style of criticism against genetics that we have come to know in this debate has finally gone the limit, with charges of "fraud" and "fakery" now that Burt is no longer here to answer for himself or take warranted legal action against such unfounded defamation.

This calumny, interestingly enough, found an eager mouthpiece in *The Sunday Times* medical correspondent Oliver Gillie, whose own recent book (*Who Do You Think You Are? Man or Superman—the Genetic Controversy*)[1] is a flagrant attack on all manner of research on human behavioral genetics.

Not scientific criticism, but "calumny"—this was Jensen's characterization of the attacks launched by Burt's critics. But he also reported in some detail his own findings:

After Burt's death, I assembled all of the many technical articles on the genetics of IQ that Burt had ever published *in the course of his 60 years as a researcher*. On the basis of these, I published a detailed analysis and critique of Burt's total empirical contributions to the field (Jensen, A. R. "Kinship correlations reported by Sir Cyril Burt" *Behaviour Genetics,* 1974, 4, 1–28). The article contains complete tabulations, taking up 10 elaborate tables and graphs of all of Burt's empirical findings on kinship correlations, which are the basis for his genetical analyses of individual differences in mental ability. In all of this cross-tabulation and analysis, I carefully pointed out every single error, inconsistency, and statistical or methodological ambiguity I could find in the whole of Burt's work—*20 such instances in all.* No one else, to my knowledge, has done a more thorough and objective job of scrutinizing Burt's work and pointing out its defects, as well as its strengths. *No errors or inconsistencies in Burt's work have been reported since, that were not noted in my 1974 article.* These peculiarties in Burt's reports are thus all clearly laid out in proper perspective, so that the interested reader may easily judge the whole matter for himself.

It appears that virtually *all of Burt's errors are of a rather trivial nature, and none is scientifically crucial in the sense that it would change any of his conclusions.* There are several misprints later corrected by Burt himself; most of the rest are transparently careless mistakes, omission of sample sizes, or even reversals of some numbers, that occurred in copying tabular material from an earlier article into a later one, while a few discrepancies remain unexplainable without undue speculation. Although the errors and inconsistencies may indicate carelessness, *they show no evidence whatsoever of "fakery" or an attempt to bias the results:* The errors *do not go consistently in any one direction. Even the statistically most stupid undergraduate could do a neater job of faking his quantitative results, if that was his aim. . . .*

It is noteworthy that a leading American geneticist, Professor Newton Morton, has made a detailed statistical comparison of British kinship correlations (most all of them from Burt's studies) with those of all the parallel studies done by American investigators, and he finds the differences between the two sets of results to be statistically nonsignificant. Professor Morton writes: "Whatever errors may have crept into his [ie Burt's] material, *they do not appear to be systematic."*

The italics in the above passage are mine, and serve to emphasize a number of considerations so telling and crucial as to deserve the clearest possible statement and enumeration:

1. In Burt's work of *over 60 years,* only *20 errors* had been found.
2. No additional errors had been reported since Jensen's 1974 account.
3. All the errors were trivial; they did not "go in only one way" (favorably for Burt's arguments), and were in no way such as to affect his conclusions.
4. The errors and misprints alike showed no evidence whatever of conscious or deliberate fraud.
5. Had such "fakery" been intended, it was most transparent and had been most clumsily carried out.

All these are extremely important facts and judgments, coming especially from the man who, expert in these matters himself, had studied Burt's work more fastidiously and meticulously than anyone else. Why, then, having arrived at such firm conclusions, did Jensen change his mind? There were at least two reasons.

First, he was persuaded by Hearnshaw's findings; by the balance, fairness, and impartiality of his account. Jensen felt himself unable to do any other than accept the apparently convincing evidence presented, such as that of Burt's diaries. Unhappy though he had been by the many conflicting claims and charges, he felt himself bound to conclude that:

> The Burt puzzle was pieced together several years after Burt's death, by his biographer, Leslie Hearnshaw, a noted historian of psychology (*Cyril Burt, Psychologist,* Cornell University Press, 1979). Ironically, Burt was convicted by his own personal diaries and correspondence files, which were given to Hearnshaw by Burt's sister. There could not be found a shred of evidence that Burt had collected any new data on MZ twins reared apart since about 1952, after he retired from his professorship. Yet he went on writing articles on twins and the heritability of IQ supposedly adding more and more cases to his twin collection, as late as 1966. . . .
>
> Hearnshaw's biography of Burt and his detective work in exposing Burt's deceptions is fascinating but sad—the story of a genius gone awry.[2]

In the same way, he felt bound to accept Hearnshaw's explanations of these latter-day "delinquencies" in terms of Burt's personality and character traits and his misfortunes: his vanity, broken marriage, illness, and so forth. A second reason, however, stemmed from his own personal experience:

> In the last year of his life, in personal correspondence with Sandra Scarr, a psychologist at Yale, he reported the IQs of three more sets of MZ twins reared apart, twins whom he had presumably just found. There was never any evidence of their existence, and when I visited Burt at about the same time that he was writing to Professor Scarr, he never mentioned his new finds to me, even though a major topic of our conversation was genetic research on twins.

This one lack of corroboration made Jensen think that Burt was at least capable of deceit, thereby lending weight to Hearnshaw's verdict. In my own correspondence with Jensen, while (as we have seen) solidly condemning the BBC film, and still upholding Burt's standing and achievements in "his great career as a psychologist," he was nonetheless quite frank in the statement of his continued judgment:

> I pretty much accept Hearnshaw's verdict. I feel most confident (although not 100% confident) that Burt "invented" data on some (perhaps as many as 20) of the MZ twins reared apart. I have seen no adequate reason to suspect fraud on anything else Burt has done. The discrepancy between Burt's letter to Professor Sandra Scarr and things he told me in person rather convinces me he was capable of deceit, although, of course, other, more charitable explanations of the discrepancy are possible. I have been favorably impressed by what seems to me to be Hearnshaw's honest and objective scholarship regarding these matters. In the absence of a stronger counter case on Burt's behalf, I have seen no basis for rejecting Hearnshaw's judgment regarding the available evidence. If there is a basis for a different verdict, I will be most happy to learn about it.[3]

Clearly, Jensen still remains by no means "100%" convinced of Burt's supposed misdeeds, and, in his most recent letter, has mentioned reasons for a revival of his doubts. "Dismayed" by my own verdict about the level of some of Hearnshaw's scholarship, he says: "I have taken his report as fully accurate, and had based my own thinking on it," but one other, and quite new, factor had arisen. He wrote in July 1987:

> Professor William Shockley (797 Esplanada Way, Stanford, CA 94305, U.S.A.) has performed an interesting analysis on Burt's twin data and compared the results with the same analysis applied to other sets of MZ twin data. It is an analysis of the form of the distribution of twin differences, plotted on normal probability graph paper. Neither Burt nor any other twin researchers have ever used this type of analysis of twin differences. The interesting finding is that the analysis reveals certain rather systematic departures from "normality"—and this feature shows up not only in Burt's data but in several other sets of twin data. Since no one knew of this type of analysis until after Burt's death, it would seem surprising that Burt or anyone else would have faked twin data in such a way as to show this particular feature. When I displayed Shockley's analysis at the annual convention of the Behavior Genetics Association in Minneapolis a couple of weeks ago, several persons in the audience later commented to me that the result caused them now to question the claim that Burt's twin data were phony.

Professor Jensen, then—on the grounds of his own substantive findings a staunch supporter and defender of Burt—has been genuinely torn by the apparently conclusive evidence of Hearnshaw's official biography, but is now again in an open-minded condition of doubt. Even so, he has never been in any doubt whatever about the *conclusions* Burt upheld:

> Scientifically, the one important conclusion that we may draw with complete confidence is that, even if all of Burt's findings were thrown out entirely, the picture regarding the heritability of IQ would not be materially changed. The scientific weight of all of the remaining massive and newer evidence and modern quantitative genetic analyses, in numerous studies by independent investigators using somewhat different methods, now far surpasses that of Burt's own pioneer research. Yet the evidence *sans* Burt leads in *toto* to essentially the same general conclusions that we find in Burt's major writings on the heritability of intelligence, viz, that, in accounting for individual differences in IQ, genetic factors considerably outweigh the existing environmental influences.[4]

The changed position of Professor Hans Eysenck, however, although consistently and completely agreeing with the same shared conclusion of Burt and Jensen (the three have never differed at all on this!), is very different. The swing of a pendulum from one extreme to another is an accurate analogy. Despite all the Clarkes have said about the existence of apparently poisonous conflicts between Burt and Eysenck from the late 1940s onwards, when the scandal broke with Gillie's article in 1976, Eysenck was, without any qualification whatever, completely on Burt's side. Confirming all that Miss Archer and Charlotte Banks had claimed—about Marion Burt's distress on learning of the charges against her brother (let alone Hearnshaw's later communication to her of his acceptance of their truth)—this was the letter he wrote to her from the Department of Psychology at the Maudsley Hospital (the Institute of Psychiatry) on November 16th:

> Dear Dr. Burt,
>
> Thank you very much for your letter of November 13th. It is very sad to think that you have been put to this distress, and altogether I cannot find it in my soul to forgive Dr. Gillie for this intemperate and absurd attack on your late brother. I have no doubt whatsoever that his

integrity in this matter cannot be impugned, and certainly the so-called evidence published does not in any way suggest fraud or faking of results.

I am sorry to say that I have no copy of the interview you mention but I enclose copies of two letters I sent to the Times and one I sent to the Sunday Times, all of which have been published and which you might like to send on to Professor Hearnshaw. I am also writing a piece on this whole affair for Encounter, a monthly magazine quite widely read in America and this country by the intelligentzia, defending Sir Cyril and pointing out that nothing that has happened upsets in any way the conclusions to which he came. There will also be a debate on Thames Television between Dr. Gillie and myself some time in the near future: it will be taped on Thursday but I don't know when it will be played.

I think this whole affair is just a determined effort on the part of some very Left Wing environmentalists determined to play a political game with scientific facts; I am sure the future will uphold the honour and integrity of Sir Cyril without any question.

With best wishes,

Your sincerely,

H. J. Eysenck

From that point on, Eysenck was not only the most loyal but also the most painstaking and indefatigable of Burt's defenders. In the *Sunday Times,* on November 7, 1976, he fully adopted and supported Jensen's position:

The rather sensationalised charge by your medical correspondent, Oliver Gillie (October 24), that Sir Cyril Burt faked his research data, and that this throws serious doubt on the strong determination of intelligence by genetic factors, is hardly borne out by the facts. There certainly are inconsistencies in the figures published by Sir Cyril, as first pointed out by Professor Arthur Jensen (not, as Gillie says, by Professor L. J. Kamin). It is a far cry from this fact to the accusation that the data on which the figures are based were faked; it seems more likely that in the absence of computer facilities, which would have made the calculations easy, Burt carried over certain figures from earlier analyses in spite of the fact that he was collecting additional cases all the time. This is of course inadmissible, and makes it impossible to rely on these figures in the future.

The accusation that he obtained his figures "by guesswork" is wide of the mark. In the days when Burt was collecting his original data, standards of measurement were less high than they are today—which is not unusual in the hard sciences either. . . .

Finally, let me deal with the view that beliefs regarding the importance of heredity in the determination of individual differences in intelligence are related to a person's political beliefs. This is simply not so. Burt himself was left-of-centre; J. B. S. Haldane, the geneticist and a former leading member of the communist party, was a firm advocate of the genetic view; J. B. Watson, the founder of the behaviourist school, and a firm conservative, believed in 100 per cent environmentalism. Ideological assumptions are red herrings. What matters above all is to continue the research and discover with ever greater precision what the facts are.

Errors and insufficiencies there may well have been in Burt's work, but no evidence of fraud; and in the *Times* a few days later, having shown how Burt's "estimations of hereditability" fitted perfectly well with those of other researchers, he defended Burt equally strongly.

The absurd accusation levelled against him of "fraud" and "faking" hardly need rebuttal; there simply is no evidence which would support anything other than the charge that he made errors of estimation and calculation as Arthur Jensen pointed out in a published article several years ago. (The ludicrous charge relating to his two young lady collaborators not being "discoverable" has been properly refuted by John Cohen.)

What is serious is that charges of this nature should be made without a shadow of proof; that a man of Sir Cyril's standing should be judged guilty without trial; and that well known facts concerning his errors should be blown up in this absurd fashion, years after their discovery, to make a journalistic debauch. This degrades the academic atmosphere in which scientists have to work, and can only please ideologues uninterested in the actual facts of the case.

These were the first among a series of letters and articles, in all of which Eysenck defended Burt against the charges of fraud, upholding both his scientific standing and his personal character. He did in fact write the article for *Encounter* (January 1977, pp. 19–24) promised in his letter to Marion Burt, and this, while taking Burt to task for the *mistakes* revealed by Jensen, again completely rejected the charges of fraud. "The suggestion that Burt 'faked' his data must, I think, be rejected out of hand as having no support in any of the facts brought forward by his accusers." Accepting

Jensen's critical treatment of Burt as being "uncompromising but fair," Gillie's treatment, he wrote, "strikes me as unspeakably mean and senselessly derogatory." Any misbehavior of Burt's was nothing, he claimed, to compare with that of these critics who "made Burt's known lapse into a sensationalized crime; who accused him, without a shred of proof, of fraud, of faking data, and of other much more serious crimes . . . and who acted in deliberate disregard of the mainstay of our conception of law and justice which says that a man is presumed innocent until found guilty." All this, clearly and without the slightest doubt, was very decidedly in support of Burt.

Then, however, with the appearance of Hearnshaw's biography, came a change; something that surprised even Hearnshaw himself. "From the pro-Burt faction," he wrote, "there has been not a murmur of dissent. I expected them to be at my throat; but even Professor Eysenck appears calmly to have accepted my conclusions, and Professor Jensen has manfully recanted his former views on Burt." This last judgment, as we have seen, was something of an overstatement, but certainly with Eysenck the change began to assume a strange character. On the one hand, he continued to defend his earlier support of Burt:

> Professors Cohen and Jensen, and I too, defended Burt when Gillie's original accusations were published because *at that time* the evidence was partial and hearsay. Proof was later furnished by Professor Hearnshaw in his biography of Burt, because he had access to Burt's diaries and other papers, but it still seems to me that the original accusations by Gillie were insufficiently based on fact to be taken seriously. . . .[5]

Gradually, however, Eysenck began himself to make "revelations" that seemed flatly to belie his earlier good opinion. Even before the biography appeared, Eysenck had clearly become aware that Hearnshaw was writing it, and appearing to have become susceptible to the influence of the Clarkes and others, seemed to be changing his testimony as to Burt's character. Gillie, indeed, taunted him with his statement of just such changes in an article Eysenck published in May 1978.[6] Now he was at least voicing doubts, but supporting them from his own experience:

> Is it conceivable that a scientist acknowledged as a world figure should stoop so low as to fake his data? It would be unrealistic to deny the

possibility. Ptolemy, Newton, Mendel and others have been similarly accused, on what appear to be reasonable grounds; eminence by itself can be no defence, and may indeed tempt a person to "prove" by invention of data what he "knows" to be right. The faking of data would probably only be undertaken on the scale suggested by someone rather odd as far as personality is concerned, and there can be no doubt that Burt was extremely odd in many ways, as I can testify from personal experience. He was in the habit of rewriting (without acknowledgement) contributions by other psychologists to the *British Journal of Statistical Psychology,* which he edited for many years. He once rewrote a fairly friendly review of one of my books, contributed by an eminent statistician, making it extremely hostile, without asking the reviewer's permission; he than rewrote my reply, only reinstating the original text when I protested! On at least one occasion he invented, for the purpose of quoting it in one of his articles, a thesis by one of his students never in fact written; at the time I interpreted this as a sign of forgetfulness. These and many other examples suggest a complex, odd and rather tortured and turbulent soul under that Pickwickian exterior; whether this oddity extended to the wholesale faking of data is of course quite another question. Should we proceed on the basis of considering a man innocent until he has been proven guilty? Should we come to the verdict of "not proven" of the Scottish Courts?

Eysenck could now, at least, seriously entertain the possibility! "Tizard and the Clarkes," he said, "have come to the conclusion that Burt was guilty of faking and I do not think their views can be readily dismissed." With the publication of Hearnshaw's book, his persuasions in this changed direction deepened. In the *Listener* of April 29, 1982, an article by Eysenck appeared under the title "Burt's Warped Personality Led Inevitably to Fraud." The introductory (editorial) paragraph said: "When Sir Cyril was first accused of fraudulently inventing data, Eysenck sprang forcefully to his defence. Further research established beyond doubt that Burt had indeed been guilty of massive fraud"; and Eysenck, who had contributed to a radio program on "The Burt Scandal," was introduced as trying to explain such questions as "Why Burt did it?" and "How did he get away with it?" Very clearly, Eysenck had now changed his mind. During the course of his article, commenting on the kinds of misfortune and stress to which Hearnshaw had attributed Burt's "delinquencies," Eysenck argued that, severe though this stress had been, stress by itself does not produce the particular type of reaction Burt showed. This requires a certain type of personality, and this type of personality was certainly present in Burt.

Outwardly, Burt presented a very normal, helpful and often charming front; many people were taken in by this, but behind this façade there was a whole mass of pathological emotions looking for expression. Hearnshaw hints at these pathological neurotic tendencies, and quotes some incidents which illustrate the very odd type of behaviour which Burt would show upon occasion. As one of his students I was subjected to a degree of hostility which gave rise to a number of highly unusual and certainly abnormal types of behaviour. Burt was indeed well known to show hostility to all his best students, possibly because he feared that they might usurp his position or because he disliked any form of criticism; it is difficult to know the reason. Many famous men have shown a similar tendency, but it did not usually show itself in severely psychopathic actions such as the following.

When my first book was published, a review of it appeared in Burt's journal, written by a very well-known British statistician. The review was extremely critical and indeed hostile, to an extent which is quite unusual in scientific publications. Ten years later I met the statistician whose name appeared under this review; he told me then that he had in fact written quite a good review of my book, but that without his knowledge Burt had completely rewritten it, and then published it under his name, without consulting him! This surely is not normal behaviour in academic circles.

Several students of mine, who had been registered with Burt for administrative reasons, found that when their results favoured my theories Burt made them rewrite their conclusions so as to be critical of myself; he also altered the papers they published on their work. On occasion he was not above inventing studies which did not exist, in order to support his views. Thus, in one of his papers he referred to work by Asenath Schonfeld on humour. When Asenath became one of my first research assistants I asked her about this work, as I had written about sense of humour myself; she told me that she had at one time considered working in this field, but had decided against it. The conclusions Burt quoted from her work were purely imaginary. All this happened well before the time that the various blows of fate recounted by Hearnshaw descended upon Burt, and I think we have the right to conclude that Burt's personality was warped, and thus presented a fertile ground for stress to produce the kind of behaviour which led to his disgrace.

Certainly many people were suspicious of him long before the final denouement; Professor L. L. Thurstone, perhaps the leading psychometrist of his generation, told me in confidence that he refused to take anything Burt wrote seriously, or to pay attention to any claims he made.[7] Professor Penrose in this country has been quoted in a similar vein. Burt's fraud, therefore, is in line with his personality, as expressed on previous occasions. . . .

According to Eysenck's new testimony—rooted in his own experience—Burt had now to be judged as having long given evidence of gross dishonesty, calculated deceit, the most reprehensible behavior, and indeed, of being a "psychopath." Burt's tragedy, he could now conclude, "was that the superior quality of his mind was not supported by a character of even average strength and quality; truly a case of an idol with feet of clay!" The question that at once springs to mind is very stark and very simple. Why, knowing this from the late 1940s onward, had Eysenck been "reluctant to believe in Burt's guilt" and "so surprised at the accusations against him?" Why, indeed, had he so strongly come to Burt's defense? "The answer, of course," Eysenck wrote, "is that most people are guilty of small dishonesties, but few are found to commit a really serious crime. The psychopathic behaviour Burt had shown towards me, for instance, whilst seriously affecting the prospects of a young student, were hardly 'crimes' in the sense that his later fraudulence was."

We have noted earlier Eysenck's final pronouncement in the BBC's *The Intelligence Man*. By now, it was not only a conclusion as severe as that of the Clarkes (indeed, of Kamin and Gillie too) but it even employed their kind of language:

> He really is to me a mystery wrapped up in an enigma. Outwardly he was always polite, gentlemanly, kindly, helpful and so on, but the evidence indicates very conclusively that he was very vengeful, hostile, aggressive, and extremely devious. . . . Psychopaths unfortunately are usually able to conceal their motivation and their wrong-doing extremely well. They are the typical "con men," and in a sense of course Burt was a "con man."

Burt was now both the "psychopath" and the "con man."

I leave the reader to compare Eysenck's judgment as to Burt's integrity and probity expressed in his letter to Marion Burt with that expressed in these later writings and his final broadcast testimony. Voicing no conclusion of my own, I also leave the reader—

as a member of the jury—to reflect upon the nature of these changes of judgment; the kinds and degrees of the differences involved in them. Do not the two extremes at the utmost ends of the swing of a pendulum form an accurate description? And is there not something strange, something questionable, in the grounds adduced for the judgments expressed at either extreme?

Meanwhile, there is one other fact that deserves the clearest and strongest emphasis: *Every item in the new catalog of charges drawn from Eysenck's personal experience (even when it involves references to others) lies wholly within the realm of hearsay.* But this can be clarified (while calling for the relevant evidence) in the list of questions requiring public answers, which can now be clearly drawn up.

Questions Requiring Public Answers
1. Why, possessing the knowledge of Burt's psychopathic personality, character, and behavior to which he later testified—so many-sided and firmly grounded in his own personal experience from his late student days onward—did Eysenck initially write in such a fulsome manner to Dr. Marion Burt assuring her of Burt's "honour and integrity"?
2. Why, too, possessing this knowledge, did he not make it plain from the very beginning in the controversy with Burt's detractors? Why did he not mention it then? Why was it kept hidden?
3. Who was the very well-known British statistician whose favorable review of Eysenck's first book Burt completely rewrote without his knowledge?[8] Why, too, did this reviewer, having been so grossly and improperly misrepresented (indeed, *completely* misrepresented), wait for 10 years before (and then only on the occasion of a chance meeting) informing Eysenck about it? Where are the original and final manuscripts of this review that give evidence of this editorial malpractice?
4. Who were the "several students" who had been forced to rewrite their conclusions in such a way as to be critical of Eysenck? Where are the manuscripts to be found that give evidence of this? Which were the papers (that Burt had altered) publishing their work, and in which journals were they published? Which, too, were the studies Burt invented to support his views? Where are the occasions of Burt's mention of these studies to be found?

Precise details are essential to lift these charges at all above the level of hearsay.

5. On the assumption that the Clarkes were among these "several students" (Eysenck's statement clearly implies that there were more), the questions addressed to them must also be addressed to Eysenck: In the case of the Clarkes, by "the papers publishing their work" does he mean the *abstracts* of their theses? In what ways were these abstracts published by Burt inaccurate and misleading? In what ways were they critical of Eysenck? These abstracts are printed here (p. 120 and p. 123), so that it should be easy for both the Clarkes and Eysenck to point these matters out clearly.

6. What were the kinds and degrees of hostility to which he (among others comprising "the best students") was subjected by Burt? What precisely were the obstacles put in his way, and in what ways precisely were the Clarkes used as pawns in Burt's battle? Why, together with Aubrey Lewis, did he warn the Clarkes that they might not get their Ph.Ds, and on what grounds? What evidence of these kinds and instances of hostility and obstacles can be provided, or at least indicated, other than the word of the Clarkes and Eysenck themselves?

    In the absence of such evidence, is it not perfectly possible that any enmity, hostility, and interdepartmental feuding that existed could have originated in, and continued to come from, the Clarkes themselves, or Eysenck, or Aubrey Lewis and the Maudsley, and not necessarily from the side of Burt? Is it not possible that Burt might well have had well-founded reasons for any feelings of suspicion, distrust, or animosity he might have harbored? Along these lines, it is clear that without evidence unresolvable conjecture can endlessly follow upon conjecture, but the conjectures can with equal validity move in both directions.

7. What precisely is the actual evidence for Burt's "invention of studies which did not exist" in the Asenath Schonfeld case? What exactly was Burt's reference to her work? What were the "conclusions quoted from it" and what was improper about them? Similarly, what is the evidence on which Thurstone's judgment of Burt's work rested? Suggestions have been made (by Cronbach, see p. 153) that Thurstone himself had to a

noticeable and significant extent "underplayed" Burt's contribution, and may himself have been jealous of Burt's achievements and reputation. In these, and any other cases mentioned
in a similar fashion, evidence must be adduced before judgments
asserted on the basis, and at the level, of pure hearsay can be
accepted. Until this is done, they should not be used in such
ways to add dimensions that clearly contribute to the blackening
of Burt's reputation. This is no more than a heaping of unqualified and unchecked contumely onto a man not there to reply.

Let the evidence relating to questions 3 and 7 be produced. Then
the issues can be properly judged—but not before.

I hope that my emphasis in this relatively short section has
become completely clear. Jensen and Eysenck are indeed both
"leading scientists" of considerable stature and influence. Just
because of this they have quite justifiably been of great significance
in the controversy. In particular, their acceptance of Hearnshaw's
judgment carried great weight at the time of the biography's publication, in seeming finally to clinch the case against Burt, in seeming
to set the seal of authority upon the verdict of guilty. In the case of
Jensen, this change of opinion—understandable and genuinely
based—was however by no means final. His mind has remained,
and still remains, open. I have therefore mentioned his position,
but it has required no further question.

In the case of Eysenck, however, things are very different. The
total about-face in his stance—the complete reversal of both testimony and judgment as to Burt's character, the readiness to con-
demn Burt almost without restraint just as he was once fully ready
to defend him, and the augmentation of this latter-day appraisal
with a catalog of comments purely within the realm of hearsay—
raises doubts and questions of the most grave and serious kind.
Having once outrightly dismissed and shown his profound distaste
for Burt's detractors—as being "intemperate and absurd," "unspeakably mean and senselessly derogatory," he finally decided
like Hearnshaw and with Hearnshaw to join their ranks. Is this not
strange? Is not the changing content and character of his testimony,
from first to last, also very strange? Does it not call for the fullest
kind of explanation and justification, bearing in mind that a man's
character and scientific reputation are at stake?

Notes

1. It is noteworthy that Gillie's own book was advertised in the footnote following his first 1976 article denouncing Burt.
2. "Straight Talk About Mental Tests" (letter). *AEP Journal* 6(3): 1984.
3. August 25, 1984.
4. Letter to the *Times*, 9 December 1976.
5. Letter to the *Listener*, 22–28 May 1982.
6. "Sir Cyril Burt and the Inheritance of the IQ." *New Zealand Psychologist* 7(1): 8–10.
7. See our earlier comment on this judgment, p. 153.
8. I was able to ask Professor Eysenck (while discussing the Burt affair over dinner with Victor Serebriakoff) if he would tell me the name of this statistician. His reply was "I would . . . if I could remember."

8

The Sociologists of Education

A Final Allegation

With one exception only, our cross-examination of Burt's detractors is now complete. The exception, however, is one of the utmost importance. It is the one allegation of Gillie's that was earlier deliberately set aside, so that at the stage of critical inquiry we have now reached, it could be considered separately and given the detailed attention it requires.

Having charged Burt with the racism and class discrimination that he identified with the extreme beliefs of the eugenics movement, and with having influenced the Wood Committee's report "in confirming the policy of segregating the mentally subnormal so that they would not reproduce," Gillie went on to say that Burt

> also advised teachers that 'innate general intelligence' as measured by tests was the most important factor determining success in the classroom—*so underrating the importance of social factors.*

Because he believed (as he believed his surveys and deductions showed) that the mental ability of individuals—their general, cognitive ability and their marked special aptitudes—was chiefly determined by heredity, Burt was said to have paid scant attention to environmental conditions, factors, and influences, attributing little importance to them. Furthermore, he was said to have "underrated" them with specific regard to "determining success in the class-room," to the performance and achievement of children in

187

schools. It is necessary now to take issue with this criticism, because a great deal hangs on it. In particular, it brings up for our consideration an entirely new field of investigation, an entirely different body of literature that (rightly or wrongly, whether justifiably or not) came to be of great weight and significance in the criticism of Burt and in the creation of a certain public image—a stereotype—of his position.

Though rooted in some of the same issues underlying the testimony of those of Burt's detractors we have already considered, this new area of research, evidence, and argument had a much earlier origin, was of a much wider nature, and went far beyond this testimony. It was indeed a very positive and wide-ranging body of research in its own right, resting on its own intellectual grounds, and was by no means simply a negative carping against Burt. At the same time, in ways that I hope to show, it came to represent in academic and public opinion alike a position ranged against that of Burt. In many ways it also came to be falsely stereotyped—perhaps for no more substantial a reason than that at least one of the people working within its field did enter into public dispute with Burt. (False stereotypes, it seems, are the intellectual and ethical positions that become effectively operative in the arena of public debate.) Not at all open to cross-examination in the way that has been possible so far, the testimony arising from it differs from everything we have considered so far. It is, however, every bit as important, raising issues that lie at the very heart of the problems of postwar education, and must therefore be dealt with no matter how great the difficulties.

The truth seems to be that since the end of the Second World War, three enormous misrepresentations have developed and become entrenched in academic and public opinion: of the area of social investigation I will describe (of leading work within the sociology of education), of Burt's own position, and of the relationship between the two. The picture has emerged of two diametrically opposed and decidedly contending positions, each entailing quite definite, distinct, and different assumptions and policies, both within education itself and beyond this in many of the wider aspects of society. Putting this simplistically for the moment, the one has been considered "hereditarian and elitist," supporting selective secondary education and therefore perpetuating social inequalities and class privilege; the other "environmentalist and egalitarian," advocating the abandonment of all selection, the ending of class privilege, and the achievement of social justice and equality of treatment for all. It is perhaps too much to say that the drawing up of these two opposed positions has been entirely intentional, but the fact that the issues involved have entered into the arena of politics—indeed, party politics—coupled with all the heated arguments attending the formulation of legislation and the working out of practical policies, has certainly made it seem so. Deliberate ideological motivation and argument has certainly entered in, clouding truth over, sharpening the caricatures, and making it all the more difficult to draw the distinction between science and politics. The best way forward, therefore, seems first of all to elaborate a little further the caricatures we have drawn so far.

The Caricatures: An Introduction

The distinctive area of work I have in mind lies within the "sociology of education." Following the end of the war, the effort to create a newly conceived welfare state involved a fundamental concern to clarify, in effective social, economic, and political terms, the nature of social justice. One core consideration in this (at least for many) was the presence or absence of the possibility of social mobility, the desire being to achieve a society in which individuals (whatever their social and class origins) would have the opportunities (entailing appropriate and effectively available avenues) to move to that level of occupation, and its attendant status, that their abilities and merits deserved. This clearly implied a direct challenge to, and criticism of, privilege; indeed, a direct attack on arbitrary privilege. At the heart of it, something which had itself resulted from the same concerns and motivation, was the 1944 Education Act and, clearly, a desire for its effective *implementation*.

The concern of a considerable number of politically motivated sociologists was therefore focused upon the extent to which the equality of opportunity and the "parity of prestige" among the different kinds of secondary schools, which were proposed in the newly instituted "secondary education for all," was actually achieved. The dominant focus, in short, was on social class and educational opportunity, and arguments began to rage as to which *form of secondary school organization* (which *kinds of school*—the tripartite division into grammar, technical, and secondary modern schools; multilateral or bilateral schools; comprehensive schools; and so forth) was the most appropriate form for the actual achievement of the clearly declared aims of the Act.

At the London School of Economics, under the leadership of Professor David Glass, a wide-ranging scheme of research was initiated to investigate all aspects of social mobility; and one important part of this (it is hardly too strong to say the very heart of it) was the inquiry into the part played by *education* in either reinforcing the existing hierarchy of statuses in society (cementing and perpetuating the very close association between fathers and sons within each social class), or in serving as an effective avenue of social mobility (loosening this association, upwards or downwards). Social mobility, with little critical consideration, was assumed to be good and desirable. All children (whatever their social origins) should have the opportunity for education and training to the level and in the directions warranted by their abilities and talents. Only with this opportunity, and with the actual achievement of this education and training for all, would individuals enjoy the fulfilment their abilities deserved, and would the tasks and skills needed at all levels of society be undertaken and carried out at the best possible levels of excellence.

Intransigence in moving towards this situation (on whatever basis of privilege or power it rested and was enforced); any obstruction of the achievement of such social mobility; meant for individuals and society alike a wastage of abilities and talent. Equality of opportunity in education, besides being ethically just, was therefore also a practical necessity for the achievement of this social end. This research therefore set out to investigate all the factors involved in the existing system of *educational selection;* especially in the processes of selection for *secondary and higher* education. Some of the later work stemming from this research orientation probed into dimensions going far beyond the "educational system" as such (as the research developed and moved more into specific fields: "the home and the school," sociolinguistics, and so on); and these developments we shall consider.

Centrally and crucially, however, it was success or failure at the age of 11 plus (on the basis of some variant of the 11-plus examination) for selection to the *grammar school* that was seen as the key that opened or left closed the door to subsequent occupational and professional advancement, and so to all the corollaries of the higher levels of social status. For success at this crucial turning point of selection, the children of middle-class families were thought to have, and were shown to possess, very considerable advantages; the children of working-class families to suffer very serious disadvantages. Environmental factors, therefore, rather than inherited factors, seemed to exert the crucially determining influences over the manifestation, measurement, recognition, selection for grades of education, and subsequent development of the levels of mental ability among children.

On the basis of this picture, reinforced by the findings established by these researches, the educational and political position was strongly advanced that the *selection* of children at the age of 11 plus for different kinds of education, and their consequent *segregation* into different kinds of school at that age, was socially unjust and socially divisive. The actual achievement of social justice, both in education and in the wider pursuit of "life chances" in the enjoyment of opportunities to move up the scale of social status and social class; the effective elimination (or at least substantial avoidance) of the wastage of human resources, for both individuals and society; required the elimination of the 11-plus test, the abolition of selection and the entire existing system of segregated schools, and the replacement of them by a uniform system of comprehensive education in comprehensive schools. In all communities, just as all children, whatever their social differences, attended common primary schools, so they should all pass into common comprehensive schools for their secondary education; such schools also, therefore, being communities containing a cross-section of all the groups in society. And many arguments were then presented for the advantages of the nature and provisions of these new kinds of schools, as against those of the old. The "educational ladder" conception of educational opportunity underlying the system of selection at 11 plus, which perpetuated class inequalities and was elitist, should be replaced by this new *egalitarian* conception of the new "secondary education for all." The work of the "sociologists of education" was such as to support and uphold this position throughout all the heated arguments of the 1950s, 1960s, and onward, and it does not seem unrealistic to say that (caricature or not) it is a position still firmly held by many.

The polar opposite of this position was the one of which Cyril Burt came to be seen as perhaps the most outstanding exponent. Believing that intelligence was largely established by heredity, Burt unashamedly did believe that selection for secondary education *should* take place, and that children *should* then be given the *different* kinds of education most appropriate to their differing levels of ability and their specific aptitudes. He did believe that the distribution of intelligence throughout the whole population of any society was largely established by heredity; that the conditions of social classes—though they might well affect the encouragement, development, and fulfilment, or the discouragement, limitation, obstruction, and perhaps even atrophy of this in individuals—were very far from determining it, and that there were therefore limits to which changes in the organization of schools or in systems of educational administration could change it. He could not accept, therefore, that the "equality of opportunity in education" could either sensibly (in a factual and functional sense) or justly (in an ethical sense) be thought of in terms of *equality of treatment*. Equal opportunity in terms of the fullest consideration of each individual's abilities and talents should mean the making available of as *wide a diversity* of provisions as possible to meet and fulfil the variety of their needs. For these reasons, therefore, he advocated not only the retention but also even the extension of different kinds and levels of education. To use the terms employed by sociologists of education, he therefore came to be seen as perhaps the most influential theorist of a reactionary nature, retaining the "educational ladder" conception, upholding the Hereditarian as distinct from the Environmentalist view concerning the determination and distribution of intelligence, upholding selection and the retention of some kinds and degrees of *differential* and segregated education (as against what was thought to be the egalitarian view, and also upholding elitism as against those who desired equality and the elimination of social class, class differences, and class privilege.

Burt came to be viewed, in short, as the arch-representative, the stereotype, of all that was right wing, conservative, reactionary, and backward-looking in these post war educational controversies; and it was as such that he was increasingly attacked by those (chiefly from the sociology of education) who, on the left, advocated their own position as being the more humane and progressive.

Out of these controversies those stark polarities emerged that have remained the source of the most sustantial and controversial issues in education ever since, continuing to exert (now as deeply if not intractably embedded assumptions) the most powerful influences in educational and political thinking. Each polar opposite has become labeled as being on the side of, or standing opposed to, "social justice." The Hereditarian elitist—supporting testing, selection, and the provision of different kinds and levels of education—is reactionary, unjust, a perpetuator and defender of privilege. The Environmentalist egalitarian—supporting the abandonment of all these things and their replacement by the comprehensive school—is progressive, humane, just, and the enemy of privilege. The latter upholds and furthers social justice. The former denies it, and stands in its way. Hereditarian versus Environmentalist; those who uphold selective education (including segregation and streaming) versus those who uphold comprehensive education (including, at its extremes, mixed ability teaching). Elitist versus egalitarian: these are the kinds of starkly differentiated and opposed positions that have come to be established, and that now form the subjects of public discourse, including that of educationalists themselves.

Clearly this is not the place for a wide-ranging critical appraisal of all that has gone into the sociology of education, or even of all that has gone into the study of social mobility. My concern in what follows will be to establish two things only. First, I want to demonstrate beyond any doubt whatever that it is a complete fallacy to suppose that Burt and the sociologists of education were ranged on opposite sides on the central issue of heredity, environment, and intelligence. I want to show that the oppositional caricatures I have just drawn up are quite unfounded as far as Burt and the sociologists of education are concerned; that they rest on unsound, false assumptions, and contain misunderstandings of the most fundamental and misleading kind. Strange though this may sound at this point, I want to show quite clearly that, far from adopting a position fundamentally different from that of Burt, and opposed to it, the research of the sociologists of education proceeded exactly along the lines of his own analysis, used the same assumptions, itemized and focused attention upon the same social and environmental factors, and came to the same conclusions.

The wonder is that there could ever have been any misunderstanding of this, and my second aim stems from it. It is to show, equally conclusively, that the specific allegation that Burt underrated the importance of social (and environmental) factors is totally false.

To demonstrate this, it is necessary, first, to consider the position of Burt and that of the sociologists of education separately so that they can be clearly compared.

Heredity and Environment: Burt

It cannot be said too strongly that no one having more than the slightest acquaintance with Burt's work could possibly have arrived at the judgment stated by Gillie. Burt certainly did believe that the level of an individual's mental ability (including some particular aspects of it) was largely determined by heredity, and was in this respect a Hereditarian. We have already said enough on this, and will later note some of his wider supporting arguments. What is equally and just as abundantly clear, however, in all his writings, is that he was just as intensely aware of, and just as deeply convinced about, the many ways in which environmental conditions and influences could stand in the way of the *manifestation* of such ability, the *recognition* of it by educationalists, the adequate *evidencing* of it in *tests* and in *school performance,* and its adequate *development* and *fulfilment* in the child's *educational career.* All his surveys demonstrated to his satisfaction that the distribution of wealth throughout society, and the consequent and very variable environmental conditions within which families lived, were such as to give some children privileged opportunities in education, sometimes to levels of provision going far beyond their own level of ability, and to present others (a massive majority) with a range of obstacles that prevented the recognition and development of their abilities, resulted in educational opportunities that fell far short of what their abilities needed and deserved, and that were well nigh impossible to overcome. No one could have been more conscious of the importance of such conditions and influences than he; no one could have more strongly emphasized them or shown greater concern about them; and few could have been more active in working to overcome them for those who suffered from their disadvantages. The fact that Burt was a Hereditarian by no means meant that he was not, in many important ways, also an Environmentalist. The exclusive polar opposites, in short, were false. Let us briefly, but nonetheless in sufficient detail, make clear Burt's position on these environmental influences and note the analysis of them that he actually undertook.

Burt had had clear, immediate, first-hand knowledge of these wide inequalities of opportunity in the surveys he had conducted in Liverpool, Birmingham, and London, but it was in *The Backward Child,* first published in 1937, that he analyzed the social factors underlying them systematically and in detail.

It is hard to understand how anyone reading this book could possibly fail to become aware of Burt's deeply felt humanity in exploring the nature, kinds, and problems of disadvantage and backwardness in children, and of his intellectual exactitude in studying them. With the greatest care, he distinguished several different categories. Intellectual were distinguished from temperamental subnormalities (the intellectual manifesting themselves "primarily by a delay or an arrest in mental progress"). Innate was distinguished from acquired subnormality.

> A deficiency that is inborn or inherited can never be cured; a shortcoming that is not inherited, but springs from lack of health, from lack of opportunity, or from such accidental cause, is, in theory at any rate, remediable. . . . We have to discriminate . . . between the boy who *cannot* learn, except within the narrowest limits, and the boy who *can* learn, but for some reason or other has never actually done so. The former may be re-called 'innately retarded', or, in one word 'dull'; the latter 'educationally retarded' or *merely* backward', implying by the phrase that the child is backward *in school work only* and not in *natural* development.

General subnormality was also distinguished from specific subnormalities; the "dull" from the "defective." His analysis therefore resulted in a carefully clarified scale of retardation, from children who were "slightly retarded" to those who were "retarded to a serious and extreme degree." But the scrupulous care Burt exercised in drawing up this scale, his awareness of the complex relationships between inherited and environmental factors, and his dominant and constantly prevailing focus of concern on *the individual child,* may be clearly seen in the summary conclusion of his own introduction:

> The lines of division, however, are by no means clear-cut. The defective merge into the dull, and the dull into the normal: those who are subnormal intellectually may display subnormalities in temperament as well, and, time after time, it proves almost impossible to decide whether a particular child's backwardness springs chiefly from innate and ineradicable weakness, or from environmental handicaps, or from both conspiring together towards the same unhappy result. Each child, therefore, must be considered as a unique individual. His psychological classification is nothing but a means to an end, a practical aid rather than an indisputable point of scientific diagnosis.

If this orientation (of a pragmatic kind), and these persuasions, unfitted him for being a *scientist* in psychology, he might well be thought the better for it! In fact, of course, they clearly demonstrated his scientific exactitude.

In the same scrupulous way (and quite contrary to Kamin's testimony), Burt also gave the most detailed account of the tests he employed; and a point of quite central importance must be noted very clearly here. It is, very simply, that no reliable estimation whatever of the degree of intractability of a child's apparent "backwardness" in his or her educational career, or of the extent to which, because of social factors, a child's performance in school has apparently fallen below his or her level of ability, is at all possible without some earlier and established appraisal of what that level of ability is! Any estimation of a wastage of human resources, a falling short of the promise of ability—whether relating to the individual or to society—requires an earlier measurement of such resources, of such ability. Indeed, it rests upon it.

Burt worked clearly on this assumption, finding it essential (1) to assess the mental ability of individuals by carefully constructed and clearly described objective tests (the most reliable, that is, that could be devised); in order (2) to discover, and measure, the extent to which *their actual and subsequent performance in schools* was or was not backward. A measurement of mental ability, a measured potential, was essential before it was at all possible to measure the extent to which children either fell below it or attained a level above it in their actual school achievements.

He also insisted that the tests of ability should be such as to probe effectively beyond those surface appearances that in large part were probably only reflections of the child's environmental context: the range of literacy, numeracy, and cultural awareness, and the extent and quality of his or her vocabulary. In both group and individual tests, therefore, Burt deliberately included both verbal and nonverbal sections. In addition, however, he also required investigations going beyond intelligence tests alone. There had to be, for example, a *physical* examination of a medical and "anthropometric" nature (the latter including a record of the child's course of growth and development, in height, weight, onset of puberty, menstruation, and so forth). In addition, a study of the social context was necessary: of the child's *home circumstances, family history, personal history* (as pieced together from information to be derived from parents, teachers, the social visitor, the medical care of the doctor) and the *school report* (including a report on the child's *conduct*). The grounds for arriving at the most reliable measurement of the child's ability, and then of his or her subsequent school performance and level of achievement in relation to this, were therefore very meticulously laid down.

One of the most impressive aspects of Burt's study (perhaps the most moving) was his detailed revelation of the ways and the extent to which environmental disadvantages brought about educational retardation by sheer *physical* causation, such as serious illness in the early life of children during the preschool period. His description of the development of children—in terms of height, weight, the ossification of bones, dentition, pubescence, and so on, all coupled with chronological age and intelligence—were enormously revealing of the radical and chronic effects of severe degrees of deprivation and malnutrition. Even moreso were his descriptions of physical defects and defects of health—of hearing, sight, speech, enlarged tonsils and adenoids, recurrent cattarh, stunted growth, spinal curvature, marked malnutrition, rickets, St. Vitus dance (chorea), epilepsy—to give only an indicative list of examples. All these were related, too, in his analysis, to kinds of experience, degrees of attention and concentration, patterns of attendance, and problems of behavior, all of which affected the child's responses to school life and school performance.

To read this book is to become overwhelmed by the kinds of deprivation suffered by so large a proportion of children and their families so recently in our history; but it is also to be overwhelmingly appreciative of the contribution Burt made (together with his many colleagues and assistants) towards the alleviation and overcoming of them by the systematic survey, presentation, and analysis of the facts in his surveys—at a time, it must be remembered, when governmental authorities (central and local) were needing and seeking ways of reliably *identifying* the kinds, degrees, and causes of "backwardness" so that they could then know how most adequately to treat them. Reliable knowledge was a necessary foundation for effective action, and this Burt's work undoubtedly supplied.

Here, however, our focus of interest and concern must be on what Burt had to say about the effects upon mental ability and school performance of *social and environmental factors,* and it is of central importance (for our later comparison) to see that in a substantial chapter of some 44 pages these were itemized and analyzed very systematically as those *social and scholastic conditions* that could be said to be among the chief causes of educational backwardness.

Burt began by reporting one basic finding (chiefly demonstrated in his Birmingham and London surveys) that there were very considerable *regional* (and *local*) variations in the *distribution* of backwardness. This led to a consideration of the different social conditions prevailing in these areas and districts—a comparison of death rates, birth rates, and rates of infantile mortality; the incidence of juvenile delinquency; the provision and qualities of schools; the extent and degree of poverty, poor relief, and unemployment; the conditions of overcrowding in neighborhoods and homes; and the size of families. Burt correlated the extent of backwardness with each of these. The highest correlations, for example, were with infantile mortality (.93) and overcrowding (.89); with poverty the correlation was .73, with unemployment .68. But Burt did not simply or readily assume any explanation in merely material terms. He was not sure quite what these correlations entailed, but he found statistical regularities suggesting that intricate, intimate, and difficult to locate and clarify social dimensions (such as kinds and elements of family relationships) were involved. He found, for example, that "the average number of children in families containing at least one backward child is 4.6; in families containing at least one scholarship winner it is 3.3." *Family size* therefore seemed to be significant, but so did the quality of care provided by *the mother* in each family.

> I must emphasize that the injurious agencies are by no means exclusively physical or economic. Lack of space, of sunshine, of fresh air, of adequate and proper food, exposure to infection and to climatic changes, inability to procure medical attention, an initial weakness attributable in part to weakness inherited from the parents and in part to the mother's own ill-health or malnutrition during pregnancy—all this no doubt may help to destroy many young lives among the poor, and leave others permanently impaired. But the most frequent and conspicuous feature is the want of proper maternal care—in a word, the inefficiency of the mother. Often this itself is a result of her poverty and consequent poor health; occasionally it is a result of her erratic temperament; but in a large number of cases, perhaps in most, it seemed the inevitable outcome of her own subnormal intelligence. But whatever may be the remoter factors at work, there can be little question that ill-health during early infancy, before ever the child comes to school, is one of the most important causes of backwardness during the school period itself.

Still, the indications of Burt's overall findings were very clear:

> The coefficients plainly imply that it is in the poor, overcrowded, insanitary households, where families are large, where the children are dependent solely on the State for their education, and where the parents are largely dependent on charity or relief for their own maintenance, where both birth-rates and infantile death-rates are high, and the infant's health is undermined from the earliest days of its life, that educational backwardness is most prevalent.

Even so, he still believed the extent to which these environmental factors were *determining* influences was by no means clear. The close association between the material handicaps of families and the extent of backwardness among children in schools was, however, firmly established:

> To conclude off-hand that in each individual case poverty is the main cause of dullness or incompetence would be neither just nor logical. A

bare smattering of biography is sufficient to refute that simple induction. Bunyan, the tinker, Faraday, the blacksmith's son, Sextus V, the child of a shepherd, Adrian VI, the son of a bargee, Burns, Cook, Giotto, all sons of peasants, d'Alembert, the foundling picked up one Christmas night on the snowy steps of a Parisian church, Romney, Opie, Inigo Jones and Abraham Lincoln, each the son of a carpenter—these and many like them have risen to the loftiest intellectual eminence from the lowliest social spheres. The poorest tenements of London contain many youthful geniuses, some of whom win—more of whom merit but fail to win—a free place or scholarship at a secondary school or college.

Stupidity, therefore, is not the inevitable result of poverty, though poverty seems its commonest concomitant; and to discover more precisely how the two interact, an analysis, not of districts, but of individual cases, will be required. Is it the lowest stocks and the dullest families that gravitate to the slums, and there, by their poor intelligence, perpetuate and even aggravate the squalor that they find? Or do the under-feeding, the over-crowding, and the many daily deprivations, tend to devitalize minds that originally were normal? And if they devitalize some minds, how is it that they leave others apparently unimpaired?

This stated the heredity versus environment question very plainly. Burt then proceeded to examine each particular feature of the social environment in some detail. For our purposes it is enough to note his clear recognition of these features, and to see what they were. It is important, however (bearing in mind our later examination of the work of the sociologists), to note them quite precisely.

First, he examined the *school conditions* in each area: the record of attendance at each school (and the reasons given for absence); the qualities of its teachers, their degree of efficiency, their career conditions (of promotion), and so forth; the nature and efficiency of each school's organization. But then he considered the social conditions beyond the school:

1. *Economic conditions of homes* (their level of income, degree of poverty, and so forth).
2. *Material conditions of their dwelling-places.*
3. *Intellectual and cultural level* of the *parents* (the level of knowledge, stimulation, and encouragement they provided within the home).
4. *Emotional and moral conditions* of the *family* ("the moral atti-

tudes, the cultural background, the emotional relationships between the different relatives''.
5. Conditions (involving a consideration of the same factors) of the
neighborhood within which the particular families lived.

All of these were described and analyzed in some detail, and in
view of what we shall later find in the writings of the sociologists
and education, it is of interest and importance to notice the special
emphasis Burt placed upon certain factors.

When discussing the ''intellectual conditions'' of the home, he
drew a contrast between two working-class families: the lively and
stimulating life of a small family with adequate means, as against
the life of a family suffering from the many-sided limitations of
poverty. In the first, the father was ''a workman with an intelligent
interest in his work,'' the mother ''a woman with the inclination
and the freedom for intellectual pursuits,'' and the two parents
joined together with their children in conversation, games, and
other social activities, including visits to places of interest. Here a
wide range of ''pre-school information and out-of-school acquire-
ments'' was enjoyed and established before school attendance
began, and was continued and extended throughout the child's
ongoing school life.

The life of the family in the poorer home was, by contrast,
culturally impoverished. The point of great interest and significance
here, however, is that Burt's attention was quite specifically focused upon the area of *sociolinguistics:* seeing clearly, and emphasizing the crucial importance of the nature of the *vocabulary*
(impoverished or otherwise) used by the family, and available to
the children of the family, and in relation to the degree of limitation
of the range of perception and experience available to them within
their life-situation. In the culturally impoverished home he described, Burt wrote (italics mine) that the parents

> know astonishingly little of any life except their own, and have neither
> the time nor the leisure, neither the ability nor the disposition, to impart
> what little they know. The mother's conversation may be chiefly limited
> to the topics of cleaning, cooking, and scolding. The father, when not
> at work, may spend most of his time 'round the corner' refreshing a
> worn-out body, or sitting by the fire with cap on and coat off, sucking
> his pipe in gloomy silence. *The vocabulary that the child absorbs is*

restricted to a few hundred words, most of them inaccurate, uncouth, or mispronounced, and the rest unfit for reproduction in the school-room. In the home itself *there is no literature that deserves the title;* and the child's whole universe is closed in and circumscribed by walls of brick and a pall of smoke. From one end of the year to the other, he may go no farther than the nearest shops or the neighboring recreation ground. The country or the seaside *are mere words to him,* dimly suggesting some place to which cripples are sent after an accident, visualized perhaps in terms of some photographic 'souvenir from South-end' or some pictorial 'memento from Margate,' all framed in shells, brought back by his parents on a bank-holiday trip a few weeks after their wedding.

The meagreness of the general information possessed by such a child is difficult to credit. To illustrate its amazing paucity, I may cite the results of a small inquiry made among pupils from the lower standards in one of the poorest quarters just outside the City. The children were mainly between 7 and 8, thorough little Cockneys, having spent, with few exceptions, the whole of their short lives within earshot of Bow bells. Of these town-bred boys and girls, nearly 350 in number, 46 per cent., I found, had never to their knowledge seen any other animal besides a horse, a cat, and a dog; 16 per cent. thought a sheep much larger than a cow; 23 per cent. had never set eyes on a field or a patch of grass, even in a Council park; 64 per cent. had never travelled in a train; and 98 per cent. had never seen the sea. With an intellectual background such as this, *how many of the statements conveyed to them by teachers or by reading-books must remain mere meaningless formulae with no mental picture to correspond!*[1]

It is especially interesting to note Burt's emphasis upon the limited *quantity* of words, the sheer *range* of the vocabulary, as well as upon their extremely limited *qualitative* nature and kinds of *experiential reference* (coupled, of course, with the absence in the home of any "literature that deserves the title").

At the same time, Burt was by no means guilty of seeing a child's experience within a materially poor home and neighborhood as being necessarily lacking in richness of perception, observation, activity, excitement, and food for the wide exercise of imagination and profitable learning—by contrast with a child's experience in some more well-to-do homes and areas. Burt knew and had enjoyed Robert Louis Stevenson's essay "Apology for Idlers!" The child from a poor home could enjoy the life of the streets and gain much from it.

Should the lad live near a railway terminus, or close to a busy thorough-fare with its large and inviting shop windows or lively bills and posters on the hoardings, he will often pick up, during his desultory rambles, some vivid and fragmentary notions about the civilized world of to-day. Many a small child has gleaned a knowledge of money values from the tickets in shop windows; has practised reading from the huge advertise-ments on the hoardings; and has learnt his geography of England from an illuminated map outside a station. But at times, it must be confessed, the features of the city streets are all too stimulating. The East-ender is tempted to shirk shcool for the fun of prowling round the docks; and the West-ender to spend in the picture palace or the fun fair hours that should be given to healthy recreation out of doors.

The London street, he added, quoting with approval from Steven-son, is "that mighty place of education, the favourite school of Dickens and Defoe."

Just as certainly, however, for some well brought up children in well-to-do neighborhoods, the life of the streets was so monotonous as to be almost nonexistent. Respectability had choked to death any semblance of life in it.

If the child's ramblings are limited to those genteel suburban areas, where nothing is to be seen but row after row of red-brick villas, or block after block of tenement buildings, where 'Respectability' (in the phrase of the American satirist) 'stalks the byways unashamed,' what is there to stir his imagination or to kindle his childish interests? In these dull but decorous districts, the code of the inhabitants is severely against their children 'being seen in the streets.' Hence, even when there is the stimulus of stores and stations and picture-palace placards near at hand, and thrilling episodes to be witnessed from the kerbstone, the prudent parent, not wholly without reason, will forbid her boy to loiter outside the house. The shopping is done, not by the child, but by the mother; the child stays at home and plays in the small back-yard. And so he loses, not only fresh air and companionship, but the sharp-ness of eye, the readiness of response, and all the titbits of miscellane-ous information that the street arab, less vigilantly supervised, preco-ciously snaps up for him.[2]

But there is another striking example of Burt's insight in one other well-marked emphasis he made within the over-all presenta-tion of his findings. When summarizing his conclusions as to the degree of influence exerted by each of the features of the home and neighborhood environment on the educational performance of the child in school, he quite deliberately emphasized the role of the mother as being probably the factor of greatest importance among them all.

> If . . . I were to single out the one feature in the home which showed the closest relation to the child's school progress, it would be, not the economic or industrial status of the family, but the efficiency of the mother. We have already noted how closely this conditions the child's physical development during the first few years of life. But in later years it has an immediate influence, no less profound, on the child's whole intellectual growth. At the same time, by affecting his comfort, cheerfulness, conscientiousness, and bodily fitness from day to day, it acts through subtler channels, indirect as well as direct. Wherever the child's mother is lacking in intelligence, in temperamental stability, or in general force of character, where she is indifferent to the mental welfare of her family, or herself overburdened by domestic worries or by frailties of heredity and health, there the child's whole mental and moral development suffers together.[3]

Even these emphases within Burt's overall survey are not enough, however, to indicate the considerable degree of importance he attached to features of the environment as being such as to exert profound qualitative influences on the nature, direction, and level of aspiration and achievement of a child's performance within and beyond the field of education. There was one other emphasis— indeed one other entirely distinctive strand or dimension of reality and analysis (frequently completely left out of account by his critics)—that Burt believed to be of the greatest importance. With his consistently maintained focus of attention and concern upon the *uniqueness of each individual child,* Burt believed that *neither* genetically established *heredity* on the one hand *nor* objectively given features of the *environment* on the other (whether considered separately or taken together in their interconnections) were enough for a satisfactory explanation of a child's personal development. Given a certain inherited endowment, given a certain environmental context, each child, with its own nature, temperament, and dispositions, was *an experiencing and learning individual,* accommodating himself or herself creatively to the people, qualities of life and society, models and goals of behavior, and ideals and values, that he or she encountered. In short, *character* (something involving personal choice, decision, will, commitment, self-discipline, endeavor, and in all of this, *creativity*) was also centrally involved.

Throughout his entire lifetime of work, Burt held this position. He *never* maintained that the inherited basis of mental ability was enough for understanding the nature of a child's educational career or the degree of achievement or fulfilment in it (or indeed, for understanding the distribution of such degrees of achievement throughout society). He *always* maintained that environmental factors and influences were of crucial importance, for better or for worse. But he also always insisted on this central importance for individual and society alike of individual *character,* which indicates once again how far his conception of *education* went beyond the formal pattern of instruction provided in schools within the educational system. This emphasis on environmental factors, an understanding of them and realization of their importance on the part of teachers, for the purpose of devoting themselves effectively to the cultivation of the mind of the individual child, was very clear throughout *The Backward Child* itself. Indeed, in that book, it was perhaps the most dominant emphasis:

> The characteristics of the backward child's home, family, and neighborhood I have discussed in some detail, because, though older teachers must be sufficiently familiar with all I have described, the inexperienced have still to learn what a powerful influence is exercised upon their pupils' work by circumstances outside the school walls. In huge cities like London, the teacher often lives miles away from his pupils; and, though the parents may come to the school, the masters seldom visit the homes. It is only when a teacher has moved from one district to another, and taught a wide variety of children, that he begins to appreciate how differences in social conditions may entirely alter the type of mind with which he has to cope. . . . Our next step, therefore, must be to turn from the environment to the child itself (p. 134).

This emphasis was also repeated and insisted upon in what was probably Burt's last article:

> Intelligence is by no means the only factor determining the child's educational progress. There are the special abilities and disabilities that emerge and mature during the years of growth; there are his qualities of temperament and character—the ambitions that he cherishes and the aims that he forms. These, like general intelligence, are also largely

influenced by the child's inborn constitution; but they are far more liable to be swayed by the conditions and events of his daily life, at home, at school, and wherever he meets his boon companions.[4]

One remaining feature of Burt's position, however, also needs the clearest and strongest of statements. Though certainly wanting children of high intelligence ("gifted children") to be given the most excellent level of educational provisions their ability deserved (whatever their social origins), and being to that extent a convinced and confessed "elitist," Burt was far from being elitist in any narrow sense of looking down on those who had been endowed with lesser capacities, or of thinking that only a diminished degree of consideration need be devoted to their claims. In addition to advocating the public provision of scholarship places so that children from financially disadvantaged families could enjoy opportunities at the same level of "higher" education, he also wanted all children, at all levels, to be given the same consideration, and to enjoy those educational opportunites and provisions that were the most appropriate to their own abilities and special aptitudes. He advocated the richest diversity of provisions possible to maximize such opportunities. In relation to this, he was opposed to the simplistic notion that this could be achieved by the imposition throughout the country of one particular kind of school. He was most decidedly not, on the basis of either principled or practical considerations, opposed to the comprehensive school; only to the political and educational idea that this one kind of school would be universally effective; could achieve these educational ends satisfactorily in all areas and in relation to all conditions of social fact.

Aware of the wide differences in the distribution of population in the different geographical regions of the country; similarly aware of the different collective conditions of the concentrations of population in the different areas and districts of large cities, towns, and conurbations (and therefore of the considerable variations in the qualities of different "catchment areas"); he thought that the most appropriate kinds of schools in different areas would necessarily differ, for different factual and administrative reasons. It was simplistic, furthermore, even to believe that one kind of school ("comprehensive" school, "secondary modern" school, or whatever) would ever be qualitatively the same throughout the country simply by carrying the same name. Given the varying actuality of social facts, each "category" was bound to contain widely differing specific instances. Burt therefore, argued for an open-minded and experimental approach to this question; the essential thing being a clear-minded realization of the need for careful assessment and selection if the provisions made (in whatever kind of school) were in fact to meet the really existing educational needs and objectives. This was also stated with perfect clarity in the same latter-day article.

Burt's position on the matter of heredity and environment was therefore completely clear, as is the obvious absurdity of the assertion that he either ignored or underrated social and environmental factors and their influences. Let us now consider, by way of comparison, the position on this same matter of "the sociologists of education."

Heredity and Environment: The Sociologists of Education

By "sociologists of education" I mean that group of researchers who worked within the context of the study of social mobility initiated by David Glass, and some of those individuals whose work stemmed directly from it. Quite specifically, I mean (1) David Glass himself, Jean Floud, Hilde Himmelweit, and F. M. Martin, who were among the contributors to the first book *Social Mobility in Britain,* which, published in 1954,[5] set out, in a number of connected studies the entire scale and project of the research; (2) Jean Floud, A. H. Halsey, and F. M. Martin, who produced the small but influential book on *Social Class and Educational Opportunity* in 1957[6]; (3) J. W. B. Douglas and his team, who produced *The Home and the School* in 1964[7] (and later, in 1968, All Our Future[8]); and (4) Basil Bernstein and his colleagues, who produced the series of volumes on *Primary Socialization, Language and Education* between 1970 and 1975.[9] All these studies[10] shared the same focus of concentration and concern: the actual nature and extent of social mobility in Britain; the educational system of selection for grammar school places at the age of 11-plus as the crucial avenue that determined it; the inequality of opportunity and the injustice of this (resting on class differences); and the several social conditions, influences, and mechanisms (such as 'socialization") that underlay and most probably sustained these inequalities.

All were postwar studies rooted in the same facts, injustices, and social and educational problems pointed out (and demonstrated) by Burt in his 1943 paper. Burt's had been a forward-looking diagnosis offered *before the end of the war;* the work of this group was a body of social research *continuing after the war*—investigating the extent to which the same facts, injustices and problems remained and, in particular, how far the changes brought about by (or at least envisaged in) the 1944 Education Act were proving successful in providing a remedy. Extensive and detailed, this whole body of postwar research was and remains, obviously, open to a wide range of criticisms, by no means entirely of an adverse or negative nature. The very concept of "social mobility" (and of "perfect mobility" set up as a statistical criterion for its measurement) and of its desirability, is itself open to question, as are many of the assumptions and methods employed. Here, however, the consideration facing us is simple and direct. Given the adversarial caricature we have drawn up, that which became so firmly established, of Burt as the right-wing Hereditarian-inegalitarian-elitist still favoring testing and selection and, on this basis, a differential range of opportunities and provisions; versus the sociologists of education as the left-wing Environmentalist-egalitarians opposing testing, selection, and segregation, the "educational ladder" conception of opportunity and its elitism, and favoring the equal provision of comprehensive education for all; given this, we have to ask what was the difference between the two? In what crucial and distinctive ways did the position of the sociologists of education differ from that of Burt? In their actual work—in its assumptions, concepts, methods, conclusions, and emphases—what was the essential difference?

The answer—astonishingly—is: *none!* Quite literally, *there were no differences at all!* To make our comparisons as convincingly argued and telling as possible, it might be best to begin by voicing a quite fundamental criticism of the account we have given of Burt's own position. The objection could be raised that the demonstration that Burt did in fact take environmental factors and influences into account does not in the slightest degree alter the fact that he was a Hereditarian. His position was, and always remained, that heredity was the chief determinant of the differences of mental ability in children, and therefore of its distribution throughout the population of any society, and that the influences of features of the environment (in many ways, and for good or ill) were only upon its course of development. The position of the Environmentalist, however (it might be said), is much more radical than this. The Environmentalist claims that children are born equal; that there is no evidence to suggest otherwise[11]; and that the different mental abilities of children are brought into being, are literally *caused by,* the environmental conditions and influences to which they are exposed: by everything (family, kin relationships, neighborhood, class, religion, quality of culture, linguistic usages, and so forth) that together, in the totality of their complexity, comprises their situation. Here, it is not to our purpose to enter into any argument about these opposed positions; they simply serve to sharpen the starkness of our answer.

Let me make a number of quite forthright statements that may well seem utterly unbelievable at this stage, but that will be seen to be completely true.

Not one of these sociologists of education was an Environmentalist as so defined. Not a single piece of evidence was ever produced in the entire range of the research to demonstrate that mental ability was environmentally determined, and for the simple reason that this possibility was never either posed or faced. The studies never made any proposals, or reported any conclusions, on the matter. The closest approach to any consideration of it was its being raised simply as a question by Floud, Halsey, and Martin, but it was never at all investigated. The fact is that not one of these sociologists at all doubted that intelligence was in large part established by heredity. On the contrary, all their studies rested on the assumption that it was. The entire focus of all these studies was upon the ways in which—given the existence of a certain (and a measurable) endowment of mental ability in children—social conditions, factors, and influences could operate in such ways as to obscure it, stand in the way of its recognition (in the tests for selection), development, and fulfilment; so leading to inequalities of opportunity and injustices in educational provisions; and therefore to subsequent injustices in occupational opportunities with their correlated statuses in society, to the underdevelopment of individual talent, and to social wastage. The emphasis throughout was not on the environmental causation of mental ability but on the ways in which social and environmental conditions influenced the accuracy of recognition of it and the child's subsequent school performance and entire educational career, with all that this entailed for life in society thereafter. This—as can be plainly and readily seen—was a position in no way whatever different from that of Burt.

Furthermore, in seeking to measure the kinds and degrees of influence exerted by environmental factors, all these studies employed carefully devised intelligence tests to establish the level of the child's mental ability. Each of them— specifying the tests used (and particularly using nonverbal as well as verbal and "attainment" tests)—measured the mental ability of the child (established his or her "measured potential") so that they could subsequently measure the child's school performance and level of achievement against this, and so assess the effects upon it of the several environmental features. The two points we have mentioned before were again very clearly evidenced here. First, there would be no possibility whatever of measuring the effects of environmental factors if there was no reliable measurement of the child's intelligence beforehand. To assess the effects of environmental influences actually requires—necessitates—some earlier (or at least independent) measurement of the child's mental endowment; and this mention of an independent measurement leads directly to the second point. All these studies assumed that the carefully constructed intelligence tests they employed (nonverbal as well as verbal) did measure the child's level of mental ability *independently of their environmental contexts;* independently, for example, of *their class origins.* It was accepted, throughout the research, that the objective tests of intelligence did provide a satisfactory and reliable measurement of mental ability, operating across all the boundaries of social class and being independent of them. Had this not been so, again, the exercise of trying to measure the effect of environmental influences upon this given mental ability would have been rendered pointless and impossible. The method employed by all these sociologists of education, then, was by intelligence tests to measure the mental ability or "measured potential" of children, and then to compare this with their subsequent school performance and educational career, in order to discover and demonstrate the influence of social and environmental factors. Again, this can be seen to be in no way whatever different from the assumptions and the method employed by Burt.

Other exact similarities and agreements could be just as forth-rightly stated: the fact, for example, that these sociologists favored the use of objective tests in the assessment and selection of children as against any reliance on the subjective judgments and appraisals of teachers; the fact that all the environmental factors actually specified and considered (home conditions, qualities of parents, family-size) were the same as those itemized by Burt; the fact that those selected for special emphasis (vocabulary and linguistic us-age, the role of the mother) were also the same. Let us pursue these matters with specific and exact reference to the studies themselves.

Social Mobility: David Glass

In this first study, the investigation of educational opportunity in relation to social mobility did not go far. It is of immediate interest, however, to note the classification of occupations (and ''social grades'') on the basis of which movement between the social classes was measured (table 8.1[12]). This classification can be com-pared with that employed earlier by Burt.[13]

The educational avenue to social mobility was very decidedly emphasized, but the study of it was still limited, pointing to the restriction of opportunity before the 1944 Act and the hopes for its extension afterwards. Distinguishing between the ''educational lad-der'' conception of opportunity (and provisions) and that of ''the policy of secondary education for all,'' and claiming that ''the educational system has become the primary agency of occupational and social selection,'' Jean Floud showed in her study of the educational experience of the adult population how limited oppor-tunities had been for earlier generations, especially for children of the semiskilled and unskilled working class, and looked upon the 1944 Act as the provision of a new framework of reform:

> It constitutes a promise of change in the nature and distribution of educational opportunity which, if it materializes, will almost certainly be accompanied by considerable changes both in the social hierarchy of occupations and in the degree of mobility within and between occupations.[14]

TABLE 8.1.
Social Grading

1 *Occupation*	2 *Standard Classification*
Medical Officer	1
Company Director	1
Country Solicitor	1
Chartered Accountant	1
Civil Servant (Exec.)	2
Business Manager	2
Works Manager	2
Nonconformist Minister	2
Farmer	1
Elementary School Teacher	3
Jobbing Master Builder	3
News Reporter	3
Commercial Traveller	3
Chef	4
Insurance Agent	4
Newsagent and Tobacconist	4
Policeman	5
Routine Clerk	5
Fitter	5
Carpenter	5
Shop Assistant	5
Bricklayer	5
Tractor Driver	6
Coal Hewer	5
Railway Porter	7
Agricultural Labourer	6
Carter	6
Barman	7
Dock Labourer	7
Road Sweeper	7

Hilde Himmelweit also claimed that "secondary education of the grammar school type" had come to provide "the main avenue for upward social mobility for the children of the 'working class' " and that "*successful* attendance at a grammar school" was becoming "increasingly the necessary first qualification for entry into salaried occupations." Her study, based upon questionnaires and tests administered to over 700 young adolescent boys in London grammar and secondary modern schools, showed again that working-class children from the lower occupational grades were underrepresented in grammar schools, and indeed, that some boys possessing high IQs in secondary modern schools revealed some errors of assessment and selection. In giving the basis of calculation of such underrepresentation, Dr. Himmelweit echoed Burt's own findings, and actually quoted the source of his agreement.[15] Variations in IQ *within* occupational groups, she said (repeating Burt's frequently reiterated point), were generally greater than those *between* them, and therefore very large groups (like those of the semiskilled and unskilled workers) were likely to contain a larger absolute number of children with the requisite ability, compared with much smaller (middle-class) groups with a higher average intelligence. Furthermore, her assumption here, too—specially mentioned in a footnote—was that "intelligence was to some degree genetically determined."[16] In seeking explanations of this underrepresentation, the environmental factors discussed (and their effects) were also the same as those indicated by Burt: the fact, for example, that lower-working-class children did less well on attainment tests in the selection examination; that family size and the ordinal position within the family seemed significantly correlated factors, as did the cultural level of parents and homes and the presence (or absence) of the knowledge, stimulation, and encouragement they gave; and other similar, and by now reasonably well-known, influences.

Similarly, the factors affecting the child's school performance after selection were the same, including those underlying and influencing teachers' assessments of these performances. The degree of industriousness, responsibility, and apparent moral and social characteristics (including manners of behavior) shown by pupils were seen and judged by teachers as being notably different among children from different homes: middle-class teachers approving of middle-class children. The same differences in the features of family and social background were also found to affect such things as the seriousness of children's concern over their "progress" in school performance, their degree of participation in extracurricular activities, the extent to which they had favorable facilities for doing homework, and the attitudes they held towards the possible extension of their education beyond school-leaving age. In all this, too, the active interest of parents in their childrens' education, their visits to the school, their support of extracurricular activities, were found to be important. Success within the grammar school was therefore still found to be "partly determined by the boy's class membership," and Dr. Himmelweit's conclusion was that "the change since the Education Act of 1944 has not yet made itself felt in the climate of the school."

These findings were complemented in a study by F. M. Martin; but the most decided emphasis on the significance of grammar school education for social status and social mobility was that made by David Glass himself, together with J. R. Hall, in their chapter on "Education and Social Mobility."[17] It was, they claimed, "the type of secondary schooling" that most affected "the degree of association between parental and filial status," and here "it is the significance of the grammar school (or its equivalent) which stands out sharply." A grammar school education meant the continuity of a high association between the status of fathers and sons in the higher occupational groups, but a lowering of this association in the lower groups. Even so, the overall picture showed that "education as such appears to modify, but not to destroy, the characteristic association between the social status of fathers and sons."

Clearly there was nothing here that ran at all counter to Burt's own description and analysis of the situation; neither was there any greater scale or degree of rigor in the investigation—despite the fact that these researches were now being undertaken by social *scientists* seeking knowledge, not *pragmatic officials* (as Burt had for a long time been) undertaking surveys for use by local authorities. One strand of doubt, however, ran conspicuously throughout the whole of the book: the question as to how far the 1944 Act was being effectively implemented. Would this legislative change, and the intentions embodied in it, actually bring about the results desired? Would equality of opportunity be achieved?

Social Class and Educational Opportunity:
Floud, Halsey, and Martin

Social class and educational opportunity was the matter specifically addressed, in their book,[18] by Jean Floud, A. H. Halsey, and F. M. Martin. They shared the assumptions that education had come to play "the crucial part in the processes of occupational selection and mobility," that the "decisive event" within this process had long been the selection or rejection for secondary education at eleven-plus, and that marked inequalities of opportunity had existed in this process of selection. They believed that the changes following the 1944 Act had been such as to *intensify* the significance, in public awareness, of this entire process of educational selection and therefore the degree of *competitiveness* within it. "Equality of educational opportunity," they believed, had become firmly established in public and professional opinion as "equality of economic and social opportunity through education in a secondary school," with the consequence that "what had been intended as a qualifying examination" had been converted into "a severe competition for secondary school places." The crucial competition, furthermore, though focused on *grammar school places,* was no longer for these school places alone. Success or failure in the eleven-plus examination, now that there was "secondary education for all," had come to mean success or failure as a total person, a decisive labeling of individuals for their places and their life-chances in society for the whole of their lives afterwards. The study therefore set out to document the effects of "the post-war educational revolution" by giving an up-to-date account of "the social distribution of access to grammar schools" in relation to "the social distribution of ability as measured by intelligence tests," and in order to do this satisfactorily it was deliberately limited in scope, confining itself to a detailed examination of two areas that differed in significant ways.

The South West Educational Division of Hertfordshire was a relatively prosperous area with a wide variety of small and medium-sized firms, engaged in many kinds of manufacture, employing a wide range of skills, suffering very little from poverty and unemployment, and was therefore well-suited to "provide the maximum response to post-war measures of educational reform." The community in *Middlesbrough,* by contrast, rested upon heavy industry (iron and steel and related trades, with a dearth of light industry) and suffered the severe fluctuations of employment/unemployment, and well-being/poverty, that were attendant upon its changing fortunes. During the 1930s it had suffered greatly from the Depression, thirty percent of its workforce having been unemployed. Though no two areas could ever be said to be completely "representative" of the nation as a whole, these two communities, with their extreme differences, were thought to offer at least the ground for worthwhile comparative study. The findings could be expected to be of wide significance. What, then, were these findings?

Perhaps astonishingly, the results of the study demonstrated that class inequalities in the selection of children for grammar school places had been well nigh completely eliminated! Even by the early 1950s, equality of educational opportunity in this sense had in fact been achieved. All the children whose abilities warranted grammar school education had in fact been selected for such education, whatever their social and class origins. This was so important a conclusion that its definite statement by the authors themselves needs to be noted. Bearing in mind that their declared object was "to look more closely than was possible on a national scale into the part played by the educational system in the process of educational selection, and at the impact of the Education Act of 1944 on the particular role of the grammar schools," their conclusion was quite plain and unambiguous:

> In the years of our enquiry in both areas, virtually the full quota of boys with the necessary minimum IQ from each occupational group in the population were awarded places in grammar schools. If by 'ability' we mean 'measured intelligence' and by 'opportunity' access to grammar schools, then opportunity may be said to stand in close relationship with ability in both these areas today. Though they are not in any strict sense representative areas they are by no means untypical of their kind, and we may reasonably conclude that in very many, if not in most, parts of the country the chances of children at a given level of ability entering grammar schools are no longer dependent on their social origins.[19]

The conclusion seems to have surprised even the authors themselves:

The very close similarity in both areas between the numbers of children of each occupational group who were allocated to grammar schools in the years of our enquiry and the numbers who might have been expected to gain admission had places been allocated on the basis of intelligence test performance only, is the more surprising when it is recalled that the selection procedures employed were fairly complex and included several different measures of ability.[20]

They were led, therefore, to scrutinize the nature of the eleven-plus examination and the methods of selection in each area, as these included at least two elements that went beyond "intelligence test performance." These were (1) the subjective judgments of the head teachers of primary schools and (2) the large weighting of the attainment tests in English and arithmetic, which (like the estimations of teachers) had long been supposed to reflect differences in the child's social and cultural background. These were subjected to detailed examination (particularly "at the border-line of success") in a completely fair and open-minded way—with a fairness and open-mindedness, it may be said, and a faithfulness to facts discovered, that marked the whole of this investigation—and the outcome was that neither factor proved such as to affect their earlier conclusion. As to the subjective judgment of Heads: "Our analysis gave no indication of any such bias"; and as to the relationships between English and arithmetic test results and the IQs of middle-class and working-class children, these were so variable as to carry no evidence of any influence that would have changed the actual selection decision. Even after this careful check, therefore, the authors' conclusion remained quite definite:

It seemed justifiable to conclude, therefore, that neither subjective bias nor diversity of performance in attainment tests, relative to intelligence, is in fact prejudicing the chances of working-class children. The present differences in proportion of the contribution of the various occupational classes to the grammar school intake can be explained almost entirely in terms of the unequal distribution of measured intelligence.

Our findings as to the social distribution of measured intelligence are closely consistent with those of earlier enquiries, and provide an adequate explanation of these differences. Virtually the full quota of boys with the requisite minimum IQ from every class was admitted to grammar schools and the distribution of opportunity stands today in closer relationship to that of ability (as measured by intelligence tests) than ever before.[21]

This, however, was not the end, and not the whole, of the study. These findings referred purely and simply to "access to grammar school places" in relation to the distribution of "measured intelligence," and the authors went beyond this in two ways—though one of these was by no more than the raising of a question.

In the first place, arguing that to think of educational opportunity only in terms of selection at eleven-plus was far too narrow and limited a conception, they claimed that the unequal influences of class differences had now come to show themselves at other significant points in the school and educational careers of children. Though a marked nationwide similarity in the attitudes of parents in the direction of supporting their childrens' education was discovered (indeed, that "what are often taken to be characteristically 'middle-class' attitudes and ambitions in the matter of education are, in fact, widespread among parents much lower in the occupational scale,") it was found that the influences of family and social background (including some traditional expectations in the two different communities) did affect the length of grammar school education; in particular, the decision whether or not to enter *the sixth form* and, if entering, to complete the course of work there. Strangely, once that particular hurdle was past, it did not affect the moving on, beyond the school, to university. It was *the point of entry into the sixth form,* and, if entering, *the completion of sixth form courses,* that seemed now to have become the new turning-point of significance.

> The great improvement already noticed in the proportion of working-class boys remaining at school beyond the age of compulsory attendance has not resulted in a greater proportion of them completing the grammar school course in the approved way by obtaining a leaving certificate. In fact, as a group, they are primarily responsible for the size of the hard core of pupils who leave without a certificate.

> In each area about twice as high a proportion of working-class boys as before the war take Higher School Certificate. But whereas before the war there were in neither area any notable class differences in the proportion of boys taking Higher School Certificate . . . from 1948–50, for which years comparable figures are available, the class differences were very marked in both areas. In South West Hertfordshire more than half of the sons of professional and business men and more than one-third of the lower middle-class boys left with Higher School Certif-

icates, as compared with only just over a quarter of the working-class boys. In Middlesbrough the relevant proportions were one-third, one-fifth, and 13 per cent, respectively.

Those working-class boys who stay to take the Higher School Certificate have a much greater chance of proceeding to a university . . . but the chances that a boy from a professional or business family would reach a university were in 1948–50 still twice as great in South West Hertfordshire and almost three times as great in Middlesbrough, although it is worth noting that this increase at the university level is no greater than that already noted at the Higher School Certificate level. That is to say, *social* as distinct from *academic* selection is at work *at the threshold of the Sixth Form,* but is *not* at work to any extent worth noting (in these two areas) *at the point of entry to the university* for those who manage to secure the necessary qualifications.[22]

Having pointed to this remaining inequality, the study went on to consider which social factors were responsible for it; which had come to be the commonly recognized kinds of social and environmental differences that exercised influence upon educational performance. These included the large regional differences in educational provisions throughout the country; the differences in the qualities of schools; the material conditions of homes and neighborhoods; the distribution of incomes; the size of families; the cultural level and attitudes of parents; and, given these, the relationship between the home and the school. All these were examined, with varying degrees of importance attached to each. For our purpose, however, it is important only to notice the one or two facts relating to the work of Burt.

The environmental factors thought to be the ones most likely to act on the mental ability of children in such ways as to affect their opportunities for selection and their subsequent performance and careers in and beyond school were, of course, exactly the same as those outlined in *The Backward Child.* Nothing was new here. Similarly, the basic method employed was exactly the same: namely, that of comparing the child's actual performance and career with his or her "measured intelligence." Nothing whatever was new either in substance or method; only the formulation and design of the study (as a comparative study of two communities) and some of the specific findings—that, for example, educational opportunity had in fact been *successfully* extended to a point of equality as far as selection for grammar school places was concerned. Nothing whatever in all this was different in conception from the position of Burt. Nothing contraverted either his methods or his findings. Yet no reference was made either to the work of Burt in general or more particularly to the environmental features to which he had specially called attention in *The Backward Child*. Is this not strange, when reference was made to other studies of the 1930s (such as those of Moshinsky and Gray) that were far more limited?

Perhaps equally important, however, is a final consideration. Floud, Halsey, and Martin did also voice their doubts as to how far ability could be equated with "measured intelligence." Part of their dissatisfaction on this point lay in the often-repeated fact that measured intelligence frequently rested on an overweighting of the verbal skills and attainment tests—which might be no more than a simple reflection of a child's class and cultural conditions; no more than "acquired responses." All this, however, was already very-well-trodden ground, and their question seemed to go beyond it in at least voicing the possibility that intelligence might at least to some extent be *environmentally determined;* in the more fundamental sense, environmentally *caused*. Their disquiet did at least lead them to raise the fundamental Environmentalist question. Just as they thought access to grammar schools a far too narrowly conceived criterion of "educational success," so they thought the IQ "an arbitrary criterion of ability (in view of the extent to which intelligence tests reflect current educational organization and practice, and measured intelligence represents a set of acquired aptitudes)."[23] In their final conclusion, having so clearly demonstrated the close fit between IQ and grammar school selection, they nonetheless went on to say:

> Yet the problem of inequality of educational opportunity is not thereby disposed of.
>
> We have considered some of the material and cultural differences in the environment of the children who succeed, as distinct from those who do not succeed, in the selection examination for secondary education, and we have shown how the success of children varies with the distribution of these features of the environment even at the same social level. Since measured intelligence is so closely related to the results of

the selection procedure our findings are relevant to the problem of the influence of environment on intelligence test scores. But this was not our direct concern, and the features of the environment we have selected for study cannot, of course, be regarded as *social determinants of intelligence*. Nevertheless, though they touch on less fundamental problems, certain conclusions do emerge concerning the part played by differences of environment in *the social distribution of educational opportunity*.[24]

The italics in this passage are mine, and again, we need note only a few points. First, there is nothing in this which is at all foreign or contrary to Burt's position. He had himself clearly pointed out the environmental factors affecting the social distribution (and inequalities) of educational opportunity. Second, although vaguely intimating (it was no more than this) that—*beyond influencing intelligence test scores*—some environmental factors might possibly be *determinants* of intelligence, it was explicitly stated that this could not be so regarded here! The question had been raised, but the claim was not made. Indeed, it was explicitly disavowed. And third, therefore, this study did not at all, in any way, advance an *Environmentalist* theory of the determination of intelligence as opposed to a Hereditarian theory; nor did it suggest or provide any evidence whatever in support of such a theory. Just like Burt, it measured educational *performance* against *measured intelligence* to clarify the nature and extent of *educational opportunity* among the children of the various *occupational grades and social classes*.

The study's conclusion was that as the gross material deprivations of the interwar years were being progressively eliminated, so were all the conditions of inequality of opportunity attendant on these. In some respects (such as selection for grammar schools) they had been eliminated almost completely; but now "the social factors influencing educational selection" were "revealing themselves in more subtle forms."

The problem of equality of educational opportunity is now more complicated than when it took the simple form of the need to secure free access to grammar schools on equal intellectual terms. With the expansion of educational opportunity and the reduction of gross economic handicaps to children's school performance the need arises to understand the optimum conditions for the integration of school and home environment at all social levels in such a way as to minimize the educational disadvantages of both and to turn their educational advantages to full account.[25]

There was nothing here with which Burt would have disagreed. No opposing position had even been attempted, let alone established.

The Home and the School: J. W. B. Douglas

The researches of J. W. B. Douglas and his team[26] were such that they might well have been supposed specially designed to study the area to which Floud, Halsey, and Martin had pointed: "the optimum conditions for the integration of school and home environment." Stemming from the same concern about the inequalities of opportunity in education, and from the same realization of the *complexity* of the environmental features and influences that were most probably responsible for this, their work focused entirely upon the relationships between homes and schools in different regional, class, and neighborhood conditions, and examined these by following a whole cohort of children through their educational careers from primary school onwards. The cohort included (apart from illegitimate children and twins) "all children born during the first week of March, 1946, to the wives of non-manual workers and of farm labourers, and one quarter of those born to the wives of other types of manual workers and self-employed persons," thus constituting a very wide-ranging sample. The declared purpose was "to describe the test performance of children coming from different home backgrounds and to relate them to the results of the secondary selection examinations," with the basic assumption that "when assessing social class differences in secondary selection, interest centres on those children who are competing for grammar school places in the 11 + examination." Douglas shared the belief of Floud, Halsey, and Martin that, although it had not been originally intended that selection for secondary schools should be by competitive examination, following the 1944 Education Act that was what it had become. Failing to heed the warnings of a Board of Education statement of 1943, it had come indeed to subject children to "the strain of a competitive examination on which not only their future schooling, but their future careers may depend." Douglas, however, was critical of the earlier book's conclusion that inequality and wastage had been "pushed forward into the grammar school," and claimed that these were still evident in the process of selection itself.

Again, however, our own purpose is only to look at the assumptions and methods employed, and briefly to note the study's chief findings to the extent necessary to compare them with the position put forward by Burt.

The research was particularly detailed in that it tested the intelligence of children twice: at the age of eight years and three months, and then again just before they were eleven, a few weeks before they were to sit for the eleven-plus examination. The tests were of the same kind as those employed by Burt. They were *group tests,* and were *supervised by the children's teachers.* As with Burt, teacher-assistants administered many of the tests, not the investigators themselves. At age eight, the test had four components: picture intelligence, sentence completion, reading, and vocabulary. At eleven, the same reading and vocabulary tests were repeated, together with a new intelligence test (diagrams and words replacing pictures) and an arithmetic test in place of the sentence completion. It is important also to note that like those of Burt, these tests were careful to employ nonverbal as well as verbal elements, and to give both verbal and nonverbal scores. All these results (at each age) were converted into overall "T" (test) scores that are akin to IQs.[27] These two succeeding scores of "measured ability" were then compared with each other and with the actual examination results, success or failure in selection for grammar schools, and subsequent school-performance, in order to assess the influence upon them of environmental factors.

The chief points to be noted are these. First, Douglas and his team were quite definite in their acceptance of the existence of a level of mental ability established by *heredity.* Though examining the ways in which environmental conditions could influence the development or the retrogression of this ability, and believing indeed that they did exert such influences, no claim whatever was made to the effect that intelligence was *environmentally determined.* The position put forward by this research was not Environmentalist in this sense. Douglas was quite clear and specific about this:

When considering the relation between environment and educational opportunity, I recognise that *innate endowment* may well be the most powerful influence in determining the level of achievement at school. But even if outside factors such as the parents' interest and encouragement, home circumstances, or the quality of teaching have only a small effect on performance, their combined action may lead to a considerable waste of talent owing to the exclusion from grammar schools of children who, given other homes or other schools, would have succeeded in getting there. There is evidence that extreme poverty of the environment (such as surrounded mill children in North Carolina, or canal boat children in England), leads to a *progressive deterioration in academic ability*.[1] At the other extreme, some families have a tradition of making the best use of their brains and their lives and this may depend more on methods of upbringing than on inherited traits. In such families the children are stimulated in numerous ways and are kept busy playing games that demand thought, and so from their earliest years acquire a totally different attitude to learning. I am not, of course, talking here only of 'innate' intelligence, but of the ability to succeed in school studies, which requires qualities of will and continuity of effort. Failure to acquire these will lead to a waste of ability that no redistribution of grammar school places or refinements of 11 + selection can avoid.[28]

[1]Jordan, A. M. (1933). Neff, W. S. (1938).

It may be noted in connection with this statement (1) that Burt had already noted the limited "academic" ability of canal boat children, and had indeed deliberately introduced nonverbal tests to probe beyond these socially induced and acquired limitations; and (2) Douglas also stressed Burt's own emphasis that, in addition to the existence of both inherited and environmental factors (in an objectively "given" sense), additional qualities of *individual character and motivation* ("will and continuity of effort") were also involved, and were not to be ignored.

Second: What, then, were the environmental features to which Douglas drew attention? The interesting and noteworthy fact is that the headings of his chapters and the sections within them are almost exactly those of the features distinguished by Burt in *The Backward Child*. The material conditions of houses, homes, and neighborhoods—the existence (or lack) of kitchen, bathroom, piped water, and running hot water; the degree and extent of overcrowding; the existence (or lack) of health services (ante- and postnatal services, health visitors, and so on)—and the effects these had on the schoolwork and homework of the child; the cultural, intellectual, and educational level of the parents and the home environment; the kind and degree of parental encouragement; the size of the family and ordinal position in the family; the material conditions of schools, their record and reputation, and the quality of their teachers—all these were considered exactly as Burt had considered them, though now of course within a more detailed, more carefully designed and controlled empirical investigation. Furthermore, particular emphasis was placed on the same features, as for example on the importance of the role of mothers:

> We know that for many young children it is the early contacts with their mothers that are likely to have the greatest influence on learning, and at later ages, too, it is often the mother who is more concerned than the father with school problems, and has the closest contact with the teachers. Because of this it seemed that among the survey children the mothers' influence on performance in school and in the tests might transcend the fathers'. . . . At any rate these observations show that it would be unwise to ignore the social origins and standard of education of the mothers when devising a new social classification.[29]

Third, we may simply note that Douglas found that all these conditions of the environment *did* exert important influences on the subsequent educational *performance* and *achievement* of children when compared with their earlier *measured ability,* and that inequalities of opportunity remained that should be remedied. But all this, of course, was precisely what Burt had noted, and which by the inclusion of the intelligence test in the selection examination he had actively sought to remedy. Furthermore, as far as the selection of children possessing the required ability for grammar school education was concerned, this research, just as strongly as that of Floud, Halsey, and Martin, did show that equality of opportunity had to a very large extent (one could almost say completely) been achieved. This is clearly shown in Tables 8.2 and 8.3.[30]

First of all, a large measure of agreement was in fact discovered between the results of the tests at the age of eleven (given before the eleven-plus examination) and the actual results of the examination itself. The comment accompanying Table 8.2 was: "While the only children who are certain of going to grammar school are those who score 70 or over in the tests, few of those who score between

TABLE 8.2.
Grammar School Places by Test Score

				Level of Test Score at Eleven				
	48 or less	49–51	52–54	55–57	58–60	61–63	64–66	67 and over
Award of grammar school places	% 0·2	% 2·7	% 9·2	% 27·2	% 47·9	% 83·8	% 85·5	% 91·9

TABLE 8.3.
Grammar School Places by Social Class

	Middle Class		Manual Working Class	
Test scores at eleven years	Upper	Lower	Upper	Lower
	% at Selective Secondary School	% at Selective Secondary School	% at Selective Secondary School	% at Selective Secondary School
54 or less	40·1	17·0	10·2	7·9
55–60	80·3	65·9	49·8	51·6
61 and over	99·0	93·9	96·3	92·3

61 and 69 fail to get places.'' Converting T scores to IQs, this meant that almost all children with an IQ of 116 or over were successful in gaining entry to a grammar school, and those with an IQ of 130 were certain of a grammar school place. Elsewhere Douglas also reported that

> Certainly at the higher ranges of measured ability (T scores of 61 and over) lower manual working class children are as likely to enter selective secondary schools, as children from any other social class. It is only at

lower levels of ability that their opportunities are restricted and that social inequalities are pronounced. This is shown in the following table [Table 8.3].

It is interesting to note in Table 8.3 that at the IQ level of 116 and over, the children of the upper manual working class gained a higher percentage of grammar school places than did those of the lower middle class, and that the percentage of the latter was only marginally higher than that of the lower manual working class. The achievement of a very close approximation to equality of opportunity in the selection for grammar school education was therefore clearly confirmed in this independent investigation.

In reporting this, however, Douglas seemed at least implicitly to disapprove of this clearly demonstrated "segregation by ability" of the children attending "state" schools. By contrast, the independent schools admitted children of a much wider range of ability, but still achieved generally good educational results. Douglas commented:

> Perhaps the middle class children who go to selective secondary schools have special qualities of character that later help them to succeed in their studies, even when their performance in tests given at the age of eleven is below that needed for grammar or technical school entry. This is no justification for social class inequalities in the distribution of selective secondary school places. These educationally desirable qualities of character are hardly likely to be inborn and limited to the middle classes, and if we are to make full use of the potential talent of the nation's children, they should be fostered in all social classes.

Mental ability was largely determined by heredity, but the qualities of character shown to be favorable for its development in the experience of the social classes enjoying more fortunate environmental conditions should be extended to the families and children of the less fortunate classes, just as—insofar as possible—their economic and cultural conditions should also be improved. This was Douglas's position—again in no distinctive or crucial way differing from that of Burt.

It is not strange once more, however, that neither Burt nor *The Backward Child* is once mentioned in this book—with chapter headings (and the specific environmental features they dealt with) so closely similar to those already set out by Burt as to be almost a mirror-reflection of them; employing the same methods of testing subsequent performance against initially measured ability; with the same emphasis of concern upon the clarification and remedying of the inequalities of educational opportunity in society? The survey was extended to study the record of the same children through the period of secondary education itself, in the book *All Our Future*.[31] In that report, Burt was mentioned once. In what respect? With regard to left-handedness![32]

Two important emphases remain.

The first is the fact that the tendency in the first study (*The Home and the School*) to claim that environmental conditions brought about *changes in measured intelligence* as well as differences in school and examination *performance*—thus at least suggesting the possibility of some environmental determination of the level of intelligence (some Environmentalist causation of measured intelligence)—was quite explicitly corrected, rejected, and abandoned in the second study (*All Our Future*). The first claim had rested on the fact that the measured intelligence of the two tests at ages eight and eleven showed differences that were then taken to be significant. In particular, the test at age eleven showed a relative improvement in measured ability among children from the middle classes, and a relative deterioration in that of the children who came from the less fortunate classes and environmental contexts. When, however, the children came to be tested again, later in their educational career (at age fifteen), the findings necessitated a change in this judgment:

> The importance of the home influences in the pre-school years was obscured in *The Home and the School* by the fact that there appeared to be an increasing social class gap in test performance, between the ages of eight and eleven. This was interpreted as indicating the growing influence of the environment on the measured ability and attainment of primary school children, an interpretation that, with the additional information available, must now be modified. The divergence of the intelligence test results seems to be a temporary artifact of the stresses of secondary selection rather than the result of real changes in the ability of the boys and girls. . . . The gap between the social classes in non-verbal test scores is not greater at fifteen than at eight, and while there is a slightly greater gap between them in attainment at fifteen, this is largely owing to the high scores made by the uppermiddle class boys and girls. It seems then that once the pupils are grouped by their family

background, the main characteristics of their test performance are determined by the age of eight and possibly earlier, though how much earlier we do not know.[33]

This, of course, is an enormously important "modification," bringing the position of the Douglas research entirely into agreement with that of Burt; strongly supporting and reinforcing the probable truth of the assumption that there does exist in each individual a given level of mental ability that does not develop noticeably beyond a certain age. This level of general intelligence *was* measurable independently of environmental conditions. It *did* seem to be innate, and *not* to be determined by these conditions. It *did* remain the same, depsite the continuing influences of these conditions. It *did* remain measurable in ways that were valid despite all the boundaries and conditions of social class. Furthermore, this was now demonstrated and confirmed by this new evidence— following an intensive, detailed, highly sophisticated, and totally independent investigation. Any tendencies that had arisen in this research to move towards an Environmentalist position with regard to the determination of intelligence were therefore fully and finally discarded. The findings and convictions that remained were only to the effect that environmental influences affected the *performance* and *achievement* of children in their later years, and the degree of fulfilment (or the falling short of) their "measured potential." The inequalities of opportunity, whether in selective secondary education or the system of comprehensive education, had now therefore to be explored in terms other than those of class inequalities in the mental abilities of children and the social distribution of intelligence:

The conclusions . . . are that, in the selective secondary system which existed between 1957 and 1962, social inequalities in educational opportunity could have been greatly reduced by raising the standards of many of the existing schools, by increasing the provision of grammar, direct grant and technical schools and by removing local inequalities in the provision of selective places—*these inequalities are largely historic and bear little relation to the ability of the pupils living in each area.* A general improvement in the staffing and amenities of many of the schools and the elimination of local discrepancies are, and will be, *no less necessary* in the comprehensive system of secondary education which is now evolving.[34]

The last emphasis to note, however, is that the findings and conclusions of this research, including this last "modification," were such as to suggest the very considerable importance of the family and the earliest environmental influences upon (and experiences of) the child *during the preschool years*. It was likely, Douglas claimed, that it was

> in the pre-school years that the mental development of many children is stunted by the intellectual poverty of their surroundings. Here is a wide field for study. . . . The first need is to measure more fully the impact of the family on the early processes of learning and on the acquisition of incentives before children leave school.

This research ended, in short, by calling for the study of "primary socialization," and that is precisely what was then undertaken by Basil Bernstein and his colleagues.

The Sociology of Language: Basil Bernstein

One of Burt's early realizations, as we have seen, was that in intelligence tests, in seeking the most accurate assessment possible of a child's mental ability, it was a mistake to pay attention to *verbal* performance alone, or even to overweight it. Like *attainment tests,* the linguistic skills of children could be very much a reflection of their family and cultural backgrounds. It was for this reason that he had deliberately incorporated *nonverbal* elements into his tests and, again as we have seen, he particularly drew attention, when describing the cultural deprivation of disadvantaged families, to their *limited vocabulary,* coupled with the impoverished range of experiences to which their limited stock of words referred. This—though in his case being influenced by other sources (such as Whorf and Sapir)—became the entire focus of Bernstein's work. His orientation of interest and concern stemmed directly from the sequence of studies we have decribed—from the orientation shared by Glass, Himmelweit, Flout, Halsey, Martin, and Douglas—and his aim in his research was the same. It was important, he claimed,

> to understand what underlies 'the complex of attitudes favourable to educational and social mobility'. That is, those factors which influence working-class children who do less well at grammar schools, leave

early, and fail to assimilate the grammar-school ethos; factors which influence those working-class children who tend to do less well on verbal tests of intelligence than on non-verbal tests, and those factors which influence educational attainment in basis subjects.

The continuity within the context of the entire scheme of sociological research was clear. But Bernstein's entire focus of interest lay in his persuasion that *language* was the factor of predominant importance at the heart of the process of *socialization*. People who in their families, work groups, and communities faced, experienced, and had to come to terms with the same material and social world; sharing its same demands, circumstances, challenges, and opportunities in working out their way of life, though to some extent differently in their differing class conditions; came (among other things) to develop an appropriate fabric of *communications* with each other. In terms of intellectual awareness; of emotions, sentiments, and values; of large aims and more limited and specific objectives within the world as they experienced it, and the structure and conditions of society as they knew it; a particular vocabulary and linguistic usage was generated: of speech usage and a formulated framework of language that was a reflection of the life-reality they faced. The language and linguistic usages of a family, an occupational (or other kind of) group, a social class, a community, would be an entire *orientation* of perception and experience *relevant* to its life situation; and *different* families, classes, and communities, with *different* life experiences, would engender *different* linguistic usages. Established within social situations over time, these became objectively existing sociocultural conditions that, through the subtle and complex processes of early learning within their families (the processes of *primary socialization*), were passed on, in living fashion, into the very nature of children. Biologically born offspring became human persons through this sociocultural process. Their orientations to the world were initially derived from the orientations of perceived fact and value about them. And the chief vehicle of this orientation was the language of the family, community, and class, into which they were born.

On this basis, Bernstein elaborated a sophisticated analysis of kinds of *linguistic codes* (first distinguishing a *public* from a *formal* language; later an *elaborated* from a *restricted* code) and their operation in different social classes (chiefly middle and working classes) and in different types of families. It was on this basis that he offered his account of the inequalities of educational opportunity rooted in *social class*. Middle-class children, though being aware of a restricted code relevant to their own class, were born and brought up within the wide-ranging experiential reference and cultural richness of an elaborated code of language that in particular was not *context-bound* but *instrumentally* orientated, assuming and expecting certain kinds and degrees of control over life and the environment and both giving and enabling a wide range of freedom and *personal* creativity. Lower-working-class children, with limited family backgrounds, were by contrast confined to the restricted code of language of their own group, a code which *was* context-bound and *noninstrumental,* its vocabulary and usages being confined to, and confining, the solidarity of the group's experiences and perceptions; yielding little orientation towards degrees of personal freedom beyond this.

These, of course, are the very slightest sketches of Bernstein's conceptual analysis, but it is clear how he analyzed class inequalities in these terms. The elaborated code of middle-class children, within the material and cultural advantages of their families, equipped them with a rich vocabulary, linguistic skills, and speech usages, which enabled them to perform well in verbal and attainment tests in particular. Working-class children, even though possessing high levels of mental ability, did not have these advantages. In nonverbal tests they might well reveal their ability but, limited by a restricted code of language, their performance in verbal and attainment tests would be likely to be much lower. But this was not all. Bernstein also offered an analysis of the nature of *educational transmissions* in schools, suggesting that the processes of teaching and expected learning in schools (resting on the elaborated code) were in keeping with the orientation of middle-class children but foreign to the experiences of working class children—thus accounting for their failure to "assimilate the grammar-school ethos" and (in relation to other attitudes) for the attitudes they held towards leaving school early.

Bernstein's work, of course, is noted not only for his conceptual and theoretical analysis but also for his very detailed empirical investigations, and he did in certain directions demonstrate the inequalities he had hypotheticallay predicted. One example may be noted, his finding of a considerable discrepancy between the verbal and nonverbal scores of a sample of working-class boys (though this was not found among boys from the middle class):

> For the working-class group all the verbal IQ scores are within the average range of the test but thirty-six subjects (59 per cent) scored above average on the non-verbal test while eleven subjects (18 per cent) scored between 120 and 126 + IQ points. In other words, 18 per cent of the group made scores which placed them in the top 5 per cent of the population. A general relationship held. The higher the score on the non-verbal test, the greater the discrepancy between the scores on the two tests. In relation to the higher ranges *of the Matrices test the language scores were severely depressed.* This general relationship between the two tests for the working-class group was *not* found for the middle-class group.[35]

The wastage of potential ability among the working-class boys was described like this:

> It seems apparent that a great deal of potential ability is being lost as the greater proportion of these boys are functioning at an average or below-average level of ability and educational attainment in formal subjects. . . . On matrices scores eighty of the subjects might have been potential candidates for grammar school; in fact only six went to grammar school, five to a technical school and three to central school, and none of this group of fourteen benefited in terms of attainment in examination. Of the total group 20.7 per cent have potential ability for grammar school but would, and perhaps did, fail as a result of educational attainment and showing on verbal tests.[36]

Again, however, our purpose is not to present a detailed account of Bernstein's position, but only to consider it in relation to that of Burt. And again, it is perfectly plain that in all that has been touched upon so far, there is no difference at all. This, indeed, becomes all the more evident when some of Bernstein's emphases are noted.

Throughout the whole sequence of his investigations and papers (which are very variable and changing), Bernstein was at great pains to make it clear that he was offering a *sociology* of language, speech, and linguistic usage; that the *communication structures* that differed among different groups, different types of families, and different social classes in different communities, were *socially* generated. In the developing nature of individual persons as they grew from birth to adulthood within their social contexts, these structures were *socially* and psychologically creative, and the inequalities of linguistic and cultural equipment to face and experience the formal educational system of society that they entailed for individuals were *socially* engendered within the context of social impositions. Only a *sociological* causation, he believed, could explain the qualitative differences arising from the effects of social conditions upon the same *psychological* basis. "What appears vital," Bernstein wrote, "is the separating out of sociological and psychological factors in order that constructive methods may be worked out to prevent the wastage of working-class educational potential." *Socialization* was the process of gradual accommodation to the socio-cultural environment whereby, stemming from the particular endowment inherited in his or her biological beginning, each individual *person* came creatively (involving his or her individual responses and developing character) to be made; and in this process certain social groups were especially important agencies. "Socialization" refers to

> the process whereby the biological is transformed into a specific cultural being. It follows from this that the process of socialization is a complex process of control, whereby a particular moral, cognitive and affective awareness is evoked in the child and given a specific form and content. Socialization sensitizes the child to the various orders of society as these are made substantive in the various roles he is expected to play. . . . The basic agencies of socialization in contemporary societies are the family, the peer group, school and work. It is through these agencies, and in particular through their relationship to each other, that the various orderings of society are made manifest.[37]

Throughout, then, Bernstein distinguished the sociological from the psychological level of his attempted explanation of educational inequalities, but this similarity of his position to that of Burt is made more completely clear by his insistence that these communication structures and their effects were *independent of measured intelligence*. Like Burt and all these sociological researchers prior to Bernstein, Bernstein also accepted the existence in individuals of *innate intelligence*. He accepted that this could be accurately measured—especially by nonverbal tests—and indeed it is only because he could establish this measured potential that he was then able to measure any deterioration or wastage, or unexpected levels of achievement, in subsequent levels of performance. It is necessary to note, and to emphasize (given the nature of the controversy), that this statement that Bernstein did in fact maintain this, is true. Particular "forms of communication" would "shape the intellectual, social and affective orientation of children, but, he held, they did not determine their level of intelligence. There was no Environmentalist theory of the determination of intelligence here. Let us confirm this clearly.

"These planning orientations," Bernstein wrote, "are independent of intelligence as measured by two reliable group tests." Again, "speech orientations to the two codes and the planning processes which they entail are independent of measured intelligence indicated by the tests used." And again, "thus in this country children from these respective social strata [the middle and working classes] will be exposed to different orders of learning and so their resultant modes of self-regulation and orientation will be different, irrespective of their levels of innate intelligence." Elsewhere, too, he wrote that within different social class contexts, children would be differently "equipped affectively and cognitively to respond to the grammar-school opportunity, despite the level of their measured potential."

Bernstein's entire position, then, rested on the recognition that different levels of intelligence existed in individuals (implying, therefore, a given social distribution of intelligence) independently of social and environmental factors, and that the intelligence of individuals could be validly measured independently of these factors—and could be successively measured throughout their educational career, whatever their success or failure in selective examinations or their varying performances and attainments in schools. All this was fully accepted by Bernstein. In all his work, he always supposes it; never raises any argument against it; and, of course, no possible basis for an assessment of any subsequent "wastage" or inequalities in educational selection would be at all possible without it. It is also notable that though Burt is mentioned only once throughout the whole series of books, he is nonetheless mentioned both positively and favorably. When again emphasizing the fact that children of families in poor environments experienced great disadvantages and inequalities in the process of selection for educational opportunities despite their high levels of measured intelligence, Bernstein wrote:

> Here we have been aware of the educational problem since the pre-war writings of Sir Cyril Burt. His book *The Backward Child* is probably still the best descriptive book we have.

This was said in a paper delivered at Teachers College, Columbia University, in New York, in 1969, and published as chapter 10 in *Class, Codes, and Control* in 1971. Clearly, Bernstein was aware of Burt's work and approved of it. Indeed, never did he at all take exception to it or state any disagreement with it. No allegations against Burt or his ideas came from this direction.

A final point deserves mention. In agreement with one of Burt's own emphases, and in keeping with its later reinforcement in Douglas, Bernstein and his colleagues also stressed the particular importance (among the agencies of socialization and the links between the home and the school) of *the role of the mother*. So important was this found to be in this whole matter of language and communications that it was found worthwhile (if not necessary) to set up a "maternity communications index," and a great deal of the subsequent research was carried out on this basis and along these lines.

The crucial finding was that if a mother was "open-minded" and "open-ended" in her communications with the child; thinking and feeling within the family towards all the situations and developments outside it, especially those of the school; able to go with her child imaginatively into his or her school experience, sharing it, discussing it, supporting and helping it—then, in *all* social classes, the educational progress of the child was most favorable. If, conversely, a mother was "closed" in mind and attitude; emotionally and inwardly bound to the family; diffident, unimaginative, not disposed to enter into the alien orbit of her child's schoolwork; unable to offer understanding, support, and help—then, again in *all* social classes, the educational career of the child was obstructed. Obviously, the most marked disadvantages here were found in the families of the semiskilled and unskilled workers, but in *all* social classes good maternal communications had beneficial results and bad maternal communications resulted in grave obstacles.

We are back, with ever-increasing substantiation and now with the full support of modern empirical studies, to the well-known conviction of Pestalozzi: "Whoever has the welfare of the rising generation at heart cannot do better than consider as his highest object *the education of mothers.*"[38]

Conclusion

This brief survey of the sequence of work of this highly influential group of sociologists of education demonstrates beyond doubt that the adversarial caricature with which we began—that these scholars were left-wing, egalitarian Environmentalists, rejecting the innate basis of intelligence, being entirely opposed to selective education, fully in support of comprehensive education, and standing in direct opposition to Burt, who was a right-wing, inegalitarian, elitist Hereditarian, paying little attention to social and environmental influences and the inequalities of opportunity in selective education, and being fully opposed to comprehensive schools—is, in fact without foundation. It is totally false and misconceived. No matter how deeply embedded it became, and has remained, in both academic and public opinion, it is a myth! There is not a shred of evidence to support it.

Certainly these scholars were left-wing in that—being aware of the inequalities of educational opportunity attendant upon differential class conditions—they wished to improve the material and social conditions of working-class families to reduce or eliminate these inequalities by giving working-class children the kind and level of education their measured ability deserved. But so, in exactly the same way, was Burt. In a very real sense, the work carried out by the sociologists of education was a direct follow-up of the problems described and identified by Burt in the 1930s and specifically pointed out in his 1943 paper (looking forward to the postwar years). Their investigations—more detailed, more sophisticated in their survey and experimental design—were in fact seeking to explore more fully the degree of causal significance of all the social and environmental factors that Burt had listed in *The Backward Child*.

It is interesting to note as well that—although pointing to the sources of inequality in the selective system involved in allocating children to different kinds of secondary education, and even (in Bernstein) voicing the concern that, as the eleven-plus examination had become more competitive, it had become a "legitimation of social inequality by individual failure"—there was not in the entire body of their work any deliberate, unqualified, and outright advocacy of comprehensive education. When mentioned, as in Douglas, the comprehensive system was, indeed, itself warned against the self-same problems as those attending selection and segregation. The evidence of all these studies was also that—given the selective system, and within it—equality of opportunity had in fact *to a large measure (indeed, almost entirely) been achieved.* But whether in the selective or the comprehensive system, the aim throughout was simply to improve the material and cultural conditions of working-class families as far as possible towards the standards of those in the middle classes, so that the inequalities of opportunity could be minimized, and—again, as far as possible—eliminated. To see this with complete clarity, we might note the comments of David Glass himself.

In *Social Mobility,* while indicating the newly emerging arguments for and against the comprehensive school, Glass by no means envisaged an abandonment of selection. His statement was that

> there are two major possibilities of reducing the sense of frustration or grievance which may otherwise accompany the new social mobility. First, it does not follow that an *élite,* even if selected for 'measured intelligence', need be so distant in social prestige from the rest of the population as has been the case in the past or as may be the case if present trends continue. In the nineteenth century, in order to minimize the cost of public education, the State took action which resulted in lowering the prestige of school-teaching as compared with that of other professions. It is not difficult to envisage deliberate public and private action which would, conversely, help to raise the prestige of, say, skilled manual work relative to non-manual occupations. Secondly, employment in occupations requiring high ability and long training and carrying high social status need not be the only means of gaining social prestige; there are other ways of serving the community and there should, correspondingly, be other paths to social prestige.[38]

A hierarchy of statuses, and a process of educational selection and differential provisions of education and training for the functions on which they rested, need not be such as to stand in the way of a shared experience of community. In his introduction to *The Home and the School,* too, Glass made it very clear that he most decidedly did not regard the children of the middle and working classes as being in any sense different in kind, and he was equally clear that, in wanting the conditions of working families raised, he was not at all desiring any *reduction* in the conditions or opportunities of children from the middle classes. Again, it may be noted that the significant qualification in the following statement is that of *"given levels of measured intelligence."*

> In order to avoid any misunderstanding, I should like to stress two points. First, for given levels of measured intelligence, working-class children, if they have good housing conditions, attend schools with high success records, and receive substantial parental encouragement, respond in the same way as middle class children. Secondly, the implications of the analysis are that the inequalities of the situation should be removed, *not* by depriving middle class children of a helpful environment, but by providing a comparable environmental stimulus for working class children.[39]

It is also of significance to note that whether in the selective or comprehensive system, Glass still very strongly favoured the retention of "objective tests" of mental ability for educational purposes. These were, he believed, of essential value for guidance, and other methods of assessment were much more likely to carry class (or other kinds of) bias.

> Nor would the abandonment of the present 'objective' selection tests help if the secondary school system remains unchanged. On the contrary, the replacement of such tests by, for example, teachers' reports might simply result in a less justifiable selection of children for the different types of secondary education. 'Objective' tests would be very valuable if used for purposes of guidance.[40]

Here, again, the agreement with Burt is evident. "Measured intelligence" was not only the necessary basis for measuring educational opportunity and the influence of environmental factors, it was also the best guide for the provision of education at the most appropriate level; and again this was true whether within a selective or a comprehensive system.

The separate caricatures, then, of the Environmentalist and the Hereditarian positions alike, and the additional caricature of their supposedly diametrical opposition to each other, simply had no basis. That it arose, became entrenched, and in particular, that Burt became dubbed in so taken-for-granted a way as a right-wing elitist and an arch-enemy of equality of opportunity and the comprehensive school can only be explained, it seems, by the *politicization* of the whole issue in public controversy and the fact that, within the arena of party-political controversy, it is caricatures that count. There may, however, be just one more reason.

If there is one among the sociologists of education who is difficult to understand here, it is A. H. Halsey. In the increasing criticism to which Burt was subjected in his later years, Halsey, it seems, was the chief and probably most conspicuous figure, and it may be that the position of "the sociologists of education" came to be identified with that which he adopted. In several papers, Halsey disagreed with Burt not (it seems) on the actual existence of inherited intelligence in individuals, but on the question of its distribution in social classes. The controversy between them focused upon social class, educational opportunity, and social mobility. Again, we need not enter into the nature of the controversy itself, except to perhaps note that as far as can be seen, no actual evidence was at all advanced by Halsey that would support any theory of the environmental determination of intelligence. Indeed, one surprising fact that seems to emerge from a survey of this entire literature is that not *one single item* of evidence has *ever* been produced for such a theory by *any* investigator; all the arguments being in fact focused upon the nature and extent of the influence exerted by environmental factors upon inherited differences—which is quite a different question.

The only thing we need note here, however, is that in the controversy, Burt always addressed Halsey with complete courtesy, pursuing the argument in the proper and (one would hope) customary manner of academic debate. Yet after Burt's death, Halsey deliberately, publicly, and forthrightly added his voice to the chorus of Burt's worst detractors, making public pronouncements that regrettably it is impossible to describe except in terms of gratuitous nastiness. He found it necessary for example, to preface an article in the *Listener*[41] (which was not really concerned with Burt at all, but with a discussion he had had with Jensen) with the following remarks.

The sorry story of Sir Cyril Burt as a diligent fraud has been aired on Radio 4 and discussed in these pages. Professor Eysenck (29 April) has blandly joined the condemning chorus only to be reminded by Oliver Gillie (Letters, 6 May) of how energetically implicated he was until after the evidence of L. Hearnshaw's biography *Cyril Burt, Psychologist* (1979) had confirmed what Gillie, Professor L. Kamin and Professor D. D. Dorfman had previously documented. The question is whether it matters just how far Burt was a young or an old delinquent. The answer differs according to whether one is concerned with the pathology of persons or of institutions. As to Burt the person, my view remains as expressed in a review of Hearnshaw's book.

The rake's progress has been most succinctly described by Professor Lankester-Jones of the Australian National University as a slide from obsession through pseudo-science to outright fraud. Hearnshaw's temperate explanations are not convincing. He suggests that Burt learnt to be a *gamin* in a London Board school, and that a classical education contains like dangers in that pupils are trained to 'fake' essays in the manner of Demosthenes or Cicero. He notices Burt's tragic incapacity for straightforward sexual relations as evidenced by a failed marriage, odd secretaries and housekeepers, and fantasy women like Miss Conway. He invokes Burt's misfortunes, such as the loss of research records during the war and the affliction of Ménière's disease, but he cannot establish any tight relation between these vicissitudes and Burt's flawed character.

There is a shortage of evidence. Burt was punctiliously reticent even in his diaries, leaving us in ignorance of his intimate relations in family, school or marriage. As a man he will probably remain enigmatic. I suspect that if we knew more we might find him a victim of a peculiarly English form of marginality. He was gifted, but not gifted enough to be rewarded by assured membership of the English 'intellectual aristocracy'. His school, Christ's Hospital, was eccentric to the magic circle of the most famous public schools, and he was not quite among the cleverest boys of his year. His college, Jesus, was not among the glittering Oxford societies, and he didn't quite get a First. Nor did he go on to a fellowship but to an assistant lectureship at Liverpool.

But these, too, are conjectures, and probably not worth much further research on their subjective consequences. The charitable thing now is to leave the man's grave in peace, to acknowledge that he concerned himself with matters of scientific importance, and to concentrate our attention on the problems he failed to solve.

This was Halsey's comment on a man, now dead, who had always dealt honorably with him in the exchanges of scholarly discourse. In no uncertain manner, Halsey here lined himself up in the ranks of Kamin and Gillie; like the Clarkes, it seems, ready to press the case against Burt even beyond the boundaries of Hearnshaw's judgment; superficially reiterating the one-sided mention of Dorfman (again, as had become customary, with no mention whatever of Stigler); not touching in the slightest way on any actual evidence in the controversy; but being content simply to give tongue to a distasteful personal smear, and thinking it fit to broadcast this in the widest sense to a radio audience. Why, one wonders, such gratuitous and widely disseminated defamation? And why such slanderous language: "a diligent fraud," "a young or an old delinquent," "the rake's progress," "a slide from obsession through pseudo-science to outright fraud"? Why such condescending slights on Burt's supposed ability: "gifted, but not enough to be rewarded by assured membership of the English 'intellectual aristocracy' . . . not quite among the cleverest boys of his year . . . didn't quite get a First. Nor did he go on to a fellowship but to an assistant lectureship at Liverpool."

Is there not an unpleasant smell of academic snobbery here? Perhaps the less said the better about the self-congratulatory conception of one's own level of ability that one must possess to deem oneself fit to exercise judgment in such a condescending manner on a man of Burt's intellectual stature; but it is enough to point out that in judging others in this manner, one is publicly exposing a judgment on oneself. These, says Halsey, are "conjectures." Then why make them at all, or mention them so casually, totally without support, and without further and more sensitive consideration? Why such straightforward slander, and such appalling and plainly wounding innuendoes to the effect that Burt's "tragic incapacity for straightforward sexual relations" was evidenced by "odd secretaries and housekeepers"? How did Halsey, or Hearnshaw for that matter, come to have such godlike insight as to be knowledgeably aware of Burt's supposed "incapacity for straightforward sexual relations"? And was a thought ever given to the fact that Burt's last secretary, Gretl Archer—by no means "odd" to anyone who knew her, and certainly unshakably loyal in her defense of Burt—was still alive? The one secretary described by Hearnshaw, but by no means disparagingly, as "neurotic and withdrawn," was Miss Bruce, and the truth seems to have been that Burt had given her much needed help and support, and she had served him diligently and loyally over many years, something for which he had made full public acknowledgment. Nothing, surely, can either justify or excuse media gossip of this kind, especially on such an insensitive and deplorable level as this.

This descent to personal smears in the quite uncalled-for spreading of defamation was, however, the one stark exception among the sociologists of education. The work of these investigators (including, in his research, that of Halsey himself) was, as we have seen, scrupulously undertaken; and did not, as has come to be commonly supposed (perhaps just because of conspicuous public statements such as Halsey's), stand in opposition to Burt in the slightest degree. The highly influential caricatures had simply never existed. The only question that stands out glaringly at the end of this section is for Halsey alone. Why, allying himself so demonstratively and completely with Burt's detractors (after Burt's death), did he think fit to do so with an utterance of such a distasteful and disreputable kind?

Notes

1. All this may be compared with the sociolinguistic researches of Basil Bernstein and his colleagues. Burt was fully aware of the contemporary literature on this subject (of Luria and others).
2. Cf. the findings of the Newsons in *Four Years Old in an Urban Community*. London: Allen & Umwin, 1968; Pelican Books, 1970.
3. Cf. Bernstein again (below, p. 236–7) and Douglas, J. W. B., *The Home and the School*. London: MacGibbon & Kee, 1964.
4. "Intelligence and Heredity: Some Common Misconceptions," *Irish Journal of Education* 3 (2): 75–94; 1969.
5. Routledge & Kegan Paul.
6. Heinemann.
7. MacGibbon and Kee.
8. Peter Davies.
9. All published by Routledge & Kegan Paul.
10. Other studies and books stemmed from this same research orientation, but were not so relevant to our purpose as these that I have selected.
11. See Burt's arguments supporting the Hereditarian case.
12. Glass, David (ed.), *Social Mobility* in Britain. London: Routledge &

Kegan Paul, 1954, p. 34. The different numbers given for farmers, coal hewers, and railway porters indicate the very slight differences in the estimation of the statuses of occupations that the inquiry discovered in the general public.

13. See p. 54. The *detail* of the occupation and grades covered in Burt's Tables deserves special note.
14. *Social Mobility* in Britain, pp. 122–23.
15. *The Sub-normal School Child,* vol. 2. London, 1950.
16. *Social Mobility* in Britain, pp. 144–45.
17. *Social Mobility* in Britain, chapter 10.
18. *Social Class and Educational Opportunity.* London: Heinemann, 1957.
19. *Social Class and Educational Opportunity,* p. 139.
20. Ibid., p. 53.
21. Ibid., p. 58.
22. Ibid., pp. 122–23. My italics.
23. Ibid., p. xix.
24. Ibid., pp. 143–44.
25. Ibid., p. 149.
26. Douglas, J. W. B., *The Home and the School: A Study of Ability and Attainment in the Primary School.* London: MacGibbon & Kee, 1964.
27. T scores were designed so that the average score for all children in the population was 50 and the standard deviation 10. The IQ had a mean of 100 and a standard deviation of 15. The authors provided a formula for converting T scores into IQs: IQ = 25 + 1.5 (T score).
28. Douglas, *The Home and the School,* p. 31. My italics.
29. Ibid., p. 43.
30. Taken from *The Home and the School,* pp. 20 and 123, respectively.
31. London: Peter Davies, 1968.
32. It is interesting to note that during recent years scholars in the Soviet Union have finally abandoned their long-held insistence that left-handedness is environmentally determined, and now accept that it is genetically based.
33. Ibid., p. 177.
34. Ibid., p. 185. Italics added.
35. *Class, Codes and Control,* vol. 1. The matrices test referred to was the Raven Progressive Matrices 1938 test, a *nonverbal* measurement of intelligence. It is interesting to note that Bernstein, like Douglas, took an IQ of 116 as the minimum requirement for grammar school entrance, and it will be remembered that almost all children with this level *did* achieve grammar school places.
36. Ibid., p. 31. It must be noted that these boys were tested at ages ranging from fifteen to eighteen.
37. Ibid., p. 174.
38. Pestalozzi, *Educational Writings.* London: J. A. Green, Edward Arnold, p. 239.

38. *Social Mobility in Britain*, p. 26.
39. P. xx.
40. P. xxii.
41. "Race Is a Poor Clue to Any Important Human Traits." May 20, 1982, p. 14.

9

Final Summary Note

This consideration of the sociologists of education—disproving Gillie's final allegation that Burt "underrated the importance of social factors"—brings to a close our cross-examination of the witnesses for the prosecution: the testimony of those who had made, and then greatly extended, the charges of "fraud" against Burt.

The evidence we have assembled has demonstrated beyond reasonable doubt—in my view beyond all doubt—that this testimony, throughout, has been of the nature of a long-sustained campaign of vilification. At best (adopting the most charitable view possible) it has been shown to contain grave flaws of interpretation, careless errors, incorrect charges, and the publication and widest broadcasting of deliberate distortions and oversimplications, in an ongoing and mounting polemic that has seemed at least in large part to be rooted in ideological rather than scientific motivation. At worst, it has been shown to be marred by personal smears so grave and distasteful that Hearnshaw's own judgment that it has had some of its origins in long-standing personal grievances and has shown outright malice in its inordinately extensive and relentless antagonism, seems fully justified. However this may be, whatever the truth may be that underlies these matters, the evidence itself, as it stands, has been set out clearly, as have the questions to which this, and our cross-examination, have given rise.

Clear public answers to these questions—in the service of truth—are now required from those who have pressed their many charges. If they are able to meet the criticisms made, and show that the evidence is in fact such as to uphold all the claims they have based upon it, then all well and good. Their case will be proved. If not, then a public retraction and apology is surely called for. The defamation of Burt must be removed. And if no answers at all are forthcoming, the only assumption remaining must be that the account of the evidence given here is the correct account, and that the charges of Burt's attackers fall to the ground. The defamation, in this case too, will be removed.

In any event, we are now in a position to move towards a clear summing-up. In themselves, our cross-examination and the evidence we have been able to assemble during the course of it have been enough to settle many issues outrightly and satisfactorily. On some matters, the facts and the truth have been shown to be unassailable. These at least, then, can now be itemized and set out clearly. Essential in itself, such a summary statement at this juncture will also have another important advantage. By way of a process of elimination, it will make clear what, if anything, requires further consideration on the basic question of fraud itself; and this, too, we must examine with scrupulous care. It is not our objective or concern to whitewash Burt, whatever the evidence. Whatever the character of Burt's detractors, whatever the personal or ideological grounds of their attacks upon him, no matter how many of their charges against him we have been able to dismiss, the crucial question remains: was Burt in fact guilty of fraud?

The answer I will give—certainly on the minimal basis of being able to establish ''reasonable doubt,'' but also as I believe on more substantial grounds that go a good deal further than this—is that he was not! But the grounds and arguments for this verdict will be for you to judge. If this judgment is found correct, however, it will clearly call for a serious rehabilitation and reconsideration of Burt and his work. His relevance to the problems faced by education in society today, and perhaps by any educational system in any society at any time, may well prove to be of vital importance, if these are ever to be satisfactorily addressed and resolved. It may be, in short, that there is something of perennial truth in the position for which he stood.

III
MALFEASANCE AND FRAUD?

SUMMING-UP, ADDITIONAL
EVIDENCE, AND VERDICT

10

Malfeasance?

Malfeasance is a word used by Hearnshaw, which I take to mean "official misconduct." It does seem the most appropriate word to use for the overall disrepute into which Burt has fallen. It is official, professional, and above all, scientific misconduct of which he stands accused.

We have seen, however, that many of the charges of such misconduct made against him, including many of the smears in which they have been embedded or with which they have been directly linked, have gone far beyond accusations of fraud proper. As the first step in our summing-up, a list of these can now be clearly identified and rejected. Our cross-examination and the evidence adduced have clearly demonstrated the points covered in the following sections.

Eugenics

It is not true that Burt was "saturated" in the literature of the eugenics movement; that he accepted and adopted its more extreme views; and that his approach to secondary school selection was tainted with the same kind of judgment as to the "superiority" and "inferiority" of various kinds of groups that, in Germany, came to be manifested in the extermination policies of the Nazis. There is no evidence to support any judgment of this kind. In particular, it is not true that the entries in Burt's early notebooks used as such evidence were either the views of his Oxford lecturers or his own. They were systematic notes on an essay by Pigou in a book that was highly humane in its sympathy for the disadvantaged in society and in its emphasis on the necessity for social reform.

Racism

It is not true that Burt "inspired" the work undertaken by Jensen and Eysenck on race and intelligence—this has been denied by Eysenck himself—or that he was in any way guilty of racism. "The insinuation of 'racism' made against him," said no less a person than Sir Andrew Huxley (president of the British Association in 1977), "is absolutely without foundation. If he looked forward to social consequences of his work, it was not in the repression of minorities with a poor showing on his tests, but in the prospect of upward social mobility of individuals who did well."[1] (We may also note the emphasis here upon Burt's own continual focus upon *individuals*.)

Social Class

It is not true, similarly, that Burt was in any way guilty of thinking of social classes in terms of "superiority" or "inferiority," or of any kind of class discrimination. It is not true that, rooted in the eugenics movement, he exerted influence on the Wood Committee in such a way as to "confirm the policy of segregating the mentally sub-normal so that they would not reproduce"; and indeed, this itself is a simplistic and false caricature of that report's recommendations. Burt's interest and concern was always focused upon *individuals;* insisting always that the range of ability *within* each social class was wider than that which existed *between* them, and that all individuals should be given the education their particular abilities and talents deserved, whatever their social origins. His continual and consistently held objective, too, was to extend the range of opportunities to those families and individuals who suffered from the obstacles rooted in social disadvantage.

Intelligence and Income

It is not true that (specifically in his 1943 paper) Burt maintained, or ever believed, that the unequal distribution of income in society was either factually explicable or morally justifiable in terms of the unequal distribution of intelligence alone, and that this state of affairs—"good, beautiful and true" according to Kamin—should be left unaltered. He was by no means of a laissez-faire persuasion. In all his surveys, Burt drew attention to the appalling conditions in which the families of the lower-income groups lived, and the entire emphasis of his 1943 paper (its primary objective) was to demonstrate the inequalities of both educational opportunity and educational provision among the children of financially disadvantaged families, and strongly to advocate a remedying of this situation.

Heredity and Environment

It is not true that, believing intelligence to be largely determined by heredity, Burt at all underrated or failed to take into account social and environmental factors, and their influences upon educational selection, school performance, and the whole educational career of a child. On the contrary, he listed these very clearly, offered a detailed description and analysis of them, emphasised their importance, and pointed out those features that were apparently of special significance among them (such as the vocabulary available in the family and neighborhood, and the role of the mother)—features that were subsequently emphasised in the same way by the sociologists of education.

Right-Wing Elitism

It is not true, in the entire public debate about the influences of heredity and environment, that Burt was in any narrow or restrictive way a right-wing elitist, standing in stark opposition to the sociologists of education (and others) who were, by contrast, left-wing, egalitarian Environmentalists. The position of Burt and these sociologists was exactly the same. On the basis of the most reliable measurement of ability they could establish, they sought to assess the influences of those environmental factors that seemed obstacles in the way of its fulfilment, hoping to identify, understand, and remove them. The caricature of two positions standing in a stark polarity of opposition to each other was false. It is not true, either, that in continuing to insist on the necessity and correctness of careful assessment, selection, and the provision of appropriately different kinds and levels of education, Burt was on the grounds of any principle wholly opposed to the "comprehensive" school. That kind of school might well be the best kind for some areas; the fault lay (he believed) in thinking that it *must* be the best for *all* areas, and therefore politically imposing it universally. This aspect of the caricature, too, was false.

Dedication and Obsession

It is not true that Burt was "dedicated to" or "obsessed by" the Hereditarian theory of the determination of intelligence. He simply, as a scientist, reported his consistently discovered findings that heredity *was* the chief determinant both of levels of general intelligence and some marked special aptitudes, and furthermore, that all the other serious studies in the field were in agreement with these findings. But he also pointed not only to the more gross effects of environmental factors and conditions but to their more subtle, important, personal influences in engendering aims, values, ideals, models for purposively directed efforts and attainment, and in sustaining motivation, which individuals experienced within their families and other social contexts, and which essentially involved their own personal temperament and character, their own progressive self-knowledge, their own exercise of will and discipline, and the assumption of their own personal responsibility for the ordering of their own lives. This, too, at least some of the sociologists of education emphasized (as, of course, many other educationalists of all times have emphasized.) Burt also noted that despite all the opposition of Environmentalists to the Hereditarian findings, none had ever produced any *empirical evidence* for their own theory of the determination of intelligence, whereas he had advanced a number of clear grounds and arguments (to be considered later) for rejecting it. These grounds went far beyond his study of identical twins.

Data, Sources, Methods of Investigation

It is not true that Burt was guilty of scientific misconduct in the carrying out of his surveys, in the methods he employed, or in the presentation of his findings. The following specific allegations of this kind made against him must all, on the basis of the evidence we have presented, be rejected:

1. It is not true that, in his many studies, Burt did not give "even the most elementary information" about "how, where and when his purported data were collected." Every study (whether reported in book or article) provided such information in detail, and if the references made in them—including footnotes—to earlier studies (for information on tests used, methods employed, and so forth) are in fact checked, the information mentioned will be found.
2. It is not true that Burt did not give the sources of any information he used other than that stemming from his own investigations. In fact, he always gave such sources in meticulous detail; and always acknowledged the people who had given him assistance, no matter how specific and limited their help might have been.
3. It is not true that he did not specify the particular kinds of IQ tests he used in his surveys. These were in fact always specified in detail—though, having been fully described in some places, they were not then so described in every place, brief references to the earlier and fuller descriptions being made. Burt wrote books and articles in a period when one could suppose, as a common scientific assumption, that when significant sources were recorded in a footnote, reference to them would be made.
4. It is not true that Burt was guilty of "shoddy work" as an "applied psychologist," or that being an applied psychologist stood in the way of his being a reliable scientist. Burt possessed all the qualities required of, and marking the work of, a scientist: not only in standards of competence (his work stands the test of comparison with that of any other psychological or social scientist of his time) but in the scientific veracity with which his work was pursued. His methods of work, for example, in the Birmingham Survey, the Vocational Guidance Survey, or in that of the Wood Committee, were very clearly outlined. Furthermore, these tests, surveys, and presentations of findings were all undertaken in the closest relation to independent studies by other authorities who were experts in their own fields: Dr. Lloyd in the Birmingham study; Dr. Lewis in the Wood Report; Frances Gaw, Lettice Ramsey, May Smith, and Winifred Spielman in the study of Vocational Guidance (the Industrial Fatigue

Research Board, which commissioned this latter study, also contained scientists of the rank of C. S. Myers, E. H. Starling, and Sir Charles Sherrington). Burt's investigations were planned, undertaken, and their findings subsequently presented, in close relation to theirs (all of which are there to be checked and verified). Were all these authorities, closely collaborating as colleagues, themselves fraudulent, or deluded, or deceived by "shoddy work" on the part of Burt? Such a possibility is simply not believable.

5. It is not true that Burt's statistics were proved faulty by Dorfman. Dorfman's own criticism was shown by Stigler, Cohen, and others to have rested on misunderstandings of a quite fundamental nature. Yet in the ongoing vilification from Gillie, to Hearnshaw, to Halsey, Dorfman alone was continually repeated; the critics of Dorfman were ignored.

6. It is not true that, in his earlier papers, Burt was guilty of plagiarizing from the writings of Winch. The evidence plainly demonstrates this. Glibly repeated by Gillie without, it seems, any checking of the facts, this was immediately expanded into the allegation of a movement "from early plagiarism to outright fraud," but for such a wildly extended claim there is no evidence.

Indeed, in complete contradiction to all these charges, the entire body of Burt's work (from the earliest papers on mental testing, through the several large-scale surveys, to the final papers) is marked by the most remarkable degree of continuity and consistency. The references made by Burt in each of his succeeding books and papers to what had been done and established in his earlier work really did refer back to these earlier findings. He really did assume that what had been clarified or established in an earlier publication need not be repeated in full later. There really was a cumulative building up of a body of conceptualization, tests, methods of study, collected facts, and theoretical observations in the entire sequence of his work. One fault of ideologically selective criticism—resting on the perceptual orientation of a political polemic—is that it never does examine a body of work *as a whole;* it has neither the time nor the concern for this; but simply selects, distorts, and inflates in the direction of its own ends. But if it is still true that truth matters, then all these claims and counterclaims need to be examined against the totality of Burt's work itself. If this is done, the judgments here stated will be found to be substan- tiated and correct.

Confidence Trickster and Psychopath

It is not true that Burt was guilty of at least those specific charges on which it has been claimed that he was deceitful, devious, underhanded, and aggressive in his undermining of colleagues; that he was guilty, in short, of both professional misconduct and personal mischief-making. Quite specifically, it is not true that he wrote articles on behalf of the Clarkes and published them deceitfully under their names. Such articles never existed. They were only the brief abstracts of their theses, and they were not published in any special way by Burt, but simply on the basis of an ongoing journal policy laid down by a previous editor. It is not true, either, that these abstracts were changed in such ways as to slant them against Eysenck. This, at least, is in no way evident.

It should also be noted, in relation to this testimony that Burt was a "con man" and a "psychopath," that it all emanates from one source: the Clarkes, and subsequently, Eysenck, who latterly came to adopt their kind of language. All these charges—that Burt placed every obstacle in the way of Eysenck, using the Clarkes as pawns in his battle; that Aubrey Lewis and Eysenck warned the Clarkes that they might not get their Ph.D.s; and so forth—are no more than hearsay, and hearsay originating and remaining only within this one small group of people who were closely related in (apparently) a particularly vexed early situation. What is required here is *evidence,* and we have made clear the questions to which answers are required. Without testable evidence, it is just as feasible a possibility that the (evidently) poisonous conflict existing between Lewis, Eysenck, and the Maudlsey Department on the one hand, and Burt and University College on the other, stemmed from the Maudsley side, as it is that it stemmed from the side of Burt. It is at least a possibility that Burt may have had every justification in being wary of any manipulations and machinations emanating from their direction. Anyone at all acquainted with more than the surface of academic life knows very well that the most evil skulduggery can come from sources that have every appearance of being the most respectable.

Minimally, then, on the basis of having been demonstrated beyond reasonable doubt, but going far beyond this in that much of the evidence presented has decisively proved it, the views, character, conduct, and work of Cyril Burt stand cleared of all these defamatory charges. This in itself constitutes a very subtantial clearing of Burt's name; and all the charges we have been able to dismiss need to be very clearly and carefully noted.

The ground has now been cleared, however, for a completely unobscured concentration and summing-up on the question of fraud itself.

Note

1. *Times Higher Education Supplement*, October 7, 1977.

11

Fraud? The Minor Charges

So that no issues are missed, we will consider separately the charges of fraud formulated by Gillie and Hearnshaw (those made by Kamin, the Clarkes, and others, being covered by these two). Three of these may be called minor charges simply in the sense that the evidence presented in our cross-examination has dealt with them satisfactorily—in a definitive way—and they therefore call for no further demonstration or argument. They can be listed and dismissed briefly.

Guessing the IQs of Adults and Parents

It is not true that Burt—in any simple, casual, or arbitrary sense—guessed at the IQs of adults and parents and then went on later "to treat these guesses as hard scientific data." Gillie made this one of his charges of fraud. We have seen, however, that the IQs of adults related to occupational gradings were drawn from other existing sources (records of tests from the United States Army and from the British Civil Service), and that very considerable care was taken by both Burt and his several colleagues (described and exemplified clearly in the Vocational Guidance study) in their estimation of the IQs of parents. The methods employed were clearly stated and systematic, and were the best that could be formulated in the face of obvious and very real difficulties. Furthermore, far from putting these forward as "hard scientific data," both Burt and his assistants pointed out their limitations and shortcom-

259

ings. All of this went far beyond any matter of mere guessing and—the crucial point—reveals no evidence whatever of fraudulence.

Working Backwards to Invented Data

It is not true (and could not be true) that Burt "worked backwards . . by supplying data to fit predictions of his favourite genetic theories and thereafter "appeared to offer hard scientific proof where it did not exist." This was another of Gillie's charges, but we have seen that it was a large-scale extension of the one claim (which Cronbach called "the smoking gun") that, responding to a request by Jencks for a limited amount of data, Burt took a week to supply it. Hearnshaw claimed that had the raw data or the test scores been readily available, this could have been supplied within half an hour. With reference even to this one specific occasion, however, it was known that Burt during his later years was under continual pressure from requests in correspondence, and Cronbach, for example, wrote: "After a witness describes the junkheap of test sheets and calculations he saw in Burt's attic, it becomes easy to see how an aged man, able to work only in brief spells, would take a week to assemble a table." But the dismissal of any charge of fraud in this matter rests on far wider considerations.

There is no evidence whatever of any "invention" of data in the empirical surveys Burt carried out, just as there was no call of any kind for any such invention. We have seen, too, that these were undertaken in close conjunction and cooperation with other highly qualified authorities, each of whom was conducting his or her own independent but closely related, simultaneous work (as part of the same surveys). No working backwards from invented data could possibly have entered into this work, and even in relation to the later twin studies, where the charge of inventing data has been particularly made, similar considerations arise. Any full examination of Burt's tables in the articles from 1955 onwards make the very idea of inventing data by working backwards from *all* the correlations there presented simply preposterous. It would be a sheer impossibility. If it is considered "miraculous if not impossible" that two correlations should agree to three decimal places, how much more miraculous would be the work of inventing data sufficiently detailed to produce (by working backwards) *all* these three decimal correlations?

But there are two other points of very considerable and (to my mind) convincing weight. First, Burt used to work over the data, and his statistical work on them, in great detail with no less a person than John Fraser Roberts, the leading geneticist (at one time at Guy's Hospital Medical School and with the Medical Research Council). How would any invention of data, working backwards from desired correlations, have escaped the notice of a scholar of such caliber? Dr. Fraser Roberts has publicly registered his support for Burt in the press correspondence following the "scandal," but a paragraph from one of his letters to me (November 2, 1984) deserves quotation here (italics added):

> Burt and I were close working neighbours for several years—he at University College and I at the London School of Hygiene and Tropical Medicine and then at Great Ormond Street. During this period we saw a lot of each other, usually at my office. *He would bring along his basic data* and our meetings almost invariably involved only the two of us. We were both fascinated to discover the most accurate and sensitive methods for the measurement of intelligence and for assessing the effect of inherited factors on subsequent performance at repeated IQ tests on both normal and subnormal subjects. This shared interest kept us in close touch with each other and we had very many sessions discussing techniques and *going through each other's data together most thoroughly.* We were also from time to time co-examiners for Ph.D. theses from candidates working in this field. We both enjoyed our contacts and found them mutually helpful. Looking back on our long association I can only assure you that I always held Burt and his work in the highest esteem and never had the slightest reason to change my opinion.

It deserves mention, too, that Dr. Fraser Roberts did not work in London until 1946, so that his long association with Burt was one taking place entirely during the postwar years. It is surely inconceivable that any fraudulent working backwards from correlations to the invention of data could have gone unnoticed in the mutually detailed working over of each other's basic data that Fraser Roberts records. There is also the second supporting consideration: in their own detailed examination and consideration of the errors and misprints found in the tables of figures in Burt's later papers, both Jensen and Eysenck claimed that none of these were serious; that it was by no means the case that they were always and predictably such as to favor and support the argument Burt was advancing; and—again the crucial point—that they gave no sign whatever of deliberate fraud.

A misguided extension of an assumption *once* voiced in relation to *one* very specific and very limited request for information, this must therefore be dismissed as not in any way constituting a credible charge of fraud. There is simply no evidence for it.

Falsifying the History of Factor Analysis

It is not true that Burt deliberately misrepresented "the early history of factor analysis" in order to belittle the part played by Spearman and, in so doing, to claim originality for himself. Stated as a charge of fraud by Hearnshaw (the claims made by Burt about his early work were, he said, "completely false"), we have seen this to be completely unsupported by evidence. Criticisms of the most fundamental kind were clearly stated by Cronbach, Banks, and Joynson, pointing to quite basic misunderstandings at the root of Hearnshaw's account, and to these Hearnshaw has not yet replied. We noted these criticisms to some extent during our cross-examination of Hearnshaw's testimony, but to demonstrate this point quite conclusively now, a little more detail seems necessary and worthwhile.

Cronbach had shown that Burt had been stimulated to tell the story of factor analysis in his own way by what he regarded as a mistaken account given by Thurstone; an account that evidently underestimated the contribution of British psychology, and also "underplayed Burt's influence and ignored his priority" in some aspects of the subject that he had, in fact, pioneered. A full consideration of all that was involved in this would make "Hearnshaw's reading seem tendentious" and "defuse the charge." It is worthwhile to note here that there was at least the possibility of some envy, some "playing down," of Burt from Thurstone's side, so that any adverse comments about Burt from Thurstone (which Eysenck, later, certainly seemed to take seriously) should not, perhaps, be taken at their face value as proving any fault in Burt. Charlotte Banks, however, carried this criticism much further, being able to demonstrate that Hearnshaw was guilty of quite simple errors and mistatements; that he was confused on some of the statistical matters on which he insisted (for example between the tetrad equation and the proportionality equation and the order in which these had been used by Burt and Spearman); that he misrepresented the relationship between Spearman and Burt; and that indeed he was fundamentally mistaken about the actual claim Burt had made. "Burt did not claim to have originated the idea [of factor analysis] nor to have been the instigator of the necessary formulae. He only claimed to be the first to do it in psychology." (It is important, however, since all of this involves statistical technicalities, to note Dr. Banks' crucial points in full detail: see Appendix 2.)

These criticisms constitute a rebuttal of Hearnshaw's charge of the most fundamental kind. As we saw earlier, they have also been fully endorsed by Joynson. This third minor charge of fraud must therefore be dismissed unless or until Hearnshaw satisfactorily meets these criticisms and provides a credible ground for his claim. Charlotte Banks and Joynson have been relatively lonely voices, and it seems have simply been ignored. This seems yet another example of a charge of fraud against Burt having gained wide currency, wide acceptance, and considerable influence, without any detailed checking of the facts and the statements made.

Burt was not guilty, then, of these three specific charges of fraud, any more than of the broader charges of malfeasance listed earlier. Again—bearing in mind the well-nigh unbreakable strength of academic and public opinion, once entrenched—it needs to be clearly and carefully noted that Burt now stands cleared of them. Only the major charges of fraud now remain.

12

Fraud? The Major Charges

The charges of outright fraud remaining are four:

1. The Case of the Missing Ladies—the invention of assistants who never in fact existed.
2. The improper use of their names as the authors of articles, sometimes in joint authorship (with Burt) and sometimes under their own names alone; and to this may be linked the more general allegation of the impropriety of writing under pseudonyms.
3. The fabrication of data when no data could have been collected, and no data existed (this referred chiefly to the later twin studies, but also to the 1969 article in which Burt claimed that some decline in educational standards had taken place between 1914 and 1965).
4. The reporting of the invariant correlations of various kinds (to the third decimal place) despite increases in the number of twins studied; something held to be "miraculous, if not impossible."

These can rightly be considered the major charges of fraud in that they are allegations of the gravest and most definite kind of calculated deception; of the deliberate falsification of scientific findings, both in the purported collection of facts and in their presentation. They can also be considered major charges in the sense that they are the most difficult about which it is possible to arrive at a completely satisfactory judgment. The evidence we have brought during our cross-examination has already proved much; in each case, a good deal more can be said; but the difficulty lies in the absence of really conclusive evidence, and on some matters this difficulty seems insuperable. We are almost bound to be left, therefore, with judgments that can do no other than rest on a careful balance of probabilities. Despite the difficulties, however, we must now, in full seriousness, meet Gillie's central charge that this was "this most sensational charge of scientific fraud this century," consisting in essence in the possiblity that Burt "published false data and invented crucial facts" in support of his theories. I say "in full seriousness" when perhaps I should better say "not contentiously." At this point, we must remind ourselves that—despite my forthright criticism of the testimony of the prosecution (because I have found it wanting in many ways), and despite my forthright arguments in defense of Burt (because I believe that on all the issues we have considered he is in the right, and to be justified)—we are not here as *participants* in the controversy. Our aim is simple and single: to establish the truth in so far as this proves possible. Let us now, then, consider each of these final allegations in turn.

The Missing Ladies

Among the great many assistants acknowledged by Burt in his publications covering the work of some sixty years, attention has been focused, as we have seen, upon Margaret Howard and J. Conway. To these, however, we must now add Miss M. G. O'Connor, mentioned in his 1969 article for the Irish Journal. About the first two assistants I do not think that there can any longer be any dispute. Testimony to the existence of Miss Howard was quite definite, not only from John Cohen, a loyal supporter of Burt, but also from Donald MacRae—in all senses other than that of wanting to establish the truth, a disinterested witness. Miss Conway was less certain, but the idea that she should have been "invented" as early as the writing of Burt's 1943 article for what was then such a limited contribution is just, in itself, a pointless absurdity. In any event, we have seen that Gillie himself, after two years of the most thorough searching, came to the conclusion that the two ladies had most probably existed, but after his discovery of Miss Molteno, had decided that the "mechanism" of Burt's fraud was somewhat different. He used the names of real people, but attributed to them work that they did not do. In Miss Molteno's case, Burt never attributed to her the work about which Gillie questioned her, and so on both counts—that of inventing people and that of not inventing them but falsely attributing work to them—Gillie's charge simply dissolves into nothingness. Other points, however, need to be made about these two ladies.

First, some testimony to their existence, and the nature of this testimony, has not been sufficiently emphasized. Both Gillie and Hearnshaw mentioned Dr. William Hammond's recollection of having been tested by them, but it was little more than a mention. Dr. Hammond's memory, however, was very firm. The following is a quotation from a letter he wrote to me in November 1984, when I was still making inquiries after the BBC film:

> I myself am quite sure about the existence of the two researchers but I am afraid I have bad news for you concerning the credibility of my own evidence. Following my writing to Prof. Hearnshaw, I got a letter from a woman doctor from Hull (who I think with a husband were largely instrumental in the attack on Burt—but I have forgotten the names). In it she referred to my letter to Hearnshaw in which I had named Miss Howard as the tester. I contradicted this saying that it was Miss C. who did the testing, she being dark haired whereas Miss H. was fair. It was in fact the dark one who administered the test, but when I checked up I found that I *had* named Miss Howard. I felt so devastated by that slip that—to my shame—I did not follow it up and pass this information on to Prof. Hearnshaw. Ordinarily it would not be of great moment that I had momentarily confused the hair colours of the two ladies, but my mistake is doubly unfortunate—especially as it is Hearnshaw's published version which perpetuates my mistake.

> Just to make it clear that the whole thing was not a fabrication on my part I remember very clearly the professional yet common sense way in which the Stanford Binet test was administered (not at all like the prissified character travestied in the BBC production). . . .

Hammond then went on to describe the test and dwell on particular details, but the above passage is of interest in a number of ways. Inadvertently, it gives evidence of the industry of Ann Clarke in pursuing and questioning any testimony in support of Burt, and also of the close liaison that seems to have existed between Hearnshaw and the Clarkes. However, the chief qualities shown in it that deserve emphasis are (1) its sheer honesty and (2) its complete lack of stridency, pretentiousness, and anything of a polemical or contentious kind. It is testimony that can be trusted; its genuineness is patently obvious. In testimony of the same nature—with recollections of a firm kind, but sufficiently honest not to claim too much in terms or precise certainty—Charlotte Banks remembers the one-time delight of Miss Bruce (Burt's secretary) at finally having found ''Miss Conway's stuff on twins'' after a period of some weeks during which (being evidently very inefficient in filing) she had been unable to turn it up following a request for it by Burt. There is, therefore, additional personal testimony of this kind that serves to reinforce the quite specific and certain evidence of Cohen and MacRae. There are also, however, considerations of a broader but quite firm kind.

One slight point, but one nonetheless worth mention, is that in initially claiming that the two ladies had been invented, Gillie said, in rather lampooning fashion, that they were ''the fantasy of an ageing professor who became increasingly lonely and deaf.'' Miss Conway, however, was mentioned in the 1943 article in relation to work done over some fifteen years prior to that date—during a period, in short (up to that time), when Burt was between 45 and 60 years old: hardly of great age, certainly not lonely, and certainly not yet troubled by deafness. But other points are more substantial.

Though there was some documentary evidence (whatever it might be worth) of a Miss Howard in the membership lists of the British Psychological Society, much was always made of the absence of any documentary evidence of the existence of the two ladies. It has to be borne in mind, however, that a very large number of Burt's assistants were voluntary assistants (head teachers, teachers, local authority administrators, and various kinds of social workers), who were only too ready to take part in the investigations but were never recorded as employees. This was also, and particularly, true of some social workers of that time who were not even included as appointees on any official lists; the category of ''care committee workers'' is one example. Documentary evidence, any official record, of a large range of assistants was therefore not likely to exist at all, and this fact is particularly relevant to Miss Conway, who was chiefly referred to by Burt in connection with child care work and tests made of children boarded out in fosterhomes. And here there is one curious fact that might ultimately prove to have a great deal more than curiosity value.

It has become a widespread assumption, so much so as no longer to be at all questioned, that the 'J' in J. Conway stood for 'Jane.' This, however, may be quite without foundation. In the 1943 paper (where she is first mentioned) no initial at all is given, and in the later papers only the initial 'J.' It *seems* (no more than this!) that the name of Jane stems only from an assumption on Jensen's part, but for which there is no actual evidence. Might there not be other possibilities? I myself, knowing that Miss E. R. Conway (a prominent and influential Liverpool headmistress) had been on the Hadow Committee and must have known Burt's work well, no doubt in London as well as in Liverpool and Birmingham, wondered whether any relative of hers might have been among Burt's helpers; I looked into this quite thoroughly but nothing came of these inquiries.

Then accidentally and coincidentally (though over a period of a little more than the past two years), a number of other items of information emerged that, taken together, seem to me to be possibly of the greatest significance.

Firstly, towards the end of 1987, Mr. Alan Neate, until fairly recently Keeper of the London County Council records, discovered that a lady named Miss H. M. J. Conway "appeared in certain L.C.C. staff lists just before the war as an assistant organiser of childcare work in the Public Health Department." On checking this, he found that Honoria Mary *Joynt* Conway started with the LCC in 1936. Beginning on a temporary basis in March, she was appointed to the permanent post in December, having been recommended for this on the grounds of having fulfilled her duties "in a most satisfactory manner." The name Joynt was not hyphenated with Conway, and may well have been, therefore, an unusual first name. This was a far cry, of course, from anything approaching substantial evidence, and no definite claim could be based upon it. Even so, it was documentary proof of the unquestionable existence of one J. Conway who was employed by the LCC during the very period to which Burt referred, working in the particular area that he specified—in the organization of child care work.

Then, however, came a coincidence that was totally unexpected. In September 1989, I had a letter from Dr. Geoffrey Cohen (the son of Professor John Cohen) of the Department of Statistics at the University of Edinburgh. He told me that, among his father's papers, he had just discovered a closely typed set of notes (of some eighteen pages) on *"The Techniques of Correlation and of Analysis of Variance and Covariance—With Special Reference to Problems of Educational and Vocational Psychology,"* written by Burt in the early 1940s (the evidence suggested 1942–1943) for circulation among his students and colleagues. His specific reason for mentioning this was that "on page 4 Burt cites "Miss Conway's study on 'Three Different Methods of Teaching Reading' (an unpublished thesis)." He added: "You may already know about this, but if not it is yet more evidence (if any were needed) for the existence of Miss Conway." I did *not* know about this, and Dr. Cohen was good enough to let me have a full copy of the notes. It may be noted, in passing, that Miss Conway's name was not cited alone, but was one among many such acknowledgments—of a Miss Harwood and a Miss Longman, for example—even in the same immediate context. Can it possibly be believed, without even going further, that Burt would give the name of an invented assistant in a document of this kind?

However it proved possible to explore the matter further. I had long been in touch with Mrs. Emma Robinson, in charge of theses at the University of London Library, and at once asked her whether the thesis mentioned by Burt was recorded. She told me that it was not, but that this was because it was not a higher degree thesis but, more probably, the kind of dissertation offered in a teacher's diploma. She then had an assistant look into the question of where this might have been presented, and the only possibility proved to be that of a Miss Honoria Mary Joynt Conway who had completed a teacher's diploma at King's College (London). I at once got in touch with King's, and the administrator in the Postgraduate Office was able to let me have the document recording Miss Conway's registration (in October 1931) and her "passing" of the teacher's diploma in 1932. This document, besides giving details of Miss Conway's address and the schools she had attended, also stated her date of birth, November 20, 1908. From this I was able (from the Registrar of Births and Deaths) to get a copy of her birth certificate, which showed her place of birth (103 Pepy's Road, Wimbledon) and that her father was a journalist. It also, as a matter of interest (although her father's full name was Walter Bernard Joynt Conway), recorded her first names as Honoria, Mary, and Joynt. I was also able, recently, from Mrs. Robinson, to discover that she had taken her first degree at the University of Dublin—but that, at the moment, is as far as my inquiries have been able to go. Let us, however, simply bring together the facts that have come so far and so unexpectedly from Mr. Neate, Dr. Cohen, Mrs. Robinson, King's College, and the Registrar of Births.

We now certainly have full documentary evidence of the existence of a Miss Conway during the period in which Burt mentioned her assistance. She was born November 20, 1908, at 103 Pepy's Road, Wimbleton, London; her father being a journalist, the maiden name of her mother having been Gorevan. (Her mother's full married name being Margaret Mary Conway: that is without the use of the name 'Joynt'—making it quite clear that this was, indeed, a *first* name.) She attended two schools: St. Andrew's Convent, Coventry Hall, Streatham; and Studley Court, Stourbridge, Worcesterhire. She read for her first degree in the University of Dublin, gaining a second class honours in history. In October 1931, now almost twenty-four years old and living at 41, Oakdale Road, London S.W. 16, she registered for a teacher's diploma course at King's College, London. A year later, by the age of twenty-five, she had passed this diploma. It is a possibility that, after this, she was for some years a teacher, but what is certain is that she was appointed to the staff of London County Council on a temporary basis as assistant organizer of child care work in March 1936, and having undertaken this work satisfactorily, was then appointed to the permanent vacancy occurring on December 7th, 1936. This, on the basis of reports by the school medical officer and the clerk of the council. That is to say, between the ages of twenty-eight and twenty-nine she became fully engaged in the area of child care work.

All these are straightforward facts. A Miss Conway existed who was well qualified academically, and who at the age of twenty-five was qualified as a teacher (and, either then or later, had written a thesis that Burt knew and recommended); and who, certainly from 1936 onwards, was officially employed by the LCC in the field of child care. This, moreover, is certainly the Miss Conway Burt recommended in his notes of 1942 to 1943. In short, the age, qualifications, and areas of work and experience of this Miss Conway are entirely such as to fit with the acknowledgments of her help, in his publications from 1943 onwards, which Burt made. But let us touch these facts only lightly with two conjectures and one question.

As to conjectures: First, is it not well nigh certain that, during her teacher's diploma course between 1931 and 1932, that Miss Conway would be bound to be aware of Burt and his work at University College? In all probability, indeed, there would be links, at this level of teacher training, between the two colleges in the University of London. Second, since Burt recommended this Miss Conway in his notes of 1942 to 1943, can it be seriously in doubt that this was the same Miss Conway whose help he also acknowledged in his published paper of 1943? Furthermore, does not Burt's awareness and mention of her earlier dissertation suggest that (whether or not for a few years she became a teacher) she could have remained in touch with his work from the date of her teacher's diploma (1932) onwards? Whether or not this was so, what is certain is that for some seven years at least before the 1943 paper (from her appointment in 1936), this Miss Conway was working (in the organization of child care) in the area from which she could have drawn, and in which she could have provided, the limited assistance and information that, in that paper, Burt claimed.

As to the question, it may be asked: Is it not extremely unlikely that the initial 'J' (as indicating a first name) would refer to "Joynt" when the family name may have been "Joynt Conway?" Is it not extremely unlikely that a person, by way of her first name, would call herself, or be called, Joynt? It certainly seems so, but here we must recall our earlier point that the now widely held assumption that 'J' referred to "Jane" has no basis in evidence. Even Gillie says as much. To the best of my knowledge, whenever and wherever Burt refers to his assistant in articles or footnotes, he never uses an initial at all. It is always simply "Miss Conway." Also, as we saw, her first names as recorded on her birth certificate are Honoria, Mary, and Joynt. The only place in which "*J*. Conway" is used is in the articles that Burt wrote under her name. In short, the use of Joynt as her first name may never in fact have arisen.

For now, however, I will stop short of arguing more strongly about the case of Miss Conway, for fear of seeming to claim too much. I have gone into such detail only because it has been so long, and so dogmatically, claimed that no documentary evidence of the existence of any such person is to be found. The documentary evidence presented here certainly does prove the existence of such a lady, one whose work was definitely known to Burt, and who was sufficiently qualified and appropriately employed to provide the assistance he claimed. But it is the case, I concede, that the identity of this Miss Conway with Burt's assistant of that name cannot be finally, as yet, confirmed. To my mind, however, all of this evidence has a high degree of significance—and grounds for such confirmation may yet be forthcoming as it is explored further.

The case of the second "missing lady" presents no difficulty. We noted earlier that there was documentary mention of a Miss M. A. Howard in the membership list of the British Psychological Society in 1924; that John Cohen remembered her well during the 1930s; and that Donald MacRae had (in person) received an article and proofs from her in 1949 and 1950. There is therefore no problem here.

All the facts presented here (quite apart from the slight conjectures connected with them—but these too) are remarkably consistent with the contributions and collaboration from both Miss Conway and Miss Howard that Burt claimed; but there is also a remarkable and parallel continuity and consistency in the work undertaken during these years that he attributed to them.

Throughout, Margaret Howard was mentioned with regard to her mathematical ability, and her assistance was recorded in articles of this nature. The acknowledgments of Miss Conway's help, however, are more interesting as they have a very direct bearing on the testing of twins and the continually extended gathering of data.

Miss Conway was first mentioned in the 1943 paper for having contributed findings related to 157 children boarded out in foster homes. In the 1955 paper—the first comparing the correlations of identical twins reared together and apart with those of other siblings reared together and apart—she was mentioned in the same way, as having continued and extended her study of foster children (to 287) and having been particularly engaged in seeking more cases of identical twins. Burt's acknowledgment follows:

> In the [1943] paper just cited, I gave correlations obtained originally from surveys in the London schools, and supplemented them by further

data collected by Miss Conway, who had been responsible for the final computations. Thanks to numerous correspondents, she has since been able to increase the number of cases, particularly for the small but crucial groups of monozygotic twins reared together or apart. The total numbers now amount to 984 siblings, of whom 131 were reared apart; 172 dizygotic or two-egg twins reared together; 83 monozygotic or one-egg twins reared together, and 21 reared apart. By way of contrast, she has also secured data for 287 foster children.

It is important to note, for the purpose of tracing the consistency of the successive reports, that in this 1955 paper (the first full study of identical twins) Burt also commented in a footnote:

> Of the monozygotic twins, only 19 were found in London: and, owing to the distances involved, we have been obliged to depend for measurements of the rest either on research-students or on local teachers and doctors (to whom we must extend our sincerest thanks).

In 1943, the number of identical twins reared apart was 15; by 1955, the extended researches had increased this to 21.

In the Bingham Lecture (delivered in May 1957, published in 1958) Burt simply said that as a result of this persistent research "he and his co-workers" had now "collected over 30 such cases." In the article of November 1958 appearing under Conway's own name, the claim was made that "since the last review of our own cases was published (1955) our collection has been still further enlarged. . . . The number of cases of . . . identical twins reared apart from early infancy now amounts to 42"; and again, the continuity of the search for cases of twins "through personal contacts" and the study of children "boarded out" is the kind of work emphasised. In Burt's final paper on this matter (in 1966), the number of identical twins reared apart had been increased to 53, and again the direction of the ongoing search—in schools, through children boarded out in foster homes, and through personal contacts ("cases to which our attention was drawn by colleagues or correspondents")—was the same, as was the nature of Miss Conway's contribution. Burt's acknowledgment here follows.

> In the initial survey a few of the children living outside London were originally tested by the local teacher or school doctor; but these have all been since re-tested by Miss Conway. I should like once again to

express my indebtedness to all who have assisted in this way, particularly to my former assistant Miss V. G. Pelling (who helped with the
earlier surveys until her untimely death), to Miss Molteno, Mr. Lewis,
Miss Howard, and Miss Conway, as well as the various teachers and
school doctors who frequently supplied physical and medical data.

It is to be noted here that a retesting (by Miss Conway) was
mentioned of the cases (outside London) previously mentioned in
the 1955 paper. Every succeeding paper and reference followed
with complete consistency upon the one published earlier, and in
this last acknowledgment both Howard and Conway were mentioned among the names of others (Pelling, Molteno, Lewis) whose
existence has been well attested beyond doubt. Does not the
parallel consistency of all these facts suggest, at the very least
"beyond reasonable doubt," the actual existence of these two
ladies? Does not the idea that this detailed degree of consistency
was conducted and sustained throughout a sequence of publications
covering a period of over thirty years, and a sequence of studies
covering a period of some forty-five years—all for the perpetration
of a final "fraud"—seem in itself beyond all bounds of credibility?
Is not the altogether hypothetical view (for which there is no
evidence whatever) that Burt would have carried out a calculated
fraud from 1943 onwards—beginning with minor footnotes, and
gradually building up with complete consistency to the increased
numbers and complex tables of correlations of the last two articles—impossible, really, to maintain? And throughout this long
sequence of work, with the most openly published statements and
pronouncements in conspicuous public lectures, were all the other
assistants mentioned in conjunction with Howard and Conway
totally unaware of these names listed in acknowledgments alongside
of their own? Was this entire assemblage of authorities, editors,
and collaborating assistants involved in Burt's researches totally
blind and unaware? It is asking a lot, surely, to believe this. And
where—the crucial question again—was the fraud? The findings
were consistent throughout. Nothing in Burt's later papers tried to
advance a position that was not there in his earlier studies. Why
such an elaborate "invention" of assistants simply to repeat findings that were substantially the same as those he had long ago
presented? We will come back to this. Meanwhile, one final consid-

eration on this one matter deserves mention. It can best take the form of a question.

Had Burt wished to perpetrate a deliberate fraud in these studies, would he have sprinkled his published books and papers so liberally with names that could be seen to be fictitious (or at the very least strange and dubious) by all those engaged in research with him? What was to be gained by so many relatively minor footnotes of a false kind—none of which, at the time of their making, could possibly have foreseen those that were to follow? Had he wished to hide, obscure, or fake his findings, would he have gone to such fastidious lengths in ways bound to be vulnerable to question and discovery? Had fraud been his aim, would it not have been much easier, much less dangerous, much wiser, to leave his text naked of references; never to mention sources, derivations, or assistance? Putting this in another way: might it not have been Burt's very generosity of detailed acknowledgment, his meticulously continued practice of acknowledging all help given him, no matter how small the contribution might have been, that proved the giving of a hostage to fortune? Only two out of the scores of assistants mentioned proved questionable, yet they were enough to call down upon him the charge of fraud.

We must not forget, however, that there was also a third "missing lady," Miss M. G. O'Connor. The same attention has never been devoted to her, and as yet no proof has been forthcoming of her existence. It does not seem profitable, however, after what has been said about the other two ladies, to dwell on Miss O'Connor here, because Burt only referred to her (in the 1969 article) as having compiled a certain table of data on school attainments from 1914 onwards, and we will have to consider this separately later: the crucial question again being, where was the fraud?

For now, however, we must deepen this question about the missing ladies by considering its second chief aspect. What of the charge that Burt himself wrote the articles published under their names, and what was the significance of this for the charge of fraud?

Authorship and Pseudonyms

We are faced here with real and inescapable uncertainties, and must first of all face the difficulties to which these give rise.

Gillie made much of the fact that Gretl Archer joined the Burt household in 1950, never met either Miss Conway or Miss Howard, and herself testified that it was Burt himself who wrote some of the later articles bearing their names, particularly those bearing the name of J. Conway. She has confirmed this last point to me in private conversation, saying indeed that she questioned this with Burt, expressing her feeling that it was something he ought not to do, but that Burt for one specific reason insisted on doing so. There is no reason whatever to doubt this testimony, and we will come to Burt's reason in a moment.

However, between 1950 and 1958 Miss Archer was almost entirely employed on domestic duties because Miss Bruce, Burt's secretary, was still alive. Only after her death in 1958 did Miss Archer fully take over Burt's secretarial work. This means that all the relevant papers up to those published in 1958 (those of 1943, 1955, the 1957 Bingham Lecture, and most probably the "Conway 1958") would have been typed by Miss Bruce, leaving (among this sequence of articles) only the 1966 article to Miss Archer. There is, as we have seen, a complete continuity and consistency in the 1943 to 1958 sequence; no problem at all arises in the sequence of tables presented here; and we have also seen, in at least some personal testimony of Charlotte Banks, evidence to suggest that Miss Bruce *did* have knowledge of Miss Conway and her collected data. Certainly it would be her, if anyone, who would have had intimate knowledge of the part played by "the two ladies" in Burt's researches. The only thing that seems certain is that it was Burt himself who wrote the papers *after* 1958; to be as completely certain as possible, perhaps the "Conway 1958" paper should also be included, as this was published very late in 1958. There is, however a measure of doubt about this that could be important, but this was followed by a further "Conway" article in 1959 (consequent on the earlier article, and being a reply to a criticism by Halsey), and then by the 1966 article containing the last table of twin (and other) correlations—the only table, really, in which difficulties arise.

Thinking of Miss Howard first, it would be Miss Bruce who had typed "The Multifactorial Theory of Inheritance and Its Application to Intelligence"[1] and "The Relative Influence of Heredity and Environment on Assessments of Intelligence,"[2] both of which appeared under the joint names of Burt and Howard. The latter was only a relatively brief piece in the "Notes and Correspondence" section of the journal, but both included very exacting and sophisticated mathematics, and there is no reason whatever to doubt the close collaboration of a mathematical kind claimed between the two authors. There were, however, three smaller pieces after 1958; these continued the same arguments, and we will look at Burt's reasons for continuing such "join authorship" in a moment.

Second, however, on the way in which Miss Conway entered into the sequence of twin articles, a good deal that is quite clear can be said. There is absolutely no question and no difficulty about the papers of 1943, 1955, "Burt 1958" (the 1957 Bingham Lecture), and 1966, because Burt himself was the sole author of these. Miss Conway entered only by way of Burt's acknowledgments, and we have noted the complete consistency exhibited by these. The only paper in this sequence under Conway's own name was that of 1958—"The Inheritance of Intelligence and Its Social Implications—and this was significant in reporting the correlations of the larger number of 42 twins; an increase of 21 from 1955. This was then followed by a 1959 reply to a criticism by Halsey. We will consider possible explanations of these in a moment, but first let us note the reason Burt gave for using their names in this way (whether in joint authorship or alone), and other reasons that have also been suggested by those who knew him. There seem to have been four reasons in all.

Burt's own specific reason was simply that of *deserved acknowledgment*. Both Howard and Conway had contributed greatly (he insisted) over a long period of time in collecting data, administering tests, computing the results, and (in Miss Howard's case) helping with detailed mathematical formulations. They had been among his chief assistants (two, he claimed, of his *three* chief assistants), and he therefore felt that they should be given the full acknowledgment of joint authorship; something he also practiced with other assistants. We will come to the use of Conway's name alone in a moment.

Others have given other reasons. It was chiefly in conversation with Miss Archer that these were mentioned, but I have heard them in various forms from others, too. It has been said that although Burt was no longer in touch with either Howard or Conway, his sense of the debt he owed them for their contributions over many years was such that he wanted the same recognition to continue. It has been said that the reason he was no longer in touch with them was that they had emigrated and he no longer knew their whereabouts, and indeed, that the continued recognition might lead them to get in touch with him again. It has also been said that, such questions of loyalty aside, Burt was very sensitive to the prevailing feeling among academic colleagues that he published too much; something disreputable, it seems, and a source of criticism, from those who never produce much themselves. This criticism seems to have increased with the increasing pressures of controversy as the Hereditarian–Environmentalist arguments, and those relating to social mobility and educational opportunity, grew. This reputation of overproductivity—of being too prolific (as though large quantity was a necessary indication of inferior quality)—was (again, it has been said) a consideration that prompted him to take to pseudonyms and bring names other than his own into the arena of public argument; and all this, too, in addition to his sense of humor (according to Hearnshaw): the delight he took, perhaps, in exploiting his editorial opportunity of sprinkling the journal with different points of view, and (according to Banks) enlivening the pages that suffered from a dearth of other contributions. All of these reasons and accounts, however—though no doubt having genuine sources and having genuine degrees of plausibility—lie in the realm of hearsay, and there seems little point in attaching too much importance to them. The one reason clearly stated by Burt himself, and plentifully evidenced throughout his work, was that of *deserved acknowledgment*. Whether this was a sufficient justification for using the names of Howard and Conway as he did is a matter for our judgment, and I have already recorded what seems a feasible judgment: that, whatever else it might or might not have been, it was certainly a foolish thing to do, opening the door to criticisms from his opponents. However, it is a reason that is at least understandable; something carrying genuine weight.

The crucial question, however, is: What in all this constituted the fraud? Essentially, it seems to lie in Gillie's charge that Burt "attributed to people work they did not do," coupled with Hearnshaw's similar charge that Burt attributed work to the two ladies (Conway in particular) that they could not possibly have done during the period he specified. What is the truth on this matter? What in fact did the sequence of papers claim?

This, necessarily and unavoidably, has to be a little repetitive if matters are to be made perfectly clear.

The 1943 paper acknowledged the correlations reported by Miss Conway from her study of 157 children boarded out in foster homes (most probably during the 1930s and early 1940s), also mentioning the number of 19 identical twins discovered in the early London survey (15 having been reared apart). The 1955 paper acknowledged her assistance in retesting the same 19 cases; extending her data on foster children to an increased number of 287; and by following up information received from correspondents, increasing the number of identical twins reared apart from 15 to 21. It should be noted here that Gillie's claim that "in 1955 Burt reported that Conway was collecting data and undertaking final computations" is not true. Burt's statement was that Conway *had* been responsible for the final computations of data covered *in the 1943 paper*. In the 1957 Bingham Lecture ("Burt 1958"), no reference to Miss Conway was made. Burt referred only to his "co-workers," claiming that by that date "over 30" cases of identical twins reared apart had been collected. In the 1958 paper under Conway's name, the brief mention of new data came only towards the end by way of comparison with new studies by Eysenck and Shields, and there was no claim of new studies by Miss Conway herself. The very limited statement (presuming that Burt wrote it) was only this:

> Since the last review of our own cases was published (1955) our collection has been still further enlarged. . . . Our earlier cases were encountered during the routine inspections of children brought up in residential institutions under the L.C.C.: not infrequently it turned out that the child in the institution was a twin, and that the other twin had been left with the mother or with relatives. Among our later cases most were discovered through personal contacts; and, as a result, many of them came of educated parents, usually school teachers or members of a University staff: when the pair was separated, one twin generally remained with the mother and shared her cultural environment, while the other was boarded out, usually with persons of much lower intellectual status. . . .

> The number of cases of this type—all identical twins reared apart from early infancy—now amounts to 42.

In the 1966 paper, the data referred to were still predominantly those gradually accumulated from the earlier surveys onwards, and Miss Conway's assistance (together with that of others) was still closely related to this. There was no claim of new investigations on her part. The predominant emphasis was on a reworking of the old, and on her contributions of the past.

The plain upshot, then, is that no fraudulent claim was made about the assistance of Miss Conway, or as to the period in which it was undertaken, despite the fact that the 1958 and 1959 papers appeared under her name. On the contrary, the record of her assistance, and all the references to it, are remarkably consistent throughout the entire sequence of articles. Burt may well have been unwise (as Miss Archer suggested to him and as we have said) to publish these articles under Conway's name, but there is no evidence of fraudulent claims in them, and this will be seen even more definitely when we come to consider the charge that Burt had fabricated data. But to press the question as far as it will go, why, in these two articles, did Burt practice what, on the face of it, was a plain deception? And why do this when, no new claims or changed arguments being presented, it seemed totally unnecessary? In trying to answer this, we must bear in mind that Burt was far from being afraid to enter into public controversy and bear the brunt of adverse criticism. What, then, could his reasons have been? Only two possible reasons seem at all conceivable: the one that he had stated himself, of *deserved recognition;* and the other, that of bringing into the growing controversy over intelligence, education, social class, and social mobility, a name other than his own, a participant other than himself.

This paper was quite specifically directed at the question of the distribution of intelligence in social classes, offering a criticism of the views advanced by some of the sociologists of education. It is difficult to believe, however, that the second reason mentioned above can have carried much weight, as the positions outlined and argued in it were those of Burt; the only possible virtue of it being, perhaps, the appearance given of someone else arguing in support of Burt—but since Conway was known to be such a close colleague of his, this itself could not have counted greatly. Only *deserved recognition* remains, and something of a clue might lie in the nature of the figures presented. All the acknowledgments in the preceding articles made it clear that Miss Conway had been chiefly responsible—by her following up of correspondents and personal contacts—for increasing the number of identical twins discovered, and for retesting and updating the data of those discovered earlier. The increase from the original 15 (in 1943) through the 21 (in 1955) and the "over 30" (in May 1957) to the 42 (in 1958) was evidently chiefly the outcome of her efforts. The first reporting of the new correlations of the larger number of twins reared together and apart (particularly of the new number of 42 reared apart) was in this 1958 paper, and in the table presenting them *only the two columns of correlations on these twins were new; all* the rest of the table (*all the other columns in it*) was exactly the same as the table of 1955. This table, in short, offered an updated computation only of the newly enlarged number of twins, and this may well have stemmed almost entirely from (or even been almost entirely) the work of Miss Conway. Although in the table the figures were still presented under the joint names of Burt and Conway, might it not have been Burt's gesture of recognition of her work (perhaps more substantial in this than in what had gone into the earlier papers) to publish this article under her name alone? And having done this, might it not have been a necessary corollary to have the 1959 article appear under her name too, as this was a follow-up reply entirely contingent upon Halsey's criticism of the 1958 article?

This, of course, cannot possibly be regarded as a firm explanation approaching anything like certainty. All one can say is that it is consistent with all of the facts and with Burt's known practices, and since no elements of deception or fraud are to be detected in either of the two articles (the arguments and facts presented are perfectly clear in both), an explanation of this kind carries more force than any other, and something more can be said on this when we consider the supposed fabrication of data.

Before this, however, we must touch briefly on the wider charge that Burt frequently wrote under pseudonyms. Hearnshaw's comment is worth recalling:

Fictitious contributions were a convenient device whereby Burt could express his views, and call attention to his achievements, in the statistical journal, without his too obviously monopolising space. . . . No doubt this exercise, which other editors are known to have indulged in, tickled Burt's well-developed sense of humour, as well as very often providing him with excuses to expound his own view under his own name by way of reply.

Hearnshaw himself claimed to have counted "more than forty" such fictitious persons, but here again we are surely in the realm of conjecture impossible to verify one way or another. Let us, however, fully concede it. What then? What evidence was there of fraudulence in this? Also, bearing in mind that evidently the pages of the journal were not easy to fill, and that Burt worked so hard and contributed so much out of his own pocket to support it; and bearing in mind his "well-developed sense of humour" and, as Hearnshaw tolerantly recognized, the fact that it was by no means an otherwise unknown editorial practice—was this so unpardonable a thing to do?

However this may be, the crucial point, is only this: There was no evidence in all of this scientific fraud. Miss Mawer's (Mrs. Carke's) judgment still seems the most relevant: that she could quite see Burt "finding it amusing to bamboozle the over-confident, but a calculated major scientific fraud is another matter." It remains only to be said that the many mentions of both Howard and Conway in the whole sequence of articles, the many acknowledgments of their assistance, and even the appearance of their names in coauthorship or (to a very limited extent) as sole authors, made absolutely no difference to their factual substance, the arguments, and the positions they maintained. Why, then, mention them as Burt did? The only reason that seems at all plausible is that of *recording an appreciation of their collaboration and help that was quite genuinely felt and meant*. This can be seen to have further dimensions as we turn now to the third major charge of fraud.

The Fabrication of Evidence

Here we are on much firmer ground. For the substantiation of *this* charge, perhaps the most serious, there is absolutely no conclusive evidence. Burt's detractors claimed that two sets of data were invented: the increased number of twins in the later studies (from 1955 through 1958 to 1966), and that offered in the *Irish Journal* article on the basis of which Burt was said to have claimed "a

deterioration in educational standards." Following our consideration of the missing ladies, let us first continue our examination of
the charge against the twin studies.

Hearnshaw, readily conceding that the numbers of twins in the
1943 and 1955 papers were validly reported, categorically denied
that any new data could possibly have been collected from the mid-
1950s onwards; his ground for this flat assertion was his claim that
the record of Burt's diaries was "decisive," proving "the pretence
of on-going research . . . a complete fabrication." We have seen,
however, that Hearnshaw's own account of the diaries is radically
questionable to the point of seeming completely unreliable. We
have also seen in the twin articles themselves (whether under the
name of Burt or Conway) that the extended and enlarged data of
the later papers stemmed from two sources: (1) primarily from a
more detailed retesting and working over of the material collected
in the earlier surveys (in Liverpool, Birmingham, and London), and
(2) from cases brought to the attention of Burt and his co-workers
by correspondents and other personal contacts. Indeed, it was the
second source that explained why these later cases were increasingly children of professional parents. Let us consider each of these
sources in turn.

There is no doubt whatever that Burt was *continually* working
over, more and more meticulously, the large collection of test
scores accumulated from his several early surveys. All who have
testified to this collection of data have agreed about the enormous
quantity of it, the jumbled way in which it was heaped together,
and—particularly as a result of the wartime evacuation and the
unknown degree of the destruction of some of it in the bombing of
University College—the questionable degree of its coverage. Much
here can only remain in the realm of the unprovable, but some
things at least are certain. It is known that the packing of boxes
and sacks of documents and the test sheets from schools for the
evacuation was a great muddle, with no one quite knowing what
was sent where (whether to University College or to Aberystwyth);
but that several sacks were taken to Aberystwyth and "thrown into
a damp and dirty coal cellar there," where they remained until the
return to London, when they were emptied out into a great pile on
the floor of a room in Burt's flat. It was only gradually, after his
retirement, when he was able to work more thoroughly on his

accumulated material (there had never been time in Aberyswyth) that Miss Archer began to sort through the papers as Burt required them, and Miss Archer had in fact a very clear memory of the test scores among them. There was, she said,

> a quantity of very long scrolls, bound in a light gray cover, which unwound to a length of a metre or so, each containing several sheets. Each sheet was divided into many columns, each column containing the test scores of one pupil. Below were the subjects tested (Arithmetic, Reading, Intelligence, etc.), and a test score was recorded against each. There were perhaps six or even seven such subject-headings. Some pupils and their scores were marked with distinctive crosses—of differing colours—and these *might* have been indicators of twins. . . .

All those who knew Burt well and remained in touch with him after his retirement—Miss Archer, Professor Valentine, Charlotte Banks, Robert Reid (for whom Burt wrote a regular article throughout the seven years before his death), and others—knew that he was continually reworking this earlier data and drawing upon it. Perhaps the clearest testimony of this was Valentine's. Pointing out that it was only after his resignation from his LCC appointment that Burt "at last had time to begin sorting out and analysing the immense fund of data he and his coworkers had amassed," he continued: "Indeed, he is still occupied in analysing some of it to throw new light on current questions as they arise." This was written in 1965! In the last (1966) paper, the actual comment on the number of twins then included bore references chiefly to work of the past:

> It will be seen that the number of monozygotic pairs we have studied now amounts to 148, of whom fifty-three have been reared apart. Of the ninety-five pairs who were reared together, the majority attended London schools; thirty-seven came from areas outside London: nearly half of these were encountered during an investigation I was asked to carry out for the Birmingham Education Authority; several were discovered in the Warwickshire area, where my family lived; and the rest were cases to which our attention was drawn by colleagues or correspondents. In each of the fifty-three pairs reared apart one child at least was a Londoner in all but eight cases. All had been separated either at birth or during their first six months of life. . . .[3]

After Burt's death, the greater part of the accumulated data remaining was destroyed by Miss Archer on the advice of Liam

Hudson (a strange recommendation indeed). So again, the actual nature of the data can never possibly be demonstrated. What is certain, however, is that throughout his retirement, Burt was continually reworking it, and the increased size of the number of children covered by, and represented in, the successive tables in his articles (not only of twins reared apart) could well have stemmed substantially from this source. There is also direct evidence in the articles themselves both of this reworking of existing data and of its extension by information received from correspondents and personal contacts.

In the very latest of the controversial articles on twins,[3] Burt took issue with Shields, who had criticized him for a lack of "twin information" in his 1943 paper (an incredible criticism knowing, as we now do, the nature of that paper). Quite justly, Burt replied:

> He regrets that I have 'given no other information about the twins brought up apart'. The paper which he cites, however, was concerned primarily with the 'influence of innate ability and parental income on entrance to universities', and the mention of twins was merely incidental. For further information I expressly referred to previous L.C.C. Reports, and explained that my own research students were still 'working on data obtained for twins up to the outbreak of the war'. After the war a fuller account was printed in the same journal (Burt, 1955), and the statistical evidence set out in some detail by my co-workers and myself in one of the more technical periodicals (Burt and Howard, 1957; Conway, 1958). Both the earlier and the later publications, however, seem to have escaped Dr. Shield's attention.[4]

He added that in addition to the "further cases of separated twins brought to our notice as a result of these discussions . . . more information has now been obtained for the earlier cases from the follow-up enquiries." The "working on earlier data" had clearly continued up to 1955, but also went on continually after that date. In addition, it is highly significant to note that, continually and consistently—from the 1943 article right up to the year prior to the publication of the 1966 article—Burt was publicly *requesting* information on twins; indeed, it is not too much to say *advertising* for knowledge of them. Throughout, Burt had maintained that the generally held assumption that identical twins were *rare* was a *mistake,* and emphasising this, had urged other investigators to look for them more carefully. In the 1966 paper, he wrote:

Most writers (e.g. Shields, 1962, pp. vi, 9) apparently suppose that *'monozygotic* twins who have been separated from early childhood are of great rarity.' This we believe to be founded on a misconception. At the time of our main survey the number of twins among children born in London (excluding those who were not British) amounted to 1.4%; and of these nearly a quarter must have been monozygotic. This follows because among twins generally about 38% are of unlike sex; and among dizygotic twins the number of pairs of like sex must be approximately equal to the number of unlike sex. Monozygotic pairs are always of the same sex. Hence about $100 - 2 \times 38 = 24\%$ of all twins must be monozygotic. Twins brought up together usually attend the same or neighbouring schools, and even after full allowance has been made for the higher mortality of twins during pre-school years, the proportion discoverable by school visiting alone is far less than would be expected from the number of those born. What happens is fairly clear. Many mothers are unable or unwilling to rear two children at the same time; but they are generally reluctant for it to be known that they have arranged for one of the children to be removed at or soon after birth. Since the actual placements are often carried out by the local authority or by some public body, a psychologist or social worker who is also a member of the staff can usually obtain full particulars for a large number of such cases. Hitherto most of the published researches have been undertaken by outside investigators who have no access to these confidential records. *May we therefore urge that other educational psychologists, who have the advantage of being on the staff of a local authority, should conduct similar inquiries along much the same lines?*[5]

In the 1955 paper, however, admitting that the number of identical twins reared apart he had by that time discovered was still small (21, and "the outcome of a quest that has lasted for over 40 years"), he had already written:

There is a natural prejudice against separating twins, especially if their sex is the same, and we should like to repeat our appeal for further cases.

And in the *News Letter of the Association of Educational Psychologists* in 1965 (number 3, and mentioning precisely the same number that appeared in the 1966 article), Burt, still (through this News Letter) in contact with a wide range of his earlier students, was advertising for more twins:

During the past 50 years my colleagues and I have kept a careful watch for cases of this kind—"identical twins reared apart from infancy. At first we could discover only a handful. But as soon as our results were published, more cases kept coming in, and we have now located as many as 53 pairs. *We should still be grateful for additional names and addresses.*

It is also important to note that this contact and communication with past students went on until, literally, a month or two before Burt's death. Hearnshaw makes much of the fact that Burt was increasingly deaf, so much so as to have been unable to have received any information about twins by telephone. It is true that Burt suffered from increasing deafness, but I have a tape (generously loaned by Robert Reid) recording a conversation in Burt's apartment (between Burt, himself, and a Dr. Zimmermann from Los Angeles) that took place only a few months before Burt's death, giving no evidence of difficulty in hearing. Robert Reid also frequently spoke to him on the telephone. Hearnshaw's evidence is therefore very far short of being conclusive, even here. The detail of the additional cases derived from personal communications (as distinct from the "test figures" of those from the earlier surveys) may also be seen in the description given in the (Conway) 1959 paper. There, referring to the "range of the social and cultural scale" in the cases discovered, it was quite plainly said that

owing to the fact that many of the cases were ascertained through personal contact, it so happened that there was an appreciable number of pairs (11 out of 42) in which one of the twins was brought up in a household which Dr. Halsey would certainly class as belonging to his highest category: the head of the household was a university or school teacher, a 'business owner', a 'manager', or the like. In three of these cases the child had been adopted; and here the other twin was in one case left with its mother (a charwoman, whose husband—a dock-labourer—was almost continually out of work), and in a second case sent to an orphanage: in the third case the child was left with its middle class parents, and so does not directly concern us here. In the remaining six cases, where the twins were children of parents belonging to the 'professional' classes, one member of each pair remained with the parents. Of those who were not brought up by the parents, three were sent to an orphanage, one was boarded out with an impecunious member of the child's own family, two were boarded out with foster-mothers of the 'unskilled worker' class, and two with foster-parents who were of an uneducated type but in moderately comfortable circumstances, that is, they belonged to the lowest cultural, though not to the lowest economic, class.[6]

There is therefore no evidence whatever to substantiate any charge of fradulent fabrication of data in the twin studies. The destruction of the raw data (including the test scores) itself places any proof of its nature totally within the realm of the unprovable, but this has only served the quite unfounded speculation of Burt's detractors. There is every reason to suppose that the reworking of the records of past surveys and the additional cases brought to Burt's attention by his repeated requests and the increasing discussion of the matter were the sufficient grounds for the enlargement of the sample covered in his later tables; and the sheer *consistency* of the account formulated in the sequence of the articles gives very solid support to this supposition.

The other charge of having fabricated data was leveled at the table of evidence presented in Burt's *Irish Journal* article, but even Hearnshaw refers to this as having been only "partially fabricated," and an examination of it quickly leads to the conclusion that this whole matter was something of a tempest in a teacup. Nonetheless, it should be dealt with.

Again, the much disputed data (such as it was) came only at the end of an article that was centrally concerned with some common misconceptions encountered in considering the subject of intelligence and heredity, and at a point where Burt was simply questioning the widely prevailing view that with the improvement in environmental conditions and educational provisions there had been a parallel improvement in the standards of attainment in educational performance (and, indeed, in levels of measured intelligence). He doubted this, expressed these doubts, and was bitterly attacked and condemned for having claimed that there had been a general deterioration in these standards. Such sweeping criticisms were completely unwarranted, and it is best simply to see exactly what Burt did say, and to see the exact nature of the data he presented. Having discussed the findings for intelligence, he turned to *school attainments*[7]

For a comparison of school attainments I am indebted to a study carried out by Miss M. G. O'Connor. She has compiled data from various surveys and reports from 1914 onwards, based on tests applied by teachers or research students. They relate to the last year of the primary school (age 10 to 11). The data are presented in Table 1 [Table 12.1].

TABLE 12.1.
Comparison of School Attainments, 1914–1965

Year	Intelligence	Reading		Spelling	Arithmetic	
		Accuracy	Compre- hension		Mechan- ical	Problems
1914	100·3	101·4	100·1	102·8	103·2	101·3
1917	100·1	95·3	96·5	94·7	91·1	92·5
1920	100·0	100·0	100·0	100·0	100·0	100·0
1930	98·6	100·7	105·2	100·8	103·4	94·7
1945	99·3	90·8	91·1	89·5	88·9	93·2
1955	99·8	95·1	96·9	93·8	91·4	95·5
1965	99·5	96·7	99·4	94·6	95·5	97·6

The figures in the table are medians; those obtained in 1920 (the year of the survey reported in *Mental and scholastic tests*) are taken as 100. The most striking feature that emerges is the zig-zag fluctuation in each of the subjects tested, never very large, and due mainly, it would seem, to the effects of the wars and the subsequent recovery in each case. As the Plowden Report (10) and other investigations have amply demonstrated, there has been, since the end of the last war, a substantial improvement in the basic subjects—most of all in comprehension of reading. Yet even so, especially where accuracy is concerned, the level reached in each of the three R's is still below that which was attained in 1914, when teachers concentrated almost all their efforts on these fundamental processes. If we took the medians for that year as standard, then the decline would be still more obvious: the figures for spelling would be only 91.1 and for mechanical arithmetic 92.5. A comparison of essays written by average school children in 1914 and fifty years later reveals yet more obvious signs of decline, at least so far as the formal aspects are concerned. Certainly the later specimens are, on the whole, more imaginative, more amusing, and (as one of my colleagues puts it) 'freer from inhibitions.' But judged from a practical and prosaic standpoint, there is a marked falling off in clarity, factual accuracy, and respect for evidence and logic. For this, I fancy, psychologists themselves are partly to blame. Piaget and his followers have led many teachers to accept the traditional notion that reasoning does not develop until the age of eleven or later (a view which I hold to be quite contrary to the experimental evidence) and that during the primary stage the chief aim should be to develop imagination, self-expression, and what it is the fashion to call 'creativity.'

All such comparisons are admittedly precarious. But the figures I have quoted appear to be the best we can get in the way of objective data. And there is in addition a cumulative mass of vaguer evidence pointing in the same direction. In connection with the 'preliminary examination' (preceding the annual scholarship examination) which the LCC instituted for a while, booklets of group tests for intelligence, English and arithmetic, were carefully prepared. These have since been published, and are still used by teachers and examiners on a fairly wide scale in different parts of the country. Here too the results bear out what I have already said. Quite independently a number of other investigators have reached somewhat similar conclusions, based on studies on their own.

Several points can be noted quite clearly in this quotation, and each deserves emphasis. First, no claim whatever was made here of any collection of *new data,* or the administering of any *new tests* to primary school children. The table was no more than a bringing together of the ''various surveys and reports of others'' in an attempt to measure performance before and after the *base* of 1920. Hearnshaw himself readily conceded that reports existed for the years 1917, 1920, 1930, and 1945—and actually cited these in detail—but claimed that the details for years 1914, 1955, and 1965 were ''more difficult to explain.'' It is clear, however, that Burt had been testing children from 1913 onwards, and that during the later years he and others would have been well aware of the studies conducted then. We will touch on this matter again in a moment.

Second, Burt did indicate, even here, the ''vaguer evidence'' that existed—which was considerable—and also made it clear that he was well aware of the evidence presented by (and undertaken for) the Plowden Committee, some of it stemming from the National Foundation for Educational Research. It also has to be borne in mind that Burt's data related to ''the last year of the primary school (age 10 to 11),'' so that, for example, the evidence provided by the preliminary examinations before the scholarship examination, or later, ''mock tests'' prior to the eleven-plus examination, would be directly relevant.

Third and quite clearly, Burt most certainly did *not* argue, however, that there had been *a general or total deterioration (or decline) in standards.* On the contrary, he pointed to the ''zig-zag fluctuations'' (probably due to the effects of wars) and to the fact that some *improvements* in standards had been achieved. His only claim was that the view of a general ongoing progress was questionable, and in particular, that, with changed methods of teaching, the evidence seemed to suggest a decline in accuracy in "the three R's," subjects that for him were very basic. But here it is worthwhile to return briefly to my point that Burt, in the later years, was well aware of the findings of ongoing studies, and in his comments on them had already made these same points, without at all, at that time, raising an uproar of opposition. In the "Conway 1958" paper (which we have presumed written by Burt), the findings of Floud, Halsey, and Martin on the measured intelligence of children in the different social and occupational classes in S. W. Hertfordshire (in 1952) and Middlesbrough (in 1953) were examined. These were then compared with findings for London children for the years 1922 to 1927; the comparison demonstrating that "the improvement in social circumstances had in no way produced a rise in the level of intelligence as assessed by the intelligence tests." The chief point of this reference, however, is that to this Burt added a footnote (p. 174):

> I may add that, so far as the limited data available go, the re-application of the older tests to pupils now attending London schools shows very little difference so far as intelligence is concerned, but a slight decline in arithmetic and spelling: on the other hand, in tests of comprehension in reading there seems, if anything, to be a slight improvement. However, before such results can be accepted, a systematic survey of carefully selected samples would be essential. Even then, it is to be remembered, there have been appreciable social changes in many areas, and nowadays families move in and out of London on an even larger scale than before.

Quite clearly the same points were made here in 1958, the same judgments on some declining some improving standards, and with clear reference to the findings of sociologists during the 1950s, as those made in the 1969 article—yet to the best of my knowledge no outburst of condemnation attended them then. It is important to recall, too, that Burt's diaries showed him continually trying to obtain examples of children's compositions from schools to compare with those written in earlier times, and still clearly in touch with colleagues who could supply him with these.

Another point, however, rests very much on the word *seemed*.

Burt, as is quite evident, was far from claiming anything approaching *certainty* for either his data or his conclusions. He simply thought that a case had been presented for *questioning* prevailing assumptions, and stated this with perfect clarity.

> Commenting on 'the alleged decline in educational standards over the past fifty years' Professor Vernon rightly notes the difficulty of procuring samples which can be safely regarded as comparable. This caution applied equally to the figures set out above. Yet, even if we make the most liberal allowance for this and other sources of inaccuracy, we must at least acknowledge that they present a strong *prima facie* case against the unverified claims so often advanced for large-scale improvements during the last half century.[8]

In giving reasons for his conclusion that Burt's later figures were "fabricated," Hearnshaw went to strangely exaggerated lengths. From 1955 onwards Burt, he said, had no right of entry to London schools, had no research funds at his disposal, and "*the whole massive operation* involved in ascertaining changes in standards . . . left not a trace in Burt's *detailed diary entries,* nor in his *carefully filed correspondence.*" But Table 12.1 quite plainly did not rest at all on a "*massive operation of testing.*" To speak of it in this way was to misrepresent its very nature.[9] It was, and only claimed to be, merely a compilation of existing (and variable) tests and surveys. No crucial certainty was claimed for it, only that it presented the grounds for a *prima facie* case calling for consideration. We have also seen that Burt's diary entries were decidedly *not* detailed; indeed, that they gave a far from complete record. And we have already mentioned, and the testimony from all sides agrees, that a very considerable amount of Burt's correspondence was not carefully filed; indeed it is most probable (writing so many letters in longhand, having only limited secretarial assistance) that much of it did not even have copies. Hearnshaw's emphasis on these charges is therefore itself highly questionable; the grounds of his claims are open to very considerable doubt. Indeed, they appear quite false. It is as though, intent on proving his case, he went to unwarranted lengths to over-prove it.

The one thing that does remain true, however, is that Miss M. G. O'Connor does remain a third missing lady. She has not yet been traced. While there is substantial evidence of various kinds for the actual existence of Miss Howard and Miss Conway, there seems to be none so far for the existence of Miss O'Connor.[10] This is one element, therefore, on which Burt's detractors can still legitimately dwell. What difference the question of her existence makes to Burt's *argument* is difficult to see, but on this issue, at present, the evidence can do no other than "stay silent." We are, in this case, in the realm not so much of the unprovable, but of what, so far, remains unproved.

Hearnshaw's verdict was that "in three instances, beyond reasonable doubt, Burt was guilty of deception. He falsified the early history of factor analysis; he produced spurious data on monozygotic twins; and he fabricated figures on declining levels of scholastic achievement." We have shown, well beyond reasonable doubt, that each of these charges is at the very least decidedly unproven, but much more probably, false. It is Hearnshaw's verdict, far more than the work of Burt to which these charges refer, that is most open to grave doubt.

But one other major charge remains.

The Invariant Correlations

Our final consideration of this last charge must once more, of necessity, be a little repetitive. The evidence brought in our cross-examination established some things conclusively. To this, however, new evidence and new arguments now have to be added. This will involve some very specific and precise details, and some complications, about which it is essential that we should be very exact. The best procedure, then, is to summarize as concisely as possible the position established so far, so that what follows can then be meticulously clear.

Initial Summary of Cross-Examination

We established conclusively that no problems whatever arose in and throughout the whole sequence of papers published between 1943 and 1958: 1943, 1955, "Burt 1958" (the May 1957 Bingham Lecture), and "Conway 1958." There were, in these articles, no "invariant correlations" that were problematical or required special explanation. There was no inconsistency or difficulty in the numbers of twins reported or in the tables presented. This may be checked again by referring to the tables and arguments on pages 68 to 76.

The 1943 paper presented no table. It simply reported the discovery (among all the sibling relationships) of 19 identical twins, 15 of them reared apart. The 1955 paper reported the increase in the number of identical twins to 104—83 reared together, 21 reared apart—as well as an increase in the number of other siblings, and for the first time presented a full table of correlations. The "Burt 1958" paper (the publication of Burt's 1957 Bingham Lecture) did no more than precisely repeat, in every detail, the entire "Mental and Scholastic" section of the 1955 table, leaving out the physical measurements. *Every* correlation in this paper was exactly the same, and *exactly to the third decimal place,* as those in the 1955 paper, for the simple reason that it was a lecture-quotation of this table—nothing more. Kamin, however, out of thirty-six correlations repeated, perceived and drew attention to *only two,* the .944 and .771 of the identical twins reared together and apart, recording these calculations as the results of a new study of "over 30" twins.

The "Conway 1958" paper reported only an increase in the number of identical twins reared apart, to 42. No increase in the number of other siblings was reported, not even of identical twins reared together, and in the table presented *only* the correlations for the identical twins were changed. The rest of the table *in its entirety* was exactly repeated; some forty-four correlations being again repeated in exact detail to the third decimal place. In this *first change* in the number of identical twins reported and studied since that reported in 1955 (which had itself reported a gradual increase from 15 to 21 over a period of 12 years), the correlations shown between them were *in every respect different. Not one* "invariant correlation" to the third decimal place was at all involved. We noted earlier, as a point of importance, that in this table, as was quite specifically claimed, *only* these correlations were recalculated; the rest were reported exactly as they had previously stood. The precise statement was:

The number of cases of this type—all identical twins reared apart from early infancy—now amounts to 42. . . . Since the data previously published (1955, p. 168) related only to the smaller sample then available, I give a more complete and up-to-date set of correlations in the table.

In all this, two points[11] already touched on before deserve special emphasis. We have noted the requests for information about twins repeated by Burt and his assistants from 1943 onwards, and the continued and more precise retesting of existing cases and the search for new pairs of twins carried out by Miss Conway. It seems quite clear from the reports in the sequence of papers that this search had been predominantly directed to the discovery of identical twins *reared apart*. Even by 1966 the number of those *reared together* had only increased to 95. By 1958, therefore, the number reared together could not have increased greatly beyond the number reported in 1955 of 83. The closeness of the correlations in the first columns of the 1955 and 1958 tables suggest and seem to reflect this, and this deserves note.

One other fact deserves clear recall and particular mention. In correspondence with Jensen about one of Jensen's own articles (that of 1968 in which he had reproduced Burt's 1955 and 1958 Bingham Lecture tables), Burt had already pointed out (long before any controversy arose) that the .944 figure for the group test of identical twins reared together was a typographical error. The correct figure was .904, and had been "unwittingly transferred into his 1958 article," Jensen wrote, "in which he had simply reproduced his whole table from . . . 1955." In all the tables up to the point of 1958, therefore, the .944 figure should have been .904.

The plain upshot is that there is therefore not the slightest evidence of anything remotely approaching fraud in the entire sequence of articles from 1943 to 1958. Quite literally, *no invariant correlations relating to different numbers of identical twins were presented in these tables at all*. Given the controversy, this is an astonishing—but nonetheless completely true—conclusion. It also has an equally plain corollary. Any fraud in the matter of "invariant correlations" can only possibly lie in the table presented in the 1966 paper. This is reproduced here as table 12.2.

The 1966 Table: Facts and Questions

What points emerge from a careful analysis of table 12.2 and of the article in which it appeared? Each of these deserves separate note and consideration.

TABLE 12.2.

Correlations for Mental, Educational, and Physical Characteristics

	A. Burt et al.						B. Newman et al.		
Number of pairs* …	Mono-zygotic twins reared together 95	Mono-zygotic twins reared apart 53	Dizygotic twins reared together 127	Siblings reared together 264	Siblings reared apart 151	Unrelated children reared together 136	Mono-zygotic twins reared together 50	Mono-zygotic twins reared apart 19	Dizygotic twins reared together 51
Intelligence									
Group test	0·944	0·771	0·552	0·545	0·412	0·281	0·922	0·727	0·621
Individual test	0·918	0·863	0·527	0·498	0·423	0·252	0·881	0·767	0·631
Final assessment	0·925	0·874	0·453	0·531	0·438	0·267	—	—	—
Educational									
Reading and spelling	0·951	0·597	0·919	0·842	0·490	0·545	—	—	—
Arithmetic	0·862	0·705	0·748	0·754	0·563	0·478	—	—	—
General attainments	0·983	0·623	0·831	0·803	0·526	0·537	0·892	0·583	0·696
Physical									
Height	0·962	0·943	0·472	0·501	0·536	−0·069	0·932	0·969	0·645
Weight	0·929	0·884	0·586	0·568	0·427	0·243	0·917	0·886	0·631
Head length	0·961	0·958	0·495	0·481	0·506	0·110	0·910	0·017	0·691
Head breath	0·977	0·960	0·541	0·510	0·492	0·082	0·908	0·880	0·654
Eye colour	1·000	1·000	0·516	0·554	0·524	0·104	—	—	—

Figures for boys and girls have been calculated separately and then averaged. In columns 3, 4, 5 and 6 the correlations for head-length, head-breadth, eye colour were based on samples of 100 only.

Writing and Revision: Dates and Circumstances

There are a number of telling facts and questions about the actual writing and revision of this article that seem at least in part to explain why, in several ways, it seems out of keeping with those that preceded it. These present, however, a rather confused picture about which it is extremely difficult to be clear. Hearnshaw himself has much to say on this.

He claims that (according to Burt's diary) the article was written in one week, between May thirteenth and nineteenth, in 1964; that it was revised on June twelfth "before being sent off to the *British Journal of Psychology*"; and that "further revisions" took place during 1965. It was published in 1966. Hearnshaw also claims that, "written in haste and anger," the article was essentially a response to Burt's critics in the developing Hereditarian/Environmentalist controversy; particularly a reply to criticisms raised by Shields and McLeish. Hearnshaw also points out that throughout this period Burt was "heavily involved in other activities": reporting on twenty-one manuscripts for Allen and Unwin, writing other articles, examining, reviewing books, and "writing hundreds of letters." Furthermore (he was then over 80 years of age), Burt was aware that his mental powers of attention, reasoning, concentration, and accuracy were, to use his own words, "deteriorating very markedly." Hearnshaw quotes him (from letters to his sister Marion) as saying "My mind seems to be ageing. Three quarters of an hour's logical thinking is as much as I can do at one spell . . . and what I write has to be checked and re-written many times before it is fit for the printer. Most of the mistakes are quite childish." Hearnshaw's summary on these matters was: "Carelessness, then, partly the result of haste and partly the result of emotional involvement and declining powers, was assuredly a contributory ingredient in the final product." He goes on, of course, to accuse Burt of deception (over the part played by Miss Howard and Miss Conway), but what can be added to these details by way of both facts and questions from an examination of the article itself?

Some questions arise over the matter of dates. The article itself (published in 1966) states that it was received by the journal on September 8, *1965,* (strangely out of keeping with Hearnshaw's date of delivery). We have also seen that it was Easter 1965 when

Burt advertised for more twins in the AEP News Letter, saying then that the number of identical twins reared apart had been increased to 53. There is therefore confirmation of consistency in this respect. Again, it is clear that the emphasis in Burt's search had been upon identical twins *reared apart;* the number of those *reared together* having only increased from 83 to 95 over the period of ten years or so. It is also evident in the article itself that it was indeed written within the context of the growing heredity versus environment controversy. The critics Burt noted were Woolf (1952), Stott (1956), Lewis (1957), Maddox (1957), Halsey (1959), and McLeish (1963), but he was more immediately stimulated to write (or revise) his own article by articles on mental inheritance by Liam Hudson and Dr. Hammerton, which were followed by correspondence in the *Listener* between June 24 and July 17, 1965. The article has every appearance of having been written, in short, as an immediate response to what Burt regarded as a false usage of the term *intelligence,* and was an attempt to bring together the findings of the several studies of identical twins reared together and apart. The curiously delayed date of the year of publication therefore rather belied its urgently controversial nature, and this is even more particularly so in view of Hearnshaw's evidence that the first writing of the article was as early as May 1964. What these details make clear beyond doubt, however, is that this article was written in haste, as a presentation of facts and arguments to counter critics; was much revised on a number of occasions during a period of (apparently) almost two years, each time (evidently) taking into account new criticisms that had arisen; and during a period when Burt was both extremely busy with other matters and increasingly vulnerable to inaccuracies in his own writing and in his reading of typescript and proofs.

A final matter of fact that should be noted (whatever its significance might be) is that *no other increase in the numbers of siblings studied was reported.* The entire emphasis of the study was on the identical twins reared together and apart, the calculated correlations of the other categories being there by way of comparison but without any claims as to any general or overall increase in their size.

With these background points in mind, what is to be said about the actual figures that have been so much in dispute?

Columns and Correlations

Examining the first two columns of identical twins reared together and apart, it can be seen that *no* correlations are the same in the "mental and scholastic" measurements of the 1958 and 1966 tables. There are no "invariant correlations" here. The only repeated correlations are those of *physical measurements,* and we will consider these separately in a moment.

Examining next the first two columns in the 1955 and 1966 tables (table 3.9) (and bearing in mind that the .944 figure in the earlier table should have been .904), it can be seen that in the "mental and scholastic" measurements there are *three* repeated correlations (to the third decimal place): the .771 for the "group test" of identical twins reared apart, the .925 "final assessment" of identical twins reared together, and the .862 "arithmetic" figure for identical twins reared together. The figures for *physical measurements* are again very close, though slightly different, but they are precisely the same (apart from those for height) as the 1958 figures. What can be said about these three "invariant correlations" among the "mental and scholastic " measurements?

It seems to me arguable that it is only the .771 for the group test of twins reared apart that is really (statistically) surprising. Even so, why should it be considered bogus? It is true that the number of these twins had increased from 21 in 1955 to 53 some 20 years later, but the figure of .771 (based upon a *group test*) was the *only* invariant correlation in all the three tables presented. (In passing, we may recall that the correlation in 1943 was .77, and will question a little later the significance, whether for a charge of fraud or otherwise, of the difference of .001.) Had Burt wished to carry out a deliberate fraud, would it not have been the easiest thing in the world for him to record a slight change in this figure? The unqualified, quite unguarded recording of the "invariance" itself is almost such as to vouch for its truth—and for Burt's openness and integrity.

The two correlations among the identical twins reared together, though questionable, do not seem difficult to accept. The number of these twins had risen only from 83 to 95; the 83 were still by far the preponderant continuing group within the final overall total, so that a close agreement in correlation was more to be expected.

Furthermore, the .925 was Burt's "final assessment" figure for mental measurement; it is not known (as far as I am aware) what adjustments he took into account in arriving at this figure from the group and individual tests; and again, had he wished to defraud, the figure could easily have been slightly changed. The arithmetic figure could also be the outcome of one of the more "measurable" scores; but we will come back to that later. Meanwhile, something quite specific has to be said about the correlations of physical measurements.

Physical Measurements

Throughout this whole sequence of studies and articles, Burt made it quite clear that (apart from the fact that these were of less interest to him than the mental and scholastic measurements) his calculations here were only and consistently based upon *small samples*. The *number* studied did not vary with the increase in the total number of siblings, as did (obviously) the other tests. They were deliberately limited to a smaller size throughout. In the 1955 paper, Burt's comment was:

> The figures for head-length, head-breadth, and eye-colour are based on much smaller numbers in every batch. Eye-colour . . . was added because, of all readily observable traits, it is immune from environmental influence.

And in the 1966 paper, these correlations were based on "*samples of 100 only.*"

The criticism, particularly in these cases, that any invariant correlations were "miraculous" or "impossible" because of the large increase in sample size, and were therefore to be regarded as fraudulent, simply did not apply. Indeed, the great probability— since apart from height these correlations for the identical twins are exactly the same in the 1958 and 1966 tables—is that Burt simply did not bother to calculate them.

Totals and Calculations: Confusion

The remaining questions relate to the correlations of the mental and scholastic measurements among all the other siblings, but it seems almost pointless to attempt any precise analysis here as we are bedevilled by a sheer lack of knowledge of the totals involved, and it seems at least very doubtful whether there was any continuity in these totals other than those of the identical twins. Thus, for example, the 1955 article reported an overall total of 984 siblings. In the 1966 table, the total is 826. In the 1955 paper, a number of 172 dizygotic twins reared together was reported. In the 1966 paper, the total is 127. From the 1955 to the two 1958 papers there is consistency, since (apart from the identical twins) the correlations still all refer to the 1955 totals. But in the 1966 table, the totals (again, apart from those of the identical twins) seem almost haphazard. Furthermore, it is almost as though *some* recalculations had been made, but all had not been completed, and therefore, where this was so, the earlier figures were simply repeated. Thus (to come back to it) the *arithmetic* calculation seems not to have been carried to completion (and hence, perhaps, the repeated correlation on this even for the identical twins); and the "mental measurements" for the "unrelated children reared together" seem well-nigh untouched. Haste and incompletion, then, seem to be the features "writ large" in this last table.

There are two other considerations, however, which seem to carry additional weight.

Misprints?

The first is the possibility (indeed, it seems probability) of very hasty and careless *typesetting* and *proofreading*. The manuscript was clearly with the editor of the journal for a long time; was evidently subjected to many revisions and alterations; and seems to have been printed with little care. It is clear from the text that at least *one* plain printing error went uncorrected. In the text, Burt said:

In our own set of results the outstanding feature is undoubtedly the high correlation for 'intelligence' between monozygotic twins even when reared apart—0.87, as compared with 0.54 for dizygotic pairs reared together. . . .

In the table, the figures shown are .87 and *.45;* and given the two figures of .55 and .52 above the .45, this *.45* should clearly be the

.54 referred to in the text. In many other places similar possibilities of careless mistakes in typesetting, and a lack of notice and correction at the proofreading stage, can be suspected (for example, 506/536; 492/472; 524/504; 116/110; 545/548; 267/269). Clearly there was some carelessness; but this of course in no way constitutes evidence, it is a possibility only—but a possibility that certainly seems plausible from Burt's side, given his known and admitted proneness, at that time, to inaccuracies.

Haste

The second possibility is simply that of *haste*.

Hearnshaw claims that this article (in the heat of controversy) was written in *"picque"*—indeed out of irritation, annoyance, and *"anger"* at his critics. It is difficult to find any evidence of these elements of feeling in the 1966 article, but as we have seen, there is plenty of evidence suggesting that the extended material, and the several revisions of it, may have been put together in haste. The new total of 53 cases of monozygotic twins reared apart was already mentioned by Burt in Easter 1965. The discussions following the articles by Hudson and Hammerton appeared during June and July, and the journal registered the final receipt of the manuscript on September eighth. In it, Burt had brought together the findings of other investigators (Newman, Freeman, and Holzinger, 1935; Juel-Nielsen and Morgensen, 1957; Shields, 1962, for example), and presented his own updated table to compare his results with theirs. It is well-known that Burt had to do his own calculations very painstakingly on an old handcalculator. And the evidence makes it clear that these late revisions of an already much-revised article were written and added between mid-July and the end of August.[12] The differing degrees of completion of some rows of calculations (arithmetic, unrelated children reared apart, and so on) may simply be accounted for by this sheer *haste* of preparation—in order to counter, as quickly as possible, the conceptions, claims, and criticisms of the Environmentalists that Burt believed to be radically false and misleading.

A final comment seems worthwhile on the difficulties presented by doubtful totals, possible misprints, and the obvious fact of haste all combined. One of the greatest (indeed, I believe insuperable) difficulties in the way of arriving at any certainty of judgment about this 1966 table, when comparing it with those of 1955 and 1958, is that the *totals* throughout are not clearly stated, or even really ascertainable. Whatever the totals were in 1955, at least the consistency of the correlations remained until, and in, the tables of 1958— because apart from the new number of identical twins, which was clearly stated, they remained the same. Only in the 1966 table, however, are the totals stated at the head of the columns, and again, apart from those of the identical twins, which are clearly stated, these do not seem consistent with totals mentioned not in the earlier *tables* but in the earlier *texts*. We have seen that in the 1955 text a total of 172 dizygotic twins reared together is mentioned. In the 1966 table, the total given is 127. Is this a case of another error in typesetting and carelessness in proofreading? It is also difficult to be certain about the other totals: so much so as almost to suggest that the 1966 table represents a set of incompleted calculations of such totals as it had proved possible to deal with. Certainty, alas, is simply not possible here.

Direction of Errors

The one fact that *is* certain, however, is that the certain errors, the uncertain possibilities of errors, and the inconsistencies of totals, are so irregular in their nature and direction that they *cannot possibly be adduced as proof of the deliberate manipulation of them on Burt's part in support of his theories*. As we have seen, they present a kind of confused amalgam of errors. Some of them seem to have no significance whatever; no bearing one way or another on Burt's central position and argument; and are certainly so uneven that—the crucial point for us—*they cannot possibly be construed as a careful attempt at fraud*. The judgment maintained by Marion Burt, Eysenck, Jensen, Cronbach, and Cattell (to mention the commentators of the highest reputation we noted earlier) is amply proved: that these errors were far too undiscriminating and far too *clumsy* to be in any way conceived as *calculated fraud*.

There are two final considerations.

The Vulnerability of Exactitude

Just as it may have been Burt's very generosity, his fastidious practice of acknowledging the name of every personal assistant who had given him help, that exposed him to the charge of the missing ladies, might it not also have been the case that it was Burt's very zeal in trying to achieve the most exact mathematical and statistical precision possible that rendered him vulnerable to critics? Why, one wonders, try to carry calculations of this kind to the third decimal place? In correlations of this kind, what significance has a difference of .001? And had Burt deliberately wanted to commit fraud, what would have been easier than to tack on, or take off, a third decimal figure? Had he reported "invariant correlations" to *two* decimal places only—to .77, for example, a figure other quite independent investigators had also reported—would the same fuss have arisen? Would the same claim that the statistical consistency proved fraud ever have been entertained? It is extremely doubtful.

Age

Lastly, we might note again that when making this particular effort to mount (and keep up-to-date) a quick reply to meet and disprove the claims of his critics, while busily involved in many other demanding activities, Burt was over 82 years of age. Working alone, with very little assistance or secretarial help, perhaps at that age errors resulting from haste and a failure to sustain the concentrated scrutiny necessary to see a manuscript safely through the process of proof correction, could be understood.

What, then, is the most feasible judgment at which we can arrive on this last major charge of fraud: on the significance of the "invariant correlations"? The truth, it seems, can best be stated in two parts. First, in the whole sequence of articles and tables from 1943 to 1955 to 1958, there is no lack of clarity, no evidence of inconsistency, and no ground whatever for suspecting any misleading manipulation of the reported correlations. Second, it is the 1966 table alone that contains errors and inconsistencies. Not one of these, however, constitutes any evidence of fraud. The results claimed do not differ from those already established in the earlier papers. The figures that are open to question do not have significance in any one particular direction, statistical or theoretical. They are far from being such as uniformly to support Burt's position.

And indeed, the uncertainty about the continuity of totals, the irregularities, the apparent incompleteness of some of the calculations, and the several repeated correlations among them, actually prove of lesser significance the one invariant correlation of the identical twins reared apart that has been singled out as the focus of concentration of Burt's detractors. The significance of this one correlation repeated to the third decimal place—as far as the proof of fraud is concerned—is actually much reduced by the revelation that other (three-decimal) correlations are repeated that do not carry this connotation at all. Indeed, the total focus of the detractors on this one correlation alone is shown quite clearly to be a selective emphasis for argument, if not a selective perception on their part.

The allegation, then, that the "invariant correlations" were evidence of fraud on Burt's part must be dismissed. It does not stand up to a searching examination of the facts. The probability most supported by the evidence is that, having managed to gather knowledge of an increased number of identical twins reared apart, and wanting to use this extended material to best advantage in opposing his critics with stronger evidence, Burt was guilty of presenting it in too rushed a manner, in an incomplete and ill-prepared form (amended and altered as new arguments arose)—a form that in some of its details did not tie in consistently with his earlier papers. These apparent inconsistencies and mistakes seem also to have been compounded by faults in typesetting that remained uncorrected in proofreading.

The allegation of impropriety in connection with the "invariant correlations" is therefore seen, like the other allegations, to rest on insufficient grounds. Beyond reasonable doubt, the evidence points to other explanations, and this brings to an end our consideration of the major charges of fraud proper. What overall verdict, then, are we now in a position to pronounce?

Notes

1. *British Journal of Statistical Psychology* 9(2): 95–131; 1956.
2. *British Journal of Statistical Psychology* 10(2); 1957.
3. "The Genetic Determination of Differences in Intelligence: A Study of Monozygotic Twins Reared Together and Apart." *British Journal of Psychology* 57:1; 1966.

4. Ibid., p. 140. Burt also pointed out his 1943 comment that his research students "were still working on data obtained for twins up to the outbreak of war."
5. Ibid., p. 141. Italics added.
6. Conway, J. "Class Differences in General Intelligence:II." *British Journal of Statistical Psychology,* pt. 1 (12 May 1959): 8.
7. "Intelligence and Heredity: Some Common Misconceptions." *Irish Journal of Education* 3(2); 1969.
8. Ibid., p. 90.
9. It is both interesting and important to note that Joynson investigated Hearnshaw's claims about this "massive operation" in very considerable detail (*The Burt Affair,* pp. 208–211). They rested, it turned out, upon a newspaper report in the *Guardian* of November 7, 1969. Joynson asked a colleague (Miss Lander) in Nottingham University Library if she would obtain a copy for him. She was unable to trace it, even after seeking the help of the British Library and the Newspaper Library in London. Unknown to Joynson, she then approached Hearnshaw himself requesting either a photocopy or a confirmation of his reference. Hearnshaw's reply to her (October 20, 1984) said: "Unfortunately, I cannot help you in your inquiry. The reference came from a secondary source, but I cannot now remember what it was, and I have dispersed a lot of the rough notes that I collected for my book on Burt. I have checked through my remaining files, but can find nothing relevant." Joynson concluded: "Hearnshaw's prime evidence for Burt's guilt in this final accusation was a newspaper article which he had not bothered to check. It was not merely second-hand evidence of an obviously unreliable kind. It was third-hand evidence, and he could not even remember where it came from. Yet he had quoted it as if he had seen it himself. If Burt had done this, instead of Hearnshaw, what would the critics have made of it?"
10. Bearing in mind, however, the record we have mentioned of a Miss M. A. Howard, it is at least worthwhile to note that there is a similar record of a Miss N. M. O'Connor in the membership lists of the British Psychological Society (1924–1936).
11. It is also worthwhile to note that the three columns recording the correlations of Newman, Freeman, and Holzinger were also attached to Burt's table—in parallel with his own—and these too were exactly repeated.
12. It would be of great interest to know the history of this manuscript while in editorial hands at the journal; what the revisions were, when they took place, and in particular, at what point the table itself was submitted or included in its final form. A good deal could be clarified with such knowledge.

13

Verdict

In all its essentials, the case for the defense has now been completed. Consistently bringing to a close my legalistic form of argument, I will now simply address you, as a jury, to summarize the case presented, indicate the conclusions that are now quite firm, and briefly articulate the verdict that on the basis of all the evidence, deductions, and arguments put forward I believe that justice requires.

Fraud? Guilty or Not Guilty?

The Initial Focus on Twins

We have seen that, from the beginning, the very nature of the accusations against Burt and his work were such as radically to misrepresent them. Burt had never designed or conducted a "classic study" of twins. His major surveys (in Liverpool, Birmingham, London) on the identification and distribution of "backwardness"; of the social conditions that contributed to this; of the delinquency arising from it; of the clarification and design of tests for the most reliable measurement possible of grades of mental ability—and all for the guidance of governmental authorities in working out remedial treatment—had all been completed long before the specific question of twins arose. The significance of twin studies emerged only within the context of these much wider investigations, and indeed in their very beginnings were initially voiced (in 1943) with particular reference to Burt's recognition of the educational inequalities of opportunity and provision alike suffered by families and children living in financially and socially disadvantaged conditions. His clear concern was that this situation, too, should be remedied. Only in the postwar controversies surrounding the subjects of educational opportunity, social class, and social mobility, did the study of twins come specifically to the fore, and even then (1955) it was still rooted in, and derived from, the data of the earlier surveys. Within the entire body of Burt's work, the study of twins was chiefly presented in the four papers between 1955 and 1966—when Burt was already between 72 and 83 years of age, with the greater part of his work (certainly his broad empirical investigations) already behind him.

The Extension of the Charges

We have also seen, however, how once having seized upon apparent flaws in this one limited area, and powered, it seems, by strong ideological aims and arguments, Burt's detractors quickly spread smears against his character and his supposedly underlying assumptions and beliefs (eugenics, racism, class discrimination, elitism) to bring the entirety of his work into disrepute. From the late twin studies, this was quickly extended backwards to the 1943 paper; back even further to the 1921 Birmingham study; then back further still to Burt's earliest papers and the charge of plagiarism. The extended defamation of Burt—to destroy his entire reputation, blacken his character completely, and to employ the charge of limited fraud to explore and disclose deception, unreliability, and deficiency in the whole of his work—was almost like the public diagnosis of a rapidly spreading disease, the discovery of a germ that was bound to entail the infection of the whole. But the fever seems only to have been one caught by Burt's detractors. Once having discovered what they took to be a particular poison in him, it was as though they could not rest with anything less than his death; and, as Cattell suggested, the hope may well have been that with his death, his intellectual position would die with him.

Cross-Examination: A Testimony of Inaccuracy and Vilification

Our cross-examination demonstrated that the testimony of the handful of those responsible for this attack (it was never more than a handful) had, in fact, developed into a long-sustained campaign of vilification, plainly indicating its animosity. We saw on strictly analytical grounds that the very *facts* on which claims were made, on which charges were rested, were falsely represented. The early notebook entries on which Kamin based his charges of Burt's supposed eugenicism and racism were *not* Burt's own beliefs, *nor* those of his lecturers, but simply his notes on Pigou. The 1943 paper did *not* justify the distribution of income in society on the grounds of the distribution of intelligence (as being "good, beautiful and true"); it was, in fact, aimed at demonstrating the *unequal* opportunities of children suffering social disadvantages. Burt's 1958 (1957 Bingham Lecture) paper was *not* a new study of "over 30" twins; its table being an exact repetition of part of the 1955 table. The work of Miss Molteno on which Gillie rested his account of Burt's "mechanism of fraud" was in fact *not* what Burt had claimed at all. The early papers of Burt did *not* show any evidence of "plagiarism." Hearnshaw's insistence on the "decisive evidence" of Burt's diaries was an *unwarranted* emphasis; the diaries were far from complete. The charge that Burt had fraudulently misrepresented the history of factor analysis appeared to rest upon a *fundamental misunderstanding*. Many such examples of straightforward but quite crucial errors in the reporting or representation of facts were conclusively laid bare.

Our cross-examination also proved that some personal testimony—in ways difficult to understand—had rested on a deliberately inaccurate (if not deliberately falsified) picture of its very foundations, and had been curiously slanted in the (long-sustained) nature of its presentation. The "articles" against which the Clarkes so long protested were shown *not* to be articles at all but simply the abstracts of their theses; yet their misleading statement and protestation was persistently repeated over many years. Other examples of this kind were shown to fall entirely within the realm of *hearsay*—the hearsay of only a particular group—carrying no confirming evidence whatever.

Stridency and Intemperate Language

Throughout this testimony of Burt's detractors, we have seen ample evidence of the strident tone of voice and the intemperate language in which their accusations were expressed. This has not been the language of impartial, critical, scientific scrutiny, but the sensational, exaggerated, popular language of the press, radio, and television. Gillie in particular has sprinkled the pages of many newspapers and journals with his talk of "fraudster," "confidence trickster," and the like. But Ann Clarke, and even Eysenck, have used the same kind of language, referring to the "con man" and "psychopath" on radio and television. We have also noted the quite unnecessary distastefulness of Halsey's written comments.

A Testimony Lacking Credibility

The upshot of all this is that the testimony of those responsible for prosecuting the charges of fraud against Burt—including their reporting of evidence, their representations of such evidence, their modes of argument, and their language of disputation—has been shown at best to be gravely lacking, and at worst to be totally lacking, in serious credibility. Even a case of criminal justice, or one of civil claims and counterclaims in the courts, would be conducted with a certain expected comportment of civilized procedure and language. These were intellectuals engaged in the discourse of scientific criticism, yet they made use of the worst kind of derogatory language to be found in popular journalism. The disgraceful nature of at least a great deal of the testimony (though Hearnshaw in large part could be counted an exception to this) was therefore all the more marked.

The Minor Charges Dismissed

Our cross-examination, with its revelation of factual evidence and its clarification of arguments, itself provided sufficient grounds on which it was possible to dismiss the many charges of malfeasance and scientific misconduct insofar as these referred to the broad range of Burt's work. The charges of racism, class discrimination, right-wing elitism, underrating the influence of social and environmental factors, shoddy work, and scientific misconduct in the carrying out of his surveys—all these were disproved. Certainly in full keeping with the standards of his time, and comparably with any other work of his time, Burt *did* give information as to how,

where, and when his data had been collected; *did* give the sources
of his information; *did* acknowledge his assistants and the sources
of information from studies other than his own; *did* describe the
several kinds of intelligence tests he used. He did *not* casually and
arbitrarily guess the IQs of adults and parents; was *not* guilty of
"poor work as a pragmatic applied psychologist"; and was *not*
proved guilty of statistical "fraud" by Dorfman. None of these
charges stood up to serious scrutiny, and the full evidence rebutting
them was made completely clear.

The Major Charges Dismissed

Going beyond this, however—setting aside the character of
Burt's detractors and the nature of their testimony alone—we were
then able, with equal clarity, and again on the grounds of demonstrable evidence, to show that none of the major charges of fraud
proper could be at all sustained. We noted that because of the
difficulties presented by the destruction of documents, by war and
after Burt's death, that much had to remain in the realm of the
unprovable. Even so, we saw that the evidence that *did* exist was
sufficiently substantial to render all the charges doubtful and to
support very different explanations of the facts. Apart from Miss
O'Connor (a remaining problem) the "missing ladies" were shown
not to be missing. Some very positive testimony for their existence
had been provided, together with at least some documentary evidence; and, more telling than this, we saw that the very consistent
nature of the acknowledgments of them and of the nature of their
work went a long way in itself towards verifying their existence. We
also saw that Gillie had himself in large part conceded this, but had
then rested his claim to have discovered Burt's "mechanism of
fraud" upon an interpretation of Miss Molteno's work that was
unfounded. We saw that Burt's use of their names in coauthorship
or (on one or two occasions) as the sole authors of articles, though
on the face of it unquestionably foolish, and on any count unwise,
had at its root at least some serious considerations that could not
simply be brushed aside, and in one or two instances might have
arisen (and then necessitated some continuation) within the pressures of mounting controversy. We saw that any broader practice
of writing under pseudonyms (the actual nature and extent of which

cannot be known), though, again, perhaps unwise, was by no means necessarily a matter of misconduct; that there was certainly no evidence of this; and indeed, that some of it could have been rooted in the lack of other contributions. The crucial matter, however, is that there was no evidence in the whole of this of *fraud*. Nothing was said in the articles bearing (in part or in full) the names of Howard and Conway that was not totally consistent with Burt's other articles. Nothing was there by way of fraudulent additions or alterations. Nothing was there with any discernible intention of deliberately misleading the reader.

We saw that the charge of fabricating data could not be upheld. Much evidence was given of the retesting and reworking of earlier data, the deliberate and continual requesting of (or advertising for) information on additional cases of twins (especially identical twins reared apart), and the continual following-up of information derived from correspondents and personal contacts; all of which could well have increased the numbers to those finally reported. The "invariant correlations," such as they proved to be, were also shown to have minimal significance (to give the matter the strongest emphasis it deserves) for any charge of fraud; most probably no significance at all. Much misrepresentation had entered into this matter, there being no problem whatever in the whole sequence of papers from 1955 to 1958. Only the 1966 paper raised difficulties and questions; but these were such a confused amalgam as to render any overall and certain conclusions impossible. Again, however, what was shown to be certain was that this constituted no evidence of fraud on the question of the claims made about the correlations relating to the identical twins reared apart, the area that had been the source of the most crucial criticism.

Judgment

The only verdict that can satisfy the evidence—on the clearly established basis of "reasonable doubt" alone, but also, as I have argued, on grounds of factual evidence and argument going far beyond this—and the verdict I ask you to return (bearing in mind that you are the collective and universal jury of the scientific world), is that of not guilty!

Truth and justice alike require it.

IV
QUESTIONS AND CONCLUSIONS

14

Remaining Considerations

Flaws and Faults?

Some conclusions follow from the verdict I have advocated, and I would like to close with these. Bearing in mind, however, our commitment to impartiality, I would like to stop for a moment to ask a limited question, one that, as we attempt to answer it, will lead to other accounts of Burt's personality and character that call for the most serious analysis, consideration, and judgment—having so far, it seems, been accepted without criticism. My aim throughout, made clear in my preamble, has not been to "whitewash" Burt, whatever the evidence, nor though defending him to indulge in the one-sided rhetoric practiced by the prosecution. I have argued that according to a careful examination of the evidence, Burt was a man of integrity; a man who, from his earliest youth onwards, had a humane concern for those condemned to live in the materially and culturally impoverished conditions of post-Victorian society; a man who sought to identify the misfortunes of such underprivileged families (the permanently debilitating effects of early childhood illnesses, the retardation of mental and personal development, the inequalities of opportunity in education, occupation, career, and conditions of social comfort and privilege alike); a man who sought to establish reliable knowledge about the distribution of these misfortunes so that appropriate help could be provided to alleviate them and to extend the range of opportunities available to all.

I have demonstrated by an analysis of his work that he was

317

indefatigable in his pursuit of accuracy in the surveys he conducted, and in the nature of the tests by which he measured both the distribution of abilities and the influences of the environmental features that seemed the most formidable obstacles standing in the way of their most appropriate fulfillment. I have insisted that the continual focus of his attention and concern was upon the *individual child* and the best possible provision of the *most appropriate* education in relation to his or her level of ability and special talents. And I have argued that he was consistent throughout the entire body of his work in his arguments on the question of the hereditary basis of intelligence and the effects of social and environmental conditions upon it.

We have also seen that he was a man who energetically and tenaciously took issue in open, public argument with those whose views he believed to be radically mistaken; and I have argued that in these arguments he was right! (We shall look at his additional and more conclusive arguments in a moment.) He stood firmly by his scientific findings and convictions; his energy did not fail him even in very old age in meeting his opponents in continuing, even mounting, disputation; he was an antagonist to be reckoned with— of outstanding achievements, qualities, and intellectual stature. All this we have clearly seen in all my arguments so far. Nevertheless, given the latter-day controversy and the charges that subsequently arose from it, there is a question that must be asked.

It follows from what we have said that Burt was not a man who was easily going to give way to pressure or opposition—whether in his departmental affairs, his journal-editing, or his scientific arguments—and, though chiefly in hearsay, we have seen views expressed as to his "difficult" nature in all these respects. He was not the man to give way before what he believed to be ludicrous misrepresentations of his position, or before insufficient arguments. He was not the sort of man to fall silent in the face of opposition, or easily to admit defeat. He was clearly a clever man; a man of great ability possessing an extraordinarily wide fund of knowledge, in almost all the areas he touched to an "expert" level; and clearly he had had long experience of the slings and arrows of the more outrageous features of academic life: the contentiousness of colleagues and committees, interdepartmental conflicts, and (it seems) quite vitriolic editorial disagreements. He would certainly not after all these experiences in his many-sided career be anything of an "innocent abroad" in meeting attacks in disputation; and there is no reason to suppose him more morally impeccable than our common human nature allows. It seems sensible to assume that he would be ready and capable of meeting the tactics and strategy of others with tactics and strategy of his own. The question we have to ask is this: Major calculated scientific "fraud" aside, does the evidence we have uncovered suggest that Burt was guilty nonetheless of *flaws* and *faults* in the conduct of this latter-day dispute in his career that did seem to make plausible the charges against him and render the presentation of his later findings so questionable as to be unsatisfactory, making them therefore of little or no use (as Kamin claimed) for subsequent scientific work?

On the face of the evidence we have considered, it seems to me that any impartial answer to this question must be "yes." Whether or not they were justifiable, on grounds about which it is impossible to be fully certain, some of Burt's actions do undoubtedly seem to have been questionable, and two things at least can be said.

First, whatever the reasons given for it, if it was the case (as the evidence does seem clearly to show) that Burt himself wrote the articles published under Miss Conway's name alone, and published them as part of the important exchange of views on the "twin controversy," this was certainly unwise and was clearly a deception. Given Miss Archer's testimony as to her own sense of disquiet about this, her expression of this disquiet to Burt, and his insistence (whatever the validity of the grounds he gave) on doing it nonetheless, this action has to be regarded as having been deliberate. It also has to be said that there seems no reason whatever why coauthorship (rather than sole authorship) would not have been quite sufficient to meet Burt's professed desire to make full acknowledgment of the very considerable extent of Miss Conway's help. This action, then, must be regarded as a deception.

Second, his haste in presenting the table of correlations in his 1966 article (incomplete, muddled, and repetitive in many ways, and variously altered in several revisions) may be said to have proved him strongly motivated to press home his side of the controversy at the expense of some accuracy, so rendering this last presentation of findings so filled with unexplained irregularities that—any question of fraud aside—it was such as to be unusable as a basis of reference for testable scientific work. (I am pressing this point very hard, however, in the service of impartiality, being very conscious of the fact that these irregularities may well have had, in terms of our earlier considerations, quite sound and satisfactory explanations.)

Let us put these matters very barely, boldly, and succinctly.

During the last six years of his life, in the context of this one pressured disputation, Burt did show himself capable of deception—which does imply some deviousness—and also of some carelessness over accuracy in the reporting of findings and calculations in seeking to prove his own arguments right and those of his opponents wrong.

How are we to explain this? What reasons have been given, and can be given, for these flaws and faults?

Explanations?

Vanity

One element of explanation commonly agreed among friends as well as opponents who knew Burt well lay in his great *vanity;* his *pride.* Burt had a high opinion of his own abilities, and of the standing of his own work. He was proud of his many achievements, and enjoyed the high and worldwide reputation these had earned for him as one of the most leading and eminent authorities in his field. Now in retirement (it was said), increasingly under attack from critics of lesser ability and achievement—deploying either sheer misconceptions or, as it seemed, deliberate misrepresentations of his positions, and using unfounded arguments—he did not like, and was unwilling, to vacate this platform of leadership, to relinquish this eminence, and see the recognition of his leadership fall away. As part of this, he similarly did not like to see the system of education (with its increased degree of educational opportunity) that he had worked for, being, as he saw it, despoiled and destroyed by simplistic political arguments and policies. Furthermore, he still firmly *believed* that his position was right; that his findings and his views were correct and justified; that his opponents were misguided and wrong; and therefore made even more insistent and energetic efforts to demonstrate their shortcomings and to defend, reinforce, and retain the centrality and truth of his own position and his own personal supremacy.

This, then, is one explanation that has been offered: Burt became (as some psychologists might put it) "ego-involved" in the dispute; his vanity drove him beyond scientific propriety and caution; and it is certainly an explanation resting on grounds that are quite understandable.

Jensen, for example (by no means an adverse or hostile critic), says that "his personal vanity was considerable, according to many of his former associates. "Strangely," he continues,

> Burt in his old age really had no need to prove any point for which there was not already substantial evidence from other studies. Apparently he could not bear to see others outshine him in the field in which he had so long been the kingpin. The fear of falling from his high status and being regarded as a scientific has-been in his old age was probably too great a threat to his ego.[1]

This, then, is the explanation of Jensen's suspicion (more or less convinced by Hearnshaw "although not 100% confident") that Burt *might* have been guilty of inventing some of the last increase in the number of identical twins reared apart, though he has seen "no adequate reason to suggest fraud in anything else Burt has done."[2]

Raymond Cattell, too, also a loyal supporter of Burt, shares this point of view. Any suspicion of fraud in Burt, he believes, could only arise in relation to the later papers, and only

> in the minute matter of these few twins reared apart. I know the rest of his work well, and it is all solid and brilliant. I have no explanation other than perhaps a certain untidiness in his recordings to explain the matter at issue. I agree with Professor Jensen that if he had a personality flaw it was in terms of a certain vanity, which may have caused him to overstep the mark. However, as I have said in my review of the biography by Hearnshaw, the biography completely misses the point of describing the social scene with which he had to deal, which in the 60's was a very biased one, in which he had to fight every inch of the way.[3]

Even here, and even if grounded on his vanity, Cattell clearly thinks that Burt's tenacity in disputation could have had its justification.

Vanity, then, together with injured pride, provided one understandable explanation. A considerable if not overweening personal vanity was evidently thought to be the one marked flaw in Burt's character. Hearnshaw, though noting and agreeing with this judgment, did, however, feel it necessary to offer a second and very different explanation. But before turning to this I cannot resist the temptation to stop and ask a question.

When approaching a judgment of this kind—deciding whether a man has been so vain, so attached to the intellectual position in which he believes and which he has long and successfully worked to establish; so jealous too of the distinction and high reputation he has been accorded and has long enjoyed; that he becomes calculating to the point of adopting some deviousness in meeting attacks from colleagues that seem not only unfounded but even deliberately distorted and tainted with some underlying ideological and personal animosity—is it not a fitting question to ask "Let he who is without fault cast the first stone?" What man is free from vanity, from ego-involvement in the work to which he has devoted himself, from a desire to defend both it and himself against attacks that so frequently stem from envy rather than any concern for the truth and, deployed with deviousness, aim at bringing down others' reputations as a way of lifting up their own? Who remains wholly free from the tangle of intrigue and manipulations that commonly ensues, and within in it, remains entirely untainted by it and blameless of devious and questionable behavior? How many, at the end of a long career in corridors of high responsibility (whether in academic or other areas of social or political life) in which ambition, contention, and corruption are rife—no matter how morally upright they are, or think themselves to be—could truthfully say that they had been always free from such flaws?

My own suspicion is that if capital punishment were to be inflicted on all those guilty of such offenses, the corridors of power would be swept unrecognizably clean. All those who had been in high places would be found swinging from the nearest trees. As one limited example, consider those who have attacked Burt: Kamin, Gillie, the Clarkes, and Eysenck (in the later stages of the controversy). Are these scholars and journalists possessed of personal vanity? Have they been ego-involved to any marked degree in their intellectual cause? Have they been motivated so strongly as to have been careless in their reporting of evidence in an effort to prove themselves right and their opponent wrong? Have they been so attached to their position as to have allowed calculation and deviousness to enter into their sustained attacks? Have they, under the sway of such ego-involvement, such attachment, allowed deliberate distortion, deliberate misrepresentation, to enter into their disputation? And should not such scientific criticism—if it was indeed of this kind—be properly judged to be scientific fraud? What does the review of the evidence suggest?

I will not try to answer this question, leaving it open for your consideration.

I want, however, to rest a very definite statement upon it, and one that, in these respects deliberately judges Burt badly.

Along the lines on which I have just been arguing, some of Burt's deviousness in meeting the ways of criticism of his opponents is open to at least another interpretation. When I was discussing these matters (such as the charge of deviousness) with Robert Reid, who also knew Burt very well, his comment was: "All it means was that he was a good committee man." Presumably, in general, in areas of academic contention, Burt was so astute and wily as to displease his opponents; perhaps better than they, in short, at the power game. And perhaps, in this latter-day controversy, he was doing no more than meet like with like; something clearly believed and indicated by Cattell's strong cautionary point, that we should remember "the social scene with which he had to deal, which in the 60's was a very biased one, in which he had to fight every inch of the way."

The definite point I wish to make here is that if Burt was guilty of some deception and deviousness in his conduct of the later stages of the twin controversy, this may well be quite straightforwardly explicable in terms of the common evils in which men are embroiled in their struggles for the success or failure of their contending positions; an explanation, it must be clearly noted, that does not at all excuse it. Burt's conduct, in short, could have been tainted with these same evils. He may have behaved wrongly, as men do behave wrongly, in such situations and within the context of such rivalries and pressures. My own persuasion is that these faults are not at all evidenced in the 1966 paper. That paper, still arguing the case for the genetic determination of differences in intelligence, still works back over Burt's earlier findings in the same consistent way as that exemplified by his earlier papers, bringing together for consideration the many findings of others, and I believe the confused figures of Burt's table are explicable in terms of the several factors we have outlined before. The only demonstrable and evidently deliberate deception seems to have been the publishing of the papers he had written himself under the name of Miss Conway (and to a lesser extent of Miss Howard), and we have no choice but to judge this on a balance of probabilities in the light of the evidence as we have outlined it.

My essential point, however, is that if Burt was guilty of flawed conduct on these two matters, it was, within the context and conditions of opposition he was facing, to be explained in terms of deliberate wrongdoing. Putting this barely, boldly, and succinctly again, the evidence as it stands suggests that in these one or two ways (in one with more certainty, in one more doubtfully), Burt may well have behaved both foolishly and badly.

I have been at some pains to state this clearly, thinking it necessary as a clear prelude and foundation to a satisfactory consideration of the much more elaborate explanation put forward by Hearnshaw—an explanation I find quite incredible, just as I find it incredible that it should ever have been seriously entertained and accepted by others, without, it seems, any searching criticism.

Pseudologica Phantastica

This is the term Hearnshaw used to refer to the general confusion, many "contradictory statements," and "diminished veracity" that, he claimed, characterized Burt's later writings (published papers and letters alike). It seems, however, a much more fitting title for Hearnshaw's own conjectural account of the development of Burt's personality, his conjectural biography of Burt's inner life. For Hearnshaw, any account of Burt's "delinquencies," "aberrations," "falsifications," "malfeasance," and the like, in the straightforward terms of wrongdoing—in calculatedly dealing with opponents in the commonalty of corruption and, during the process of this, becoming himself tainted with it—was not enough. A satisfactory explanation had to have deeper roots. Burt's alleged attack on Spearman, supposedly attempting to depose him so that he himself could be seen in the prior and superior position (which, we may recall, evidently rested on a basic misunderstanding), was, said Hearnshaw, "almost a classic example of the killing of the father king. And indeed it is more than probable that there were pathological features in this bizarre saga." This is strange language, but it reveals the keynote of the only kind of explanation that would satisfy Hearnshaw: *pathology!*

In a moment we will analyse Hearnshaw's explanatory account, listing and commenting on the pathological elements he thought discernible. Before this, it is necessary to note the detailed and graphic account he also gave of Burt's very busy and troubled period of retirement, between 1950 and 1971.

Still having very limited financial means, Burt "was compelled to work right up to the end of his life just to make ends meet." His college pension was inadequate. He did not receive any state pension until he was 80. He had, therefore, to continue bearing a heavy load of examining, lecturing, reading and reporting on manuscripts for publishers, and editing. All these undertakings were carried out with his customary and well-known thoroughness, and throughout he continued to produce articles, finally completing his last book, *The Gifted Child,* just before his death. It was within the context and ongoing pressures of this workload that the controversies over social class, the distribution of intelligence, the inequalities of opportunity in education, and social mobility arose, particularly from some among the sociologists of education, though as we have seen, no radical difference to Burt's basic position was to be found in their work.

The controversy, however, particularly as this continued with Halsey, made it increasingly seem so, and as Hearnshaw said (in this clearly agreeing with Cattell), in the 1960s these attacks on Burt "became more venomous." Burt himself, writing to his sister, said "The labour educationists who are all out to build what they call a classless society, keep launching ludicrous attacks on my views." He was surely right. The attacks *were* ludicrous! And it was under the stress of these controversies (claimed Hearnshaw) that some personality traits that had been deeply established and were at least discernible earlier in his life grew in such ways, and to such an extent, as to assume an increasing degree of dominance in Burt's nature, becoming more conspicuous in his behavior and his work. The true explanation, claimed Hearnshaw, lay in an understanding of Burt's personality. "The psychologist himself," he said, "must be psychologised." Then followed what probably ranks (as Freud might say) as the best "Just So" story in the whole history of psychology: Hearnshaw's story of "How the Professor got his Pathology." The story was as follows.

Burt was certainly highly intelligent, with an unbelievably well-stocked mind—with vast stores of knowledge and great intellectual gifts. His knowledge ranged widely beyond psychology and the social sciences into the fields of history, religion, music, ancient and modern languages, literature, and philosophy (also ancient and modern), and all this is substantially evident in his work (some not yet published). His nature was also that of the disinterested scholar: apolitical, unworldly, not interested in wealth or social status, disliking and shunning social gatherings. In all this as well, despite his many academic contacts, he seemed essentially a very lonely man. About all this, Hearnshaw was quite decided and clear. But there was, he claimed, another side to the coin.

Behind or beneath Burt's intellectual nature there was also an intense inwardness, a fear of emotional involvement. Linked with this, Burt was also, undoubtedly ambitious, with a strong impulse toward *domination,* though this domination took the form of believing in and seeking to impose his own *intellectual supremacy.* In this, he was egotistical, exalted, grandiose, as revealed in his very youthful preoccupation with his own aim of *self-perfection* during his life in the world. "The trouble," said Hearnshaw, "lay in his personality." What were the elements that went into the formation of this?

The seeds of Burt's subsequent pathology were first implanted in his "mixed ancestry," claimed Hearnshaw. He was part Saxon, part Celt—of a divided genetic constitution. It is also probable that there was a genetic basis for the much later onset of Ménière's disease. Marion Burt, recalling much of Burt's behavior in his earliest childhood, believed (and had said) that the evidence suggested that her brother's "semi-circular canals were innately not very effective." Some factors, then, were to be traced to his genetic endowment. Burt was a lonely figure at the most basic psychosomatic and psychological level. There was an innate instability in his psychosomatic makeup. In his earliest years, however, environmental circumstances also exerted telling and formative influences on this.

The roots springing out of the germination of these inherited seeds were set in the ground of certain circumstances of Burt's earliest childhood, during the first nine years of his life. Though his father was a professional man, a doctor, their home was in Pretty France, in London, and the family was hard-up. Their economic level was "barely above the bread-line" and they lived in squalid surroundings. Burt also had to attend the local board school, and had to mix with "the mob" of the local children. Here it was that he deeply imbided the "gamin culture" of the children he mixed with and learned the "grim art of gamin survival": an art he was never to forget. But then a "deep duality" was established in his personality, adding to that of his mixed Saxon–Celtic stock, by a sharp break in family circumstances.

When Burt was nine years old, the family moved from this "tough urban environment to the medieval peace of an isolated Warwickshire village," a sharp break that "must have been an incredible change." There, Burt went to the centuries-old grammar school, with its smaller classes and classical fare, adapting well and quickly to the relative security of his new situation, and coming evidently to love the country. Even so, Hearnshaw claimed, a lasting split was created in Burt's nature between the gamin character of the Londoner and the more settled character of his life in Warwickshire, a "major reason" for the duality in his personality that was to endure. From that point onwards, Burt's life and personality continued on a course that seemed relatively smooth and secure.

During the 1930s, however, and increasingly from then onwards, things began to go wrong. At the beginning of this period, it may be noted, Burt would be forty-seven years old. During the last thirty years of his life, in particular, he suffered a number of setbacks. His marriage, which had taken place in 1932, soon ran into difficulties, was unsatisfactory, and ended (his wife leaving him) in 1952. April 1941 saw the destruction of a quantity of his papers in London air raids. In the summer of 1941 he also had his first severe attack of Ménière's disease. He experienced a break with his old department after his retirement, having evidently failed to exert any influence on the appointment of his successor. In 1963 he lost control over the *Statistical Journal* (after some sixteen years). Increasingly, too, during the later years of his life he was seeing the gradual erosion of the system of selective secondary education that to some extent he had been responsible for bringing into being. It was in facing and fighting against all these slings and arrows of fortune, and particularly against the opponents who at the same time were increasingly attacking him, that, said Hearnshaw "the gamin component of his personality came to the surface again." But, in addition, two other substantial, highly influential, and important sources of kinds of psychological orientation were discernible in him and could be identified.

The first of these was Ménière's disease. Severe attacks of this disease—involving giddiness and sickness when "the walls would spin round with amazing rapidity"—seriously incapacitated Burt for spells of several hours at a time from the summer of 1941 onwards, though these *had been preceded by nausea during 1940*. There was at that time no treatment for it, but with care, the attacks eased off, *though he was always liable to them*. In 1966, the disease intensified, but, from 1960 at least, a remedy had been available and Burt's attacks were, from this time on, "only short (20 minute) spells of instability," now with "no vomiting," and he was "able to get on fairly well" with his work. The illness stayed with Burt *throughout the last thirty years of his life* and, said Hearnshaw, "his hearing loss was permanent and disabling." This, so far, was a straightforward story of clinical facts, and I have italicized some elements of it because of Hearnshaw's later emphases; for not content with these kinds of facts alone, he felt it necessary to offer conjectures (it was never more than this) about other possible dimensions.

Some physicians, Hearnshaw went on, "though by no means all," had come to believe that Ménière's disease was a *psychosomatic* disorder,[4] brought about "in persons with a constitutional disposition as a result of emotional stress." He cited evidence to suggest that the psychological (emotional) disturbances were *primary* causes, the "*precipitating* factors," and were associated with "a particular type of personality." Ménière patients were "obsessional-compulsive types" with "perfectionist traits," "aggressive dependency, emotional liability, over-reactivity," and marked "psychosomatic liability." Furthermore, some physicians had found that the prominent stresses precipitating the disease were "marital difficulties and the loss of valued objects." Hearnshaw did not indicate how common these diagnoses were among physicians, nor did he say what the other causal stresses were. His own selection of these, however, led him to claim that it was the loss of Burt's papers in April 1941 (within the context of marital difficulties) that was "the final causative agent," and that it was the possible anxiety over the coming publication of the 1966 article that brought about the intensified attack in the spring of that year.

This very specific linking of the emergence of the disease, and the course it took, with specific events in Burt's later life is, however, strangely at variance with the other facts Hearnshaw himself presented, which we have already touched upon. Marion Burt, for example, had claimed that even in his earliest childhood Burt was troubled by vertigo, and gave several other signs of his having inherited defects in his semicircular canals. If this was so, where is the evidence of any effects of stress whatever during the nine years of Burt's early school days when, in the hard life of the board school, he was having to learn "the grim art of gamin survival"? Also, Hearnshaw claimed that Burt's marriage ran into trouble very early, and that it continued to worsen throughout the 1930s. Why were there no Ménière's attacks during that period, especially if the stress of marital difficulties was a chief precipitating cause? Also, the Hereditarian–Environmentalist controversy together with the related issues of "social class, intelligence, and social mobility" and the twin studies, began during the 1950s, and were certainly becoming more intense from 1955 onwards. Why no Ménière's attack until 1966?

The same kinds of questions could be asked in more detail about other periods of Burt's life earlier and later. Furthermore, with the relief brought about by the treatment that was by this time available, and despite the extension of the disease (to attack his right ear) in 1966, Burt had managed in fact to curtail its attacks so that they did not seriously disrupt his work. And certainly his deafness, though it did deteriorate, was not so much worsened as to render telephone conversation and ordinary conversation in his rooms impossible or even greatly difficult.[5] Hearnshaw, nonetheless, was strongly persuaded that "beneath his composed, polite exterior"

Burt was "an anxious, disturbed character." There was something "obsessionally-compulsive" about his strivings. There was "a perfectionist strand in his make-up." His "repressed aggressive impulses . . . manifested themselves in his eager controversialism." The close fit between the Ménière's syndrome (of some physicians) and Burt's pathology (according to Hearnshaw's own conjectures) was, for Hearnshaw, compelling. But this was not all!

In addition, "regressive changes" in Burt's personality and "a recrudescence of earlier patterns of behaviour" began to "obtrude both in his personal relationships and in his published work." From the late 1930s onwards, Burt became increasingly egotistical, self-aggrandizing, suspicious, cantankerous, devious, unscrupulous. This also supposedly resulted from the setbacks he began to experience then, and two things, said Hearnshaw, became apparent. First, there was "a regression to, and a surfacing of, the primitive 'gamin' element in his make-up," and second, there was the development of a "marginally paranoid condition" that he suffered during the final phase of his life. The "primitive gamin element" in Burt's makeup, of course, had only ever existed in the imaginative and creative processes of Hearnshaw's psychologizing. Apart from this, there was never any evidence of it whatever. Indeed, what a "gamin element" actually is, especially as a component of a personality, is a matter open to some question. But what of the "marginally paranoid condition"? Hearnshaw's statement about this deserves full quotation.

Paranoia in its fully developed form is generally classed as a delusional psychosis. The delusional system is commonly a circumscribed one, leaving the personality otherwise intact, and in many respects capable of perfectly normal functioning. Moreover it often occurs in the milder form of a marginal psychical abnormality, in which the delusional element is fairly inconspicuous. Characteristic features of such marginal forms of self-aggrandisement are inflated egocentricity, oversensitiveness and suspiciousness, querulousness, secretiveness, compulsive drive ('a temperament which never allows itself to flag') and hypochrondria.[6] Such a condition is regarded by Jaspers as reactive, that is primed by external events, usually of a repeated nature, in a personality with some basic peculiarity or weakness. It is also perhaps significant that paranoid conditions are not infrequently associated with hearing loss. The picture is concordant with the known facts about Burt. Self-aggrandisement and inflated egocentricity were certainly a marked feature of his later behaviour, and accounted for many of the devices to which he had recourse—the alterations, for example, in contributors' articles, and the distortions of factor-analytic history. Burt, too, was oversensitive to criticism. He was sharply on the look-out for anyone who challenged his views, and wrote 'out of the blue' to upbraid and correct them. He was deeply suspicious of rivals, particularly his own most able students, like Cattell and Eysenck. Others, who in fact admired him and supported many of his views, he disparaged and sometimes alienated because they did not wholly accept his authority. Finally Burt was most surely secretive, hypochrondrical, and compulsively motivated. He shows then all the essential marks of a marginally paranoid personality.[7]

Like the psychological corollaries of Ménière's disease selected from *some* physicians, "marginal paranoia" fitted the conjectural facts of Burt's supposed pathology like a hand fitting a glove. And so for Hearnshaw, it was compelling.

It would seem, then, that we are justified in concluding that Burt suffered, in the final phase of his life, from a marginally paranoid condition; that this condition was a reaction to the setbacks which he experienced from the late 1930s onwards; and that it led to a regressive reactivation of behaviour patterns he had acquired in the London period of his boyhood, and from the 'gamin' sub-culture in which he had been immersed. This, we suggest, is the basic explanation of the deceptions and subterfuges which marred his work in its later stages. In the end he chose to cheat rather than see his opponents triumph. To trace the origins of these defections from probity to childhood experiences would seem to receive support not only from the findings of psychology, but from the deeper intuitions of humanity:
In ancient shadows and twilights
Where childhood has strayed
The world's great sorrows were born
And its heroes were made.
In the lost boyhood of Judas
Christ was betrayed.[8]

And it was "in the lost boyhood of Cyril Burt," Hearnshaw concluded, that "psychology was betrayed." There was, he concluded, an element of "pseudologica phantastica" in the lack of veracity in Burt's later work.

Well . . . so ends Hearnshaw's biographical story; his psychologizing of the pyschologist.

I do not know how far readers will agree with me in this, but I find and suggest that this entire psychological profile of Burt's inner mental development, personality, and character, from its beginning in the inbuilt psychosomatic instability of his Saxon–Celtic genetic mix, through its "gamin-like" reinforcement in his London childhood, through the great cleavage and duality caused by the move to the isolated village in the Warwickshire countryside, and through all the later regressive and recrudescent experiences underlying the Ménière's disease and the "marginal paranoia" from which he suffered—is indeed nothing more than a "Just So" story of the most incredible kind. It makes Rudyard Kipling look like a hard realist. It is purely suppositional throughout and, although bearing the appearance of serious scholarly analysis, nowhere rests on a single piece of objective evidence. If anything could be properly characterized as "pseudologica phantastica" it is this account. What remarkable profundity of insight did Hearnshaw possess ennabling him to analyze—from documents, from speculations over the significance of biographical periods, from selected clinical diagnoses and symptoms, and from hypothetical psychological conjectures—and then to reconstruct and judge the entire personality of a man in a way few psychoanalysts would be prepared to contemplate after seven years of the most intimate talking-out on the couch? What is even more incredible is that it should ever have been seriously entertained—in itself, and as a serious explanation of Burt's misdemeanors—by others. Not only is it variably inconsistent with Hearnshaw's own portrayal of many elements and periods of Burt's life; not only is it out of keeping with, and contrary to, the testimony of many others who knew Burt well (and far better than Hearnshaw); but many elements of it that seem evidential have *no evidential foundation at all*. Let us briefly consider just a few of these to prove the point.

What, for example, is the supposed genetic and psychosomatic instability of a mixed Saxon–Celtic parentage? The literature of psychology seems remarkably lacking in any information about this. What "genetic contribution" to a "duality in personality" can be said to be demonstrated here? What is the evidence of a "gamin culture" in Burt's early school-days, and of a "grim art of gamin survival"? Hearnshaw did not even know which school Burt attended, but nonetheless filled in its supposed characteristics by quotations from Booth's description of the deplorable conditions of that *kind* of school. He also quoted an inspector's report of Buckingham Gate School—which might have been Burt's school—that said, however, surprisingly, that the discipline of the school was *excellent* and the teaching there *"full of spirit and intelligence."* But this did not stay the flow of Hearnshaw's conjectures. "Though the discipline in the school was strict," he continued, "the children themselves must have been an obstreperous crowd of little gamins." This seems, if anything, to reveal something about Hearnshaw's conception of working-class children; but the significant question is: What was the evidential source, the source of authority for such a judgment? Why . . . it was Hearnshaw's own conjectural imagination!

Where is the evidence for the "split" and "deep duality" in Burt's personality resulting from his move as a nine-year-old to the Warwickshire village—which would, one might have supposed, have been a welcome improvement and relief? There is none whatever apart from Hearnshaw's conjecture. Where is the evidence that Burt suffered undue degrees of stress from marital difficulties and the ultimate breakdown of his marriage? None is to be found. Indeed, there has been testimony to suggest that marriage was never something that Burt ever really wanted; that it was never something he was deeply or specially concerned about. He was certainly not in the least ungenerous or possessive in his relationship with his wife. He paid for the medical course his wife wanted to undertake. She enjoyed full personal and social freedom. All the evidence suggests, indeed, that his one overwhelming absorption (for better or worse) was not his marriage at all but his work. Furthermore, these difficulties were developing over a period of some twenty years—during the 1930s, followed by the wartime evacuation, the return to London, and into the early 1950s—and throughout this period, despite any such possible stress of a personal and emotional nature, Burt's eminence and scholarly work and status were by no means dimmed or diminished. Neither were they diminished, despite the end of his marriage, from the mid-1950s onwards, to the late 1960s, during the "social mobility" controversy. Burt held his own in this controversy. Indeed, it is hard to see how, in his lifetime, his eminence could ever be said to have been seriously diminished. Only towards the end of a long and enormously active and productive life was he increasingly pressed to provide some of the "raw data" underlying his reported findings, and asked questions about various aspects of them. But he was still held in the highest regard, and indeed, received the warmest tributes on his death: one of these, strangely enough, being Hearnshaw's own funeral oration. Hearnshaw himself had clearly not detected any flaws at this time.

The upshot of these considerations is that this story of psychosomatic instabilities, cleavages of personality and accumulating difficulties—this entire period of developing troubles—covered *almost half of Burt's life!* Are we to suppose that Burt was enduring these emotional stresses (these *primary precipitating causes of* severe psychological disturbance) over so extended a period, but that they were such, nonetheless, as to break out psychosomatically in the two particularly intense manifestations of Ménière's disease of 1945 to 1946 and 1966?

The entire story is one of conjecture only—supported by nothing remotely approaching objective evidence. There is only a strange stringing together of supposedly significant incidents, clinical and psychological symptoms and diagnoses, and hypothetical suggestions, all highly selective, and all to support the one contention: that the flaws in Burt's later behaviour were rooted in his personality and were *pathological,* to be explained by the resurfacing of genetically inbuilt instabilities, the "primitive Gamin culture" of his early childhood, and the like.

To what conclusion, then, are we driven, after this analysis? Or what, at any rate, is the kind of conclusion I am suggesting?

I cannot see that it is at all possible to accept Hearnshaw's entirely conjectural construction, which rests on no evidential grounds whatever. We are left, therefore, with the straightforward possibility of deliberate wrongdoing. In defending his position against the increasing animosity of his critics, Burt may have employed some tactics, some deceptions, some elements of calculated guile, which were questionable. None of these, however, were such as to promulgate fraudulent views that were not grounded on the findings of all his early investigations, and had not been long and consistently put forward and argued; and certainly they did not require, for their explanation, quite unfounded and highly speculative fictional constructions of conjectural pathology. If Burt in some ways had misbehaved; if in some ways he had been guilty of wrong-doing in his latter-day disputes with antagonists; let this be admitted; let it be considered within the context of the animosity he faced and in relation to both his own character and arguments, and the character, ideology, and arguments of his critics; and let him be pronounced blameworthy—and take the blame.

Such a judgment, however, of Burt's critics as well as of Burt himself, raises interesting questions.

Burt's Detractors

It is far more than an attempted about-turn of rhetoric to reorientate these same questions now in the direction of Burt's detractors. Some broad and fundamental, as well as some quite specific, issues are involved.

To consider, first, the character displayed by the detractors themselves. Is it not the case that our examination of their testimony, and of their manner, of initiating and then pursuing the controversy, has disclosed many instances of apparent deception, deviousness, deliberate misrepresentation and distortion, ideological obsession, an apparently obsessive compulsion in persisting in their vilification of Burt over many years—long after Burt's death—with much repetitiveness, and expressed in terms of the most intemperate and outrightly defamatory language? Have we not in many items of clear evidence seen far more disgraceful denunciations forthrightly hurled at Burt in the most public domain of the mass media than ever issued from either the mouth or pen of Burt against any of those who took issue with him? Why, then, one wonders, this powerfully and continually felt animus against Burt? What can account for it—for it has clearly gone far beyond the bounds of straightforward intellectual disagreement? Why too (and here we approach the broader issues) the powerfully and continually felt animus against any theory maintaining that differences in mental ability are to a large and significant extent established by heredity, even when such theories readily recognize the importance of subsequent social and environmental influences? Why among this small handful of Burt's accusers, and why among a large and evidently influential group of intellectuals in both Britain and America, has there been, especially since the end of World War II, such

a fanatical opposition to Hereditarian doctrines? Was this something rooted in the ethos of the social changes taking place during
these postwar years? Was it a misconceived corollary of the movements towards a greater egalitarianism and extended democracy?
Was it the outcome of a misconception of the idea of equality as a
principle of social justice? However this may be, the specific polemic against Burt does seem to have been symptomatic of a much
wider antagonism to Hereditarian theories that clearly came to
exercise powerful influence in academic and publishing circles.

It is interesting and important to see that in America, in particular, this antagonism was even spoken of as the "anti-Hereditarian
lobby," a "lobby" so powerful as to seem to have entered deeply
into editorial and publishing censorship. It is also significant that
the marked protest against this stemmed directly from the influence
of Burt. In the *American Psychologist* in July 1972 (p. 660), a large
group of some of the most eminent scientists in America were
moved to issue the following statement.

COMMENT
Behavior and Heredity

The posthumous Thorndike Award article by Burt (1972) draws
psychological attention again to the great influence played by heredity
in important human behaviors. Recently, to emphasize such influence
has required considerable courage, for it has brought psychologists and
other scientists under extreme personal and professional abuse at
Harvard, Berkeley, Stanford, Connecticut, Illinois, and elsewhere. Yet
such influences are well documented. To assert their importance and
validity, and to call for free and unencumbered research, the 50 scientists listed below have signed the following document, and submit it to
the APA:

Background: The history of civilization shows many periods when
scientific research or teaching was censured, punished, or suppressed
for nonscientific reasons, usually for seeming to contradict some religious or political belief. Well-known scientist victims include: Galileo,
in orthodox Italy; Darwin, in Victorian England; Einstein, in Hitler's
Germany; and Mendelian biologists, in Stalin's Russia.

Today, a similar suppression, censure, punishment, and defamation
are being applied against scientists who emphasize the role of heredity
in human behavior. Published positions are often misquoted and misrepresented; emotional appeals replace scientific reasoning; arguments are
directed against the man rather than against the evidence (e.g., a
scientist is called "fascist," and his arguments are ignored).

A large number of attacks come from nonscientists, or even antiscientists, among the political militants on campus. Other attackers include academics committed to environmentalism in their explanation of almost all human differences. And a large number of scientists, who have studied the evidence and are persuaded of the great role played by heredity in human behavior, are silent, neither expressing their beliefs clearly in public, nor rallying strongly to the defense of their more outspoken colleagues.

The results are seen in the present academy: it is virtually heresy to express a hereditarian view, or to recommend further study of the biological bases of behavior. A kind of orthodox environmentalism dominates the liberal academy, and strongly inhibits teachers, researchers, and scholars from turning to biological explanations or efforts.

Resolution: Now, therefore, we the undersigned scientists from a variety of fields, declare the following beliefs and principles:

1. We have investigated much evidence concerning the possible role of inheritance in human abilities and behaviors, and we believe such hereditary influences are very strong.

2. We wish strongly to encourage research into the biological hereditary bases of behavior, as a major complement to the environmental efforts at explanation.

3. We strongly defend the right, and emphasize the scholarly duty, of the teacher to discuss hereditary influences on behavior, in appropriate settings and with responsible scholarship.

4. We deplore the evasion of hereditary reasoning in current textbooks, and the failure to give responsible weight to heredity in disciplines such as sociology, social psychology, social anthropology, educational psychology, psychological measurement, and many others.

5. We call upon liberal academics—upon faculty senates, upon professional and learned societies, upon the American Association of University Professors, upon the American Civil Liberties Union, upon the University Centers for Rational Alternatives, upon presidents and boards of trustees, upon departments of science, and upon the editors of scholarly journals—to insist upon the openness of social science to the well-grounded claims of biobehavioral reasoning, and to protect vigilantly any qualified faculty members who responsibly teach, research, or publish concerning such reasoning.

We so urge because as scientists we believe that human problems may best be remedied by increased human knowledge, and that such increases in knowledge lead much more probably to the enhancement of human happiness than to the opposite.

Signed:

JACK A. ADAMS
Professor of Psychology
University of Illinois

DOROTHY C. ADKINS
Professor/Researcher in
    Education
University of Illinois

ANDREW R. BAGGALEY
Professor of Psychology
University of Pennsylvania

IRWIN A. BERG
Professor of Psychology and
    Dean of Arts & Sciences
Louisiana State University

EDGAR F. BORGATTA
Professor of Sociology
Queens College, New York

ROBERT CANCRO, MD
Professor of Psychiatry
University of Connecticut

RAYMOND B. CATTELL
Distinguished Research Professor
    of Psychology
University of Illinois

FRANCIS H. C. CRICK
Nobel Laureate
Medical Research Council
    Laboratory of Molecular
    Biology
Cambridge University

C. D. DARLINGTON, FRS
Sherardian Professor of Botany
Oxford University

ROBERT H. DAVID
Professor of Psychology and
    Assistant Provost
Michigan State University

M. RAY DENNY
Professor of Psychology
Michigan State University

OTIS DUDLEY DUNCAN
Professor of Sociology
University of Michigan

BRUCE K. ECKLAND
Professor of Sociology
University of North Carolina

CHARLES W. ERIKSEN
Professor of Psychology
University of Illinois

HANS J. EYSENCK
Professor of Psychology Institute
    of Psychiatry
University of London

ERIC F. GARDNER
Slocum Professor & Chairman
Education and Psychology
Syracuse University

BENSON E. GINSBURG
Professor & Head, Biobehavioral
    Sciences
University of Connecticut

GARRETT HARDIN
Professor of Human Ecology
University of California,
    Santa Barbara

HARRY S. HARLOW
Professor of Psychology
University of Wisconsin

RICHARD HERRNSTEIN
Professor & Chairman of
    Psychology
Harvard University

LLOYD G. HUMPHREYS[1]
Professor of Psychology
University of Illinois

DWIGHT J. INGLE
Professor and Chairman of
    Physiology
University of Chicago

ARTHUR R. JENSEN
Professor of Educational
    Psychology
University of California, Berkeley

RONALD C. JOHNSON
Professor & Chairman of
    Psychology
University of Hawaii

HENRY F. KAISER
Professor of Education
University of California, Berkeley

E. LOWELL KELLY
Professor of Psychology &
Director, Institute of
Human Adjustment
University of Michigan

JOHN C. KENDREW
Nobel Laureate
MRC Laboratory of Molecular
Biology
Cambridge, England

FRED N. KERLINGER[1]
Professor of Educational
Psychology
New York University

WILLIAM S. LAUGHLIN
Professor of Anthropology &
Biobehavioral Sciences
University of Connecticut

DONALD B. LINDSLEY
Professor of Psychology
University of California,
Los Angeles

QUINN MCNEMAR
Emeritus Professor of
Psychology, Education, and
Statistics
Stanford University

PAUL E. MEEHL
Regents Professor of Psychology
and Adjunct Professor of Law
University of Minnesota

JACQUES MONOD
Nobel Laureate
Professor, Institute Pasteur
College de France

JOHN H. NORTHRUP
Nobel Laureate
Professor Emeritus of
Biochemistry
University of California and
Rockefeller University

LAWRENCE I. O'KELLEY
Professor and Chairman of
Psychology
Michigan State University

ELLIS BATTEN PAGE
Professor of Educational
Psychology
University of Connecticut

B. A. RASMUSEN
Professor of Animal Genetics
University of Illinois

ANNE ROE
Professor Emerita, Harvard
University & Lecturer in
Psychology
University of Arizona

DAVID ROSENTHAL
Research Psychologist and Chief
of Laboratories
National Institute of Mental
Health

DAVID G. RYANS
Professor & Director Educational
R & D Center
University of Hawaii

ELIOT SLATER, MD
Professor of Psychiatry and
Editor
British Journal of Psychiatry
University of London

H. FAIRFIELD SMITH
Professor of Statistics
University of Connecticut

[1]In Item 1, preferred "substantial" or "important" to the wording "very strong."

S. S. STEVENS
Professor of Psychophysics
Harvard University

WILLIAM R. THOMPSON
Professor of Psychology
Queens University, Canada

ROBERT I. THORNDIKE
Professor of Psychology and
    Education
Teachers College
Columbia University

FREDERICK C. THORNE, MD
Editor, *Journal of Clinical
    Psychology*
Brandon, Vermont

PHILIP E. VERNON
Professor of Educational
    Psychology
University of Calgary, Alberta

DAVID WECHSLER
Professor of Psychology
N.Y.U. College of Medicine

MORTON W. WEIR
Professor of Psychology and
    Vice-Chancellor
University of Illinois

DAVID ZEAMAN
Professor of Psychology and
    NIMII Career Research Fellow
University of Connecticut

REFERENCE

BURT, C. Inheritance of general intelligence. *American Psychologist*, 1972, 27, 175–190.

ELLIS B. PAGE
University of Connecticut

Bearing in mind what has been said about the decline in Burt's reputation during his later years, it may be noted that this statement, stimulated by the Thorndike Award, was issued *after Burt's death!* Bearing in mind, too, Burt's latter-day battles with his supposedly egalitarian Environmentalist opponents, and his supposed wrongdoing in coming to terms with them, it is interesting to note in this statement the recognition that *courage* was needed—in both Burt and in the award to him of the Thorndike prize—in being even prepared to take a stand for "hereditary reasoning." Is there not something strange about the extremity and tenacity of the attacks, within science, on any hereditarian position? And has not this broader assumption and persuasion—as well, it seems, as other more personal feelings—been demonstrably at work in Kamin, Gillie, the Clarkes, and the small circle of editors and producers in the media who have provided the megaphone (so to speak) for their voice, and the slanted dramatization (as in the BBC film) of their stereotypes?

A simple question is, why has the question of "pathology" only been raised in relation to Burt? Should Hearnshaw not also be looking into the genetic beginnings and early childhood influences at work in the inner personality of Leon Kamin? What early and deeply established elements of instability might underlie the apparent obsessiveness of Gillie in so long sustaining his journalistic campaign? Might it not have been some coincidentally experienced childhood constellation of emotional shock, some telling trauma, that bound the Clarkes together in their shared and frequently repeated misrepresentation of their "abstracts" as "articles"? May there not have been some deep grounding of emotional and behavioral lability in the genetic constitution of Hans Eysenck that explains his wide swing from a total support of Burt to a total denunciation of him? And what of Hearnshaw himself? Might there not be some irremediable disposition in his personality (which we could discover if we did but "psychologize" him) that compels him to indulge in hypothetical conjecture to explain hypothetical possibilities in the absence of facts?

I hasten to say that I am far from supposing or suggesting that such pathological roots exist. There is, of course, no evidence. Nothing of the sort can or should be claimed. My only point is that it is just as likely to be so among these detractors as in the case of Burt. If the alleged misrepresentations of a dead man call for pathological explanation, why not those of the living? But I leave such questions for the jury to consider.

Our conclusions can be clear. The verdict on the charges of fraud against Burt must decidedly be one of "not guilty!"

The further questions as to his having employed any deviousness and deception in meeting his increasingly antagonistic assailants and defending the position he had long maintained, I leave to the jury's consideration; just as I leave to your consideration the nature and supposed necessity of Hearnshaw's pathological account of this.

In exactly the same way, I leave to your consideration and judgment the same questions as to the apparent misrepresentations, distortions, and widely disseminated and sustained defamations, of that handful of detractors who (all considerations of pathology aside) have so aggressively travestied the name, reputation, and work of Burt after he was dead.

The one overall conclusion I put to you, as being most certain on the basis of all the evidence we have assembled, is that the "scandal" in the "Cyril Burt scandal" lies chiefly in the disgraceful nature of the testimony of those who raised and pursued it. If the evidence we have considered is firm and true, as I believe it to be, it will not be Sir Cyril Burt who will go down in history as the perpetrator of "the most sensational fraud this century" (Gillie's words), but his detractors who will go down in history as its discredited and distasteful promulgators. That will be the substance of their achievement and their fame.

Rehabilitation and Contemporary Relevance

All that remains to be said—briefly because it is so clear—is that the name, reputation, and work of Burt now call for a public and scientific rehabilitation so thoroughgoing and conspicuous as to remove from them the defamation from which they have so long suffered; the cloud of poisonous disrepute that has so long hung over them, obscuring them from view and standing in the way of their consideration because of the public distaste that has spread with it; and the now entrenched and worldwide assumption that the charges against him were true and justified. For, strangely, once this cloud is lifted it can be seen that Burt's achievement over at least sixty years of activity and productivity as both an applied and academic psychologist, consists of an entire and thoroughly consistent corpus of work as considerable as that (if not more considerable than that) of any other British psychologist in the history of the subject. Furthermore, it is a contribution that can be seen to be pragmatically, intellectually, ethically, and politically at the heart of our changing society from Victorian times to now. It was indeed part of that changing society; a contribution that as it was made, and in its making, actually contributed to the nature and direction of that social change itself.

Following the earlier surveys of Booth and Rowntree, Burt's own surveys (which quite consciously followed upon these pioneering studies and frequently referred back to them), were a further mapping out of the disturbing economic and social conditions of widespread poverty and deprivation that, despite the many reforms it instituted and achieved, Victorian society bequeathed to the twentieth century. They identified the nature and range of the inequalities inherited by the families of Britain in the different regions, localities, neighborhoods, and communities. Focused on Liverpool, Birmingham, and then chiefly London, Burt's surveys were the essential and timely ways in which the many roots of backwardness, and the many causes of retardation, in the nature and lives of individuals were identified and measured, and (an emphasis that seems to have been long forgotten) this was a revelation of the *physical* and *medical* (as well as the psychological, social, and educational) correlates of appalling social conditions and early childhood *diseases*. Frequently, indeed, Burt's surveys were undertaken hand in glove with *medical collaborators*.

They were especially concerned, as well, to point out, among these inequities, the marked inequalities of educational opportunities and provisions, and link them with vocational guidance and the practical problems of training for occupations. Considerations about education were therefore directly linked with a consideration of the *work* of individuals, and the conditions, problems, and requirements of employment and industry. At the heart of all this, the most searching attention was given to the difficult problem of *reliable measurement,* of accurately discovering the grades and distribution of the levels of mental ability and the grades and distribution of the levels of mental ability and the special talents of children, so that having achieved this as far as possible, one would be better able to identify those environmental conditions and factors that encouraged or stood in the way of their fulfilment. This it was that led to the much *improved* ways of recognizing children's abilities (with nonverbal as well as verbal kinds of testing) by going beyond the surface appearance of class privileges and attainments, and subsequently to the *extension* of opportunities for those children who were shown to be disadvantaged. In all this, Burt's work was actually at the heart of the social progress attempted and accomplished in Britain throughout the first six decades or so of this century; it was a part of it; and it is important to see that it was largely undertaken in close conjunction with governmental inquiries and efforts (both local and central), and was in keeping with most other public inquiries and the reports of government committees of the time. This is a matter of clear public recognition.

In the Plowden Report (to take a late example of which Burt was well aware), which came to question the way in which selection in education had come to be regarded (unfortunately and falsely) as an unpleasant and permanent segregation of children at the age of eleven-plus, the progressive nature of the extension of educational opportunity already achieved was clearly recognized. In their section on "Selection for Secondary Education," the committee stated:

> Before we turn to the future, we think it right to recall the intentions of those who introduced methods of selection. Their aim was fundamentally egalitarian. It was to open the doors of the grammar schools to children of high ability irrespective of their social background. For the first 20 years after Hadow the problem was often to persuade working class parents to take up the "free places" their children had won.[9]

Also recognized was the great value of the introduction of *intelligence tests,* in which of course Burt had been by far the most central and influential contributor.

> In the past 50 years persistent efforts have been made to refine methods of selection. As a result the World Survey of Education in 1962 commented that "Great Britain has made the greatest advance . . . in developing reliable and valued methods of testing and examining scholastic aptitude and ability. Few countries . . . have yet adopted such reliable methods of standardising or normalizing the marks in assessments used for selection purposes." Any substantial further improvement in accuracy is unlikely.

In this, too the central importance of the *intelligence test* as a basis for teachers' assessments—as against *attainment tests*—was clearly and strongly emphasized.

> The N.F.E.R. [National Foundation for Educational Research], in their enquiry in Twickenham in 1956, found the greatest accuracy was achieved when account was taken both of attainment tests and of the head teacher's order of merit scaled by the results of an intelligence test. Nevertheless, the order of merit was the best single predictor. Only a slight reduction in accuracy was caused by leaving attainment tests out of the calculation. This loss of accuracy must be weighted against the effects of externally imposed attainment tests on the curriculum of the primary school. Some teachers undoubtedly prepare for attainment tests and give this preparation undue weight in the curriculum. Some authorities try to reduce the backwash on the curriculum of standardised attainment tests by including English composition in the tests, or by new English tests which allow a greater freedom of response

than did earlier types. Arithmetic tests have been constructed in which speed and computation are reduced in importance and items included which attempt to measure understanding. Although these tests are improvements they will not allow enough freedom to primary teachers if they are externally imposed. We conclude that where selection procedures continue to be used, a slight loss of accuracy is better than the risk of a harmful backwash on the curriculum, and that externally imposed attainment tests should be abandoned.

Burt's emphasis had in fact won the day, and was now both recognized and operative in selection procedures—whatever the end to which these were directed.

To all of this must be added the contribution Burt also made (within the same context of revealing social conditions and the effects of economic and social deprivation) to the understanding of juvenile delinquency. *The Young Delinquent* was as valuable a study as *The Backward Child,* and Burt himself literally trod the streets in his quest for a first-hand understanding of his subject matter. It is interesting to note that in this his investigations were very similar to those of some members of the Chicago School of sociology in America. He was certainly no ivory-tower researcher. His data, again, might not have met the sophisticated requirements of more recent research design, but derived from a grass-roots acquaintance with the people and their contextual conditions he was studying they most certainly were.

Burt was also as much concerned, however, that children possessing exceptionally *high* levels of ability should be given the education their talents required and deserved, the outcome being his last book, *The Gifted Child.* All this work was conducted with the greatest degree of accuracy that Burt and his many helpers could bring to the task (bearing in mind that these were substantial surveys undertaken in the light of the needs of local authorities and therefore requiring many assistants), and showed the greatest degree of humanity and sympathy with the people (delinquents, normal and well-behaved, or highly gifted) with whose problems he was concerned. And all these attributes and qualities of Burt's work are open to the clearest demonstration and proof by the simple test of reading the books and articles—in their order, continuity, and consistency—that resulted from them.

Burt's work does richly deserve this overall systematic reconsideration, and in the process might well be compared with the work of those who have thought themselves in a fit position to criticize him. It is a salutary and telling comparison.

This claim for the rehabilitation of the whole body of Burt's work should not, however, take our attention too much away from the narrower range of subject matter that we have chiefly had to consider: the studies of identical twins (and the question of the hereditary basis of intelligence) out of which the charges of fraud stemmed. Despite all the doubts thrown upon it by the many allegations, Burt's work, even here, calls for careful consideration and rehabilitation to at least a very considerable degree. The assumption that because of the fraud charges, his work in this area is no longer of scientific use, has been too readily and uncritically accepted, and needs to be radically questioned and challenged. Three points deserve clear statement.

First, bearing in mind Jensen's remaining caution—that with his part persuasion, part reservation about Hearnshaw's account, he is still "not 100 percent confident" as to whether there was anything false in Burt's claim to have managed to accumulate 53 pairs of twins reared apart by 1966—we must reiterate the point that (given the reworking of past data and the adding of cases obtained by advertising, information volunteered in communications, and provided by personal contacts) there is no evidence to prove with any degree of definiteness that this claim should be doubted. Even from 1943, but certainly with and after the publication of the 1955 paper—with its number of 21 twins and its table of correlations—there had clearly been a very positive effort to seek new cases. By May 1957 it was said that these efforts had managed to increase the number of 21 to "over 30," and there was therefore (given these very deliberate ongoing efforts) nothing at all implausible about the figure of 42 reported in 1958. Similarly, with the same persisting efforts, undertaken on the grounds of the continuing claim that identical twins were not as rare as was commonly supposed, there was nothing implausible about the subsequent increase by 1966 to 53. This could be made even more plausible by one other consideration that, not wanting to seem to be overweighting the argument in Burt's favor by drawing upon evidence that was not firmly founded, I have not so far mentioned: namely, the incidental possibility (mentioned by Hearnshaw) that some twins (in this last table) might have been "borrowed" from other sources. Although this is a possibility, I do not myself think that this point needs to be pressed. It is too doubtful at present to bear any firm argument. In any event, we have seen that the total of 53 was quite separately mentioned by Burt during 1965 in the *AEP Newsletter,* before the publication of the article and without any possible knowledge of later disputations. Though the 1966 table of correlations itself was a statistical hodgepodge (and we have noted the several reasons that might have been responsible for this), and therefore in itself was probably unusable as a body of data for subsequent science, there is no proven ground on which to doubt the claim as to the total number of twins.[10]

The second point, however, is quite undoubted and firm. Setting aside the 1966 table, there are no reasons whatever to doubt the soundness of all the earlier reports: 1943, 1955, "Burt 1958," and "Conway 1958." We have seen that a clear consistency runs through all these reports. The tables of correlations follow each other with no lack of clarity whatever (being in many respects the same); the charge of invariant correlations is completely groundless; and the criticisms leveled at this entire sequence of papers, up to and including 1958, have all been shown to be completely without foundation, having rested either on sheer carelessness or misunderstandings, and certainly in some respects on misrepresentations and distortions. The studies argued and reported in all these papers, then, can still rank as studies as accurately based and scientifically reputable as any others being conducted in their own day; and remain completely in accord with the findings now reported in the most up-to-date investigations in this same field (such as those, for example, from Minnesota). Even on this one very specific area of study, so much and for so long disputed, Burt deserves the fullest reconsideration and rehabilitation.

There is a third consideration here, however, that is much broader and of very considerable weight. Though they have chiefly been discussed with reference to the twin studies, Burt's arguments in support of the view that general intelligence had a largely hereditary basis were by no means confined to twin studies but went considerably beyond them, and the Environmentalists have not as yet rebutted the reasoning he advanced. As early as the 1943 paper, Burt had clearly set out *seven* grounds supporting his view.

One of these was the evidence of the identical twins reared apart: that there remained a high correlation in their measured intelligence even when, from earliest childhood, they had been exposed to the conditions and influences of quite different environments. This point needs no further mention as we have considered it sufficiently. But Burt offered six other considerations that in his view constituted undeniable evidence.

First, he pointed to the growing and general rejection of Locke's long-held view that every human mind at birth was a *tabula rasa* on which environmental influences and education could simply write their own story. Even the Watsonian behaviorists, Burt showed, acknowledged inherited differences in anatomical and physical structures, and it was a reasonable assumption that such differences (for example in the structural organization of the brain and central nervous system "and doubtless in its chemistry as well") entailed mental differences and differences of mental ability.

> Since for almost every characteristic that is not directly indispensable for mere survival, innate difference is the rule throughout the animal kingdom, it would be all but inconceivable to the biologist if human intelligence were identical in every normal individual, and if the mental defectives and the geniuses were freaks and exceptions.

Second, this *a priori* probability was in fact verified by empirical investigations that showed:

> that every intermediate grade, from mental deficiency up to the highest genius, is fully represented in the general population. Variety, not uniformity, is everywhere the rule, however uniform the environment.

Third, Burt reported his own early study[11] in which a series of tests were administered to the children of elementary schools and those (who were sons of Oxford professors and lecturers) attending a preparatory school. The study showed, he claimed,

> that the more the test was saturated with the 'general-factor', the higher were the performances of the children of abler parents; and the more it depended upon educational acquirements, the higher were the performances of the elementary children, who came from somewhat poorer homes, but who at these earlier ages had received a better grounding in the more fundamental school subjects. Further, it was in the complex

tests, i.e., in those depending most on the 'general factor,' that the correlations between parents and children, or between brothers and sisters, were found to be greatest.

Fourth, he pointed to his often reported finding that the differences between *individuals* in the *same* economic class proved to be far wider than the differences between the *averages* of *different* economic classes (a position, we may recall, fully endorsed by the sociologists of education). How, Burt asked, was this to be explained on the basis of environmentalism?

> Numerous children from the poorest homes, brought up under the most unfavourable conditions, achieve I.Q.'s of 130 or above; while others from the most comfortable and cultured homes get I.Q.'s of only 70 or below. If the high I.Q.'s obtained by the average members of the better classes are to be attributed chiefly to their environmental advantages, how can we explain the low I.Q's of so many others in those classes, or the high I.Q.'s of poorer children?

Fifth, environmental disadvantages seemed to make little or no difference to measured intelligence. How, on an environmentalist basis, was this to be explained? "Current handicaps arising from environmental conditions," Burt wrote,

> such as physical ill-health, lack of cultural opportunities, or passing emotional disturbances, as a rule make very little difference to the I.Q. when properly assessed. In following up cases of various types, I have encountered many instances where the child's home conditions have been vastly improved, and still more where they have rapidly deteriorated: yet even after five or ten years in the changed environment, the I.Q. seldom alters greatly. This conclusion is further confirmed by retesting evacuated children after two years or more in their new surroundings. Even prolonged disease or malnutrition, as Shepherd Dawson has shown, exerts very little influence, provided the nervous system itself is not directly attacked.

It is to be noted here, however, that Burt—again in his often-reported way—was far from denying the fact that environmental disadvantages could *retard* or even *impair* measured intelligence, and on this he held a quite specific point of view. The claim just made, he said, does not altogether dispose of the possibility that poverty and its concomitants may permanently impair 'intelligence.' If bad feeding, infectious disease, and the like exert any serious influence on mental ability, the damage, I believe, is most likely to be done *during the first few years of life, before ever the child comes to school:* and such impairment, I can readily imagine, might be lasting. The real question, therefore, is—how frequent and how serious are the effects of such pre-school handicaps?

And sixth, there was the evidence of children placed at an early age in residential schools, homes, and orphanages, *where the environment was virtually the same for all.* Comparative studies revealed, quite apart from the question of the degree of closeness of the correlation between their intelligence and that of their parents, that there was in fact a wide range of differences in intelligence among them. Again, how did environmentalists explain this? "Since the post-natal conditions of the children must have been much the same," Burt wrote, "it seems impossible to escape the conclusion that the difference in their IQs was the effect of a difference in heredity.[12]

Any environmentalist theory of the determination of intelligence must therefore come to terms with these arguments, in addition to that relating to the evidence of identical twins reared apart—and so far they do not seem to have done so.

Both on these very specific areas of study, therefore, and on the much wider range of the several early surveys, and in the books and articles that resulted from them—many of which were in themselves really of the nature of pioneering studies—Burt's work does call for full rehabilitation and the most serious and searching reconsideration. The centrality and importance of his place in the efforts made to assess realistically and reliably the conditions of deprivation and the many inequalities suffered by the disadvantaged families of society; and following this, to improve their lot, particularly but by no means only in education; needs to be recognized anew. A great wrong has to be put right, and work that has been of the most substantial value for psychology and the social sciences needs to be reappraised.

Apart from the matter of justice, however—central and important though this unquestionably is—this call for Burt's rehabilitation receives additional and even urgent support from a realization of the contemporary *relevance* of both his findings and his ideas to the condition into which education in our society has now fallen. This relevance is only too plain. Burt's position, based realistically on fact and impeccably on the firmest principles of morality and justice, is clearly indicative of what *education in society ought to be,* as against the sorry mess of the *educational system as it now exists,* and to which successive political "reforms" and ministerial policies since the end of the second world war have brought it.

There had been nothing in the 1944 Education Act or in governmental reports preceding it (that of the Norwood Committee is an outstanding example) to suggest that the eleven-plus examination for selection to one or other of three kinds of secondary school was instituted as a test to separate "successes" from "failures"; "superior" children from "inferior" children; branding them as such for life and segregating them into superior and inferior kinds of schools. It is painful now to see how completely the analysis and recommendations of the Norwood Committee were misunderstood and misrepresented. Indeed, it is difficult to believe that they were ever seriously and attentively read. For whatever reason, however (clearly there were many), this is how eleven-plus selection *did* come to be regarded, and this conception was in part caused, and then certainly fueled by, simplistic political interpretations along party lines. Selection in education came to be totally conceived, in blanket fashion, as an injustice of class inequality, an injustice stemming from social inequalities that served to perpetuate the class system. Equality of opportunity then came to be conceived, in opposition and by contrast, as *equality of treatment* for all, only to be achieved if all children attended *the same kind of school*—the comprehensive school. And even there the same inequalities of selection and treatment should be eradicated. "Streaming" should be abandoned. "Setting" was frowned on. "Mixed-ability teaching" alone could achieve full equality. It was also an unjust inequality that academically able pupils should end their secondary education with an examination certificate (0-levels, perhaps A-levels) whereas nonacademic children could not. The CSE qualification was therefore introduced. This failed to achieve equality, however. CSEs were decidedly thought inferior to 0 levels. These examinations have therefore been made into one, the GCSE. Since even here some would be unequal to others in performing in written examinations at the end of the course, a new system of continuous assessment, as yet of an unproven nature for teachers and children alike, has been introduced.

In all such matters, each succeeding minister of education stepped into the shoes of his or her predecessors, intent on instituting still further reforms towards fairness; to approximate still more closely to social justice; and to make education seem more evidently relevant to the experience and subsequent occupational life of the vast majority of children. Well . . . the story is all too familiar, and could be long and protracted. The question is: how did Burt regard this onward tramp of political reform, and what is the relevance of his views to the current attempts to effect a cure? It is interesting to recall that in 1969, Burt was roundly berated for even suggesting that some standards in educational attainment had fallen during this period of educational reform (including reforms in teaching methods); whereas today, twenty years later, almost everyone would with scarcely any question agree with him. It is now an almost universal conviction that, behind the glass-and-concrete facade of the new education, behind all the talk at all the conferences, there lies in fact a sprawling chaotic mess.

Burt believed that much of the ideologically motivated and politically legislated "reform" of the entire educational system was bogus—and could not be otherwise. It rested on a completely false appraisal of psychological and social (and even geographical) facts, and on so simplistic a political notion and implementation of the basic principle of equality of opportunity in education as to be completely unsound, and—even worse than inefficient—such as to sow the seeds of educational pretense and chaos. What was Burt's own position?

He certainly shared the desire for justice in education; the concern that every individual child should, as far as this was possible, have equality of opportunity to gain that education best suited to his or her abilities and aptitudes; and the persuasion that educational provisions should be of the highest degree of excellence society could achieve at all levels, if standards of thought, knowledge, accuracy, judgment, and skills, and therefore the quality of life for individuals and society alike, were to be maintained and improved. But he believed that the notion of the equality of opportunity had been misconceived under the pressure of political ideology. The duty of each adult generation was to provide each succeeding generation of children with the best education possible that for each child was most appropriate to the levels of ability and special aptitudes shown (fully bearing in mind, and taking into account, their social contexts and any privileges or disadvantages these might possess). For this, certain things were indispensable. First, a sensitive, careful, and accurate *assessment* of these abilities was required. The most reliable kind of *measurement* should be employed, and such appraisals should not be left to the judgment of teachers alone, whose values and attitudes could well be the vehicle of the very class prejudices everyone was seeking to avoid. It is worthwhile to recall that this was precisely the view of the sociologists of education, stated most succinctly and positively by David Glass. "Objective tests," he said, should not be abandoned. "On the contrary, the replacement of such tests by . . . teachers' reports might simply result in a less justifiable selection of children. . . ." Objective tests "would be very valuable if used for purposes of guidance." Glass warned only against any *simplistic* kind of selection (which was unaware of, and insensitive to, the social basis of many inequalities) and the adoption of any *rigid and simplistic basis* for it; but Burt also was insistent on this! The provision of the education most appropriate to the level of general intelligence and the special aptitudes of children positively *required* selection. But, Burt was careful to point out, it was indeed simplistic to identify selection purely with the separation of children into one or other kind of school organization, or the supposed elimination of selection altogether by the compulsory imposition of one kind of school. The organization of schools was varied for many kinds of reason in different geographical and administrative regions; indeed, the organization of even the one kind of school differed in different areas (and catchment areas); and the educational provisions (including the presence or absence of selection) that educationalists may have in mind and think desirable were not necessarily achievable by the imposition, throughout the country, of any one of them. Burt was decidedly not opposed in principle to the comprehensive school (as one kind of school among other kinds), but he thought it a myth that selection could possibly be altogether eliminated there. "Remedial classes," "special needs" classes—what were these but kinds of selection, cutting across any supposed sufficiency of "mixed-ability teaching"? And in mixed-ability teaching, except under the most favorable conditions (including size of class) and when undertaken by the most skilled and experienced teachers, it was highly improbable that the appropriately differential education the varying groups of children (let alone individuals) required could be satisfactorily provided. Again, we may recall the warning of Douglas that the many desired improvements in schools (of staff, amenities, and so forth) would be "no less necessary in the comprehensive system of education which is now evolving" if local discrepancies and social inequalities were to be eliminated.

For Burt, selection was *unavoidable* in education. In one way or another, whatever was said or professed, it *took place*. It could be done covertly, badly, and inefficiently, leaving all the same inequalities uncovered and unremedied; or it could be done overtly, efficiently, and well. His concern was that it should be done openly, on the most reliable basis, and *well*. But justice in educational opportunity and provision entailed, Burt believed, a third indispensable element: not equality of *treatment* but *appropriately differential treatment*. To think of selection in terms of whether or not it reflected and perpetuated the class system; to think of equality of opportunity in terms of equal treatment; and to think that this could be achieved by the universal imposition of one kind of secondary school organization; was for Burt, therefore, a vast mistake. We noted Burt's own statement of this earlier, but it deserves repetition here.

> In England the issues that arise have of late been canvassed chiefly in reference to their bearing on school organization; and it seems widely assumed that those who subscribe to the hereditarian view are wholly at variance with the establishment of comprehensive schools. That is by no means an inevitable inference. . . . There is no one universal scheme equally suited to every type of educational area. Recent enquiries have demonstrated that so-called comprehensive schools differ far more from one another than is commonly imagined, and the various types of organization are constantly being revised. We should therefore suspend our judgement as to the relative efficiency of different kinds of school.

> The paramount need is not equality of educational opportunity, but diversity. Each child should, in an ideal system, be provided with the peculiar types of opportunity that can best minister to his needs. Inevitably that must entail some kind of segregation or selective stream-

ing. A year or two ago a questionnaire circulated to a number of practising teachers indicated that the majority of the older (and therefore presumably the more experienced) favoured relatively homogeneous classes as being far easier to teach. "The dull pupil," said one, "when working in a class with pupils of average intelligence quickly becomes disheartened by the daily evidence of his own inferiority; the exceptionally able soon get bored and restive." But unless the teacher is prepared to sift and sort he cannot secure the intellectual homogeneity than he wants.

On this oversimplified basis of a reorganization of schools to approximate to one form only; with any imposition of undiscriminating mixed-ability teaching (coupled, particularly, with the advocacy and practice of new methods of teaching with an insufficient emphasis upon the reliable learning of foundation subjects), Burt believed that the supposed progress in having changed the educational system for the better might well prove, sadly, to be only apparent, not real. The actual outcome might be a condition of continuing educational pretence; a demoralization of teachers caught up, as they were bound to be, in a situation fundamentally untrue; a disaffection of children on a massive scale; and, coupled with all this, a marked deterioration of standards: a situation, in short, in which education would no longer be taken seriously. Education would fail both individuals and society.

Burt also believed that the continued achievement of high standards of creativity and productivity in society (in wealth creation, economic well-being, and all areas of culture alike) would be at risk if the most able children were not given the highest standards of education we could provide. The neglect of the gifted, and of the maintenance of the highest standards of intellectual excellence, as well as the neglect of the less able and the disadvantaged, could also bring social deterioration. But finally, I turn again to the one emphasis at the heart of Burt's position, which is often overlooked in appraisals of his work.

No matter how complex the theoretical considerations and empirical investigations of heredity on the one hand and environmental factors on the other, and no matter how accurate and satisfactory these might become, the central emphasis in Burt's mind, concern, and work, was always *the individual child*. With his or her inherited endowment, growing towards maturity in that particular context of environmental influences in which he or she had been placed (by birth or other circumstances), each child was encountering, experiencing, and evaluating certain aims, ideals, models for imitation, motives for this or that kind of behavior, activity, and endeavor. This growing knowledge of the world and society, with the perception of all these human qualities within it, were also accompanied by, and were a part of, the growth of *self-knowledge. The process involved was that of the self-creation of character,* and the qualities unavoidably and essentially at the heart of the making of the character of a person were those the child experienced among other people during early life. At its heart, then, education—in addition to the provision of information, the inculcation of skills, and the provision of the knowledge that had been established by mankind in times past—was (whether insensitively and tyrannically, or sensitively and with a concern for freedom of self-determination) concerned with *the creation and cultivation of personal character.* In this, it entailed dimensions going far beyond any "training for employment" or "fitting a child for society" (though these elements also had to enter). It entailed all the dimensions of the human spirit, and Burt himself was sensitively aware of these, exploring them in literature, music, and the most careful approaches to religion.

The relevance of education for Burt, then, was by no means confined to the narrow vocational relevance now being emphasized (though this had indeed figured much in his studies). It went far beyond equipping the child to live effectively and successfully within the competitiveness of the free market. It was much more closely akin to that of Matthew Arnold, who (approving the "admirable" teachings of men like Epictetus) claimed that "the formation of the spirit and character must be our real concern." Burt, like Arnold, was on the side of culture and "the Sovereign Educators" as against the prevailing philistinism (then and now) of businesspeople, politicians, and ministers of education. "As to the usefulness of knowledge," Arnold had said, "a single line of poetry, working in the mind, may produce more thought and lead to more light, which is what man wants, than the fullest acquaintance with the processes of digestion. . . ." Burt would have agreed.

Indeed, though it may seem fanciful to introduce such a point at this concluding stage of our argument, as I nowadays read Burt in detail, realizing the continuity and consistency of his emphases throughout his work, I am reminded more and more strongly of the central teaching of Maria Montessori: that education (while establishing a secure knowledge of, and secure skills in, those foundation subjects on which all subsequent learning must rest—something Burt also emphasized) should essentially concern itself with providing the right context for the growth of each child's own knowledge of himself or herself, which at the heart of the matter lies in discovering, within the totality of the child's experience, that which is *his or her own work in the world,* and how to deploy oneself effectively and satisfyingly in the creative activity of a lifetime in realizing this to the full. It is hardly too much, either, to see in this the ideal Burt set for himself, and which he followed with such a fullness of commitment and achievement. Perhaps his early inclination towards self-perfection in the world was neither as misplaced nor so open to shallow criticism as his detractors have thought. The provision of appropriate education to children was, for him, the context that was the necessary prelude to the fullness of their lives; hence his devotion to it.

The relevance of Burt is therefore plain and profound. It is interesting to note that this was recognized, even at the time of his death (in 1971), by none other than Professor Eysenck. In his tribute to Burt in the *AEP Journal,* Eysenck wrote:

> As the undoubted leader of the London School, Burt will be sorely missed not only by his former pupils, but by many to whom his ardent search for truth in the complex field of psychology, accompanied by the desire to apply whatever knowledge he might have gathered, represented the best type of scientific involvement in human affairs—long before it became fashionable to talk about 'relevance' he had devoted his life to a type of work very relevant indeed to our modern problems of community living.

Burt's position was bound to be essentially critical of the altogether too stereotyped "system" that we had in part inherited from the past, and that mistaken political engineering had in part constructed about our ears; critical of its confining and constrictive misconceptions and blunted malpractices. Indeed, it is easy to see that the subtleties of the provisions of differential education he thought desirable would have made him skeptical about the sufficiency of any "system," and again it is interesting to see that at the very end of his life he found himself completely in agreement with Professor Jensen in desiring diversity rather than uniform equality in education. In the same journal, Burt quoted Jensen with approval in this way:

> The polemics of the heredity-environment question have revolved around certain misconceptions. That individual differences are largely hereditary is now well established. The goal should not be literal equality of opportunity; individual differences and group differences must be studied—in both their genetic and their environmental aspects—for the purpose of creating an optimal diversity of educational opportunity. A vigorous renewal of scientific inquiries into the nature-nurture problem will do more to implement the humanitarian aims of a free society than the dogmatic insistence that environment alone is responsible for all important human differences.

Burt's desire, however (given the existence of the educational system) was to discover that organizational basis that could best ensure—for different children, with different abilities and talents, in different sets of circumstances—the educational provisions that it ought to be our aim to give. "Hitherto," he wrote,

> our notions about the kind of school, curriculum, and teaching methods best fitted to this or that type of child have been for the most part decided by purely theoretical deductions. What is most urgently needed therefore are systematic experiments, deliberately planned and conducted, in order to secure first-hand empirical evidence as to the merits and limitations of the various alternatives now proposed.

Educational matters, alas, are now decided not even by theoretical deductions but increasingly, by ministerial diktat and new formulations for further legislation. Perhaps, however, even as yet another straitjacket is being imposed upon us—of a national curriculum, a national system of testing at specified ages, a new examination, with new ways of continuous assessment—we would be wise to consider again Burt's counsels and, in particular at this juncture to stay still for a while, give ourselves time for thought, and above all, investigate before we pontificate and legislate.

Surely a truly radical reconsideration is now required, both of

Burt himself, and of the implications of his work, which clearly go far beyond him.

Notes

1. "Straight Talk About Mental Tests." New York: The Free Press, 1981.
2. Letter to me, August 25, 1984.
3. Letter to me, September 4, 1984.
4. *Cyril Burt, Psychologist.* London: Hodder and Stoughton, 1979, p. 278.
5. I have already mentioned the tape loaned to me by Robert Reid on which he recorded a conversation in Burt's sitting room only a few months before Burt's death (on the occasion of a visit by Dr. Zimmermann). The tape recorder was hidden in Dr. Zimmerman's handbag, but despite this the recording is reasonably clear, and Burt showed no sign of any great difficulties of hearing.
6. Hearnshaw says: "I have largely followed Leonhard in describing the symptoms of paranoia," and quotes Leonhard, K. "Paranoia and Related States." In Krauss, S. (ed.), *Encyclopaedic Handbook of Medical Psychology.* 1976, pp. 361–63.
7. Ibid., pp. 289–90.
8. Ibid., pp. 290–91.
9. *Children and the Primary School: A Report of the Central Advisory Council for Education,* vol. 1. London: HMSO, 1967, pp. 153–54.
10. See Appendix 3 for further facts of considerable importance.
11. "Experimental Tests of General Inteligence." *British Journal of Psychology* 3:175; 1909; and "The Inheritance of Mental Characteristics." *Eugenics Review* 24:180; 1912.
12. All these grounds of argument are stated in the 1943 article on "Ability and Income," pp. 90–91.

Appendix 1

Tests Employed

The Study in Vocational Guidance began in 1922 and was published in 1926. All the tests employed were described in the fullest detail by Winifred Spielman and Frances Gaw.

Oral Tests: The Binet–Simon Scale

It was noted here that the Binet–Simon Tests were probably the most efficient tests of general intelligence so far devised, and that a modification of the Stanford Revision was used. A precise reference was given:

> This revision is fully described in *The Measurement of Intelligence* by Terman (published by G. Harrap & Co.). A roneoed version of the Stanford scale revised for English children was already in existence, prepared by Dr. Burt, with the permission of Professor Terman, and the aid of many teachers in the Council's schools; this, with some further modifications, was the version employed.

A detailed description of the application of the tests was given— 30 to 45 minutes being required for every child.

Nonverbal Tests

Two methods of measuring intellignce in nonlinguistic terms were used.

Performance Tests

The details given were these, and I include the authors' footnote references as evidence of their own sources and their precise recording of them.

A scale of fourteen performance tests was used in this study. The scale was one arranged by the psychologists at the Psychopathic Hospital in Boston, Mass., U.S.A. and includes part of Pintner and Paterson's scale of performance tests,[1] part of the U.S. Army scale,[2] and Porteus's Maze Test.[3] The following were the particular tests employed[4]:

(1) Healy Picture Completion, Test I.

(2) Healy Picture Completion Test II.
These two tests consist of pictures in which holes have been cut, removing objects essential to the various actions going on. These holes are to be filled by the child with appropriate insets.

(3) Manikin Test and

(4) Profile Test.
These two tests consist of pieces of wood which, when correctly put together, represent a man, and a man's face in profile, respectively.

(5) Cube Construction Test.
This test involves the fitting together of a number of small cubes with sides coloured red and white, so as to form larger cubes with sides coloured in a definite way.

(6) Dearborn Formboard.
This test is a formboard containing six different types of figures, or insets, of simple geometrical shape, which must be rearranged and fitted into the board in certain combinations.

(7) Porteus Maze Test.
This test consists of seven printed mazes, graded progressively in difficulty, through which the child must find the way.

(8) Cube Imitation Test.
In this test, four 1-inch cubes, placed in front of the child, are tapped by the examiner in several different orders, which the child must reproduce.

(9) Goddard Adaptation Board.
This is an oblong wooden board, containing four circular holes, one of which is very slightly larger in diameter than the other three. The board is turned in several different positions, after each one of which the child must indicate the largest hole.

(10) Substitution Test.
In this test numbers must be inserted as quickly as possible for different types of geometrical figures according to a definite key.

(11) Triangle Test.

(12) Diagonal Test.

(13) Healy Puzzle " A."

These three tests are small formboards, with recesses which must be filled as quickly as possible with insets of various geometrical shapes.

(14) Goddard Formboard.

This is a large formboard, the recesses in which must be filled as quickly as possible with appropriate blocks representing simple geometrical figures.

---

[1] Pintner, R. and Paterson, D. *A Scale of Performance Tests,* D. Appleton & Co., 1921.

[2] Yoakum, C. S. and Yerkes, R. M. *Army Mental Tests,* Henry Holt and Co., 1920.

[3] Porteus, S. D., *Porteus Tests—the Vineland Revision,* Publications of the Training School of Vineland, N.J., No. 16, September, 1919.

[4] For a detailed description of these tests, with results obtained from their application to London children, see Gaw, F., *Performance Tests of Intelligence,* Industrial Fatigue Research Board, Report No. 31, 1925.

It is important to note (as it was noted then) that performance tests consisted of short problems only, *rarely containing more than five or six steps.* The authors therefore decided that it was necessary

to use a number of such tests, and to combine the results in order to get a mental age or mental ratio. The method for doing this in the present research has been to translate the scores in each test by means of a table of norms into an equivalent mental age, the median of these mental ages being taken as the child's final score. A mental ratio has then been computed for each child by dividing his mental age (as thus obtained with the performance tests) by his chronological age. These ratios will be referred to hereafter in this paper as performance ratios.

The following was their table of results.

Marks obtained in Performance Tests of Intelligence.[1]

	Cube Imitation.	Adaptation Board.	Goddard Formboard.[2]	Manikin.	Profile.[2]	Healy A.[2]	Picture Completion I.	Picture Completion II.	Triangle.[2]	Diagonal.[2]	Porteus.	Substitution.[2]	Cube Construction.	Dearborn Formboard.	Average Performance Ratio.
Norm. Median score expected for children aged 13·0–14·0	7·5	5	12·5	5	150	36·5	511·5	60	38	31·5	13·5	98	16·5	18·2	Boys 100 Girls 100 Avg. 100
Actual Score (Elementary School Children). (Median score actually obtained by children aged 13·0–14·0)	8	5	13	5	76·5	49	578	62·2	40	35	12·5	99	12	15	Boys 96 Girls 93 Avg. 94
Percentage of Subjects— Above norm	57	70[3]	57[3]	87[2]	79·5	42	69	54	45	48	12·5	46·5	20	14·5	
Below norm	43	30	43	13	20·5	58	31	46	55	52	87·5	53·5	80	85·5	

[1]All the children (52 boys and 48 girls) were given all the tests except the Dearborn Formboard, which was given to 31 boys and to 24 girls only.

[2]In these tests the smallest number indicates the best score and the highest degree of success.

[3]The median score actually obtained by the elementary shool children was the maximum score in these two tests. The percentages here given (70 and 87 respectively) refer to the children who passed with the maximum score.

A similar table showed, with similar detail, the sex differences in the performance tests.

Nonlanguage Group Test

The second method used was "Pinter's non-language group test (*Journal of Applied Psychology,* volume 3, 1919, pp. 199–214), which was described as follows (the italics being my own):

> This consists of a printed booklet containing six component tests. It is similar to most other group scales that involve the use of pictures and form relationships; and requires the subject neither to say nor to write words, but simply to underline or mark the diagrams. As regards the method by which the problem is presented, this test is almost unique even among group tests, in that the examiner must use no words in explaining the test, and must convey his meaning through gestures, and by various simple diagrams and drawings. *Pinter's scale is exceptional in yet another respect; it is suitable for subjects of adult level of intelligence as well as for children,* while most group tests which do not involve linguistic responses are suitable only for younger children. For each part of this test there is a time limit; and the scoring is in terms of the number of errors made.

When all these tests had been conducted, the results were correlated with each other and with teachers' estimates, and many observations of interest were made. It is enough for our purpose, however, to see that the test, the methods, and the procedures employed were in fact set out in the fullest detail. Burt's reference in his 1943 paper referred in fact to all this detail. Did Kamin not check this, and discover that it was so? If not—why not—before exercising his judgment about it? Is this an example of the precise method of science that he is continually extolling? But the matter must be pressed even further.

At much the same time as this study was taking place, a detailed investigation was also being carried out into the extent and problems of *mental deficiency;* and of the mentally defective child and adult. This (resulting in the Wood Report) began in 1924 and was published in 1929. The chief investigator in the study was Dr. E. O. Lewis. The other authority chiefly referred to was Dr. Tredgold. Burt's contribution was simply to provide the tests employed, and to advise in such matters. The importance of this, for our purpose, was that these tests were again set out in very considerable detail. Again, they were chiefly those of "the Binet–Simon scale and its modifications," though a few new standardized tests were added. And again, the allocation of the tests to the various age groups, was based on "the standardization made by Professor Burt with English children." These tests and their elements were set out as follows, and again I include the publication's footnotes to indicate the precision of the detail provided.

Ages I and II.
1. Eyes follow a light.
2. Grasps and handles objects.
3. Chooses sweet and not block of wood.
4. Unwraps paper before eating sweet.
5. Imitates simple arm-movements.

Age III.
1. Points to nose, eyes and mouth.
2. Knows sex.
3. Names knife, key, penny. (A and B.)
4. Gives name and surname.
5. Picture-enumeration. (O.)

Alternatives.
5a. Replaces nest of boxes.* (O.)
5b. Matches colours.† (O.)
5c. Repeats 2 numbers.

Age IV.
1. Repeats sentence (6–8 syllables).
2. Repeats 3 numbers.
3. Counts 4 pennies. (A and B.)
4. Compares lines. (B.)
5. Compares faces. (O.)

Alternatives.
5a. Discriminates forms. (O.)

Age V.
1. Copies square. (O.)
2. Triple order. (B.)
3. Repeats sentence (12 syllables).
4. Answers questions (Comprehension : 1st Series).
5. Repeats 4 numbers.

Alternatives.
5a. Gives age.

Age VI.
1. Counts 13 pennies. (A and B.)
2. Copies diamond. (O.)
3. Names 4 coins ($\frac{1}{2}d.$, $1d.$, $6d.$, $1s.$). (A and B.)
4. Repeats 5 numbers.
5. Distinguishes right and left.

Alternatives.
5a. Knows number of fingers.

---

* The nest of boxes can be bought at most toy shops ; the set used in the present investigation consisted of five boxes. The child was first shown the boxes set one inside the other. The five boxes were then placed on the table in an indiscriminate order, and the child was asked to put them back one inside the other as they were at first. A time limit of three minutes was set.

† For this test 12 coloured counters, each 1 in. in diameter, were used. The set consisted of 3 counters of each of the primary colours—red, green, blue and yellow. All the counters were placed on the table in an indiscriminate order. The investigator picked up one of them and asked the child to choose a counter of the same colour from amongst those on the table.

5b. Distinguishes morning and afternoon.
5c. Names 4 colours.   (O.)
5d. Frame patience.*   (O.)
5e. Compares 2 weights.

Age VII.

1. Recognises missing features. (O.)
2. Answers questions (Comprehension : 2nd Series).
3. Repeats 3 numbers backwards.
4. Adds 3 pennies and 3 half-pennies.   (A and B.)
5. States difference (concrete objects.)   (B.)

Alternatives.

5a. Ties bow-knot.
5b. Weekdays (with check questions).

Age IX.

1. Ball and field : inferior plan. (O.)
2. Repeats 6 numbers (once out of 2 trials).
3. Repeats 4 numbers backwards.
4. Names 6 coins ($\frac{1}{2}d$., 1d., 6d., 1s., 2s., 2s. 6d.).   (A.)
5. Gives easy rhymes.

Alternatives.

5a. Re-arranges mixed sentence (simple).†
5b. Counts stamps.   (O.)
5c. Names months (without check questions).
5d. Tells time from watch.   (A.)

5b. Names weekdays (without check questions).
5c. Defines by use.
5d. Pictures—description.   (O.)
5e. Repeats sentence (16–18 syllables).

Age VIII.

1. Answers questions.   (Comprehension : 3rd Series.)
2. Counts backwards (20–1).
3. States similarities (2 things).
4. Gives change of a shilling.   (A.)
5. Vocabulary (20 words).

Alternatives.

5a. Reading (recalls 2 items).   (B.)
5b. Definitions : Superior to use.
5c. Gives date.
5d. Repeats 6 numbers (once out of 3 trials).

Age X.

1. Names months (with check questions).
2. Makes sentence with 3 words.
3. Arranges 5 weights.
4. Draws from memory.   (O.)
5. Vocabulary (30 words).

Alternatives.

5a. Reading : recalls 8 items.   (B.)

---

* This test is a modification of Binet-Simon's test of reconstructing a divided oblong card, which we do not regard as very suitable for young children.   Instead of the divided card we used a rectangular block of wood, 4 in. by 3 in., which was cut diagonally and fitted into a wooden frame. The child was first shown the frame with the two triangular pieces fitted in it.   The two pieces were then taken out of the frame and placed upon the table in the same relative positions as those indicated in the original test with the divided card.

† This is a simpler and easier form of the test of re-arranging mixed sentences in the original Binet-Simon Scale.   (Age 12, Test 4.)   The words of the following sentence, " The cat ran after the mouse and caught it," were printed on separate cards.   These cards were placed on the table at random and the child was asked to arrange them so that the words made a complete sentence ; all the words had to be included in the completed sentence

Age XI.

1. Detects absurdities.
2. Answers questions. (Comprehension : 4th Series).
3. Gives 60 words in 3 minutes.
4. Repeats sentences (20–23 syllables).
5. Repeats 3 numbers backwards.

Alternatives.

5a. Gives right time from watch ¼-hour fast. (A.).

Age XIII.

1. Repeats 7 numbers (once out of 2 trials).
2. Definitions (abstract words).
3. Interprets fables (2 correct or equivalent).
4. Solves problem question.
5. Reverses hands of clock. (A.)

Age XII.

1. States similarities (3 things).
2. Vocabulary (40 words).
3. Ball and field : superior plan. (O.)
4. Re-arranges mixed sentences. (O.)
5. Pictures (Interpretation). (O.)

Age XIV.

1. Induction test (folded paper) (O.)
2. Arithmetical reasoning (O.)
3. Vocabulary (50 words).
4. States 3 differences between President and King.
5. Differences (abstract terms).

Peformance tests were also carried out, though with provisos:

The conditions under which our investigation was conducted made it impossible to apply Performance Tests with the care and thoroughness that is practicable at a psychological clinic; nevertheless, several of these tests were used in supplementing our examination with the scale of intelligence. They proved most valuable and helpful, especially in the examination of the young children of lower grades, the feeble-minded with verbalistic propensities, the deaf-mute and the blind. . . . The recent publication of comprehensive manuals of Performance Tests* makes it unnecessary to describe in detail in this report the tests or the forms applied, and all we need do is to give the following list of the tests applied most frequently: the Seguin Form-Board, Porteus Maze tests;† Goddard's Adaptation Board; Healy's Construction, Tests A and B; and Healy's Picture Completion Tests 1 and 2.

*A copy of these Tests is appended in the pocket at the end of this Report. The instructions regarding their use given in the following pages are substantially the same as those published in the "Manual of Directions for Primary and Advanced Examinations" for use with the Otis Group Intelligence Tests. Both the Tests and the Directions are strictly copyright, the publishers in Great Britain being Messrs. George G. Harrap & Co., Ltd., 39–41, Parker Street, London, W.C. 2, to whose courtesy we are indebted for permission to reprint part of the instructions.

†Wood, Robert, p. 222.

This list may be compared with the tests employed in the Vocational Guidance study. Educational tests (attainment tests) of reading (accuracy and comprehension), spelling, and arithmetic were administered, but what is more interesting to us here is the very detailed information set out about the nature of the *group tests* employed: in all probability those referred to by Kamin as having been "employed for over 45 years." They were described as follows:

Group Tests.

The Group Tests used in the present investigation were the Otis Group Intelligence Tests* (Primary, Form A) ; but certain modifications were made so as to make the Tests more suitable for application to retarded children.

Each child was given a script, and requested to write his name and age on the first page. The children were then requested to put down their pencils while the examiner told them what they had to do.

The following instructions* were then given by the examiner :—

" In these booklets there are pictures and drawings, and I want to see if you can answer some questions about them. You will be told to make certain marks on these pictures and drawings ; you must do exactly what you are told, and do it as quickly as possible. In order to play this little game fairly, you must not look to see what any one else is doing. I want to know what you can do yourself. You must listen very carefully to everything I say, so that you will be sure to hear the first time, because I shall not repeat anything. Don't ask any questions. You must begin as soon as as I tell you, work quickly, and stop at once when I say ' Stop.'"

Test I.—Association Test.†

" Now open the book at page 1. Notice the first row of pictures at the top of the page. There is a leaf with a little cross under it, an apple with a little ring under it, a banana with a line under it, a pear with an up-and-down line under it, and some cherries with a dot under them. You are to put the same marks under the same pictures below the line. Now look at the next row of pictures. There you see an apple, banana, cherries, etc. Put a little ring under the apple, like the ring under the apple in the top row." (Pause 5 seconds.)

" Now put a line under the banana just like the line under the banana in the top row." (Pause 5 seconds.)

" Now put a round dot under the cherries like the dot under the cherries in the top row." (Pause 5 seconds.)

" Now put under the next banana the same kind of line that is under the other banana." (Pause 5 seconds.)

---

* A copy of these Tests is appended in the pocket at the end of this Report. The instructions regarding their use given in the following pages are substantially the same as those published in the " Manual of Directions for Primary and Advanced Examinations " for use with the Otis Group Intelligence Tests. Both the Tests and the Directions are strictly copyright, the publishers in Great Britain being Messrs. George G. Harrap & Co., Ltd., 39–41, Parker Street, London, W.C.2, to whose courtesy we are indebted for permission to reprint part of the instructions.

† This test is given first because it is the simplest, and also because it impresses upon the child the necessity for working quickly.

" Now what goes under the apple ? If you know, raise your hand." (Call for an answer, and when the right answer is given say) " Yes, a little ring, the same as before. Put the little ring under the apple." (Pause 5 seconds.)

" Now put under the cherries the mark that belongs to them and do the same under the pear and apple." (Pause 10 seconds.)

" Now go right on with the other four rows and put under each picture the mark that belongs to it. Work quickly and see how many you can get done before I say ' Stop.' Ready, go ! "

Time given, half a minute.

" Stop ! Put down your pencils. Turn to the next page."

Test. II.—Picture completion test.

" On this page are twelve pictures. Something is left out of each picture. Look at the first picture and think what is left out. If you know, raise your hand." (Call a pupil for an answer. Then say) " Yes, one eye is left out. Draw the eye where it should be." (Pause 5 seconds.) " Now there is only *one thing* left out of each picture. Look at each of the other pictures and, as quickly as you can, put in what is left out. See how many you can do before I say ' Stop.' Ready, go ! " (Time 2 minutes.)

" Stop ! Put down your pencils and turn to the next page."

Test III.—Instructions Test.

" Now look at the next page—the one with the pictures of little men in the corners. I am going to tell you to do something with your pencils to each of these pictures. Listen carefully, and work as quickly as you can. Notice the pictures at the top of the page."

(1) " Now take your pencils and put a tail on the cat that has no tail." (Pause 5 seconds.)

(2) " Next, look at the little man in the upper right-hand corner and draw a line for him to stand on." (Pause 5 seconds.)

(3) " Next, look at the second row of pictures and draw a ring round the doll." (Pause 5 seconds.)

(4) " Next, find the picture of something that can run, and draw a line under it." (Pause 5 seconds.)

(5) " Next, find the picture that is between the doll and the candle and make a little cross under it." (Pause 5 seconds.)

(6) " Next, find the picture of something that gives light and can be picked up. Make a round dot under it." (Pause 5 seconds.)

(7) " Next, draw a line from the Teddy Bear's ear to the rabbit's ear that will go under the sun." (Pause 5 seconds.)

(8) " Next, find the picture of a child's plaything that has large ears, and put a little ring under it." (Pause 10 seconds.)

(9) " Next, notice the chicks and eggs in the next row of pictures and draw more eggs so that there will be as many eggs as there are chicks." (Pause 10 seconds.)

(10) " Next, find the two chicks that look most alike and cross out the one between them." (Pause 5 seconds.)

(11) " Next, notice the pictures of hands. Draw a ring round the picture of the right hand." (Pause 5 seconds.)

(12) " Next, in the two rows of little drawings below the hands, cross out each ring that has a star under it." (Pause 10 seconds.)

(13) " Next, make a dot in each square that is between two stars."
(Pause 10 seconds.)

(14) " Next, notice the large ring with a smaller ring in it. Put a cross
in the space that is in the large ring but not in the smaller ring." (Pause
5 seconds.)

(15) " Next, in the middle drawing, put a cross in the space that is in all
three rings." (Pause 5 seconds.)

(16) " Next, in the third drawing, in the corner, count all the rings, and
write the number below the drawings." (Pause 10 seconds.)

" Stop ! Put down your pencils and turn to the next page."

Test IV.—Maze Test.

" Here you see pictures of little square boxes with walls in them and little
paths between the walls. In the box in one upper corner you see a mouse,
and in the other upper corner is a piece of cheese. And there is a line from
the mouse to the cheese, showing just how the mouse would have to go,
around through the paths, to get to the cheese. The line shows the *only*
way to get to the cheese. If the mouse went into any other path, he would
run up to a wall and have to turn and go back to the right path.

" Now you will see another piece of cheese in the box in the *lower* corner
of the page. How would the mouse get to that piece of cheese ? When I
say ' Ready, Go ! ' you are to draw a line to show just where the mouse would
have to go to get to this other piece of cheese, in the lower corner. Be very
careful not to go into any wrong path. See how far you can get before I
say ' Stop,' without crossing over any wall or going into any wrong path.
Ready, go ! " (Time 2 minutes.)

" Stop ! Put down your pencils. Turn to the next page."

Test V.—Picture sequence.

" Look at the three pictures at the top of the page. They tell a story of
a bird building a nest and hatching out some little birds. You can see that
the pictures are not in the right order. Which one should come first ? "
(Call on a pupil. When the right answer is given, say) " Yes, the bird has to
build her nest first, so put a figure 1 in the little square of the picture which
shows the bird building her nest." (Pause 5 seconds.)

" Now which picture comes next ? " (Call on a pupil. When the right
answer is given, say) " Yes, so put a figure 2 in the little square of the picture
of the nest with the eggs in it, and put a figure 3 in the picture of the nest
with the little birds in it. Always put the number in the small square in
the corner of the picture." (Pause 5 seconds.)

" Now you are to do the same with all the other rows of pictures. In
each row, find the picture that should come first and put a figure 1 in the
corner of that picture. Then put a figure 2 in the picture that should come
next, and so on. See how many rows you can get done before I say ' Stop.'
Ready, go ! " (Time 2 minutes.)

" Stop ! Put down your pencils and turn to the next page."

Test VI.—Similarities.

" Look at the first row of pictures on this page. You will see that they
are all small blocks, each with a different picture. The first three blocks have
pictures with little crosses under them, and these three things—sun, lamp
and match, *are alike*—all three give light. Now look at the pictures on the
other five blocks in this row. Which of these things is *most like* the first
three ? " (When the right answer is obtained, say) " Yes, the candle, because

it also gives light.   Now put a cross in the small square in the bottom corner of this block to show that this is the one that is most like the first three." (Pause 5 seconds.)

" Now in each of the other rows, in the same way, look at the first three pictures and see how they are alike ; then put a cross under the picture among the other five that is most like the first three.   Remember, there is only *one* right answer in each row.   Ready, go ! "   (Time 2 minutes.)   " Stop.   Close your books."

The marking of the scripts.

The following maximum scores were allotted to each of the above tests :—

						Maximum score.
Test I	. .	. .	. .	. .	. .	8
II	. .	. .	. .	. .	. .	12
III	. .	. .	. .	. .	. .	16
IV	. .	. .	. .	. .	. .	16
V	. .	. .	. .	. .	. .	22
VI	. .	. .	. .	. .	. .	26
			Total	. .	. .	100

Norms.

The following norms were established by testing 640 normal children, ages varying from seven to thirteen, and with approximately equal numbers in each age-group :—

Age.							Average score.
7	. .	. .	. .	. .	. .	. .	34
8	. .	. .	. .	. .	. .	. .	47
9	. .	. .	. .	. .	. .	. .	58
10	. .	. .	. .	. .	. .	. .	67
11	. .	. .	. .	. .	. .	. .	69
12	. .	. .	. .	. .	. .	. .	72
13	. .	. .	. .	. .	. .	. .	75

Why, it may now be asked, have I thought it necessary to go into such detail? What is its significance?

First, is not the nature of the group test Burt used in his studies perfectly clear? We have seen that all the details of methods, procedures, and tests used were correctly indicated and implied in Burt's footnotes referring to LCC surveys and the Vocational Guidance report, and could have been discovered had this reference been followed up. But also, as to the nature of the group tests not located by Kamin, in addition to what has been quoted above, Burt had this to say in the 1943 paper. Considering the IQ related to university entrance and the standard deviation of the general population, he said:

> The most reliable figures would seem to be those obtained with 'group tests' of intelligence similar to *those used for junior county scholarship examinations and for the examination of ex-service candidates after the last war*. On equating the results with I.Q.'s obtained with the London revision of the Binet scale, I estimate that the standard deviation of the upper half of the curve of distribution is approximately 16 I.Q. This yields the figure for university entrance quoted above, namely, 134.7 I.Q.

This was completely in keeping with what was said and used in the studies we have mentioned, but on these group tests, Burt's footnote has this further very specific information (again, the italics are mine).

> The tests which I drew up for this latter purpose (slightly revised) were subsequently published by the *National Institute of Industrial Psychology under the title of 'Group Test No. 33.'* They were used regularly for entrants to the London Day Training College, for our own students at University College, *for investigations on vocational guidance among adults in various fields of work,* and more recently for recruits in the Army. Consequently, a good deal of data is now available. It is advisable, however, to note several complicating difficulties, commonly overlooked in discussions on the general standard deviation. (i) *The variability, in terms of the I.Q., is itself bound to vary somewhat with the type of test used: results based on group tests may differ appreciably from those based on individual tests of the Binet–Simon type.* (ii) As the efficacy of each type of test is improved, the resulting standard deviation is likely to increase: thus it is generally larger with revised versions of the Binet tests than with the original. (iii) If my own figures can be accepted, it is not the same at every age: in particular it appears to increase towards puberty, and to decline after adolescence is over, (iv) *We cannot assume* that the amount of variability above the average

(or below) can be determined by calculating the amount of variability over the entire sample, i.e., *that the curve of distribution is exactly symmetrical, much less exactly normal.* In the lower half of the population, disease and other disturbances augment the frequency of the more extreme deviations (as is shown by figures for pathological types of the imbecile grade); in the upper half the absence of a definite upper limit to the scale seems (with most tests) to prolong the upper tail still more. There can be no 'mental age' below zero; but there is no *a priori* limit to mental ages in the upward direction, so that an I.Q. above 200 is not impossible, while an I.Q. below 0 is out of the question. Accordingly, my use of tables for the normal probability integral to deduce percentages above any given borderline from the s.d. value of that borderline must be regarded as merely a convenient way of smoothing the empirical data. If figures for the higher moments could be more exactly determined, it might be better to work with a hypergeometric curve. Alternatively we can calculate the numbers above or below specified percentiles directly from the tabulated data. I have tried both these alternatives as checks; and find little change in the ultimate percentage.

The italicized lines point first to the consistency and continuity of these tests in Burt's many studies, so that our *knowledge* of the tests he used is reliable; our assumptions are soundly based. Second—and this is very important—they make clear Burt's working assumption (one could correctly say knowledge) that the measured IQ for the same individual could differ from the group test to the Binet–Simon tests. It is perfectly clear, then, why in his later twin studies (for example, of identical twins reared together and apart) he gave one correlation based on the group test, a second based on the individual test, and a third that took them both into account. There was nothing mysterious, obscure, or difficult to understand about this, as Kamin claimed. Kamin writes in great detail about the ambiguities, or rather lack of clear knowledge, of what went into the individual test (whether Stanford–Binet, performance tests, or both), but there is no doubt whatever why Burt gave both a group test and an individual test correlation and, as in every element we have uncovered so far, there was not the slightest suggestion here of any fraudulence. Everything was stated with the most open and perfect clarity. The further point is touched upon (in 1943, let us note) that it could not be assumed that "the curve of distribution" would be "exactly symmetrical, much less exactly normal." This will seem to have little significance here, but in the light of Professor Shockleys recent findings, mentioned earlier, may come to possess quite crucial significance. (see, p. 175).

Appendix 2

Dr. Banks' Criticisms of Hearnshaw

Criticizing Burt's analysis of the results of one of his earliest tests (of the boys of a preparatory school and a central school), Hearnshaw had said:

Thirteen tests were intercorrelated and the results analyzed using the tetrad equation which was derived from Spearman's work. The theoretical values calculated from the tetrads were compared with the observed coefficients . . ." and "there is no evidence in Burt's 1909 article, as he subsequently claimed, that he proceeded to subtract the theoretical figures from the observed. . . .

These statements, Charlotte Banks claimed, simply did not stand up to scrutiny, especially in the light of Hearnshaw's further assertion that "Burt's 1909 work was entirely derived from Spearman." The following are the chief points she made:

First, Burt did subtract his theoretical figures from the observed; they are on pages 161 and 162 of the 1909 article for all to see, and he did test the residuals for significance. This subtraction and testing may seem a small point, but it appears to be the nub of the whole issue. I have been unable to find in Spearman's work, published or unpublished (Spearman papers held by the British Psychological Society) an indication that he had attempted, or was even interested in attempting the subtraction of a hierarchy (theoretical correlations) from observed figures to look for further factors. If I am correct, then there seems no reason to doubt Burt's claim in *The Factors of the Mind* (1940) that "the first attempt at fitting a theoretical matrix to a set of observed correlations was, I think, that shown in Tables V and VI of my paper of

1909'', and he continues, "the residual correlations were obtained in a way which has since become fairly general" (p. 295).

Secondly, Burt did not use the tetrad equation for his analysis. This equation was used later by Spearman to show that a table of correlations could be explained in terms of a factor common to all the variables and a factor specific to each. But it was only proposed as the 'correct criterion' by Spearman well after the introduction and use of the intercolumnar correlation (Hart and Spearman, 1912) for the same purpose. In the *Abilities of Man* (1927) Spearman wrote, "it was an immense relief when the usage of this intercolumnar correlation could be dropped . . . by the discovery of the probable error of the tetrad equation''. Had Burt used the tetrad equation he could not have compared his 78 observed coefficients with "the theoretical values calculated from the tetrads''. . . .

Thirdly, Burt obtained the theoretical correlations in his paper by multiplying together the appropriate saturations, and he accepted and acknowledged a formula suggested by Spearman for this. Burt had sent his draft paper (and later the proofs) to Spearman for criticisms and suggestions. These are now missing, something that Hearnshaw fails to note; but it is clear from Spearman's reply that Burt has already constructed a hierarchy of his own, a hierarchy of which he wrote, "I am a little diffident''. Spearman answered that he did not know how Burt had obtained it, "but a prettier agreement between observation and theory is not often seen''. But, as Burt explained nearly 30 years later (Liverpool Archives: Burt-Spearman correspondence), he had been trying "various methods" and was satisfied with none of them, having landed himself in "difficulties that at the time I did not understand''. Not least of which was what to put in the diagonals of the matrix, and he accepted Spearman's formula which ignored these (as did Spearman's later formula in the *Abilities of Man,* 1927). Hearnshaw may have been misled over the tetrads because in his comments on Burt's draft, Spearman set out for the first time the proportionality equation, which obeyed the criterion of the intercolumnar correlation and on which the tetrad criterion was based using, he wrote, Burt's notation. But he gave no indication at that time of how it was to be modified and used as a criterion; moreover, there is no doubt that Burt must have had such proportionality in mind to construct his own well-fitting hierarchy. . . .

Charlotte Banks continued:

This is not the place to discuss in detail Spearman's two subsequent claims to have been the first to put forward the 'proportionality equation'. Suffice it to say Burt quoted this in his 1909 paper, making it quite clear that the equation was Spearman's.

After making other equally telling points, she concluded by making it quite clear, on the question as to who (Burt or Spearman) was the first to do factor analysis, that "Burt did not claim to have originated the idea nor to have been the instigator of the necessary formulae. He only claimed to be the first to do it in psychology."[1]

Note

1. Charlotte Banks," Experimental Tests of General Intelligence," British Journal of Psychology III: 94–177; 1909.

Appendix 3

The 53 Pairs of Twins: Additional Information

Much has been made in the past, especially by Hearnshaw ("Cyril Burt: Psychologist," pp. 246–47) of the fact that Burt had difficulty (or was much delayed) in supplying to both Professor Jencks and Dr. Shockley, at their request, a table of data on the IQs and social classes of these 53 twins. The following is in fact the table that was sent to Dr. Shockley.

Data for Identical Twins

| | Reared In | | | | | Reared In | | | |
| | Own Home | | Foster Home | | | Own Home | | Foster Home | |
Case No:	IQ	Social Class	IQ	Social Class	Case No:	IQ	Social Class	IQ	Social Class
1	68	6	63	6	28	97	5	92	1
2	71	4	76	5	29	97	3	95	5
3	73	5	77	5	30	97	5	112	R
4	75	6	72	R	31	97	6	113	5
5	78	3	71	6	32	99	5	105	4
6	79	3	75	5	33	100	3	88	3
7	81	5	86	5	34	101	5	115	5
8	82	2	82	R	35	102	5	104	R
9	82	4	93	2	36	103	6	106	5
10	83	4	86	6	37	105	6	109	1
11	85	5	83	6	38	106	5	107	5
12	86	6	94	6	39	106	6	108	R
13	87	5	93	1	40	107	5	108	3
14	87	6	97	6	41	107	3	101	2
15	89	6	102	2	42	108	5	95	5
16	90	2	80	2	43	111	6	98	5
17	91	3	82	2	44	112	6	116	5
18	91	2	88	5	45	114	1	104	5
19	92	5	91	6	46	114	5	125	5
20	92	2	96	3	47	115	2	108	6
21	93	6	87	2	48	116	2	116	6
22	93	3	99	4	49	118	2	116	6
23	93	5	99	3	50	121	1	118	5
24	94	6	94	R	51	125	4	128	5
25	95	6	96	5	52	129	2	117	5
26	96	2	93	R	53	131	1	132	4
27	96	4	109	1					

R denotes Residential Institution

Mean I.Q.	97.8
S.D. I.Q.	14.7

Correlation between Twins' (a) I.Q.'s	0.874
(b) Social status of Home	0.033

Hearnshaw says that Burt "eventually enclosed (to Shockley) the table of separated MZ twins previously sent to Jencks, but *that was all*" and that this table "*was all Shockley ever received . . .*" (this being December 19, 1969). This is another of Hearnshaw's statements, however, that proves to be untrue.

Shockley's correspondence with Burt went on longer than this. On April 5, 1971, he wrote to Burt to ask him again about this research. "One of the objections that is occasionally made about the identical twin data that you sent to me is disbelief that families of the highest social class would put their children out for adoption that places them in some cases in social class 5." He asked Burt for his comments and explanations. On April tenth—only six months, it may be noted, before his death—Burt replied at length. The letter dealt with several questions Shockley had raised, but I give below the extracts dealing specifically with that on adoption. Burt's letter read as follows:

9, Elsworthy Road,
LONDON, N.W.

April 10, 1971

Dear Professor Shockley,

Thank you for your letter of April 5 and the interesting questions you raise.

In your letter you mention, as an objection occasionally put forward, the "disbelief that families of the highest social class would put their children out for an adoption that places them in social class 5." The wording (the ambiguous plural) is, I think, a little misleading: only one child is put out for adoption, not by 'the family', but by the mother (if alive, otherwise the 'care committee').

In our data only three pairs (43, 50, 53) were in the highest occupational class. The story of 53 is typical: I have generally used it to start my discussion of twins; it is recorded in Miss Conway's paper (Brit. J. Statist. Psychol., X1, 1958, p. 184) and one or two of my own popular publications. They were children of an Oxford don who died a few months before their birth. Unable with her slender means to bring up two boys as she would desire, she secretly arranged for one to be 'boarded out': he was sent to a farmer in Wales (occupation class 4), and eventually became a successful farmer himself (Miss Conway gives his IQ in 1958 as 137; our final assessment was 132). The one who remained with his mother eventually obtained a 1st class degree (IQ 136 in 1958; 131 in 1965).

The pair numbered 45 were girls born to the wife of an elderly London professor. She died after the delivery of the second twin, who was very sickly. The father had three sons already and felt unable to cope with infant girls. The healthier twin was adopted by his cousin, a senior civil servant (class 1); the other recovered after some weeks in hospital, was then sent to an 'orphanage' for infants, and later to the wife of a farm-labourer (class 5). This girl's lower IQ was, I think, undoubtedly due to ill health in infancy.

The pair numbered 50 were the illegitimate children of the wife of a church dignitary (a well known Hebrew scholar; class 1). During pregnancy the mother went to stay with her relatives in Scotland, nominally on the grounds of her own ill health; the relatives retained the healthier twin, and the other was boarded out with a shepherd on their estate. (The mother's husband was presumed to know nothing of this misadventure, or at any rate acted as though he knew nothing).

The parents of the nine pairs in occupational class 2 were mostly clergy, teachers, or college lecturers. In this country the salaries of women-teachers and parsons is in no way equal to their nominal social status; and a mother who finds herself unexpectedly delivered of two infants at once often feels little qualm in arranging for one to be transferred to a foster-home. In these high class cases the arrangement is usually made in great secrecy; most of them came to our notice because we knew the parents personally, not because of our connection with the office of the London County Council.

[After thanking Shockley for a 'scattergram' which he had sent, and commenting on it, with some observations on occupational classes, Burt continued:]

But the occupational category really means very little. I quoted them in order to counter the common complaint that the care committee workers might have placed children with foster parents in the same socio-economic category as their own parents. What happens is that, owing to the shortage of foster homes, the care committee workers have to take the first that offers, provided the foster-mother, when first visited to make arrangements, proves to be clean, respectable and kindly. The social workers at this stage know little about the two families, except the occupations of the fathers or mothers in both families (own family and foster family). It is only later, after the annual visit of the committee's inspectors, that full details regarding material and cultural conditions in the foster-home get recorded. For obvious reasons most of those who are willing to act as foster-mothers are in class 5 (motherly women who want to make a little extra money in this way); and the actual conditions of such homes may vary widely: eg. some (it turns out) are women of good education who have married beneath their own cultural level. Others, however, may prove to be less hygienic than appeared on the first visit. In one or two cases, I believe, the health of the infant was adversely affected, and this impaired the child's developing intelligence. These are the chief ways, I believe, in which environment affected the 'final assments' The assessments depended so much on our final checks with performance tests that I don't believe cultural conditions could have affected them at all. But early infectious fevers may, I am convinced, often impair intelligence as it matures. These final assessments are given as IQs in the table I sent you in 1969.

Of the twins in column i (entered under the caption 'Own Home') numbers 3, 24, 39, 45, and 50 were brought up by relatives in London—except 50 (the other going to a relative in the country or more frequently to a foster-home). In all these cases the occupational class of the relative was the same as that of the natural parent, except number 3, where the natural parents were 'unskilled (father feebleminded) and the relatives 'semiskilled'.

The mother of the pair numbered 51 died just after they were born. The father refused them, and one twin (IQ. 125) went to a foster parent in class 4 and the other (IQ. 128) to a foster parent in class 5.

[After a few comments on the smallness of the sample of separated twins; in consequence, the statistical "non-significance" of some correlations; and the need for a comparison of data for all types of relative to consider fully the case for mental inheritance; Burt concludes:]

I hope this answers all your questions,

With all good wishes and many thanks for the other documents,

Yours sincerely . . .

It may be noted in passing that this letter, with its many details, must have been written and sent off by Burt almost by return mail—Shockley's letter being dated April fifth and Burt's April tenth. There was certainly no delay here. But why, chiefly, do I think it important to note this letter in the Shockley–Burt correspondence?

It is because this letter surely does show an immediate and familiar knowledge of the qualitative facts involved in the rather naked table of data got together in 1969. In this almost spontaneous letter, Burt shows a ready familiarity with the cases running through the entire range of the 53 pairs of twins.

Should we believe that Burt did actually have the intimate knowledge of his sample of 53 pairs of twins that this letter indicates—a sample he and his colleagues had claimed to have brought together so painstakingly over such a long period; that they had so long advertised, and so long studied? Or are we to believe, on the contrary, that in an immediate response to Shockley's questions

Burt simply sat down and, with a rich and inventive imagination, fantasized all the details there given?

One point is sure. To the best of my knowledge the qualitative details mentioned in this letter have not been noted before.[1] They do reveal a considerable qualitative familiarity with the 53 twins— the possession of considerable qualitative data relating to them— and so significantly alter the situation (as it has been so far presented) as to call, at least, for further consideration and judgment.

Note

1. I am indebted to Professor Jensen for sight of this letter. Strangely, however, in the correspondence between Professors Shockley and Jensen it emerges with near certainty that the whole of the Burt– Shockley correspondence was sent to Hearnshaw early in 1977 (Shockley sent a second set of photocopies to Jensen so that this could be done), yet Hearnshaw has never made mention of this letter. His statement (p. 247 of his biography) is very definite: "All Shockley ever received was the table for the fifty-three separated MZ twins."

Appendix 4

Testimony for the Defense: Supplementary Evidence

Now that the case for the defense is concluded, it seems fitting to cite some additional testimony from highly qualified and reputable sources that has not so far been introduced. To be both brief and systematic, three sections seem advisable: The first is a testimony as to Burt's qualities and achievements given at the time of his death by two of those who subsequently became perhaps the most influential of his opponents, Eysenck and Hearnshaw. Next is a selected sequence of the testimony given in the correspondence columns of the *Times* and the *Sunday Times*. Here I have been very sparing. Much more of value could have been included from Professors Eysenck and Jensen, Dr. Fraser-Roberts, and others of their level of eminence, but I have rigorously excluded (apart from Professor John Cohen) all those whose views have been dealt with earlier, confining myself to a limited number of letters from hitherto unmentioned scholars that also cast some light on Oliver Gillie's journalistic methods. The third section contains additional and quite independent testimony from some of those who, having worked closely with Burt for twenty years or so, and right up to the point of his death, had a far more intimate knowledge of his character and work than any of those who had made the allegations of fraud against him.

Supporters Turned Opponents

Sir Cyril Burt—A Tribute: By Professor H. J. Eysenck

Sir Cyril Burt became Professor of Psychology at University College, where he succeeded Charles Spearman, after a career in what was essentially applied work; his great contributions to education and criminology, as well as abnormal psychology, are well remembered. He continued in his work and teaching a long-established tradition, beginning with Galton (whom he had met as a boy) and Pearson, which stressed the importance of studying individual differences, emphasized the relevance of heredity to any understanding of these differences, and insisted on the value of refined statistical analysis in the unravelling of the many complex problems posed in this search. Burt's main interest was the study of intelligence, but he also made fundamental contributions in other fields of personality study. Already in the opening years of the century he had suggested a formula for the analysis of intelligence test scores which anticipated Thurstone's famous centroid method, and in his thinking, as well as in his empirical work, he always insisted on the importance of what he called "group factors", in addition to Spearman's general factor ("g"). In this way he reconciled the claims of the opposing camps—Spearman insisting on the predominance of 'g', Thurstone on what he called "primary factors"—even before the opponents had entrenched themselves in their positions; had more attention been paid to his intermediate and eclectic position, many idle wrangles might have been avoided. Unfortunately he had a genius for hiding his light under a bushel; he tended to publish in esoteric and not-widely-read journals, and even reports, formulae and results which were of great interest and importance. I still have in my possession lecture notes which he circulated and in which he would discuss original ideas and results which were never published in any orthodox form at all! He was so fertile in ideas that he seemed not to care where he dropped his pearls; had he been more careful about their disposal it seems likely that many more would have been picked up. It is my belief that psychology would have been the richer for it.

Without being an original mathematician, Burt knew his way around mathematical statistics better than almost any other psychologist; only Thurstone and Godfrey Thompson were his equals. He managed to apply this knowledge and harness it in a most fruitful manner; the contributions he made to factor analysis are perhaps best known, but his work on behavioural genetics also commands respect. He was unlucky in that his book on "Factors of the Mind" came out in wartime, when most psychologists had other things to think about, and when he too did not have time to polish it and re-write it as he would normally have done; the mass of original ideas contained in it has not received appropriate acknowledgement. He often suffered from the fact that psychologists, educationalists and sociologists who disagreed with him on points of fact or interpretation were unable to follow his mathematical arguments and proofs; this led to the farcical situation that critics would often accuse him of supporting ideas which he had explicitly rejected, or of rejecting ideas which he in fact agreed with. It is difficult to know how this type of hiatus can be overcome, other than by requiring all social scientists to acquire sufficient knowledge of mathematics and statistics to understand what is going on in their own field—it does not seem too much to ask!

When confronted with misunderstandings of his position, or wrong-headed criticism, Burt was a past-master in the art of refutation. His skill became legendary in the gentle art of slaying unsuspecting opponents, and he exercised it not only in print, but also on the public platform—I remember with joy the gentle way in which he would introduce the knife into his squirming opponent's body, and twist it with the most beatific smile on his face! He never lost his temper, always remained polite and helpful, and seemed genuinely eager to find some common ground with his opponents; impeccable manners such as he always showed are unfortunately becoming a rarity even in academic discourse nowadays. In reviewing books, too, his skill in detecting weaknesses and unmasking them with great clarity was uncanny; many an author will still remember his rising anguish as in Burt's review of his book the initial praise of whatever was praiseworthy was inexorably followed by detailed dissection of weaknesses and faults. Burt had a feeling for quantitative analysis which no mere formal teaching of psychometrical formulae can give; in a rare manner he combined literary and quantitative abilities, and bridged the gulf between the "two cultures". The only fault in his writing was the excessive reliance on footnotes—sometimes in his books one or two lines of text would be followed by footnotes taking up the rest of the page, and perhaps the next page as well!

Burt's mind never lost its exemplary clarity; only a few weeks before his death he read through the draft of a new book by A. Jensen, highly technical and full of formulae and quantitative results, and made comments and suggestions on almost every page; the book was returned to the author within three days! Few other people could have read it in that time, leave alone checked the formulae, worked out alternative ones, recalculated many of the results, and generally added much new material to the formulation and interpretation of the data. As he would have said: "The important thing is to have picked your parents well"—senile decay is very much a matter of heredity, and he was extremely fortunate in this respect. As the undoubted leader of the London School Burt will be sorely missed not only by his former pupils, but by many to whom his ardent search for truth in the complex field of psychology, accompanied by the desire to apply whatever knowledge he might have gathered, represented the best type of scientific involvement in human affairs—long before it became fashionable to talk about 'relevance' he had devoted his life to a type of work very relevant indeed to our modern problems of community living.

This tribute was published in the *AEP Journal* in the autumn of 1971, after Burt's death. This testimony, like that of his early letter to Dr. Marion Burt, may be compared with Eysenck's later denunciation of Burt, with its several dimensions.

Cyril Lodowic Burt (1883–1971): By L. S. Hearnshaw

The death of Sir Cyril Burt on 10 October 1971 has removed one of the leading British pioneers in the development of psychology as an applied scientific discipline. . . . The first decade of the twentieth century was the most revolutionary decade in the history of psychology, certainly since Aristotle's death. It was in this decade that Cyril Burt made his debut as a psychologist. He had the intellectual gifts, and the consuming sense of purpose, as well as the opportunities, to take advantage of this situation, and in this country it is to him, more than to any other man, that the applications of psychology, particularly in the fields of education and child development, are due. . . .

[His] lectureship in experimental psychology at Liverpool[1] was one of the first such posts to be established in this country. . . .

Burt lectured not only to medical students, but to students from the departments of education and social science, and before he left he had attracted a number of research students. His lectures were accompanied by experimental demonstrations, some of them of such an enterprising nature that they became known as 'Burt's musical-hall turns'. His lectures embraced not only the experimental psychology of the sense-organs, but also more adventurous topics such as hypnosis, Freudian psycho-analysis (then a complete novelty), sexual differences, and, of course, questions relating to heredity and general intelligence. It was in this last area that Burt's researches focused. He made the decision from which he never deviated in the course of his long working life, to make the psychology of individual differences (differences in ability and personality, and the genetic and social influences determining them, together with the means of assessing and evaluating them) the main focus of his endeavour. His Liverpool years were marked by the publication of four outstandingly important papers,[2] two on tests of general intelligence, one on the inheritance of mental characteristics, and one on the mental differences between the sexes. In the papers on tests of general intelligence he demonstrated that intelligence could be more effectively measured by more. complex tests than the sensory tests then commonly in use, and he developed a series of verbal tests (involving reasoning (opposites, analogies, syllogisms, sentence completion) in which he made use of his Oxford training in logic, tests which have formed models for many subsequent intelligence tests. . . .

The Liverpool period came to an end on Burt's appointment as psychologist, part-time, to the London County Council. . . . His terms of reference were (1) to carry out periodic psychological surveys of children in the Council's schools, (2) to examine and report on individual cases of subnormality, delinquency, and special giftedness, and (3) to study the psychological aspects of any specific educational problem that might from time to time arise (e.g. selection for grammar schools). This complex task Burt was required to perform unaided and in a half-time post. His achievements during this London period can only be described as miraculous. He seemed to know precisely what to aim for, and how to achieve his aims. He showed none of the uncertainties of the young investigator breaking new ground. The amount of work he got through was phenomenal, and the data he collected served as material for analysis almost for the rest of his life. . . .

The most important outcome of Burt's L.C.C. years, however, were four classic volumes, which remain among the masterpieces of British psychology—*The Distribution and Relations of Educational Abilities* (1917), *Mental and Scholastic Tests* (1921), *The Young Delinquent* (1925), and *The Backward Child* (1937). These volumes represent the high-water mark of Burt's achievement. They are storehouses of data, techniques, ideas, and conclusions, and combine technical expertise and statistical rigour on the one hand with human insight and judgement on the other. Even today they are readable, interesting, and far from outdated. . . .

In 1931 C. E. Spearman, who had been in charge of the psychology department at University College, London since 1907, retired, and Burt was a natural successor. . . . The years up to the outbreak of war were years of substantial achievement. . . .

In 1940 Burt's department was evacuated from London to Aberystwyth, and there it remained until the end of 1944. . . .
  On his return to London in November 1944 Burt settled in the large flat in Elsworthy Road, Primrose Hill, which was to remain his home for the twenty-seven remaining years of life. . . .

Retirement from his chair in 1950 at first brought little change in Burt's way of life, apart from the relief from teaching and administrative duties. . . . He remained immensely busy with meetings, lectures, broadcasts, and the editing of the new journal of statistical psychology, and old students frequently sought his advice. His more important lectures, such as the Hobhouse, Bingham, and Galton lectures, were attended by packed audiences, which indicated that he was still very much a force to be reckoned with. He continued to produce a steady stream of articles, right up to the time of his death, and his published work represents only a small part of his huge output. . . .

As a psychologist he was essentially English. The major influences shaping his viewpoint were the psycho-biology of Darwin, Spencer, Galton, and McDougall, the neurophysiology of Hughlings Jackson and Sherrington, and the brand of idealistic philosophy propounded by James Ward. In Germany he readily absorbed the teaching of the Gestalt psychologists, who had to some extent been anticipated in this country by Stout, and he looked with favour on many of the central tenets of psychoanalysis. He was markedly unsympathetic to the behaviouristic trends which began to dominate American psychology from the 1920s onwards, and which spread to this country in the 1950s. His work can be regarded as a working out of the programme, first envisaged by Francis Galton, for a psychology of talent and character, rooted in evolutionary biology and genetics, and recognizing the importance of individual differences, and quantitatively based. Towards the establishment and application of such a psychology Burt worked with undeviating consistency. There is a single thread of purpose uniting his first publication in 1909 and his last posthumous papers published in 1972.

This very consistency inevitably brought Burt into conflict with some of his younger contemporaries. Psychological fashions changed; Burt did not. It was fashionable in the first decade of the century to regard consciousness as a valid and central concept. The behaviourists rejected it; their camp followers quietly disregarded it. Burt never ceased to hold that consciousness was a central feature of the human mind, and a key topic in psychology. It was fashionable, too, before the First World War to emphasize the significance of heredity. Under the influence of behaviourism and egalitarianism heredity was supplanted by environmentalist explanations of human differences. Once again Burt stuck to his guns. The evidence, he insisted, pointed to the large role of inheritance. He continued to believe in the value of intelligence tests, and continued to support streaming in education, after these views had come under attack. He believed the evidence was on his side, and he refused to be swayed by sentiment or fashion.

There was much that was admirable in this stubbornness, and in the long run Burt may well turn out to have been right on many of these contentious issues. Nevertheless it must be admitted that Burt was somewhat impervious to the changes taking place in psychology. Not that he was not fully aware of the changes: he was indeed remarkably well informed, but he was comparatively little influenced. . . .

Burt was a great teacher, and the riches of his knowledge and expertise were showered on his students without stint. But though he gave profusely, he was less willing to receive. It was a one-way relationship, and when his pupils had fully matured, they drifted away from the master. So Burt never established a school. His work was carried out from the earliest days to the very end largely single-handed (even when he used his students as assistants), and in the long list of his publications, there are comparatively few joint entries.

In his lifetime he was widely honoured. He was knighted in 1946. He was elected a Fellow of the British Academy in 1950. He received honorary degrees from the Universities of Aberdeen and Reading, and was elected an Honorary Fellow of his old Oxford college, Jesus College. In 1965 in honour of his eightieth birthday two years previously a festschrift, *Stephanos,* was presented to him by former colleagues and admirers. And, a forthcoming event which gave him in anticipation great pleasure, the Sir Cyril Burt School for maladjusted children was opened at Beckenham in Kent just after his death.

These honours were richly deserved. As long as human beings are prepared to study their own nature and behavior with that combination of insight and scientific rigour which marked his own work, we can be sure that Cyril Burt will be remembered as a great figure in twentieth-century psychology.

Hearnshaw was chosen—as a historian of psychology—to deliver the oration and tribute at the commemoration service October 21, 1971. The biographical essay and appraisal was published in the *Proceedings of the British Academy* in volume 58, 1972, and then printed as a pamphlet in 1973. For brevity's sake, the above has had to be a much-abbreviated selection, but the entire essay is of this laudatory nature, containing nothing whatever that is defamatory. The very worst that is said of Burt is that his great talents

were not unfortunately matched by a very accurate memory, and, although he recognized his weakness, he was still not careful enough in checking all his facts. His autobiographical sketches, and some of his other writings, are, therefore, marred by factual inaccuracies, and this deficient memory sometimes led him into unnecessary controversy with colleagues—for he would tend to defend his version of events against attack.

Again, this testament to Burt's abilities, character, and work, may be compared with Hearnshaw's later statements in his biography and all the judgments he has subsequently delivered in his articles and biographical pieces.

Correspondence Columns: A Selected Sequence

From John Cohen, Professor of Psychology, The University, Manchester (the *Times,* November 10, 1976):

> Sir, I find it very sad that you should have allowed your Education Correspondent, Mr Devlin (October 25), to besmirch the good name of the late Sir Cyril Burt, a preeminent scholar of his time, and a man, as I am convinced after decades of close association with him, whose character is beyond reproach.
>
> Mr Devlin relies too heavily on remarks he attributes to Professor J. Tizard. Had Professor Tizard ventured to make these extraordinary comments during Burt's lifetime he would have found himself sued for slander and considerably out of pocket as a result.
>
> Professor Tizard, we are told, first became suspicious when he tried to get in touch with Miss Margaret Howard, one of two people at University College, London, "who were said to have worked most closely with Sir Cyril". All Professor Tizard's "enquiries drew a blank". Mr Devlin also repeats the fiction that extensive enquiries "could find no evidence that they ever existed". We are asked to believe that Sir Cyril invented two phantoms.
>
> Allow me to assure Professor Tizard and Mr Devlin that I knew Miss Howard over a period of several years at University College. She was a vivacious and pleasant young woman of flesh and blood, and mathematically competent, I recollect that she wore slightly tinted spectacles, and spoke easily, with a ready laugh.
>
> Professor Tizard finds it strange that the files of data on which Sir Cyril based an early book of his, *The Young Delinquent,* on which he started work possibly as early as 1905, were not readily available in the later sixties or seventies. I wonder whether World Wars I and II took place while Professor Tizard's back was turned. Does he not know that University College, where Burt worked, was set on fire by a bomb in 1940, that Burt was "exiled" to Aberystwyth for the duration, and that he moved house several times during this period of 50 years?
>
> During his long, and supremely productive life, Burt wrote an enormous mass of unpublished papers, reports and memoranda quite apart from his very considerable publications. He never enjoyed anything like the secretarial, storage and access facilities that today we accept as given. My own facilities have been incomparably superior to Burt's. Yet I should find it virtually impossible to retrieve experimental or statistical data compiled five or 10 years ago. Yet Burt was expected to have at his finger tips data he had collected half a century earlier.

The thoroughness in which Professor Tizard pursued his ill-fated enquiries as to the existence of Miss Howard, and the sort of "blank" he drew, should make one pause before believing his charge that Burt did worse than plant a Piltdown Skull, and that Burt "made a lot of it up". There is not a shred of direct evidence that these imputations are true, and, having regard to the method whereby they were reached, we must reject them lock, stock and barrel.

I wish to add that my own views on "intelligence" its measurement and heritability differ radically from those espoused by Burt, but I do not regard this as sufficient ground for reviling the memory of a British scientist who rightly won world-wide acclaim.
I am, Sir, Yours truly,
John Cohen

From Dr. Oliver Gillie, Medical Correspondent, the *Sunday Times* (the *Times,* November 11, 1976):

Sir, Now that Professor John Cohen has identified a Miss Margaret Howard who worked in University College in the 1930s, perhaps in association with Sir Cyril Burt (letter, November 10), may I be allowed to make some pertinent observations. The existence of Miss Margaret Howard and Miss J. Conway was called into question because no one who knew Burt in the 1950s, including Professor Cohen, appears to recall Howard or Conway at that time. The date is important because it was in the 1950s that Howard and Conway published their scientific work on inheritance of intelligence which is alleged to have been faked. Altogether they published seven scientific papers, six book reviews and a note, yet no one appears to recall knowing them during this period.

We have the word of Burt's housekeeper and secretary, Miss Grete Archer, that Burt himself said that he wrote the papers published under the names of Howard and Conway. When Miss Archer asked Burt if she could send Howard and Conway reprints of the work he said that was impossible because they had emigrated and had not left any address.

The papers by Howard and Conway were published by Burt in the *British Journal of Statistical Psychology,* which he edited. On the admission of a lecturer at University College who was closely associated with the journal, Burt was in the habit of writing "spoof letters and papers" for the journal because it was "so difficult to fill".

The addresses given under the names of Howard and Conway in these scientific papers is always University College, London, and in one case the psychology department of University College is mentioned. Since

Howard and Conway appear not to have been associated with University College at that time this is, at least, misleading.

Burt told his housekeeper that he used the names of Howard and Conway because it was they who made the original observations and so it was they who should get the credit. On the face of it this appears reasonable except that some of the papers and all the book reviews contain no original data but rather opinions which now appear to be those of Burt himself.

The mystery over Howard and Conway is of course quite distinct from the fundamental issue of whether Burt invented scientific data. Burt's reputation must ultimately stand or fall on the scientific issue.
Yours truly,
Oliver Gillie

From John Cohen, Professor of Psychology, The University, Manchester (the *Sunday Times,* November 14, 1976):

YOUR Medical Correspondent, Dr Gillie, last week made a commendable effort to extricate himself from the scrape he got himself into by his lamentable article of October 24 suggesting that Sir Cyril Burt faked his research data. But his heart does not appear to have been put into this effort, and the good name of Sir Cyril seems now to have been smeared indelibly. Dr. Gillie persists in asserting, without a vestige of "evidence" that could be admitted in a court of law, that the papers of Burt "contain faked statistics."

He cites a lecturer at University College, London, "who has asked not to be named." Why this cloak of anonymity? What is there to hide? This nameless lecturer declares that "it is well known that Burt used to write spoof letters and papers." Well known to whom? Certainly not to me. Burt used to send me pretty well all his papers and I have yet to come across a single one that could, by any stretch of imagination, be called "spoof." And what, anyway, is a spoof article?" The anonymous lecturer fails to give a single example.

Then, with reference to the phantom Miss Margaret Howard, who is no longer as discarnate as Dr Gillie imagined her to be, the anonymous lecturer adds: "I am sure there may be other of these ladies." What on earth does "I am sure there may be" mean? And why cannot one of these other ladies be named?

Dr Gillie then cites two or three people at Hull who say: "An attempt is being made to whitewash Burt." The boot, I am afraid, is on the other foot: an attempt is being made to denigrate him. Perhaps on the North East coast it is the practice to consider a man guilty until he is proved innocent.

Five years after Burt's death, the Hull group suddenly decide to make an unverified allegation about the publication of certain unspecified papers. Why did they not take action or protest while Burt was still alive?

In the October 24 article they are quoted as saying: "Since no one who knew Burt could possibly accuse him of incompetence, there remains only the probability of dishonesty." It would be just as plausible to reverse this specious plea and say: "Since no one who knew Burt could possibly accuse him of dishonesty, there remains only the probability of incompetence." But the conclusion "there remains only" would be reached by a scientific investigator only after all other "probabilities" had been explored. This the detractors have manifestly failed to do. To my mind there is a simple explanation for a relatively minute number of inconsistent figures in the vast mass of Burt's papers and publications.

I repeat that it is Burt's reputation, not his views, that I strive to vindicate.
(Professor) John Cohen, University of Manchester
Department of Psychology

From Dr. Monica Lawlor, Department of Psychology, Beford College, University of London, November 11, 1976 (the *Times,* November 16, 1976):

Sir, The classical method of dealing with doubts about the quality of scientific observations is to gather fresh evidence or to repeat experiments. Questioning the integrity of the original reporter is the last resort of the intellectually destitute. Only when the original evidence is unique, or the experiments unrepeatable, does the integrity of the scientist become the touchstone for the truth of his observations.

To compare the case of the Piltdown man to the data on the measured IQ of identical twins collected by the late Sir Cyril Burt is very misleading. The world contains an excellent supply of twins, and those dissatisfied with the standards of scientific rigour of Burt's study are perfectly free to replicate it; such a replication would involve a great deal of work but no extraordinary luck or talent.

By contrast the discovery of fossil evidence of early hominoids requires a good deal more than a willingness to dig. If proper evidence could have been obtained by mere diligence, it is doubtful if the Piltdown fraud could ever have been perpetrated, still less have remained undiscovered for so long.

How little is gained, in a scientific sense, by seeking to vilify the late Sir Cyril Burt can readily be seen by those who have followed the present controversy. On October 24 (in *The Sunday Times*) the possible non-existence of a Margaret Howard was explained to us as ". . . the fantasy of an aging professor who became increasingly lonely and deaf". Data published by doddering old men with delusions might well be unreliable, the non-existence of the lady is offered as evidence of the doddering and the doddering as evidence of the unacceptability of the data.

When Professor Cohen turned out to have a perfectly clear recollection of a flesh and blood Margaret Howard it becomes evident that her existence, or nonexistence, makes exactly no difference to the argument. Dr. Gillie with a bewildering volte face ditches the pathetic image of an old man in the grip of a disordered imagination and instead asks us to believe in a brisk Sir Cyril Burt who was "in the habit of writing 'spoof' letters and papers. . . ." As evidence for this remarkable new revelation he offers us that least attractive of all sources, an anonymous gossip, allegedly from University College.

No scientific issue can possibly be resolved at this level and in these terms: the publication of anonymous tittle-tattle about a dead scientist is as useless in forwarding scientific inquiry as throwing bricks at a live one. If the study of identical twins is critical to this debate on heredity and intelligence, which I doubt, the proper course is obvious, it is to collect more data.

The only psychological truth in anyway illuminated by this debate is the observation that scandal, particularly if it hints at feet of clay in respectable persons, never lacks a fascinated audience.
Yours faithfully,
Monica Lawlor

From Dr. A. R. Jonckheere, Department of Psychology, University College, London (the *Times,* November 20, 1976):

Sir, I am the psychology lecturer whose remarks are cited by the medical correspondent of *The Sunday Times* concerning Professor Burt's missing authors. These remarks were made during a telephone conversation, instigated by him, and lasting about an hour, during which I tried to show him how his article, starting "The most sensational charge of scientific fraud this century. . . ." (*Sunday Times,* October 24, 1976), was an example of innuendo unworthy of scientific journalism.

To give one instance, his third "charge" was "That Burt miraculously produced identical answers accurate to three decimal places from different sets of data—this is a statistical impossibility and he could only have done it by working backwards to make the observations fit his answers." But surely anyone intending to perpetrate such a fraud would hardly publish figures which are a "statistical impossibility" and so risk detection by careful scholars like Professor Kamin. The thought of Professor Burt, whose statistical acumen far surpassed that of any of his present-day critics, arduously "working backwards" and writing down fictitious intelligence test scores in order to obtain exactly the same correlations as he had previously published is not only ludicrous but equally an "impossibility."

What might have happened is that in successive publications he merely gave the same original correlation, but each time reported that the numbers involved were the total of the record he had at the time of writing. This is, of course, quite inexcusable, but is at least a feasible explanation. Moreover, unlike the cashier whose errors always seem to be in his favour, even unconsciously he would hardly have wanted to produce identical correlations but, if anything, higher ones. Those who cannot refrain from moralizing might like to try and find the phrase which captures Professor Burt's culpability: "fraud" does not seem to be it. This is not of course to say that all the anomalies that have been found in his work might have the same explanation, but simply to point out that this kind of journalism hardly contributes anything of value to the discussion.

As regards the missing authors, apparently some people seem to think that if they are fictitious then anyone who deceives his readers in this way might also stoop to fraud. So in order to throw doubt on all of Professor Burt's work, even where no anomalies can be detected it must somehow be established that these authors did not exist.

It is difficult, however, to conceive of any motive Professor Burt might have had for publishing papers with fictitious authors which could be construed to his advantage in the sense required for the allegation of fraud: their validity hardly required bolstering in this way, and authorship with unknown, inaccesible or even fictitious persons could only diminish their scientific value. Were Professor Burt to have invented them, whatever his motives they could not have been of the kind implicit in the production of fraudulent scientific data. It is in this context that my remarks appear to have suggested there was evidence for the nonexistence of these authors. Had I been asked what this evidence was I would of course have immediately retracted these implications.

It is hardly surprising that I wished to be dissociated from further articles written in this sensational style, and I can only regret that my offhand remarks were cited as considered statements to be used for the pointless moral castigation of Professor Burt—after his death.
Yours faithfully,
A. R. Jonckheere

From Professor C. D. Darlington, Magdalen College, Oxford (the *Times,* November 23, 1976). In a long letter on "Genetics of intelligence: bearing on education," Professor Darlington's comments on Burt were as follows:

> The great development of Galton's work came, as we know, from the invention of intelligence testing. The original purpose was to find some systematic or objective basis for segregating children in school in groups according to their levels of teachability. Hence the numerical indexes of mental age (MA), index of brightness (IB) or intelligence quotient (IQ).
>
> These indexes are today the basis for establishing special schools for the feeble-minded (below IQ 70) and institutions for imbeciles (below IQ 50). This principle of segregation assumes that no education will remedy the differences in innate intelligence between the three groups. And any attempt to remedy it will be wasteful if not damaging. Does anyone question this assumption?
>
> Arbitrary lines, and often cruel lines, have to be drawn in deciding what education and, later, what employment will best suit the abilities, innate abilities, of each individual in our community. But for our guidance in drawing those lines we have had the use of a century's study. In Britain the most valuable was the work of Sir Cyril Burt since as Psychologist to the London Education Authority he was able to call upon the advice of some of the most skillful and experienced statisticans and geneticists in the world: the late Sir Ronald Fisher, Professor Lionel Penrose and, most of all, Dr. Fraser Roberts.
>
> Out of this collaboration came the bell-shaped curves of variation and the correlations of kindred which are the commonplace of general biology. In turn these were related by Burt to the three great fields of his inquiry, the understanding of the human mind, the process of education, and the evolution of society. In his last work, *The Gifted Child,* published after his death, we are offered the fruits of this work, flavoured with his own deep learning and humanity.
>
> All this, we may say, was the harvest of the Galtonian and Mendelian revolutions which came together in 1900. But 20 years ago another revolution came when serious chromosome study began in man. It was largely aimed at discovering the innate origins of bodily, mental and sexual variations in men and women. By now about a million human beings have had their chromosomes examined for these purposes so that today we may claim to know more about heredity in man than in any other animal or plant.
>
> Thus another synthesis in the understanding of human heredity and intelligence began to take place. We could now distinguish between the

polygenic inheritance of Fraser Roberts' normal curves of variation in IQ and the chromosome mutations responsible for imbeciles. We could relate both the defects of the brain which are chemical or physical, and the means of its improvement, with changes in the chromosomes. In his last letter to me (April 28, 1970) Burt says that he looks forward to studying these questions. At 87 he was still eager to learn.

Additional Testimony

Memories of Sir Cyril Burt: By Robert S. Reid

It was my privilege when I took on the Editorship of this Journal in 1964 to meet Sir Cyril Burt at least four times in every year at his home in Hampstead, and to exchange many letters with him. Readers of the first issue will recall his reply to my letter when I asked him to inaugurate the "News Letter", as it was then, with what I now realise, as I look back, was rather facetious temerity. "Would you", I wrote "be so kind as to give the News Letter a "Nihil obstat: Imprimatur"?" He gently rebuked me for attributing to him the powers of the licensing Censor; that a scientist in a young and growing science could not take on this rank of intellectual superiority and omniscience; that he looked forward to a magazine in which educational psychologists could communicate and discuss with each other not only on professional matters but report experiments which would be to the benefit of children. In all, with his last article in this issue, he has contributed 20 articles to the Journal.

All his letters to me were written in his own handwriting. His articles were first written in longhand, then typed for the printer. Sometimes he would ask me what topic would be interesting to our members; sometimes he would say he would like to write an article on some subject on which people had been writing to him for his opinion. Every letter had kind and courteous inquiries about my health or what I was doing or where I had been on holiday. Like his contemporaries, the late Dr. William Boyd of Glasgow University and Dr. Robert R. Rusk also of Glasgow University and now living in retirement in Inverness, no query was too trivial to be given consideration and scholarly opinion, and above all the questioner felt that his inquiry mattered. Truly outstanding men have an innate courtesy, respect and kindness for their fellowmen.

To me, from my meetings with Sir Cyril Burt, this is the memory of him I shall always have. His courtesy and his kindness. I shall remember his talks with me in his Hampstead room, with the grand piano open with a book of Bach preludes, the pots of flowers on the tables, the huge Zimmerlinden growing in the window overlooking Primrose Hill, where in springtime he delighted in drawing my attention to the daffodils and the budding trees. "I can't walk up there now so well", he said, "but I always used to take a walk across the Hill at Regents Park to University College". He would talk of London and his school days at Christ's Hospital 75 years ago. Of Oxford at the beginning of the century, of travels on the Continent, where galleries, museums and antiquities were described as if he had only just come back from such a tour. His comments on contempoary psychologists were never pungent, but with a twinkle in his eye he might say "I've often wondered how so-and-so always manages to get a book out in time to catch a topical interest". He kept a working day to the very end. Letters were answered by return of post. I received his present article in the middle of September. "I hope this will be in time, and please do not hesitate to cut or sub-edit as you think fit". He corrected and returned the galley proofs to the printer in two days.

He was delighted when Croydon Education Authority asked him if a new school for maladjusted children could be given his name. I took him copies of the plans, and he pored over them asking reasons for several features and working out the cubic capacities of the rooms in his head, and then remarking "Oh, I see the architect has already done this in the table in the corner". In June 1970 when the Foundation Stone was laid with civic ceremony he looked forward to doing it, and only two days before the event in the middle of a heatwave his doctor told him the strain would be inadvisable, and Dr. E. J. Weeks, one of his first students when he was Professor of Education in 1926, deputised for him.

On one visit we talked of the styles in which text books on Psychology were written, their frequent discursiveness, their jargon and lack of lucid English style. I mentioned William James as a master of expression and clear exposition. He agreed. "Who do you think," he asked me, "would be the James of this century?". "I would say yourself, Professor Burt", I replied. His eyes twinkled behind his glasses, "No, I don't think so. I haven't written a text book of Psychology—yet!"

I shall miss his courteous letters. I shall miss his warm personality and friendliness over afternoon tea with him and Miss Archer his housekeeper and secretary for over 21 years. I have been privileged in knowing a great man, whose eyes, I am certain, would light up with delight if I could say to him now "Do you know this poem by Robert Burns which is annotated in the Kilmarnock edition as one of his very best in English?"

EPITAPH ON A FRIEND

An honest man here lies at rest
As e'er God with his image blest!
The friend of man, the friend of truth
The friend of age, and guide of youth.

> Few hearts like his with virtue warmed,
> Few heads with knowledge so informed;
> If there's another world, he lives in bliss;
> If there is none, he made the best of this.

This tribute was published in the *AEP Journal* in the autumn of 1971, after Burt's death. Robert Reid edited the *Newsletter* and *AEP Journal* for some twenty years. In his "Valedictory Editorial Diary" in the winter of 1984 (vol. 6, no. 5 of the journal), he also wrote:

> Some readers may still possess that first issue in which Cyril Burt, as Patron of the A.E.P., wrote an Introduction and gave his blessing to the new venture. The A.E.P. had less than 200 members then. So the flow of articles from members was a sporadic trickle and we had to borrow material from other journals and newspapers and try to write articles ourselves. Cyril Burt wrote an article for every issue to Number 9 of Volume 2 which came out the month before his death in 1971. We acknowledge our indebtedness to him for his generosity and his inspiration. But for his continuous help this Journal could well have folded as several psychological journals have done these past twenty years.

Sir Cyril Burt—A Reminiscence: By Dr. E. J. Weeks

In my young days I studied at the London Day Training College. I obtained my Diploma in Pedagogy in 1922 but, like so many others, I failed to obtain a teaching post until 1924. It was then that I decided to pursue the course for the M.A. (Education). Professor Nunn did not advise me to risk an examination in practical teaching and suggested that I follow the course for the M.A. in Educational Psychology. For two years I attended the course at King's and University Colleges where I had the joy of working under Spearman, Flugel and Bartlett.

At the beginning of 1926 I went to see Professor Burt at the L.D.T.C. Even after 45 years I still remember that meeting. Sir Cyril was then in his early forties. He was a handsome man, very well dressed and gave the impression that here was one who knew exactly what he wanted and was very sure of himself. He agreed that he would accept me as a research student and suggested that I might be interested in investigating the possibility of the existence of a general emotional factor corresponding to Spearman's 'g'.

Enquiring into my knowledge of statistics he informed me that the further work I should have to do would produce no difficulties. (I soon found out that the word 'easy' to Burt was the same as 'hard' to me.)

From the beginning Burt was kind and thoughtful. He gave me his own notes on statistics which I found to be much easier to understand than the text books I had previously used. Then he used a phrase which I shall always remember. My intellectual horizons must be enlarged. Knowing I was a chemist he surmised that I had had little time for wide reading. He suggested a few books that I might care to read. After nearly an hour he wished me a cheerful goodbye and I left in a bewildered but excited state of mind.

Thereafter once a fortnight at 5 p.m. on a Wednesday I was to meet and talk with Sir Cyril. These talks certainly did 'enlarge my horizons'.

The concepts of character, temperament, disposition, personality were exemplified by reading and studying such varied authors as Henry James, Shakespeare, Jane Austen and Cannon. Then, of course, I had to immerse myself in the works of Jung, Freud and Adler.

Sir Cyril's width and depth of knowledge was outstanding although he never made one feel that he lived and thought on any superior plane. At the final dreaded oral examination he so made me feel at ease that I had no sense of nervousness. Incidentally a question by Professor Dover Wilson on the temperament of Hamlet finally flawed me but in the end all went well. I still possess the pass list for that degree in Educational Psychology. One candidate—one pass.

Sir Cyril Burt was to give me a life long interest in educational research combined with a great sympathy for the emotional problems of young people. I am now in my 70th year but I shall always remember my old professor as a kind-hearted, severely intellectually critical, sympathetic middle aged man. He expected a high standard of clear and concise thought, a capacity for detailed and critical study and a wide general reading. I account it a great privilege that in my young days I had the opportunity to study under and enjoy the friendship of such a genius as Sir Cyril Burt.

Dr. Weeks' tribute was also published in the *AEP Journal* in the autumn of 1971.

Tributes of this kind from past students and colleagues of Sir Cyril Burt could be multiplied greatly, but, at the end of this additional testimony, I ask readers simply to weigh the testimony of scholars of the stature of Professors Cohen, Darlington, and Fraser Roberts, who had a close knowledge of Burt's work and character over many years; and of colleagues in Departments of Psychology in the University of London (like Drs. Lawlor and Jonckheere); against that of the very small handful of Burt's detractors, whose knowledge of Burt was, by contrast, extremely limited. Bearing in mind the initial stance of this book—of putting all these questions to you, the readers, as to a jury—I am satisfied now to leave the judgment to you.

Notes

1. 1908–1913.
2. [Hearnshaw's footnote] Experimental Tests of General Intelligence', *Brit. J. Psychol.* iii. 94–177. 1909; 'Experimental Tests of Higher Mental Processes and their Relation to General Intelligence,' *J. Exp. Ped.* i. 93–112. 1911; 'The Inheritance of Mental Characteristics', *Eugen. Rev.* iv. 1–33. 1912; 'The Mental Differences between the Sexes' (with R. C. Moore), *J. Exp. Ped.* i. 273–84, 355–88. 1912.

Select Bibliography

Adams, B, M. Ghodsian, and Richardson, K. "Evidence for a Low Upper Limit of Hereditability of Mental Test Performance in a National sample of Twins." *Nature* 263; Sept. 1976.

Archer, Gretl. "Reflections on Sir Cyril Burt." *AEP Journal* 6 (1); 1983.

Asimov, Isaac. "Burt, Sir Cyril Lodowic, English Psychologist." *Asimov's Biographical Encyclopaedia of Science and Technology*, 2d rev. ed. 1982.

Association of Educational Psychologists. "Sir Cyril Burt: The Essential Man." *AEP Journal* 6 (1); 1983.

Banks, Charlotte. "Professor Sir Cyril Burt: Selected Reminiscences." *AEP Journal* 6 (1); 1983.

Banks, Charlotte, and P. L. Broadhurst. *Studies in Psychology: Presented to Cyril Burt*. London: University of London Press, 1965.

Banks, Olive. *Parity and Prestige in English Secondary Education*. London: Routledge & Kegan Paul, 1955.

Beloff, Halla (ed.). "A Balance Sheet on Burt." Supplement to *Bulletin of the British Psychological Society* 33; 1980.

Bernstein, B. *Class, Codes and Control*, vol. 1. London: Routledge & Kegan Paul 1971

Bouchard, Thomas J. Jr. "Identical Twins Reared Apart: Reanalysis or Pseudo-Analysis?" *Contemporary Psychology* 27 (3); 1982.

———. "Twins Reared Together and Apart: What They Tell Us About Human Diversity." In Sydney W. Fox (ed.), *Individuality and Diversity*. New York, Plenum, 1984.

———. "Do Environmental Similarities Explain the Similarity in Intelligence of Identical Twins Reared Apart?" *Intelligence* 7; pp. 175–184; 1983.

————. "The Hereditarian Research Program: Triumphs & Tribulation." In S, Modgil and C, Modgil (eds.), *Arthur Jensen: Consensus and Controversy*. London: Falmer International, 1987.

Bouchard, Thomas J. Jr., and Nancy L. Segal. "Environment and IQ." In B. B. Wolman (ed.), *Handbook of Intelligence,* New York: Wiley, 1985.

(All Professor Bouchard's publications are associated with the Minnesota Center for Twin and Adoption Research)

Burt, Sir Cyril. A full bibliography of Burt's publications was published in 1965 by University of London Press; the following are only those referred to in the argument of this book.

Burt, Sir Cyril. "Experimental Tests of General Intelligence." *British Journal of Psychology* 3; pp. 94–177; 1909.

————. "Experimental Tests of Higher Mental Processes and Their Relation to General Intelligence." *Journal of Experimental Pediatrics* 1, pp. 93–112, 1911.

————. "The Measurement of Intelligence by the Binet Tests" (pts I and II)." *Eugenics Review* 6 (1 and 2); 1914.

————. "Mental Tests." *Child Study* 8; pp. 8–13; 1915.

————. "An Appeal for Co-operation in Research." *Child Study* 8 (2); pp. 92–93; 1915.

————. "The Development of Reasoning in School Children." *Journal of Experimental Pediatrics* 5; pp. 68–77, 121–7; 1919.

————. *Report of an Investigation Upon Backward Children in Birmingham*. City of Birmingham Stationery Dept., 1921.

————. "The Mental Differences Between Individuals." (Presidential Address to Psychology Section). *British Association Annual Report,* 1923.

————. "The Backward Child." *Parents and Children* 1 (9); 1933.

————. "Ability & Income." *British Journal of Educational Psychology* 13; pp. 83–98; 1943.

————. Mental & Scholastic Tests. 3d and 4th eds. London: Staples Press, 1947 and 1962.

————. "The Evidence for the Concept of Intelligence." *British Journal of Educational Psychology* 25; pp. 158–177; 1955.

————. "The Inheritance of Mental Ability" (The Bingham Memorial Lecture, 1957). *The American Psychologist;* 13; pp. 1–15; 1958.

————. "Intelligence & Social Mobility." *British Journal of Statistical Psychology* 14 (1); 1961.

————. The Backward Child. 5th ed. London: University of London Press, 1961.

————. "The Genetic Determination of Differences in Intelligence: A

Study of Monozygotic Twins Reared Together and Apart." *British Journal of Psychology* 57 (1 and 2); 1966.

————. "The Genetic Determination of Intelligence: A Reply." *British Journal of Psychology* 58 (1 and 2); 1967.

————. "Intelligence & Heredity: Some Common Misconceptions." *Irish Journal of Education* 3 (2); 1969. Reprinted in *Question* 4 (Journal of the Rationalist Press Association, London), Pemberton, 1971.

————. "The Mental Differences Between Children." *Black Paper Two* (Occasional Publication of the Critical Quarterly Society, London); 1970.

Burt, Sir Cyril, and Margaret Howard, "The Multifactorial Theory of Inheritance and Its Application to Intelligence." *British Journal of Statistical Psychology* 9 (2); 1956.

————. "The Relative Influence of Heredity and Environment on Assessments of Intelligence." *British Journal of Statistical Psychology* 10 (2); 1957.

Cattell, Raymond B. *Personality and Learning Theory* (2 vols.). New York: Springer, 1979.

————. "Are Culture Fair Intelligence Tests Possible and Necessary?" *Journal of Research and Development in Education* 12 (2); 1979.

————. "Cyril Burt, Psychologist." [A review of Hearnshaw.] *Behaviour Genetics* 10 (3); 1980.

————. *The Inheritance of Personality and Ability*. [Research methods and findings.] New York: Academic Press, 1982.

————. "Evolutionary Ethics, Eugenics and the Social Sciences." *The Mankind Quarterly* 19 (4); 1979 (then printed as a pamphlet [Reprint no. 15] by The International Association for the Advancement of Ethnology and Eugenics).

Clarke, Ann M, and A. D. B. Clarke, "Comments on Heredity," and "Comment on Professor Hearnshaw's 'Balance Sheet on Burt.' " See Beloff, Halla. 1980.

Cohen, John. "The Detractors." *Encounter,* March 1977.

————. "Sir Cyril Burt: A Brief Note." *AEP Journal* 6 (1); 1983.

Conway, J. "The Inheritance of Intelligence and its Social Implications." *British Journal of Statistical Psychology* 11 (2); 1958.

————. "Class Differences in General Intelligence, II." *British Journal of Statistical Psychology* 12 (1); 1959.

Cox, C. B, and A. E. Dyson. "Black Paper Two." Occasional paper of the Critical Quarterly Society, London, 1970.

Cronbach, Lee J. "Hearnshaw on Burt." *Science* 206, 1979. pp. 1392–1394.

Devlin, T. "Theories of IQ Pioneer 'Completely Discredited.' " *Times,* October 25, 1976.

———. "Heredity of little effect on IQ, Twins Survey Finds." *Times,* October 28, 1976.

———. "More Flaws Found in Intelligence Theory Data." *Times,* October 29, 1976.

Dorfman, D. D. "The Cyril Burt Question: New Findings." *Science* 201 (4362); 1978. pp. 1117–1186.

Douglas J. W. B. *The Home and the School* London: MacGibbon & Kee, 1964.

———. *All Our Future* London: Peter Davies, 1968.

Duncan, Carl P. "The Intelligence Controversy (a review)." *American Journal of Psychology* 95 (2); 1982.

Economist, The. (Anonymous column.) "Who's fault I'm Fick?" November 6, 1976.

Evans, Christopher. "Empirical Truth and Progress in Science." *New Scientist,* January 26, 1984.

Eysenck, H. J. *Race, Intelligence and Education* London: Temple Smith, 1971.

———. "The Case of Sir Cyril Burt (On Fraud & Prejudice in a Scientific Controversy)." *Encounter,* January 1977.

———. "Sir Cyril Burt and the Inheritance of the IQ." *New Zealand Psychologist* 7 (1); 1978.

———. *Intelligence: The Battle for the Mind* London: Pan Books, 1981.

———. "Sir Cyril Burt: Polymath and Psychopath." *AEP Journal* 6 (1); 1983.

———. "Burt's Warped Personality Led Inevitably to Fraud." *Listener,* April 29, 1982.

Farr, R. M. "Some Observations on the Nature of Probity in Science: The Case of Sir Cyril Burt." See Beloff, Halla, 1980.

Fletcher, R. "The Doubtful Case of Cyril Burt." *Social Policy & Administration* 21 (1); 1987.

———. "The Progressive Vendetta Against the IQ Man." *Sunday Telegraph,* August 2, 1987.

———. "BBC Character Assassination." *The Free Nation,* 12 (5); 1987.

———. "Speaking Up For Burt." *Times Educational Supplement,* December 4, 1987.

———. "The 'Scientific' Assassins." *The British MENSA Magazine,* April 1988.

Floud, J. E. (ed.), A. H. Halsey, and F. M. Martin. *Social Class and Educational Opportunity*. Bath: Cedric Chivers; 1972.

Galton, Francis. *Inquiries into Human Faculty and Its Development* London: Dent, 1907.

Gillie, Oliver. "Pioneer of IQ Faked his Research Findings." *Sunday Times*, October 24, 1976.

———. "IQ Researchers 'Did Exist.' " *Sunday Times*, November 7, 1976.

———. "Man—The Soft Machine." *Sunday Times*, November 28, 1976.

———. "Sir Cyril Burt and the Great IQ Fraud." *New Statesman*, November 24, 1978.

———. "Burt's Missing Ladies." *Science* 204; 1979. pp. 1035–1039.

———. "Burt: The Scandal and the Cover-Up." See Beloff, Halla, 1980.

———. "Cyril Burt: Intuitive Genius or Discarnate Communicator." *AEP Journal* 6 (3); 1984.

Glass, D. V. (ed.). *Social Mobility in Britain*. London: Routledge & Kegan Paul, 1954.

Greer, Germaine. *Sex and Destiny*. London: Picador, 1985.

Hadow, Sir W. H. (chairman). *The Primary School* (Hadow Report). London: HMSO, 1931.

Halsey, A. H. "Race Is a Poor Clue to Any Important Human Trait." *Listener*, May 20, 1982.

Hearnshaw, L. S. *Cyril Burt, Psychologist*. London: Hodder & Stoughton, 1979.

———. "The Decline and Fall of Cyril Burt." *Observer*, July 8, 1979.

———. "Burt, Cyril." In *Biographical Supplement to the International Encyclopaedia of the Social Sciences*, New York: Free Press, 1979.

———. "Burt, Sir Cyril Lodowic (1883–1971)." *Dictionary of National Biography*, 1971–1980.

———. "Balance Sheet on Burt." See Beloff, Halla, 1980.

———. "Commentary on the Burt Symposium." *AEP Journal* 6 (3); 1984.

———. "Burt, Sir Cyril Lodowic (1883–1971)." In R. L. Gregory and O. L. Zangwill. (eds.), *The Oxford Companion to the Mind*. Oxford: Oxford University Press, 1987. See also exchange with Joynson in *The Psychologist,* Bulletin of the British Psychological Society, 1990 (2) pp. 61–68.

Jensen, A. R. "Sir Cyril Burt: A Personal Recollection." *AEP Journal* 6 (1); 1983.

————. *Educability and Group Differences*. New York: Harper & Row, 1973.

————. *Straight Talk about Mental Tests*. New York: Free Press, 1981.

Joynson, R. B. Letter. *AEP Journal* 6 (3); 1984.

————. *The Burt Affair*. London: Routledge, 1989. See exchange with Hearnshaw in *The Psychologist,* Bulletin of the British Psychological Society, 1990 (2), pp. 61–68.

Kamin, Leon J. *The Science & Politics of IQ*. Hillsdale, NJ: Erlbaum, 1974.

————. "Heredity, Intelligence, Politics and Psychology (parts I and II)." In N. Block and G. Dworkin (eds.), *The IQ Controversy: Critical Readings*. London: Quartet Books, 1977.

————. *Intelligence: The Battle for the Mind* London: Pan Books, 1981.

Kline, P. "Burt's False Results and Modern Psychometrics: A Comparison." See Beloff, Halla, 1980.

Kohn, Alexander. "The Burt Controversy—Inheritance of Intelligence." In Alexander Kohn, on *False Prophets,* Blackwell, 1986.

MacRae, Donald G. "Spot the Lady" (letter). *New Statesman,* 96; 820, 1978.

McLoughlin, C. S. "Sir Cyril Burt: The Essential Man." *AEP Journal* 6 (1); 1983.

Medawar, Sir Peter. *The Limits of Science*. Oxford University Press, 1986.

Medical Research Council. A Study in Vocational Guidance (Report 33 of Industrial Research Fatigue Board). London: HMSO, 1926.

Moore, T. "Thoughts on the Integrity of Sir Cyril Burt." *AEP Journal* 6 (1); 1983.

Newson, J. and E. Newson. *Four Years Old in an Urban Community*. London: Allen & Unwin, 1968.

Norwood, Sir Cyril (chairman). *Curriculum and Examinations in Secondary Schools (Report of Norwood Committee)*. London: HMSO, 1943.

Nunn, Sir Percy T. *Education: Its Data and First Principles* (chap. 9, particularly pp. 120–137), 2d ed. London: Arnold, 1930.

Pigou, A. C. "Some Aspects of the Problem of Charity." In G. M. Trevelyan, et al. (eds.), *The Heart of Empire: Discussions of Problems of Modern City Life in England*. London: Fisher Unwin, 1901.

Sandiford, P. *The Foundations of Educational Psychology*. London: Longmans, 1928.

Spielman, Winifred, and Frances Gaw. *A Study in Vocational Guid-*

ance. Medical Research Council, Industrial Fatigue Research Board. Report no. 33, H.M.S.O., 1926.

Stigler, S. M. Letter (a critique of Dorfman). *Science,* 1978?

Sunday Times. Columns and Correspondence on Burt Controversy. October 31; November 7, 11, 14, 1976.

Sutherland, G. and S. Sharp. " 'The Fust Official Psychologist in the Wurrld': Aspects of the Professionalization of Psychology in Early Twentieth Century Britain." *History of Science* 18 (41); 1980.

Times, The. Letters on the Burt controversy. October 26, 27, 29; November 1, 4, 6, 8, 9, 11, 13, 17, 18, 20, 23, 24, 27, 29; December 5, 9; all 1976.

Thompson, Sir Godfrey H. *The Factorial Analysis of Human Ability*. 5th ed. London: University of London Press, 1951.

Vaizey, G. *In Breach of Promise*. London: Weidenfeld & Nicolson, 1983.

Valentine, Charles. *Cyril Burt: A Biographical Sketch and Appreciation*. London: University of London Press, 1965.

Vernon, P. E. *The Measurement of Abilities*. 2d ed. London: University of London Press, 1956.

Wade, Nicholas. "IQ and Heredity: Suspicion of Fraud Beclouds Classic Experiment." *Science* 194; pp. 916–919, 1976.

Wall, W. D. "Sir Cyril Burt: A Personal Note." *AEP Journal* 6 (1); 1983.

Winch, W. H. "Binet's Mental Tests: What They Are and What We Can Do With Them" (articles 1–9). *Child Study* 6–8, 1913–1915.

———. "Some New Reasoning Tests Suitable for the Mental Examination of School Children." *British Journal of Psychology* (7); pp. 190–225. 1914.

Wood, Arthur R. (chairman). *Report of the Mental Deficiency Committee*. Joint Committee of the Board of Education and Board of Control. London: HMSO, 1929.

Index